PUBLIC RELATIONS THEORY

COMMUNICATION

A series of volumes edited by:
Dolf Zillmann and **Jennings Bryant**

PUBLIC RELATIONS THEORY

Edited by

Carl H. Botan
Rutgers University

Vincent Hazleton, Jr.
Illinois State University

LEA *LAWRENCE ERLBAUM ASSOCIATES, PUBLISHERS*
1989   *Hillsdale, New Jersey*   *Hove and London*

Copyright © 1989 by Lawrence Erlbaum Associates, Inc.
All rights reserved. No part of the book may be reproduced in
any form, by photostat, microform, retrieval system, or any other
means, without the prior written permission of the publisher.

Lawrence Erlbaum Associates, Inc., Publishers
365 Broadway
Hillsdale, New Jersey 07642

Library of Congress Cataloging-in-Publication Data
Public relations theory /edited by Carl H. Botan, Vincent Hazleton, Jr.
    p.   cm.—(Communication)
    Includes index.
    ISBN 0-8058-0382-3
    ISBN 0-8058-0692-X(p)
    1. Public relations.   I. Botan, Carl H.   II. Hazleton, Vincent.
III. Series.
HM263.P8165   1989
659.2—dc19   88-26767
                                                                    CIP

Printed in the United States of America
10 9 8 7 6 5 4 3 2 1

Contents

Contributors

Ronald B. Anderson
University of Texas at Austin

Carl H. Botan
Rutgers University

George Cheney
University of Colorado

Caroline Garrett Cline
Southwest Texas State University

George N. Dionisopoulos
San Diego State University

Joseph Fritsch
Michigan State University

James L. Gaudino
Speech Communication
Association of America

James E. Grunig
University of Maryland

Peter K. Hamilton
Pittsburg State University

Bruce Haynes
Michigan State University

Vincent Hazleton, Jr.
Illinois State University

Donald J. Johnson
University of Wisconsin–Madison

Gary L. Kreps
Northern Illinois University

Michael H. McBride
Southwest Texas State University

Gerald R. Miller
Michigan State University

Randy E. Miller
University of Texas at Austin

Priscilla Murphy
Drexel University

Bonita Dostal Neff
Public Communication Associates

Dan O'Hair
Texas Tech University

Ron Pearson
Mount Saint Vincent University

Marcia Prior-Miller
Iowa State University

Joseph C. Scott, III
University of Oklahoma

Michael Smilowitz
University of North Carolina—
Charlotte

Keith Terry
Kearney State College

James K. VanLeuven
Colorado State University

Preface

This book evolved out of the belief that public relations can be best understood as a specialized kind of communication. If this assumption is true, we reasoned, it should be possible to study public relations as an instance of applied communication. We should be able to apply communication theory to explain and to predict public relations practice, and use public relations practice as a site for the development of communication theory.

In the spring of 1987 a conference on communication theory and public relations was held at Illinois State University. The authors wish to express their appreciation to Illinois State for support for this conference. Participants were selected for the conference on the basis of a competitive blind review of papers that addressed the topic of communication theory and public relations. Based on a desire to test the limits as well as the core of this approach to public relations, a broad definition of communication theory was used, allowing room for related social science theories to be included.

The participants met in a workshop format for 3 days using prepared papers as the basis for discussions that ranged across a wide spectrum of theoretical issues. These discussions fell into three categories: those addressing issues of metatheory, those addressing issues of theory, and those addressing issues or examples of application of theories. These three categories were later used to organize this book, although the chapters are substantially different from the original papers discussed at the conference. These changes, in part the result of conference discussion and in part the result of the editing process, have had the overall effect of putting the focus of the book even more clearly on communication theory.

Carl H. Botan
Vincent Hazleton, Jr.

I

ISSUES OF METATHEORY

The Role of Theory
in Public Relations

Vincent Hazleton Jr.
Illinois State University

Carl H. Botan
Rutgers University

ABSTRACT

This chapter lays a foundation for understanding the kinds of theory and how they are developed by addressing how metatheories effect theory development, providing a vocabulary of theory development, and assessing the prospects for theory development in public relations. The chapter concludes by warning against a premature commitment to any particular theory or methodology while urging a continued exploration of the boundaries of public relations.

INTRODUCTION

This is a book about public relations and public relations theory. The book seeks to identify and explain the theoretic roots appropriate to the study of public relations as a social science.

The book is divided into three sections. First, are issues of metatheory or world views that direct the focus of research and the practice of public relations. The chapters in the second section address particular theories or theory areas that are seen as relevant to public relations research and public relations practices. In the third section issues concerning the application of theories to practice are addressed.

This chapter lays a foundation for understanding the role of theory and kinds of theories so that the reader might employ the following chapters to best advantage. This chapter is organized into three parts. The first part addresses issues of metatheory and its influence on theory development. The second part suggests a vocabulary for evaluating and comparing theories. The schema provided draws heavily from the work of others, most noticeably Leonard Hawes (1975). Although this is only one possible schema among many, it is one that we find useful in our teaching and research. Finally, we examine the prospects for theory in public relations.

METATHEORY

Theories are fundamentally products of human endeavor, therefore theory construction may be studied like other forms of human behavior, such as communication. In fact, theory construction, as a social enterprise, is a communication-bound activity.

Influenced by points of view much like the one presented in the preceding paragraph, philosophers and practitioners of science (e.g., Kuhn, 1970; Polanyi, 1958) have argued that theory construction is not the dispassionate and objective process that it was once considered. Instead, theorists and researchers bring to this process fundamental assumptions or world views that direct inquiry and theory development.

As Grunig notes in chapter 2, the content of such metatheories, which he calls "presuppositions," may be considered "extra-scientific" in so far as they are not subject to direct observation and therefore may not be refuted easily. Presuppositions are assumed to be true. Because the obvious truth of these beliefs cannot and need not be demonstrated, they are seldom discussed; and their influence may not be recognized.

Hazleton and Cupach (1986) argued for the utility of a concept they call "ontological knowledge". *Ontological knowledge* refers to what communicators know about themselves and the world in which they exist. Such knowledge defines what a communicator assumes is possible or impossible in a given situation. A metatheory may be considered as a type of ontological knowledge, which by its self-evident nature, can blind researchers to certain paths for understanding and learning.

Pearce, Cronen, and Harris (1982) suggest two general questions, which when answered from different metatheoretic perspectives lead to different forms of research and to different theories. The first question is: "What counts as data?". The second question is: "What do data count as?".

Pearce and colleagues suggest that the first question, "What counts as data?", implies the following more specific questions:

1. "What is the appropriate unit of analysis?" Our own experience suggests that researchers and theorists disagree about the smallest meaningful unit of data. How researchers regard the often cited maxim that "meanings are in people not in words" may determine whether public relations scholars focus their study on symbols, messages, or message effects.

2. "What is the appropriate unit of observation?" In public relations should we focus on individuals, groups, or institutions/organizations? Answers to such questions are not trivial. For example, it is possible to assume that annual reports are products of individual effort rather than a product of the organization. In the first case, a researcher would seek a representative sample of practitioners. In the second case, a researcher would seek a representative sample of organizations.

3. "What is the appropriate form of data?" The most obvious distinctions are between quantitative and qualitative methods. However, finer distinctions may be made within each of these alternatives concerning appropriate measurement. For example, in a quantitative study it might be arguable that the mean, median, or mode is the correct and appropriate measure of central tendency for summarizing message strategies across public relations campaigns. In a qualitative study, the question may be the number of examples that are adequate to support a claim or the extent to which summary claims and observations may substitute for particular examples that are the focus of concern.

The second question, "What do data count as?" is informed by answers to two additional questions:

1. "What does a statistical relationship indicate?" Is a particular finding indicative of a causal or associational relationship? Although Pearce et al. (1982) do not suggest the following, we would argue that this question is also relevant in qualitative research. For example, the qualitative researcher must consider whether particular observations are indicative of temporary or enduring phenomena. This extension is possible when you consider qualitative research as instances where $n = 1$ or some other small number not suitable for traditional statistical analysis.

2. "What is the relationship between the data and the theory?" Answers to this final question are reflected directly in the ways that theories are constructed and modified as well as in the initial theory choices that researchers pursue. Researchers infer different properties from a common observation depending on their interest in uncovering laws (e.g., Berger, 1977), discovering rules (e.g., Cushman, 1977) or specifying systems (e.g., Monge, 1977).

Fundamental disagreements of the type suggested above are not uncommon. For example, Gerald Miller (chapter 3) and James Grunig (chapter 2) disagree about the nature and ethical character of persuasion. Miller argues that public relations messages are a subset of the universe of persuasive messages. Grunig considers persuasion to be only one type of public relations message. Moreover, Grunig considers all persuasion as unethical, whereas Miller sees evaluation of means and ends as necessary to assess the ethicallity of persuasion.

At the root of this disagreement are different beliefs about the motivations of public relations practitioners. According to Miller, all public relations may be motivated by desires to understand or control the environment and to gain understanding from those in the environment. It is this motivation that is central to recognition of persuasion. Grunig argues that public relations may be motivated by desires for mutual understanding; messages generated by such motivations are not persuasion, and they are ethical.

This fundamental disagreement is, at present, unresolvable. Resolution would first require an unambiguous measure of the motivations of public relations practitioners. If public relations practitioners were found to be homogenous in their motivations to influence when communicating (even if only for the purpose of achieving understanding in their public), we would conclude that Miller is correct. If public relations practitioners were found to be heterogenous (exhibiting motivations to influence as well as motivations to understand), then we would conclude that Grunig is correct. It is doubtful that either author could propose a measure that both they and we would consider an unambiguous measure of motivation. Until such a measure exists, so that the disagreement may be resolved, we will continue to evaluate these theories based on our own presuppositions about motivations for public relations.

Poole and McPhee (1985) touched on another dimension of presuppositions when they discussed what they call the theory—method complex. They suggest a reciprocal relationship between method and theory. Their discussion indirectly suggests to us the need to consider the relationship between public relations practice and theory construction in public relations.

If Poole and McPhee are correct, for example, it would be unsound practice for public relations scholars to base their research on methods drawn solely from practitioners' experience. Their contention that "methods are one's [a researcher's] point of contact with reality" (Poole & McPhee, 1985, p. 101) suggests that a priori adoption of methods may have the same assumptive force as a world view.

It is reasonable to assume that practice as well as theory building may be influenced by metatheories. Public relations practitioners bring their own world views to work with them and express these world views through their day-to-day activities.

This would lead us to argue for the need to train researchers and practitioners broadly, so as not to allow methodological assumptions to constrain productivity. In a field where creativity is a desirable characteristic, a broad knowledge of theories and methods will lead to the recognition of multiple, alternative solutions for practical as well as theoretical problems.

To summarize our discussion to this point, metatheories are assumptions about the fundamental nature of the phenomena of interest. These assumptions are frequently unrecognized and influence choices of theory as well as method. Recognition of metatheoretic assumptions is necessary before other alternatives may be considered by theorists and researchers (Littlejohn, 1983; Pearce et. al., 1982).

A supposition that underlies our efforts in writing this chapter is: In order for communication to be effective, communicators must share or come to share a common set of symbols. To accomplish this end, the next section of this chapter defines the set of symbols that we use to talk about "theory."

THEORETIC VOCABULARY

Theories may be viewed as consisting of two basic types of content: concepts and statements about the relationships between those concepts. As a minima, a theory consists of at least two concepts and a statement explaining or predicting the relationship between those concepts.

Concepts are descriptive in purpose and function. They reference the fields of human experience. Concepts vary principally in their degree of abstractness. Level of abstractness is a function of the number of differentiated exemplars that constitute instances of a concept, as well as the extent to which exemplars are directly/indirectly observable.

For example, the concept "public relations" embraces a large number of differentiated exemplars, each of which may be seen as an occurrence of the concept. Behaviors as diverse as planning a communication campaign and writing a press release are readily recognized as instances of public relations. In the case of our current example, "communication campaign" and "press release" are also "theoretic" concepts. A theory of public relations should account for our earlier observation that both of these molecular concepts are indeed instances of the molar concept "public relations."

Relationships

Statements linking concepts in a theory are logical in character. Perhaps the most common type of relationship described in theories is the *conditional* relationship characteristic of hypotheses (If A then B). Other types of relationships are also possible, such as *conjunctive* relationships (Both A and B) or *disjunctive* relationships (Either A or B).

Both the conceptual content and the relational form of the statement contribute to our understanding of types of theories. Hawes (1975) identified two fundamentally different types of theoretic statements: synthetic and analytic. According to Hawes, synthetic statements are "empirical" in nature. Their validity is a function of the content of the concepts being related. Analytic statements are logical. Their validity is a function of form or structure. Analytic statements are more abstract and general than synthetic statements.

Different criteria are relevant to the evaluations of theories constructed from these two types of statements. Theories that consist principally of analytic statements are evaluated first in terms of their internal structure and consistency and secondarily in terms of their fit with human experience. Theories that consist principally of synthetic statements are evaluated first in terms of their fit with human experience and secondarily in terms of their internal structure and consistency.

Statements

Hawes (1975) suggested three dimensions applied to synthetic and analytic statements that produce seven unique types of theoretic statements from which theories may be constructed. The dimensions are scope of the statement, source of the statement, and validity of the statement. Types of statements are facts, hypotheses, propositions, postulates, axioms, theorems, and laws.

The first dimension, scope, refers to three levels of generality. Statements may be specific, general, or universal in scope. All analytic statements are universal in scope. Synthetic statements may be either specific or general in scope.

Four sources for statements are identified by Hawes. Statements that are primary and not derived in any way from other statements are said to be "assumed." Statements that are speculative and loosely tied to other statements are "inferred." Statements that are suggested by the empirical content of a prior statement are "derived." Statements whose logical validity is suggested by the logical structure of prior statements are "deduced."

The third dimension is validity of the statement. The validity of a statement should not be confused with its truth. Validity is a necessary but not sufficient condition for truth. A statement is tautologically valid if the primary statement from which it is deduced is logically valid. All analytic statements are tautologically valid.

Three other classes of validity apply to synthetic statements and reflect the extent to which all or none of the theoretic concepts are presently observable. A statement in which all of the concepts are subject to observation is considered empirically valid. If only some of the concepts in a statement are presently observable it is considered semantically valid. Finally, a statement is syntactically valid if none of its concepts may be observed at present.

In summarizing Hawes, we find that seven types of theoretic statements are recognized from the application of these dimensions to the analysis of synthetic and analytic statements. A *fact* is a synthetic statement where the scope is specific, the source is assumed, and the validity is empirical. A *hypothesis* is a synthetic statement of general scope, derived from prior statements, and empirically valid in that a hypothesis proposes a relationship between two or more sets of facts. Facts and hypotheses are not properly parts of theory. They serve as a bridge between theory and the empirical world.

The next four types of statements, *propositions, postulates, axioms,* and *theorems* may be either synthetic or analytic depending on the type of theory containing them. Synthetic propositions are general in scope, their source is assumed, and they are empirically valid. Analytic propositions are universal in scope, their source is assumed, and they are tautologically valid. Synthetic postulates are general in scope, their source is assumed, and they are semantically valid. Analytic postulates are universal in scope, their source is assumed, and they are tautologically valid. Synthetic axioms are general in scope, their source is assumed, and they are syntactically valid. Analytic axioms are universal in scope, their source is assumed, and they are tautologically valid. Synthetic theorems are general in scope, their source is inferred, and they are empirically valid. Analytic theorems are universal in scope, their source is deduced, and they are tautologically valid.

Laws are the final type of theoretic statement examined by Hawes. Laws are analytic statements that are universal in scope. Laws are deduced, and they are tautologically valid.

Types of Theories

Although the potential for laws concerning public relations is likely to be a hotly debated issue (depending on the metatheoretical presuppositions to which researchers and theorists adhere), the formal, analytical conceptualization of theories proposed by Hawes appears to be useful for organizing theories into a limited number of types. Each of these types is defined by a common set of characteristics. Hawes (1975) identified four types of theories.

Type I theories, according to Hawes, are likely to be presented in a literary style. The primary statements of the theory are axioms. None of the concepts expressed in the theory are presently observable, although they may be empirical in character. Type I theories are characterized by a large number of statements and are the least parsimonious of substantive theories.

In order to be tested empirically, postulates must be added to the Type I theory. Theorems can be inferred from valid postulates, and hypotheses may be derived from the resulting set of statements. Facts may directly support theorems and indirectly support postulates. Most rhetorical theories, including the theory in chapter 8 by Cheney and Dionisopoulos, are Type I theories.

Type II theories consist of at least two postulates. From the postulates a theorem may be inferred, and at least one hypothesis can be derived from the theorem. Facts may directly test the theorem and indirectly test the primary postulates of a Type II theory, therefore "negative results cannot be interpreted as falsifying the primary statements" (Hawes, 1975 p. 58). The number of theory concepts subject to empirical observation influences the adequacy of any observation as a theory test.

We argue that in many respects the application of coorientation theory to public relations presented in chapter 14 by Johnson is characteristic of Type II theories. Whereas this theory is generative of useful and informative hypotheses, failure to support a particular hypothesis in a particular study may be more indicative of the inability of research methods to adequately observe the theoretic phenomena than as a direct test of the adequacy of the theory.

Type III theories consist of at least one propositional statement from which a hypothesis may be derived. Facts that support the derived hypotheses directly test the proposition. Type III theories are the most parsimonious of substantive theories. In this book, theories of persuasion Gerald Miller identifies in his chapter are most representative of Type III theories.

Type IV theories are formal rather than substantive theories. Primary statements in Type IV theories are analytic rather than synthetic. A formal theory consists of at least one analytic proposition, postulate, or axiom from which at least one analytic theorem can be deduced.

The utility of formal theories is their generality. They are models of structures on which a variety of observations can be tested for goodness of fit. The theory of games presented by Murphy in chapter 10 is a formal theory, or Type IV theory. She argues that the general structure of games, expressed mathematically and logically may be used to explain public relations behavior and as a guide to planning public relations.

If theory construction is to serve the advancement of knowledge concerning public relations, then we must be able to compare and contrast alternative theories. We suggested earlier that an understanding of metatheoretic presuppositions may contribute to such an analysis. In addition, the typology of theories identified in this section of our essay is useful in categorizing theories and research. However, neither of these directly addresses issues of practical utility. In the next section we suggest criteria that are useful in comparing alternative theories.

Comparing Theories

Direct comparison of theories is only desirable when two or more alternative theories address the same problem area or domain of investigation. Theories may be viewed as functional solutions to problems, and it is the extent to which theories contribute to solving the problems associated with understanding, teaching, or practicing public relations that will determine their worth.

A functional analysis of theory considers at least four goals. First, theories may be seen to perform a descriptive function. They provide a vocabulary for studying and talking about public relations. The goodness of fit between theories and our experiences with the phenomena they seek to describe is one way of comparing alternative theories. Here the adequacy of the concepts to model public relations is the primary focus.

The primary emphasis of the Public Relations Process model Long and Hazleton (1987) proposed is description. Its goal is to identify general concepts and variables that apply to all instances of public relations. Little attention is paid to specifying the relationships between those concepts identified in the model. The proposed model may be compared to other models and/or it may be assessed for goodness of fit against experience. The psychographical profile Scott and O'Hair propose in chapter 12 is also descriptive.

A second function of theories is to promote understanding. In addition to telling us what public relations is (description), a theory may tell us why public relations exists (understanding). The degree of satisfaction with the explanatory power of a given theory may be a function of the theory's correspondence or adherence to the auditors metatheoretic presuppositions. For example, constructivist theorists find the attitude-change research influenced by logical empiricism lacks explanatory

power because meaningfulness is a concept central to constructivist research but not to logical empiricism (see Delia, 1975; O'Keefe, 1975).

Prediction and control are also useful criteria for assessing and comparing theories. These two criteria are different but complimentary.
Prediction refers to the ability of theories to anticipate the future value of
concepts from current or past observations of those concepts or related
concepts. Control refers to the ability of theorists to systematically intervene and influence outcomes predicted by theory. Prediction may be
considered as a necessary but not sufficient condition for control.

In public relations, the general effects of favorable and unfavorable
publicity upon stock price is predictable. Favorable publicity is likely to
produce an increase and unfavorable publicity is likely to produce a
decrease in the price of a referenced stock. A theory that suggests how
practitioners could intervene in the communication process so as to determine the valence, favorable or unfavorable, of publicity would allow
for the control of stock prices. Stock prices can be controlled through
collusion between practitioners and the media, however such behavior is
both illegal and unethical. (We also note that collusion is a concept studied within the theory of games [see Hazleton, 1977] and theories about
illegal and unethical behavior might be derived from game simulations
or analogous situations.)

Finally, we consider the heuristic function of theory. The heuristic
function of theory refers to the tendency to generate research and additional theory. We suggest two factors that may be related to the heuristic
function. First, theories that deal with problem domains considered central to a field are likely to receive more attention than theories that deal
with peripheral problem domains. Second, the availability or lack of
available methods for observing theoretic concepts appears to influence
research activity. It is our experience, for example, that method-bound
theories appear to generate less research than theories that are not method bound.

Heuristic theories also are likely to be controversial. They attract op-
ponents as well as proponents. In psychology, dissonance theory (Festinger, 1957) not only generated research by Festinger's students, it generated critical attention from other theorists, including Bem (1967).

As a summary, we observe that "better" theories describe adequately
the activities and processes that constitute public relations. They enhance our understanding of the rationale and purpose underlying public
relations practice and effects of those practices. They make accurate
predictions about the influence of various environmental factors on relevant publics and suggest how, within ethical and legal boundaries, practitioners might control the outcomes that derive from public relations

.activities suggested by theory. Finally, a better theory elicits research activity in public relations and theory building.

In this section of our chapter we provide our own theory of theories. We identify and define a basic vocabulary useful for talking about the basic elements of theories and constructing those elements. We show how, from these elements, various types of theories can be constructed. And finally, we suggest extra-theoretic criteria useful for comparing and evaluating theories. In our final section we consider the prospects and promise for public relations theory.

PUBLIC RELATIONS THEORY

Public relations is a rapidly emerging social science discipline. Central to the maturation of public relations as a profession and an academic discipline is the development of a body of theoretic knowledge that differentiates public relations from other professions and other academic disciplines. The academic roots of this discipline are clearly found in departments and schools of journalism and the empirical and humanistic social sciences concerned with the study of communication.

Journalism and public relations have been viewed traditionally as crafts to be learned from skilled practitioners. This may result from two historical influences. First, early public relations practitioners were principally ex-journalists who naturally brought with them many perspectives and values from their professional training and experience. Second, in the past, public relations has been taught largely in departments of journalism (although this is no longer the case, see Neff's chapter) so that beginning practitioners often start with the values and perspectives taught for the journalistic profession.

However, the craft approach to public relations education and training does not produce the unique body of theoretical knowledge necessary for the development and advancement of a profession. For example, engineering is a profession derived from physics and the other natural sciences rather than in the construction trades. Medicine was practiced in barbershops until it was linked to the sciences of biology and chemistry. So we look toward the humanistic and empirical traditions of social science to develop public relations theory.

Both empirical and humanistic traditions are reflected in this text. The works of Cheney and Dionisopoulos (chapter 8) and Pearson (chapter 7) are examples of theory and research in the humanistic tradition. Chapters by Murphy (chapter 10); Hamilton (chapter 19); and Cline,

McBride, and Miller (chapter 13) reflect an empirical orientation. Currently, little data suggests the superiority of one tradition over the other.

The metatheories and theories that comprise the first two sections of this text must be tested through research in laboratories and field. The third section of this text is concerned with application of specific theories or the potential application of theories to research and practice.

Our personal experience with professional and academic organizations (including the International Communication Association, the Public Relations Society of America, the Association for Education in Journalism and Mass Communication, and the Speech Communication Association) is that there has been little of public relations research that is theory driven. However, there is an apparent, increasing commitment to theory-driven research as evidenced in part by this book.

In this formative stage of social-science based public relations research, premature commitment to a particular theory or methodology is inappropriate. Merely substituting a new set of restrictive assumptions for an old set would deny public relations the opportunity to explore its boundaries and develop analyses which can allow it to both draw on, and make contributions to, the vast area of human endeavors studied by the social sciences.

REFERENCES

Bem, D. J. (1967). Self perception: An alternative interpretation of cognitive dissonance phenomena. *Psychological Review, 74,* 183–200.

Berger, C. R. (1977). The covering law perspective as a theoretical basis for the study of human communication. *Communication Quarterly, 25,* 7–18.

Cushman, D. P. (1977). The rules perspective as a theoretical basis for the study of human communication. *Communication Quarterly, 25,* 30–45.

Delia, J. G. (1975). *Communication research and the variable-analytic tradition.* Paper presented at the Speech Communication association convention, Houston, TX.

Festinger, L. (1957). *A theory of cognitive dissonance.* Stanford, CA: Stanford University Press.

Hawes, L. C. (1975). *Pragmatics of analoguing: Theory and model construction in communication.* Reading, MA: Addison-Wesley.

Hazleton, V. (1977). *Machiavellianism, power, and communication behavior in the creative alternative game.* Unpublished doctoral dissertation, University of Oklahoma.

Hazleton, V., & Cupach, W. R. (1986). An exploration of ontological knowledge: Communication competence as a function of the ability to describe, predict, and explain. *The Western Journal of Speech Communication, 50,* 119–132.

Kuhn, T. S. (1970). *The structure of scientific revolutions.* Chicago: University of Chicago Press.

Littlejohn, S. W. (1983). *Theories of human communication.* Belmont, CA: Wadsworth.

Long, L. W., & Hazleton, V. Jr. (1987). Public relations: A theoretic and practical response. *Public Relations Review, 13,* 3–13.

Monge, P. R. (1977). The systems perspective as a theoretical basis for the study of human communication. *Communication Quarterly, 25,* 19–29.

O'Keefe, B. J. (1975). Logical empiricism and the study of human communication. *Speech Monographs, 42,* 169–183.

Pearce, W. B., Cronen, V. E. & Harris, L. M. (1982). Methodological considerations in building human communication theory. In F. E. X. Dance (Ed.), *Human communication theory* (pp. 1–41). New York: Harper & Row.

Polyani, M. (1958). *Personal knowledge: Toward a post-critical philosophy.* Chicago: University of Chicago Press.

Poole, M. S., & McPhee, R. D. (1985). Methodology in interpersonal research. In M. L. Knapp & G. R. Miller (Eds.), *Handbook of interpersonal communication* (pp. 100–170). Beverly Hills, CA: Sage.

2

Symmetrical Presuppositions as a Framework for Public Relations Theory

James E. Grunig
University of Maryland

ABSTRACT

Public relations theorists have borrowed theories from communication science and other social sciences, but few have developed unique theories of public relations. Scientific disciplines always have borrowed from one another, but they do not advance unless they build original theories from the borrowed concepts. In this chapter, Grunig maintains that public relations theorists must examine their presuppositions about public relations before they borrow concepts and build theory. All theories are derived from presuppositions. Unless theorists recognize the effect of presuppositions, they will blindly follow the prevailing worldview of the field. The prevailing worldview, Grunig argues, sees public relations as persuasive and manipulative. As a replacement, he proposes a symmetrical view of public relations that sees the purpose of public relations as managing conflict and promoting understanding.

This chapter focuses on presuppositions and their role in theory building, especially in building a theory of public relations. In chapter 1, Hazelton and Botan described different types of theories that have been developed in communication and explained the role of metatheory in theory building. This chapter, then, examines the effects that metatheory has had on public relations. In the past, public relations theory has ignored metatheory, but I believe that we must understand it if we are to improve both the ethical quality of public relations and its chance for success in resolving practical public relations situations.

Presuppositions are the essence of metatheory. They influence all four types of theory described in chapter 1. They consist of assumptions about the world and values attached to those assumptions. Presuppositions define the problems researchers attempt to solve, the theoretical traditions that are used in their research, and the extent to which the world outside a research community accepts the theories that result from research.

The Roman Catholic Church excommunicated Galileo for his presuppositions when he claimed that the earth was not the center of the universe. Presuppositions have produced lawsuits when evolutionary theory has differed from fundamentalist interpretations of the Bible. I maintain that presuppositions about the nature of public relations have steered research and theory in the field in a direction that I consider to be both ineffective and ethically questionable. I then suggest an alternative set of presuppositions that I believe will produce a theory of public relations that helps organizations be more effective. I also propose a theory more ethically acceptable to people outside the public relations profession than are the current principles that guide our practice.

Public relations is an infant scholarly field, although it has been practiced for at least 100 years and perhaps for thousands, depending on how tightly we define the origins of the field (J. Grunig & Hunt, 1984, pp. 13–46). One can think of many theories that apply to public relations, but it is more difficult to think of *a* public relations theory (one that has not been borrowed from another discipline). Public relations as a scholarly discipline, therefore, appears to be fragmented and not unique as a discipline.

The professional practice of public relations appears to be equally fragmented; practitioners have no common body of knowledge nor even a common set of skills. Yet one can argue that the practice is guided by a single mindset, or paradigm as Kuhn (1970) called it, that dominates the field. Such a mindset defines public relations as the use of communication to manipulate publics for the benefit of organizations. "Persuade" is a softer word often substituted for "manipulate," but changing the word does not change the mindset. Practitioners with a social conscience often convince themselves that manipulation benefits publics as well as their organizations. Again, however, the mindset remains the same.

Olasky (1984) traced this predominant mindset to the introspective psychological theories of public relations developed by Edward L. Bernays in the 1920s and called it the "Bernays paradigm." Jackall (1986) described the same mindset and argued that it differs little today from when it guided the practices of the press agents of the 1800s.

Roughly described, the dominant mindset defines public relations as the manipulation of public behavior for the benefit of the manipulated publics as well as the sponsoring organizations. The mindset carries with it a number of obvious presuppositions about the nature of human beings, the nature of social responsibility, and the nature and purpose of communication. It also suggests the relevance of some obvious communication theories, most notably theories of attitudes and persuasion. I call this mindset the *asymmetrical model of public relations* and suggest an alternative I call the *symmetrical model of public relations,* which has a different set of presuppositions and calls for a different kind of theory.

Before describing these competing mindsets, however, I introduce some concepts from the philosophy of science that help to explain the nature of scientific theory and the role that presuppositions play in its development.

PROBLEMS AND DOMAINS IN SCIENTIFIC RESEARCH

During the last 20 years philosophers of science have abandoned the idea that the purpose of science is to discover truth or to discover theories that accurately describe the real world. Instead, they have come to the conclusion that the purpose of scientific research is to build theories that solve the most relevant problems to researchers working in a scientific domain. Two terms are important in this statement and require further explanation: *problems* and *domain.*

Researchers do not, as so many of our methodology textbooks assert, formulate theories and try to falsify them with data.[1] Rather, they choose problems that researchers working in a domain believe to be important. After choosing problems, researchers develop primitive theories— vague, general hunches—about how to resolve those problems. If research provides hope that these first hunches offer promise of solving the problems, researchers pursue the theories further and gradually revise and expand their theories so that they resolve more and more problems.

Domain is a term that was coined by Shapere (1977). His concept of domain is similar to such concepts as research programs (Lakatos, 1970), disciplines (Toulmin, 1972b), research traditions (Laudan, 1977), or paradigms (Kuhn, 1970). Shapere, like these other writers, was trying to define the fields or areas of interest that can be identified within a science. What is common among these writers is the notion that common

---

[1]This antiquated explanation of science is usually called logical positivism or logical empiricism (see, e.g., Feigl, 1969). The idea that the purpose of science is to falsify conjectured theories was developed by Popper (1959, 1965). For a discussion of what the "new philosophy of science" means to public relations, see J. Grunig (1979).

problems hold these fields together. Public relations can be described as a scientific domain within the broader area of communication, although it is certainly one of the least-developed communication domains.

Scientific Domains

According to Shapere (1977), domains cannot be identified by single theories or by research traditions. Likewise, domains cannot be explained sociologically as a community of scholars, as Kuhn (1970) argued, for example. Rather, domains consist of a set of "items" that have some deeper unity: phenomena to be explained, facts and observations that have been made about these phenomena, and theories that have been used to explain them. Thus, in Shapere's view, scientists use theories to do more than explain observations. They also use them to explain other theories or simply to find a idea that unifies the domain.

It is difficult even to identify the items in the public relations domain. What are the famous studies, the competing theories, the typical methodologies? In contrast, the persuasion and attitude-change domain consists of many observations of effective and ineffective communication campaigns, thousands of experimental results, learning theories, functional theories, stimulus–response theories, cognitive consistency theories, and cognitive–response theories.

The constitute a domain, according to Shapere (1977, p. 525), the items must be related in some way. In addition, there must be something problematic about the domain (something not well understood); the problem or problems must be important; and science must be ready to deal with the problem.

Scientific Problems

Problems that scientists agree are important, therefore, constitute the core of a domain. Shapere (1977, p. 533) defined three types of scientific problems. *Domain problems* relate to "the clarification of the domain itself." The other two kinds of problems relate to the need for a "deeper account of the domain": *theoretical problems* "inasmuch as answers to them are called 'theories,'" and *theoretical inadequacies,* because the problems are with the theories themselves.

Laudan (1977) has provided further clarification of the nature of the scientific problems found at the core of a domain. In *Progress and Its Problems,* he described science as a problem-solving enterprise. He defined a scientific problem as something that is ambiguous or irregular, and said that "the function of a theory is to resolve ambiguity, to reduce irregularity to uniformity, to show that what happens is somehow intelligible and predictable" (p. 13). Laudan (1977) proposed two theses about the nature of theory:

Thesis 1. The first and essential acid test for any theory is whether it provides acceptable answers to interesting questions; whether, in other words, it provides satisfactory solutions to important problems.

Thesis 2. In appraising the merits of theories, it is more important to ask whether they constitute adequate solutions to significant problems than it is to ask whether they are "true," "corroborated," "well-confirmed" or otherwise justifiable within the framework of contemporary epistemology. (pp. 13–14)

Like Shapere, Laudan (1977, pp. 15–31) elaborated further on the types of problems that could be found in a domain (although Laudan did not use the term *domain*). According to Laudan, problems may be either *empirical* or *conceptual*. An empirical problem consists of an experiment or other kind of observation that provides a test of a theory.[2]

Conceptual problems occur with a theory itself. When they occur, scientists pay more attention to such problems than to empirical problems. Conceptual problems may be *internal*: an inconsistency in the logic of the theory. They also may be *external*: They may be incompatible with a theory from another domain, with prevailing methodologies, or with prevailing nonscientific beliefs. Laudan called incompatibility with nonscientific beliefs "worldview" difficulties—difficulties that occur when scientific theories conflict with the prevailing worldview of nonscientists. "Worldview difficulties," I believe, describe the problems of Galileo, evolutionary theory, and of public relations.

Laudan (1977, p. 71) maintained that scientists do not evaluate theories by testing them against facts or data, as most empirically oriented communication researchers assume, but by comparing them with other theories. Theories can be compared if they address similar problems. The best theories, Laudan (1977, p. 66) said, are those that solve the most empirical problems and have the fewest conceptual problems and anomalous empirical problems. Such theories are the hallmark of advanced domains.

---

[2]Laudan defined three kinds of empirical problems. *Unsolved problems* are those that no theory has solved. *Solved problems* are those solved by one or more theories. *Anomalous problems* are those that one theory can solve but that one or more competing theories cannot solve.

Mature and Immature Sciences

Many philosophers of science have attempted to describe the differences between primitive and developed sciences. Obviously, public relations is a primitive science. In primitive science, according to Shapere (1977), "obvious sensory similarities or general presuppositions usually determine whether certain items of experience will be considered as forming a . . . domain, this is less and less true as science progresses" (p. 521). In primitive science, scientists work directly with phenomena and, at times, empirical generalizations. As a domain matures, scientists develop deeper theories to connect and explain relationships among the items in the domain. Nickles (1977) added that a single theory begins to dominate a domain as it matures, and "as one theory succeeds another the domain is modified and usually enlarged" (pp. 583–584).

If public relations were a more advanced domain, we would be quarreling about whose theory best solves Laudan's conceptual problems and anomalous empirical problems. Instead, we seem to have few public disagreements, probably because we have few theories to argue about. We have few theories because we have not defined the important problems in the domain. Our first task, then, is to solve Shapere's domain problems, which means that we must clarify the domain itself.

Good Theories Are Underdetermined by Data

As philosophers of science have recognized that the purpose of science is to solve problems rather than to explain phenomena, they also have begun to realize that results of research do not have to match theoretical hypotheses perfectly, or even well, to be useful. Too often in a primitive domain like public relations, we pay great attention to the empirical accuracy of research and do not ask whether our research is related to important problems or contributes to the building of deep theories.

Laudan (1977) argued that theories seldom predict empirical results closely and that researchers, instead, search for enough confirmation of their hunches to proceed to develop a theory:[3]

---

[3]Lakatos (1970, p. 138), similarly, claimed that researchers ignore anomalies at the beginning of a research program, when anomalies abound, and search for enough verification of the theories to suggest that the theory warrants further development. Suppe (1973, p. 147) added that "there is no question whether the theory is empirically true—it's known to be false." But, he added, researchers still use such a theory "because it conveniently yields incorrect predictions, which are close enough for the purposes at hand."

Although rare, it sometimes happens that a theory exactly predicts an experimental outcome. When that desirable result is achieved, there is cause for general rejoicing. It is far more common for the predictions deduced from a theory to come close to reproducing the data which constitute a specific problem, but with no exact coincidence of results . . . for problem-solving purposes we do not require an exact, but only an approximate, resemblance between theoretical results and experimental ones. (p. 23)

Suppe (1977a) said that the evidence used to admit a theoretical proposition into a domain "always *underdetermines* the truth of the claim" (pp. 701–702). He explained elsewhere:

Examination of successful, illuminating, products of science throughout its history reveals one pervasive characteristic—the most impressive achievements of science are the ones which are underdetermined by the available data. Characteristic of science is the acceptance and rejection of comprehensive theories on the basis of available data which, in principle, are insufficient to establish either the truth or falsity of these theories. (pp. 17–18)

What This Means for Public Relations

The discussion, thus far, of contemporary philosophy of science reveals that explanation of data matters less to scientists than does the solving of important problems. Mature sciences develop deep theories to solve those problems, and the accuracy of empirical results is less important than the ability of these results to suggest a deeper theoretical integration of a domain. Yet, in most immature sciences—and communication domains provide fine examples—researchers devote far more attention to gathering and analyzing data than to building theory. Those data seldom go beyond direct observations or empirical generalizations.

In public relations, construction of deep theories should be our goal. Before we can construct such theories, however, we must clarify the problems that should be in the domain. Before we can resolve theoretical problems, we must solve our domain problems (i.e., select the problems we want to solve). To do that, we must understand where problems come from. As we see next, research traditions and extra-scientific worldviews provide presuppositions that identify our research problems for us. We must examine those presuppositions carefully if we are to understand where the public relations domain is and where it is going.

However naive it may seem, one must begin the discussion of presuppositions in scientific research with the statement that scientists are human beings. Human beings are by nature subjective creatures who have no choice but to use their minds to construct scientific theories. But to what extent does the mind and what is in it beforehand distort what a scientist sees?

Biologist George Gaylord Simpson (1964, pp. 98–99) stated, for example, that "science is man's exploration of his universe and to exclude himself even in principle is certainly not objective realism." Science historian Jacob Bronowski (1965, pp. 10, 20) added that a scientist is not a camera recording facts. "Science, like art, is not a copy of nature, but a re-creation of her . . . We re-make nature by the act of discovery." Scientists, like artists, have creative minds, Bronowski added. The creative mind sees order where others see only disorder.

The Effect of Worldview

The creative mind, however, does not observe with a blank slate. Researchers bring with them what Meehan (1968) called a conceptual framework:

> [It] serves as a selecting mechanism for the observer . . . in the same way that spectacles serve the man who is blind without them. . . . The facts do not lie before the observer, immutable and unchangeable. What a fact *is* depends on the conceptual framework through which perceptions are screened. (p. 41)

Many philosophers of science have used the German term *Weltanschauung,* which means a comprehensive worldview or mindset, to describe conceptual frameworks (Suppe, 1977a). In 1962, Kuhn (1970) introduced the first and most popular term used to describe a scientific worldview, which he called a *paradigm.* Kuhn did not state clearly what he meant by a paradigm, however, and philosophers of science have criticized the term severely (e.g., Shapere, 1964).

Masterman (1970) claimed that Kuhn used the term *paradigm* in 21 different ways in *The Structure of Scientific Revolutions.* To counter such criticism, Kuhn (1970, p. 175) added a postscript to a revised version of the book in which he redefined a paradigm as consisting of a "disciplinary matrix" and "exemplars." The disciplinary matrix is most relevant for understanding the nature of a worldview held by a scientific community. A disciplinary matrix "stands for the entire constellation of beliefs, values, techniques, and so on shared by the members of a given community."

Kuhn believed that a paradigm serves as a *gestalt* for researchers, a unified perceptual or psychological picture of reality that is more than the sum of its parts. He argued that this *gestalt* defines relevant problems and theories for scientists and serves as a psychological blinder that makes theories from different paradigms "incommensurable" (i.e., not subject to direct comparison empirically to establish which theory is best). Single paradigms dominate mature sciences, Kuhn added, and could only be replaced through a scientific revolution.[4]

Reactions to Relativism

Most philosophers of science did not accept Kuhn's relativistic picture of science. Suppe (1976), for example, argued that Kuhn's view of science:

> makes science fundamentally an irrational enterprise—an enterprise consisting of periods of uncritical dogmatic drudgery separated by occasional episodes of near-psychotic schizophrenic activity having much in common with panic, mass hysteria, and mass religious conversion. (p. 15)

Suppe (1977b, p. 498) maintained that the dogmatic aspects of Kuhn's disciplinary matrix—community, values, prejudices, and learning experiences—could be removed by recognizing that the central component of the matrix is a conceptual framework, his translation of *Weltanschauung*.

Brown (1977, pp. 101–109) reconstructed Kuhn's ideas to make them less relative. In place of "disciplinary matrix," he used the term *presuppositions*, a central concept toward which I have been working in this chapter. Presuppositions, according to Brown, are a priori propositions that the scientist sees as necessary truths. Presuppositions are not tautological (true by definition), but the scientist assumes them to be true based on his or her worldview. Presuppositions suggest empirical phenomena that would confirm the truth of the presuppositions if the phenomena could be observed. Nevertheless, presuppositions cannot be measured and re-

---

[4]Kuhn was not the only historian or philosopher of science to hold these views. He was the principal figure in a group of relativistic philosophers of science, including Feyerabend (1970), Bohm (1977), and Hanson (1958).

futed directly. Presuppositions, as described by Brown (1977), are less relative and more flexible than Kuhn's paradigms, however:

> Although presuppositions are protected propositions which are not given up lightly at the first sign of a counter-instance, presuppositions do change and a persistent failure to account for an anomaly might well lead to such a change. (p. 105)

Presuppositions and Theory

Many other philosophers have incorporated the concept of presuppositions into their explanation of the nature of scientific theory. In each case, they did so by describing two or more levels of theoretical principles in a domain. The most abstract level is that of presuppositions; the second level is that of theories or laws.[5]

Laudan (1977, pp. 70–120) incorporated presuppositions into his concept of a research tradition, a second major concept of this chapter and a term that Laudan used to describe a *Weltanschauung.* He listed several examples of research traditions: Darwininism in biology, quantum theory and the electromagnetic theory of light in physics, behaviorism and Freudianism in psychology, and Marxism and capitalism in economics. A research tradition is broader than a theory and has presuppositions that are difficult to test—Laudan called presuppositions sets of doctrines or assumptions that represent a broad type of theory.

A research tradition also contains a narrower type of theory—hypotheses, axioms, or principles that "can be utilized for making specific experimental predictions and for giving detailed explanations of natural phenomena" (Laudan, 1977, p. 71). The specific theories can be tested, but the research tradition and its presuppositions are "neither explanatory, nor predictive, nor directly testable" (p. 81).

According to Laudan (1977, p. 82), research traditions provide us (scientists) "with the crucial tools (we) need for solving problems, both empirical and conceptual . . . the research tradition even goes so far as

---

[5]Meehan (1968), for example, proposed three levels of principles: a *conceptual framework* suggests which variables should be in a *logical system* that will generate empirical *expectations.* Toulmin (1972a, pp. 123–124, 192–199) also described three levels. He called presuppositions "disciplinary principles" and theories "theoretical principles" or laws. Toulmin called his third level "hypotheses," statements based on laws that attempt to explain phenomena. Toulmin added that theoretical principles are always more ordered and logically coherent than disciplinary principles. In addition, theoretical principles change more rapidly than disciplinary principles.

to define what the problems are, and what importance should ᵥᵥ
tached to them." A research tradition, Laudan (1977) added, thus

> delimits the domain of applications of its constituent theories . . . gener-
> ates conceptual problems for its theories . . . acts negatively as a constraint
> on types of theories which can be developed within the do-
> main . . . provides vital clues for theory construction . . . and contains
> guidelines about how its theories can be modified to improve its problem-
> solving capacity. (pp. 86–93)

Most researchers are unaware of the way in which presuppositions
and research traditions are linked to problems and theories. When they
hold a set of presuppositions, they are more likely to think some research
problems are relevant than others and that certain theories are more
useful. Researchers also may be unaware of why they choose to be part of
a research tradition. For example, they may become part of a research
tradition because the presuppositions of that tradition match their extra-
scientific presuppositions. (For example, fundamentalist Christians easily embrace "creation science" as a dubious scientific research tradition
because it matches their religious worldview.) Or the presuppositions of
a research tradition may become a person's extrascientific presuppositions. (For example, B. F. Skinner supposedly raised his children according to the principles of behaviorism. Fundamentalists make such a claim
implicitly when they argue that belief in evolution is a religion.)

Controlling the Effects of Presuppositions

Once one realizes that presuppositions and research traditions influence
scientists' choices of research problems and theories, it is easy to conclude also that science is totally subjective (as did Kuhn). However, philosophers such as Laudan, Suppe, Shapere, and Toulmin argue that the
effectiveness of theories derived from different presuppositions can be
compared. Theories from more than one research tradition may be used
to link "items"—problems and theories—in the same domain. Also, research traditions can be compared by their ability to solve the same
problems.

In addition, researchers can compare theories if they can make "direct
observations"—made through neutral measuring devices that are free of
interference from the person doing the measuring or the thing that is
being measured (Shapere, 1977; Suppe, 1977a, pp. 690–693). When
direct observations are not possible, scientists can make "indirect obser-

vations" to compare theories. Although indirect observations are laden with the theory they are to measure, they can be "unloaded" by comparing them with what Shapere called "noncontroversial background information" or background theories.

Recently, yet another group of philosophers called "scientific realists" have challenged some aspects of the view of science I have just presented.[6] In particular, realists argue that theories in a mature science approach "truth," and that new theories that replace older ones incorporate the true predictions of the older theories and progress toward greater truth (see, e.g., Leplin, 1984b; Putnam, 1984). Truth means that theories *refer* to events or objects that exist in the real world, and that the "deep structure" of a theory—its most abstract level—is true, literally, as well as the observations it generates.

Realists in essence want to retain the idea from logical positivism that science is completely objective. They would like to believe that science explains what is "really out there." Laudan (1984) called this wishful thinking:

> All of us would like realism to be true; we would like to think that science works because it has got a grip on how things really are. But such claims have yet to be made out. Given the present state of the art, it can only be wish fulfillment that gives rise to the claim that realism, and realism alone, explains why science works. (p. 245)

If realism is an accurate description of science, presuppositions and research traditions would not have the importance I have ascribed to them in this chapter. Scientists would develop new theories to replace older theories, but the transition would represent a single path of progress toward truth. In contrast, I would argue that the new theory may progress toward truth but that theories developed from within a different presuppositional framework will not progress toward the same truth. Laudan (1984, p. 238) took the same position, saying that "changing ontologies or conceptual frameworks make it impossible to capture many of the central theoretical laws and mechanisms postulated by the earlier theory."

Presuppositions, therefore, play a crucial role in research and theory building. *With this presupposition in mind,* we turn to a discussion of the presuppositions that have and should affect the public relations domain.

---

[6]For example, see the volume edited by Leplin (1984a).

MODELS OF PUBLIC RELATIONS

At the beginning of this chapter, I asserted that public relations practice is dominated by the presupposition that the purpose of public relations is to manipulate the behavior of publics for the assumed, if not actual, benefit of the manipulated publics as well as the organization. The worldview holding that presupposition and the alternatives to it can be described by four models of public relations that I introduced in 1984 (J. Grunig, 1984; J. Grunig and Hunt, 1984, pp. 21–26).

The four models of public relations are representations of the values, goals, and behaviors held or used by organizations when they practice public relations—simplified in the same way that a perfect vacuum or perfect competition are simplified representations in other sciences. I have called these models "press agentry/publicity," "public information," "two-way asymmetrical," and "two-way symmetrical."

Press agentry/publicity describes propagandistic public relations that seeks media attention in almost any way possible. The *public-information* model characterizes public relations as practiced by "journalists-in-residence" who disseminate what is generally accurate information about the organization but do not volunteer negative information. Both of these models are one-way models in that practitioners who follow them give information about the organization to publics but do not seek information from publics through research or informal methods.

The next two models are more sophisticated in that their practice includes the use of research and other methods of two-way communication. Two-way communication can be manipulative, however; thus, *two-way asymmetrical* public relations programs use research to identify the messages most likely to produce the support of publics without having to change the behavior of the organization. Effects are asymmetrical because the hoped for behavioral change benefits the organization and not publics, although many practitioners believe that manipulated publics benefit also from the manipulation. As a result, the two-way asymmetrical model is the epitome of much of modern, sophisticated public relations practice. However, it also describes a model that fits within the predominant mindset developed by Bernays and others decades ago.

The fourth model, in contrast, has effects that are symmetrical—effects that a neutral observer would describe as benefitting both organization and publics. Organizations practicing *two-way symmetrical* public relations use bargaining, negotiating, and strategies of conflict resolution to bring about symbiotic changes in the ideas, attitudes, and behaviors of both the organization and its publics.

Four Models Collapsed to Two Worldviews

Previously, I have argued (J. Grunig and L. Grunig, 1986), that two of the models are asymmetrical in purpose—press agentry and two-way asymmetrical—and that two are symmetrical—public information and two-way symmetrical. In retrospect, however, only the two-way symmetrical model is truly symmetrical. Practitioners following the press-agentry and two-way asymmetrical models intend to persuade or manipulate publics. Those following the public-information model have the effect of manipulating publics, although that may not be their intent.

I would now argue, therefore, that the press-agentry, two-way asymmetrical, and public-information models are variations on the dominant worldview of public relations, and the two-way symmetrical model represents a break from that worldview. The press agentry and two-way asymmetrical models can, alternatively, be described as "craft" and "scientific" versions of asymmetrical public relations. The public-information model can be described also as the "journalistic" model, which I now see as de facto asymmetrical public relations.

Originally, I believed that the public-information model would be the dominant one practiced (J. Grunig and Hunt, 1984, p. 22). Research has not born out that contention. Organizations seem to practice several of the models together, and the press-agentry model is most popular. The two-way asymmetrical model, if practiced, is most popular in corporations. The public-information model seems to be most popular in governmental agencies, especially in scientific agencies (E. Pollack, 1984; R. Pollack, 1986). The public-information model, however, consistently has been the most difficult model to measure reliably, because organizations rarely practice it as a pure model.

Many organizations practice the two-way symmetrical model at times, but it is seldom the dominant model practiced. In addition, organizations often practice the two-way symmetrical model together with the two-way asymmetrical model, failing to recognize that communication does not have to be persuasive and manipulative if done under the rubric of public relations.

Why Organizations Practice the Models

Although our research consistently has shown that the four models accurately describe the practice of public relations in the real world (J. Grunig and L. Grunig 1989), the research until recently has not satisfactorily explained why organizations practice the four models. Originally, I developed a contingency theory that stated that organizations would practice the model of public relations best suited for their environments (J. Grunig, 1984). The contingency idea did not work. We had to conclude that as an environmental contingency theory, the models function more as a normative theory—specifying what organizations *should* do—than as a descriptive theory—explaining what they actually *do*.

Our most recent research shows that organizations use the models in two ways (J. Grunig & L. Grunig, 1986). First, the models function as situational strategies that organizations use for different publics and public relations problems—not as single organizing frameworks for all public relations efforts. Second, the presuppositions of the models function as part of an organization's ideology.

Our research shows, next, that the reasons these models become part of organizational ideology and that organizations choose them as situational strategies can be explained by the concepts of organizational power, organizational culture, and the expertise of the top public relations executive.

In brief, our research shows that the *dominant coalition* of an organization, its power elite, identifies strategic publics in the environment as the target for public relations—publics such as employees, the financial community, activist groups, or consumers. The dominant coalition then turns the problem over to the public relations director and dictates to the director which model would be an appropriate strategy. Which model the dominant coalition chooses depends on whether that model fits with organizational culture and whether the public relations director has the expertise to carry out the model.

The expert public relations director practicing the more sophisticated, two-way models is more likely to be in the dominant coalition—where he or she can influence culture, the strategic public chosen, and the situational model to be applied.

Now that ideology and culture have come to the fore as critical predictive variables, the presuppositions of the models take on great importance. In particular, few organizations practice the two-way symmetrical model because their worldview of public relations does not include that model, and they seldom have public relations personnel with the expertise to practice it. To change the way organizations practice public relations, therefore, we must change the dominant presuppositions about public relations. We look next at the presuppositions of the three asymmetrical models and then describe the presuppositions of the two-way symmetrical model.

PRESUPPOSITIONS OF THE ASYMMETRICAL MODELS

When an organization, its dominant coalition, or its public relations practitioners hold an asymmetrical worldview, they presuppose that the organization knows best. Furthermore, they assume that the public would benefit by cooperating with the organization. They assume that if dissident publics had "the big picture" or understood the organization, these publics would willingly "cooperate" with the organization.

Before publics will cooperate with the organization, however, they must be "sold" the organization's position.[7] War is also a popular metaphor (e.g., "Waging and Winning the War of Ideas" was the title of a speech at the 1986 annual meeting of the Public Relations Society of America; Feulner, 1986).

Although the asymmetrical perspective may sound like a reasonable position, keep in mind that organizations often expect publics to accept strange things as a result of "cooperation": pollution, toxic waste, drinking, smoking, guns, overthrow of governments, dangerous products, lowered salary and benefits, discrimination against women and minorities, job layoffs, dangerous manufacturing plants, risky transportation of products, higher prices, monopoly power, poor product quality, political favoritism, insider trading, use of poisonous chemicals, exposure to carcinogens, nuclear weapons, and even warfare. The list could go on and on.

This list is important because few of the organizations advocating these positions believe the practices are detrimental to the publics they ask to adopt the behaviors. In spite of these good intentions, I contend that the long-term effects of the asymmetrical models make it impossible for them to be an ethical and socially responsible approach to public relations.

Let me list a few other presuppositions that I believe are part of the asymmetrical worldview:

Internal orientation. Members of the organization look out from the organization and do not see the organization as outsiders see it.

---

[7]As I was writing this chapter, a new book came through the mail titled *Selling Science* (Nelkin, 1987), which concluded that science must have a good "image" (p. 133) before the public will accept it. "Image" is one of the public relations buzzwords that clearly has asymmetrical presuppositions behind it. Presenting a good "image" usually means selecting a few attributes of an organization, product, or cause that publics will accept and promoting those attributes and not those that publics are less likely to accept. If I were to write this book from a symmetrical perspective, I would title it *Communication with the Public About Science.*

Closed system. Information flows out from the organization and not into it.

Efficiency. Efficiency and control of costs are more important than innovation.

Elitism. Leaders of the organization know best. They have more knowledge than members of publics. Wisdom is not the product of a "free marketplace of ideas."

Conservatism. Change is undesirable. Outside efforts to change the organization should be resisted; pressure for change should be considered subversive.

Tradition. Tradition provides an organization with stability and helps it to maintain its culture.

Central authority. Power should be concentrated in the hands of a few top managers. Employees should have little autonomy. Organizations should be managed as autocracies.

Although this set of presuppositions reflects more politically conservative than liberal presuppositions, liberal groups and organizations also practice asymmetrical public relations. Most corporations tend to be conservative, however, and the aforementioned set of presuppositions represents their worldview.[8] Many liberal activist groups, in particular, use asymmetrical public relations to further their causes. When that is the case, they also seem to accept the closed-system, elitist, and sometimes central-authority presuppositions previously described.

Theories Relevant to the Asymmetrical Models

As we have seen, philosophers of science have shown that the presuppositions of different research traditions suggest both what problems researchers should attempt to solve and which theories would best solve them. The history of theory and research in public relations bears out this conclusion.

First, it is clear that the asymmetrical presuppositions of the press agentry, two-way asymmetrical, and public information models of public

---

[8]Olasky (1987) has analyzed corporate public relations from a libertarian perspective and concluded that corporations take a classic liberal approach, which favors strong government, and use public relations to seek government support and regulation that benefits them—calling it social responsibility. He also described Edward Bernays as a liberal who used asymmetrical public relations to bring about what Bernays considered to be socially desirable behaviors. More is said about Olasky's study later.

relations have suggested attitude and behavior change, means of persuasive communication, diffusion of innovations, and the effects of media campaigns as relevant problems for public relations research.

Theories chosen by public relations scholars also reflect the asymmetrical worldview. They have borrowed these theories from other domains, a practice not unusual in science. Scientists working in a domain frequently borrow research traditions and their accompanying theories and problems from other disciplines, although the theory used in the new domain usually is more of an analog of the original theory than a replica (Shapere, 1977, p. 545). In the cases of the press agentry, public-information, and two-way asymmetrical models, certain research traditions come to mind as relevant to and commonly applied to each of the models.

For the press agentry model, the study of propagandistic techniques beginning in the 1920s was especially relevant (e.g., McDougall, 1952).

The scientific study of attitude change and persuasion was especially relevant to the two-way asymmetrical model,[9] along with the humanistic study of rhetorical principles. Thus, it is not surprising that the two-way asymmetrical model is especially popular among public relations researchers in the field of speech communication where persuasion has been a tradition since the time of Aristotle.

The public-information model can be most easily identified in the approach taken to public relations by journalism schools. Often that approach has been de facto rather than intended: Students trained in journalism, and not specifically in public relations, easily have found employment in organizations as "journalists-in-residence." As a result, public relations researchers in journalism schools have found the research on the effects of public-information campaigns (e.g., Rice and Paisley, 1981) and the research on diffusion of innovations (e.g., Rogers, 1983) to be especially relevant.

Most of the research in these traditions reflects what has been called *administrative* research as opposed to *critical* research—that is, research designed to help the organization further its ends rather than to criticize the performance of that organization.[10] Recently, however, two critical studies have been conducted of what I interpret as the asymmetrical

---

[9]See Petty and Cacioppo (1981) for an excellent review of the theories developed in the attitude-change domain. It is interesting to note, however, that recent theories show that attitudes most often change when the approach to communication has been what I would interpret as symmetrical (pp. 255–269)—that is, cognitive effects must precede attitude change.

[10]For more discussion on administrative and critical research, see the volume edited by McAnany, Schnitman, and Janus (1981).

models of public relations. These studies, I believe, reveal the shortcomings of the asymmetrical models from the perspective of ethics and social responsibility.

Critical Studies of the Asymmetrical Models

Two recent critical studies of public relations, one that I interpret as a study of the press agentry and two-way asymmetrical models (Olasky, 1987) and the other as a study of the public-information model (Gandy, 1982), have reached similar conclusions critical of the practice of public relations. The studies come from the opposite sides of the political spectrum: Olasky's is conservative and Gandy's is radical. Olasky concluded that public relations as we know it should be replaced by "private relations." Gandy concluded that public relations efforts of corporations and bureaucracies should be monitored carefully to control their influence on public policy.

Olasky maintained that in the 19th century, corporations practiced what he called "private relations." Corporate executives communicated directly with the media and others outside the corporation without the need for the intervention of the public relations practitioner. Often they simply kept their business to themselves. At the beginning of the 20th century, however, public relations innovators including Ivy Lee and Edward Bernays entered the picture, helping corporations to manipulate their communication and beginning what Olasky called the "story of convoluted philosophy and tawdry practice."

Olasky (1987) is a libertarian conservative, one who believes that private enterprises should be autonomous to pursue their interests without the interference of government or outside groups. Competition should be wide open, and corporations should be free to be closed to outsiders should they choose—his concept of private relations.

Olasky analyzed landmark cases of public relations in the railroad, telephone, movie, and steel industries. Firms in these industries took what Olasky described as an elitist liberal view of social responsibility. They used public relations to seek government intervention and regulation in order to eliminate competition in the guise of supporting the public welfare.

> That story is this: For over a century, many major corporate public relations leaders have worked diligently to kill free enterprise by promoting big government–big business collaboration. Over and over again, public relations executives have supported economic regulation with the goal of eliminating smaller competitors and insuring their own profits. They have sold

such restrictions on freedom by promising better service, but their frequent inability to deliver has left a residue of public disbelief in the prom-
ises of corporate America. (p. 2)

Olasky recommended two solutions to the ethical problem of manipulative public relations: responsibility that begins at home and private
relations. Responsibility at home means dealing directly with people affected by corporate actions, not by papering over the activities with "an
extra gift to a local charity or by Thanksgiving turkeys to the faithful" (p.
151). Private relations means saying "none of your business" when that is
appropriate.

Gandy (1982) used the concept of an information subsidy as the central concept of his criticism of public relations. Decision makers, he argued, need information to make decisions, but information has a cost.
The demand for information, then, is a function of its price and the
resources available to the decision maker. "The lower the price of information, the more it is likely to be acquired. By the same token, the more
income a DM (decision maker) has, the more willing he is to spend it on
information" (p. 30).

Interested actors in the policy process, such as corporations and other
bureaucracies, may reduce the cost of information to decision makers by
subsidizing the cost of the information, thus making it more likely that
decision makers will acquire this preferred information.

Although subsidized information is not necessarily false, Gandy maintained that it is almost always incomplete. Drug companies or governmental health agencies, for example, provide free information about
their products or research but not about the products or research of
others. Subsidized information seems to be exactly the kind of information produced by practitioners of the public-information model. Information subsidies, therefore, result in indirect manipulation of publics.
They influence "the actions of others by controlling their access to and
use of information relevant to those actions" (p. 61).[11]

From his Marxist perspective, Gandy concluded that the dominant
actors in society are most able to produce information subsidies and that
the poor, consumers, and other information-poor people are least likely

---

[11]The concept of information subsidy is much like Donohue, Tichenor and Olien's
(1973) concept of "knowledge of" science as opposed to "knowledge about" science.
"Knowledge of" is the perspective from within the system; "knowledge about" is an outside, more critical perspective on the system. They found that science writers are more
likely to produce "knowledge of" science than "knowledge about." See R. Pollack (1986) to
see how these concepts distinguish between an internal and external orientation in an
organization, as described in the list of presuppositions of the asymmetrical models, and
the correlation of "knowledge about" with use of the two-way symmetrical model.

to be able to afford nonsubsidized information. As a result, public relations acts to reinforce the power of dominant groups in society.

Both these critical attacks on public relations seem reasonably on target to me, although I disagree with the political prescriptions of both. Both believe, essentially, that society would be better off without public relations. Both, however, miss the benefits to society of another worldview of public relations—the two-way symmetrical model.

PRESUPPOSITIONS OF THE TWO-WAY SYMMETRICAL MODEL

The term *symmetrical communication* may be a new one in public relations, but allusions to the concept can be found throughout the history of public relations—in the work or writings, for example, of Ivy Lee, Edward Bernays, John Hill, and Scott Cutlip (J. Grunig & Hunt, 1984, p. 42). Most of these practitioners and most contemporary practitioners did not or have not made a clear conceptual distinction between the two-way asymmetrical and two-way symmetrical models (see also Turk, 1986, pp. 8–9). In general, they confuse the idea of two-way communication with symmetrical communication and do not realize that two-way communication can be manipulative.

In the wider field of communication, several theorists introduced concepts identical or similar to symmetrical communication in the 1960s. Carter (1965), for example, incorporated Newcomb's (1953) concept of coorientation into his theory of communication and affective relations; Chaffee and McLeod (1968) initiated a major program of research on coorientation. (Coorientation occurs when two or more people simultaneously orient to a situation or object rather than a single person orienting to a situation or object.) Similarly, Watzlawick, Beavin, and Jackson (1967) distinguished between asymmetrical and symmetrical communication in their theory of interpersonal communication. Finally, Thayer (1968) distinguished between synchronic and diachronic communication in his systems theory of communication.

These symmetrical theories of communication were popular when I was a doctoral student, whereas theories of attitude change were losing their appeal (at least in schools of journalism and mass communication where I studied). As a result, their presuppositions have been part of my worldview ever since. In addition, I studied and accepted most of the presuppositions of the systems approach to organizations and communication at that time. Finally, I have incorporated presuppositions from a theory of politics called interest group liberalism into the conceptual framework of the two-way symmetrical model of public relations.

From the symmetrical theories of communication comes the following presupposition:

Communication leads to understanding. The major purpose of communication is to facilitate understanding among people and such other systems as organizations, publics, or societies. Persuasion of one person or system by another is less desirable.

From systems theories come four additional presuppositions:[12]

Holism. Systems consist of subsystems and are parts of suprasystems. The whole is greater than the sum of its parts, and each part of a system affects every other part.

Interdependence. Although systems have boundaries that separate them from their environment, systems in the environment cross that boundary and "interpenetrate" the system (Preston & Post, 1975, pp. 24–27).

Open system. The organization is open to interpenetrating systems and freely exchanges information with those systems.

Moving equilibrium. Systems strive toward an equilibrium with other systems, although they seldom actually achieve it. The desired equilibrium state constantly moves as the environment changes. Systems may attempt to establish equilibrium by controlling other systems, by adapting themselves to other systems, or by making mutual, cooperative adjustments. In the symmetrical approach to public relations, cooperative and mutual adjustment are preferred to control and adaptation.

In addition to these systems presuppositions, I include the following presuppositions in the two-way symmetrical approach:

Equality. People should be treated as equals and respected as fellow human beings. Anyone, regardless or education or background may provide valuable input into an organization.

Autonomy. People are more innovative, constructive, and self-fulfilled when they have the autonomy to influence their own behavior, rather than having it controlled by others. Autonomy maximizes employee satisfaction inside the organization and cooperation outside the organization.

Innovation. New ideas and flexible thinking should be stressed rather than tradition and efficiency.

---

[12]These presuppositions can be examined in more detail in books such as Ruben (1984), A. Kuhn (1975), Thayer (1968), J. Grunig and Hung (1984, pp. 92–98).

Decentralization of management. Management should be collective; managers should coordinate rather than dictate. Decentralization increases autonomy, employee satisfaction, and innovation.

Responsibility. People and organizations must be concerned with the consequences of their behaviors on others and attempt to eliminate adverse consequences.

Conflict resolution. Conflict should be resolved through negotiation, communication, and compromise and not through force, manipulation, coercion, or violence.[13]

Interest group liberalism. Classic liberalism, which typically champions big government, can be as closed-minded as classic conservatism, which typically champions big business. Interest-group liberalism, however, views the political system as a mechanism for open competition among interest or issue groups. Interest-group liberalism looks to citizen groups to "champion interests of ordinary people against unresponsive government and corporate structures" (Boyte, 1980, p. 7).[14]

---

[13]I am tempted to include the word persuasion here as something that should not be involved in conflict resolution. I would include the word when it refers to manipulative kinds of persuasion as are used in the asymmetrical models. Petty and Cacioppo (1981, p. 267) call manipulative persuasion the "peripheral route to persuasion." Using reasoned argument in support of one's position is an important part of conflict resolution in the symmetrical model, however; Petty and Cacioppo call this the "central route to persuasion" (p. 266). The central route to persuasion usually is the first move that people make when using the symmetrical model to resolve conflict. However, conflicting persons or systems must be willing to switch their strategy from persuasion to negotiation or compromise when the central route does not bring about the direct change in attitude and behavior they want, as it seldom does. For example, Petty and Cacioppo call the central route "a difficult way to change attitudes" (p. 266). They add, however, that persuasion by the central route is more likely to result in a permanent change in attitude (p. 268). I would add that the symmetrical model of communication, by extension, more often produces a long-term change in behavior than does the asymmetrical model—because both parties had a stake in choosing the behavior.

[14]Lowi (1979) coined the term "interest-group liberalism," although he was critical of it. He explained the term as (p. 51):

Liberalism because it is optimistic about government, expects to use government in a positive and expansive role, is motivated by the highest sentiments and possesses a strong faith that what is good for government is good for the society. It is interest-group liberalism because it sees as both necessary and good a policy agenda that is accessible to all organized interests and makes no independent judgement of their claims. It is interest-group liberalism because it defines the public interest as a result of the amalgamation of various claims.

See J. Grunig (1987) for an integration of the concept into my theory of public relations.

Theories Relevant to the Symmetrical Model

As the previous discussion suggests, several research traditions have suggested presuppositions for the two-way symmetrical model of public relations, including coorientation, systems theory, and interest-group liberalism. Also relevant are theories of conflict resolution such as those of Ehling (1984, 1985) and Fisher and Ury (1981).[15]

What is most important, however, is the fact that the framework provided by the two-way symmetrical presuppositions is producing an original theory of public relations. We are not borrowing persuasion theory or theories of organizational communication. Rather, we have built a theory of public relations both with concepts from other research traditions and with concepts that are original to the theory. I have presented parts of that theory earlier in this paper when I discussed the four models of public relations, and more complete discussions can be found in J. Grunig and L. Grunig (1989), J. Grunig (1987), and J. Grunig and Hunt (1984).

WHICH SET OF PRESUPPOSITIONS WORKS BEST?

As we end this chapter, we must ask what the discussion of the asymmetrical and symmetrical worldviews means for the practice of public relations and the building of theory to ground the field. As I showed earlier in this chapter, philosophers of science now have largely rejected the idea that science is totally subjective, even when it is based on presuppositions that cannot be tested directly. Philosophers now believe that researchers can compare competing presuppositional frameworks by comparing their ability to solve problems important in a domain. Researchers can compare theories using direct measures of concepts or by using background information to "unload" indirect measures.

I would like to end this chapter, therefore, by arguing not only that the two-way symmetrical model is a more moral and ethical approach to public relations than the other models but that it is also a more effective model in practice. Let me cite two examples of research that support that contention.

L. Grunig (1986) studied how organizations deal with activist groups and found that none of them had tried the two-way symmetrical model. In every other case, the other models failed to resolve the conflict. The result usually was litigation or continued conflict. Thus, she concluded

---

[15]See Lauzen (1986) for a review of the literature of conflict resolution and a study relating that literature to the four models of public relations.

that the two-way symmetrical model provided the only hope of success because of the universal failure of the other models.

Turk (1986) also found that only one state agency she studied in Louisiana used the two-way symmetrical model. The other models did not work. She concluded (1986):

> State agencies that rely upon public information officers to "get the word out" to win support for agency policies and programs may be overrating the ability of PIOs to influence the agency picture portrayed by the news media for consumption by those who get their information about state government from the media. (pp. 24–25)

It will take another paper and continued research to find definitive support for the assertion that the two-way symmetrical model is a more effective as well as more responsible approach to public relations. I hope this chapter stimulates such research: Even more, I hope it affects the presuppositions about public relations of those who practice and teach it. Eventually, I hope, public relations will be practiced in a way that will make it a highly valued and effective force for resolving social conflict and improving the societies in which we live.

REFERENCES

Bohm, D. (1977). Science as perception-communication. In F. Suppe (Ed.), *The structure of scientific theories* (pp. 37–391). Urbana: University of Illinois Press.

Boyte, H. C. (1980). *The backyard revolution: Understanding the new citizen movement*. Philadelphia: Temple University Press.

Bronowski, J. (1965). *Science and human values*. New York: Harper & Row.

Brown, H. I. (1977). *Perception, theory and commitment: The new philosophy of science*. Chicago: University of Chicago Press.

Carter, R. F. (1965). Communication and affective relations. *Journalism Quarterly, 42*, 203–212.

Chaffee, S. H., & McLeod, J. M. (1968). Sensitization in panel design: A coorientation experiment. *Journalism Quarterly, 45*, 661–669.

Donohue, G. A., Tichenor, P. J., & Olien, C. N. (1973). Mass media functions, knowledge, and social control. *Journalism Quarterly, 50*, 652–659.

Ehling, W. P. (1984). Application of decision theory in the construction of a theory of public relations management I. *Public Relations Research & Education, 1*, 25–39.

Ehling, W. P. (1985). Application of decision theory in the construction of a theory of public relations management II. *Public Relations Research & Education, 2*, 4–22.

Feigl, H. (1969). The origin and spirit of logical positivism. In P. Achinstein &

42   GRUNIG

S. F. Barker (Eds.), *The legacy of logical positivism* (pp. 3–24). Baltimore: Johns Hopkins University Press.

Feulner, E. J., Jr. (1986, November). *Waging and winning the war of ideas.* Paper presented to the Public Relations Society of America, Washington, DC.

Feyerabend, P. R. (1970). Consolations for the specialist. In I. Lakatos & A. Musgrave (Eds.), *Criticism and the growth of knowledge* (pp. 197–230). Cambridge: Cambridge University Press.

Fisher, R., & Ury, W. (1981). *Getting to yes.* New York: Penguin Books.

Gandy, O. H., Jr. (1982). *Beyond agenda setting: Information subsidies and public policy.* Norwood, NJ: Ablex.

Grunig, J. E. (1979). The status of public relations research. *International Public Relations Association Review, 3,* 9–16.

Grunig, J. E. (1984). Organizations, environments, and models of public relations. *Public Relations Research & Education, 1,* 6–29.

Grunig, J. E. (1987, May). *When active publics become activists: Extending a situational theory of publics.* Paper presented to the International Communication Association, Montreal.

Grunig, J. E., & Grunig, L. S. (1986, May). *Application of open-systems theory to public relations: Review of a program of research.* Paper presented to the International Communication Association, Chicago.

Grunig, J. E., & Grunig, L. S. (1989). Toward a theory of the public relations behavior of organizations: Review of a program of research. In J. E. Grunig & L. S. Grunig (Eds.), *Public relations research annual* (Vol. 1, pp. 27–63). Hillsdale, NJ: Lawrence Erlbaum Associates.

Grunig, J. E., & Hunt, T. (1984). *Managing public relations.* New York: Holt, Rinehart & Winston.

Grunig, L. S. (1986, August). *Activism and organizational response: contemporary cases of collective behavior.* Paper presented to the Association for Education in Journalism and Mass Communication, Norman, OK.

Hanson, N. R. (1958). *Patterns of discovery.* Cambridge: Cambridge University Press.

Jackall, R. (1986, October). *The magic lantern: Public relations and the shaping of plausibility.* Paper presented to the sixth international conference on culture and communication, Temple University, Philadelphia.

Kuhn, A. (1975). *Unified social science.* Homewood, IL: Dorsey.

Kuhn, T. S. (1970). *The structure of scientific revolutions.* Chicago: University of Chicago Press.

Lakatos, I. (1970). Falsification and the methodology of scientific research. In I. Lakatos & A. Musgrave (Eds.), *Criticism and the growth of knowledge* (pp. 91–196). Cambridge: Cambridge University Press.

Laudan, L. (1977). *Progress and its problems.* Berkeley: University of California Press.

Laudan, L. (1984). A confutation of convergent realism. In J. Leplin (Ed.), *Scientific realism* (pp. 218–249). Berkeley: University of California Press.

Lauzen, M. (1986). *Public relations and conflict within the franchise system.* Unpublished doctoral dissertation, University of Maryland, College Park, MD.

Leplin, J. (Ed.). (1984a). *Scientific realism.* Berkeley: University of California Press.

Leplin, J. (1984b). Truth and scientific progress. In J. Leplin (Ed.), *Scientific realism* (pp. 193–217). Berkeley: University of California Press.

Lowi, T. J. (1979). *The end of liberalism: the second republic of the United States* (2nd ed.). New York: Norton.

McAnany, E. G., Schnitman, J., & Janus, N. (Eds.). (1981). *Communication and social structure: Critical studies in mass media research.* New York: Praeger.

McDougall, C. D. (1952). *Understanding public opinion.* New York: Macmillan.

Masterman, M. (1970). The nature of a paradigm. In I. Lakatos & A. Musgrave (Eds.), *Criticism and the growth of knowledge* (pp. 61–65). Cambridge: Cambridge University Press.

Meehan, E. J. (1968). *Explanation in social science.* Homewood, IL: Dorsey.

Nelkin, D. (1987). *Selling science.* New York: Freeman.

Newcomb, T. M. (1953). An approach to the study of communicative acts. *Psychological Review, 60,* 393–404.

Nickles, T. (1977). Heuristics and justification in scientific research: Comments on Shapere. In F. Suppe (Ed.), *The structure of scientific theories* (2nd ed., pp. 571–589). Urbana: University of Illinois Press.

Olasky, M. N. (1984). Retrospective: Bernays doctrine of public opinion. *Public Relations Review, 10,* 3–11.

Olasky, M. N. (1987). *Corporate public relations: A new historical perspective.* Hillsdale, NJ: Lawrence Erlbaum Associates.

Petty, R. E., & Cacioppo, J. T. (1981). *Attitudes and persuasion: classic and contemporary approaches.* Dubuque, IA: William C. Brown.

Pollack, Ellyn J. (1984). *An organizational analysis of four public relations models in the federal government.* Unpublished master's thesis, University of Maryland, College Park, MD.

Pollack, R. A. (1986). *Testing the Grunig organizational theory in scientific organizations.* Unpublished master's thesis, University of Maryland, College Park, MD.

Popper, K. (1959). *The logic of scientific discovery.* London: Hutchinson.

Popper, K. (1965). *Conjectures and refutations: The growth of scientific knowledge.* New York: Basic Books.

Preston, L. E., & Post, J. E. (1975). *Private management and public policy: The principle of public responsibility.* Englewood Cliffs, NJ: Prentice-Hall.

Putnam, H. (1984). What is realism? In J. Leplin (Ed.), *Scientific realism* (pp. 140–153). Berkeley: University of California Press.

Rice, R. E., & Paisley, W. J. (Eds.). (1981). *Public communication campaigns.* Beverly Hills: Sage.

Rogers, E. M. (1983). *Diffusion of innovations* (3rd ed.), New York: The Free Press.

Ruben, B. D. (1984). *Communication and human behavior.* New York: McMillan.

Shapere, D. (1964). The structure of scientific revolutions [book review]. *Philosophical Review, 73,* 383–394.

Shapere, D. (1977). Scientific theories and their domains. In F. Suppe (Ed.), *The structure of scientific theories* (2nd ed., pp. 518–565). Urbana: University of Illinois Press.

Simpson, G. G. (1964). *This view of life*. New York: Harcourt, Brace & World.
Suppe, F. (1973). Theories, their formulations, and the operational imperative. *Synthese, 25,* 129–164.
Suppe, F. (1976). *Beyond Skinner and Kuhn*. Paper presented to the Committee On History and Philosophy of Science Colloquim, University of Maryland, College Park, MD.
Suppe, F. (1977a). *The structure of scientific theories* (2nd ed.), Urbana: University of Illinois Press.
Suppe, F. (1977b). Exemplars, theories, and disciplinary matrices. In F. Suppe (Ed.), *The structure of scientific theories* (2nd ed., pp. 483–499). Urbana: University of Illinois Press.
Thayer, L. (1968). *Communication and communication systems*. Homewood, IL: Irwin.
Toulmin, S. (1972a). *Human understanding* (Vol. 1). Princeton, NJ: Princeton University Press.
Toulmin, S. (1972b). *Human understanding* (Vol. 2). Princeton, NJ: Princeton University Press.
Turk, J. V. (1986). Information subsidies and media content: A study of public relations influence on the news. *Journalism Monographs* (No. 100).
Watzlawick, P., Beavin, J. H., & Jackson, D. D. (1967). *Pragmatics of human communication*. New York: Norton.

SUGGESTED READINGS

Brown, H. I. (1977). *Perception, theory and commitment: the new philosophy of science*. Chicago: The University of Chicago Press.
Grunig, J. E. (1979). The status of public relations research. *International Public Relations Association Review, 3,* 9–16.
Grunig, J. E. (1984). Organizations, environments, and models of public relations. *Public Relations Research & Education, 1,* 6–29.
Kuhn, T. S. (1970). *The structure of scientific revolutions*. Chicago: University of Chicago Press.
Laudan, L. (1977). *Progress and its problems*. Berkeley: University of California Press.
Olasky, M. N. (1987). *Corporate public relations: A new historical perspective*. Hillsdale, NJ: Lawrence Erlbaum Associates.
Shapere, D. (1984). *Reason and the search for knowledge*. Dordrecht: Reidel.
Suppe, F. (Ed.). (1977). *The structure of scientific theories* (2nd ed.), Urbana: University of Illinois Press.

Persuasion and Public Relations: Two "Ps" in a Pod

Gerald R. Miller
Michigan State University

ABSTRACT

This chapter argues for a close correspondence between effective persuasion and effective public relations because both are primarily concerned with exerting symbolic control over relevant aspects of the environment. After stipulating a working definition for the term *persuasion,* the chapter examines several limitations of the current body of persuasion research. Finally, the chapter considers the implications of two areas of recent persuasion literature, research on counterattitudinal advocacy and research on sequential message strategies, for persuasion researchers and public relations practitioners alike.

As my title suggests, this chapter rests on the conceptual assumption that effective, ethically defensible persuasion and effective, ethically defensible public relations are virtually synonymous. Because conceptual vantage points rest on definitional choices, I hasten to add that both *persuasion* and *public relations* could be and have been defined in various ways that render them vastly different symbolic animals. My own preference is to stress the overwhelming similarities of the two communicative processes, rather than placing them at loggerheads by nitpicking minor distinctions or tilting ideological windmills.

Communication, and in this instance, persuasion,[1] is humankind's

---

[1] I resist the impulse to digress to an extended discussion of whether or not "communication" and "persuasion" are synonymous; for example, whether it is preferable to con-

primary symbolic resource for exerting control over the environment (Miller & Steinberg, 1975). This bedrock claim is likely to encounter an immediate semantic roadblock because of the unfavorable connotations conjured by the term *control*: In our society, control is typically equated with Machiavellian, marketplace manipulation. As used here, control is assigned a much broader meaning; specifically, to say that people seek to control their environments recognizes the patently obvious fact that people (or at least, people who are normatively defined by society as healthy, functioning individuals) have a preference for certain environmental outcomes over others. From birth to death, people seek warmth rather than chilling cold; full bellies rather than empty ones; and respect, affection, and love rather than contempt, social isolation, and hatred. Thus, the quest for environmental control is a crucial fabric of the tapestry of our lives, a human activity as natural and pervasive as breathing. In this broad sense, then, the concept of seeking control is *amoral* just as breathing or eating is amoral; it is an inevitable aspect of *being alive*. Moreover, just as we say that anorexic or bulimic persons suffer a sickness or an "eating disorder," we opine that persons who are apparently indifferent about their environmental outcomes suffer a sickness or a "social disorder."

To say that the overarching persuasive aim of achieving environmental control is amoral, and hence, not subject to ethical scrutiny, does not, of course, imply that specific persuasive acts are exempt from ethical assessment. Quite the contrary, any message directed toward enhancing or exerting environmental control is fair game for two broad categories of ethical judgments: judgments pertaining to the *ends* sought by the persuasive message and judgments pertaining to the persuasive *means* employed in pursuit of these ends. Stated differently, ethical questions are both probable and appropriate when it comes to evaluating particular domains of control or specific symbolic strategies used to establish control. Should tobacco companies seek to control consumers' attitudes toward their product to enhance sales of an unhealthy product? Should political leaders lie to conceal the existence of certain political activities? These questions, along with a host of other ends and means issues, are sure to continue to provide grist for the mill of ethical controversy. But

---

ceptualize all communication as persuasion or to draw distinctions between persuasion and other communicative goals. Suffice it to say that even if one opts for the latter alternative, issues regarding environmental control remain paramount. For example, the communicative objective of "information exchange" is inextricably entwined with domains of control ranging from increasing task efficiency ("This information will enable you to perform the assigned task more effectively"), to enhancing communicator credibility ("This information will demonstrate I am a competent, trustworthy, and/or sociable communicator"), to strengthening relational bonds ("The time and energy we expend exchanging information illustrates that we value our relationship").

even after this fact is granted, it remains true that persuasion as a chief symbolic resource for exercising environmental control remains an indispensable and irrevocable dimension of human existence. Those who would purge it from our daily lives might as well try to legislate breathing and eating out of existence, a claim amusingly documented by noting the frustration and hostility experienced by the "anti-persuasionists" when their audience refuses to embrace their position—in the language used here, a symbolic attempt at environmental control gone awry.

Public relations, my other "P" in the pod, can also be conceptualized as a process that centers on exerting symbolic control over certain aspects of the environment. Specifically, *public relations* serves as a definitional label for the process of attempting to exert symbolic control over the evaluative predispositions ("attitudes," "images," etc.) and subsequent behaviors of relevant publics or clienteles. Granted, the domain of control is considerably narrower than the all-inclusive sense embodied in the concept "persuasion," a circumstance that may cause skeptics to charge that public relations is ethically suspect because of the particular ends sought by its practitioners. Such an argument flies in the face of logic and common sense: *Whenever control of the environment hinges on the attitudes and behaviors of others, attempts to control these attitudes and behaviors are inevitable.* If students hope to achieve good grades, they must be concerned with the attitudes and behaviors of their teachers; it would be logically absurd to counsel students to strive for the Dean's List but to be indifferent about their teachers' assessments of academic competence. To be sure, there is considerable room for ethical concern about the symbolic means used to control such assessments. If, by dint of diligent study, the student submits excellent papers and examinations (persuasive messages aimed at controlling the attitudes and behaviors of the teacher); she or he is commended; if the student relies on cheating or unwarranted ingratiation, he or she is subject to moral censure. In a loose sense, then, students serve as their own public relations agents.

By the same token, it makes little sense to say that political candidates seeking public office, governmental agencies striving for acceptance and support of public policies, or industries and businesses attempting to market their products and services—to mention but three areas within the purview of public relations professionals—should turn a cold shoulder to the evaluative predispositions and subsequent behaviors of voters, citizens, or consumers. Moreover, unless one opts to renounce entirely the social, economic, and political foundations of our society, this process of seeking symbolic control—to reiterate, of preferring certain environmental outcomes over others—is an amoral, human necessity. Even this qualification is largely superfluous, for renunciation of existing institutions would inevitably result in their replacement with others, and the business of exerting environmental control would continue unabated. Thus, as in the case of persuasion, ethical issues concerning public relations are primarily relevant to *particular* political, policy, or product ends and to the *specific* persuasive means used to pursue these ends (e.g., to attempt to sell a physically harmful or defective product or to employ deceptive or dishonest message strategies when pursuing political office).

Although much more could be said for the virtual synonymity of persuasion and public relations, I rest my general case with these remarks. The remainder of this chapter focuses on three tasks: First, I stipulate a working definition for the term *persuasion,* and I examine some of the significant implications of this definition. Next, I consider several important characteristics and limitations of the existing body of social scientific research on persuasion processes and outcomes. Finally, I suggest two persuasive problem areas that strike me as particularly promising avenues for collaboration between persuasion researchers and public relations professionals, areas that are far from virgin territories yet could certainly profit from more intensive joint explorations.

A WORKING DEFINITION OF *PERSUASION*

The definition of *persuasion* that guides my remarks represents a slight modification of one offered earlier by Miller (1987):

> The term "persuasion" refers to situations where attempts are made to modify [attitudes and/or] behavior by symbolic transactions (messages) that are sometimes, but not always, linked with coercive force (indirectly coercive) and that appeal to the reason and emotions of the intended persuadee(s). (p. 451)

This definition should prove helpful here, both because it captures key elements of the persuasive process and because it has several important implications for public relations professionals.

The symbolic nature of persuasion has been stressed in my previous remarks. To *symbolize* is to *communicate*; hence, the major interest of the student of persuasion lies with the verbal and nonverbal code systems employed by persuasive transactants. By contrast, nonsymbolic efforts at environmental control fall outside the persuasive realm, although they may sometimes be described in everyday language as instances of persuasion. Miller (1980) wrote:

> Though a Mafia hireling in a Hollywood production may remark menacingly, "It looks like you need a little persuading," as he starts to work

over a stubborn merchant who has refused to purchase mob protection, the scholarly endeavors of persuasion researchers . . . have consistently centered on the manipulation of symbols. (pp. 13–14)

Similarly, efforts at environmental control by public relations professionals are largely grounded in symbolic exchange.

To grant the primacy of symbolizing, of course, does not deny the fact that persuasive messages are often buttressed by coercive force—in the language of Kelman (1961), social influence sometimes results largely from the persuader's ability to exercise *means control* (i.e., to manipulate effectively certain rewards and punishments for the persuadees). Simons (1974) has counseled against a "drawing room" conception of persuasion that ignores the rough-and-tumble nature of many real-world persuasive exchanges. Among individuals, institutions, and nations, persuasive effectiveness often hinges on the ability *and* the willingness of persuaders to utilize coercive force. The possibility of strikes and plant closings heavily influences the persuasive give-and-take of labor-management bargaining; the specter of nuclear exchange weighs on the negotiation of a nuclear test ban treaty; the resources and inclination to provide political patronage affect a candidate's chances of securing support from powerful party allies. In a nutshell, whereas persuasion is symbolic, *effective* persuasion often requires more than symbols.

Although public relations professionals must heed this caveat, it should be emphasized that they walk a fine ethical line in selecting rewards and punishments to reinforce their persuasive messages. Inaccurate as they may be, dramatic portrayals of the world of public relations have delighted in positing the centrality of bribes, booze, bacchanals, and brothels when currying the favor of clients. Indeed, a persuasive case can be made for the claim that conscientious public relations professionals suffer an unfair disadvantage in plying their craft because of the unfavorable connotations associated with the term "public relations," in much the same way that conscientious rhetors are hampered by the negative force of such contemporary phrases as "only rhetoric" or "mere rhetoric." Thus, although public relations professionals require some control over rewards and punishments to ensure the impact of certain messages, they must select these rewards and punishments with scrupulous care.

It will seem strange to many readers that my 1987 definition of persuasion omitted the term *attitudes,* because historically, attitudes and attitude change have been viewed by most writers as the staple products of persuasive exchanges. This decision resulted primarily from the predominant conceptualization of the attitude construct as an intervening variable, a mediating process that occurs, if at all, inside people's heads and hence is not available for observation. My behavioristic biases led me to argue that the only thing persuasion researchers are ever privy to when assessing the effects of a persuasive message are behaviors, that their raw data are not *attitudes* but instead *behavioral indicants of attitudes*. Moreover, I contended that preoccupation with the attitude construct has quite likely impeded our quest for understanding the persuasive process rather than accelerating it.

A case in point can be found in the voluminous literature devoted to the so-called "attitudes versus behavior problem" (see, e.g., Cushman & McPhee, 1980; Liska, 1975), the mistakenly phrased notion that attitudes have proven to be poor predictors of behavior. Stated more accurately, the problem, if indeed it should be accorded problem status, resides in the weak correlation between verbal expressions of an attitude and other attitude-related behaviors. When stated in this way, the discrepancy is hardly surprising, for the fact that people's verbal assertions about their feelings often fail to correspond with their other actions—a social commonplace—accounts for the popularity of such adages as "Talk's cheap!" and "Actions speak louder than words." Considerable scientific mischief and misplaced effort have resulted from this fundamental confusion of the issue (see Miller, 1987, pp. 455–457, for a comprehensive discussion of this claim). As a result, the attention of many persuasion researchers has been deflected from more important matters to the pursuit of a question that is, at best, a minor problem and, at worst, a pseudo-problem.

Despite my disenchantment with the attitude construct, I have elected to include it as an element of the working definition of persuasion that guides this chapter. My reason is simple: If *attitude* is defined as an evaluative mediator that predisposes individuals to behave selectively toward some stimulus—a definition that fits nicely with the way most writers envision the construct—then it coincides closely with what most public relations professionals probably see as their major persuasive mission. Put another way, the predominant perception is likely to be that public relations professionals rely on persuasion primarily to purposefully affect the attitudes of some relevant clientele or other public. As a consequence, it seems appropriate to include the attitude construct as part of my working definition.

Two caveats accompany its inclusion. First, it should be stressed that *attitude change* is but one of three possible persuasive aims, although the term *persuasion* is commonly equated with the process of changing the attitudes of some target audience. A second persuasive objective is to *foster* an attitude (i.e., to condition a consistent evaluative response to some stimulus where no such response previously existed). This goal is particularly germane to situations involving the introduction of unfamiliar products, policies, or people. Before August 1945, no one except a few informed scientists and political leaders had any knowledge of or attitudes about nuclear energy and its many byproducts. Since that time, much of the persuasive activity in areas such as the development of nuclear power has sought to condition positive *or* negative attitudes toward building and using nuclear power facilities. In a similar vein, questions about the effects of certain product advertisements on children stem primarily from a fear that these youths will develop positive attitudes toward potentially physically or psychologically harmful products (e.g., watching attractively packaged television ads for alcoholic beverages may cause children to acquire positive attitudes regarding drinking). No matter how one feels about these issues, the point is clear: Persuasion is a powerful resource for shaping new attitudinal responses.

A third important function of persuasion is to *reinforce* presently existing favorable attitudes, or, in ordinary language, to remind individuals how wise they are for holding certain attitudes. Although this aim probably seems self-evident, I suspect it is often forgotten or ignored in the hustle and bustle of everyday, persuasive life. In the language of an old cliché, persuasion is an invaluable ally in keeping old friends as well as making new ones. Nevertheless, it is easy to shortchange this goal because of the understandable zeal to convert skeptics and foes. Prudent persuaders, public relations professionals included, profit from devoting adequate attention to attitudinally reinforcing messages.

My second caveat relates to the way the temporal relationship between attitudes and behaviors has typically been conceived. It has been common to view attitudes as precursors of behavior: The successful persuader first changes the attitudes of the target audience; and once this change has occurred, the desired behaviors are apt to follow. This traditional picture of the temporal linkage is responsible for such common expressions as, "You can't expect people to do something unless they believe in it," or "You have to get folks to accept a change before it can be instituted." Thus, we cannot have racially integrated facilities until segregationists have been "educated" to accept them; we cannot hope that drivers will wear seat belts until they have favorable attitudes about wearing them; we cannot reduce drug usage until users have developed anti-drug attitudes, and so forth.

In recent years, several students of persuasion (e.g., Bem, 1965, 1968, 1972) have questioned the assumption that attitudes must inevitably precede behaviors. Instead, these writers contend that persons frequently infer their attitudes by observing their own behavior (e.g., when asked, "Do you like Paul Newman?" an individual who has never given much thought to this query reasons, "I must like Paul Newman, because I'm always going to see his movies"). This reversal of time order has important implications for persuasion researchers and practitioners alike, for it posits that attitudes and behaviors are reciprocally rather than nonreciprocally related: *Just as attitudes may "cause" behaviors, behaviors may "cause" attitudes.* Thus, even if the ultimate aim of persuasion is defined as influencing attitudes, the best strategy for achieving this aim often lies in inducing persuadees to behave in attitude-consistent ways. This possibility is explored in greater detail during my subsequent discussion of one of the problem areas ripe for collaboration between persuasion researchers and public relations professionals.

A final implication of my working definition of persuasion pertains to the distinction drawn between appealing to reason and appealing to emotion. Both common sense and prior research (e.g., Becker, 1963) underscore the naivete of believing that reason and emotion (or in psychological terms, cognition and affect) can be neatly separated into mutually exclusive cubbyholes. Most ordinary language has emotional overtones. In our society, even phrases such as "Let's look at this logically" and "Logic reveals that . . ." carry considerable emotive force, for whom among us wishes to be pictured as a muddled, illogical thinker? Conversely, persuasive messages appealing to the emotions of intended persuadees are often structured cogently. As final revision of this chapter neared the end, the race for the Democratic Presidential nomination narrowed to Michael Dukakis and Jesse Jackson. Pundits proclaimed that Governor Dukakis relied primarily on the force of his reasoning and arguments, whereas Reverend Jackson sparked the emotions and feelings of his audience. Although this analysis was certainly on-target, no one took it to imply that Dukakis's persuasive messages are devoid of human emotion or that Jackson's are entirely illogical.

Thus, the difference between logical and emotional appeals is one of degree, not of kind. Notwithstanding this fact, the distinction is worth noting, because it is a difference that frequently makes a difference. Some public relations campaigns are primarily intended to tease the cerebrum, others to tug at the heartstrings. Consider, for instance, the differing approaches typically employed by those advocating introduction of casino gambling in a community and those opposing it. The former cite statistics purportedly demonstrating that casino gambling will produce jobs, stimulate commercial development, and broaden the tax base—in short, they reason that the advent of gambling will signal economic improvement. On the other hand, the anti-gambling campaign envisions an immoral, lawless community largely ruled by mobsters—in sum, it appeals to emotions such as fear and moral righteousness. Although concern for economic security is surely rooted in emotional soil and it is certainly not illogical to prefer the security and peace-of-mind that accompanies a law-abiding community, the fact remains that the two approaches differ in ways that are important to both persuasion researchers and public relations professionals.

In a nutshell, then, persuasion is symbolic; sometimes but not always indirectly coercive; seeks to change, foster, or reinforce attitudinal and behavioral responses; and relies on the twin, albeit overlapping avenues of logical and emotional appeals to achieve its aims. Having sketched several important implications of these crucial defining characteristics, I turn next to a brief assessment of the voluminous body of current social-scientific research dealing with persuasive processes and outcomes.

CURRENT PERSUASION RESEARCH: A CAPSULE EVALUATION

Miller and Burgoon (1978) wrote:

> Most persuasion research [relies] on a one-to-many situational context. In the traditional persuasion study, a relatively large aggregate of receiver/persuadees—a classroom of students, the members of a PTA, and so forth—is exposed to a message attributed to an individual or an institutional source. With few exceptions [a] linear, unidirectional view of the "transaction" is enforced by the fact that the message is not even presented live. Instead the persuadees read it, or see and/or hear it on video or audiotape, a procedure that prevents any meaningful reciprocal influence by the audience. After message exposure [almost always, as I shall stress later, exposure to a single message], the persuadees respond to some measure of persuasive effect, usually a paper-and-pencil assessment of attitude change. Thus, the entire enterprise closely resembles a public speaking or mass media setting, although, even here, the fit is far from perfect, because there is little opportunity for the kinds of audience social facilitation effects one would expect in real-life communicative settings. (p. 33)

This state-of-the-art assessment, proffered a decade ago by Burgoon and myself still describes the situation fairly accurately. The lion's share of persuasion research has been grounded in a *passive reception* paradigm (Miller & Burgoon, 1973, see Fig. 3.1). In this paradigm, the persuader, who is the primary symbolizing agent, encodes and transmits a message to a relatively passive audience. Even when the opportunity for audience feedback exists—and as the preceding quotation indicates, most studies do not permit this opportunity—persuadees are relegated to a relatively inactive role: Persuasion is conceptualized as a unidirectional process where the persuader *acts* and the persuadees are *acted upon*.

The investigational hegemony of this paradigm is hardly surprising, for just as persuasion has traditionally been equated with changing at-

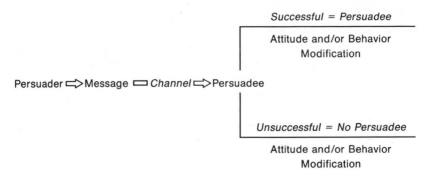

Successful = Persuadee

Attitude and/or Behavior
Modification

Persuader ⇨Message ▭ *Channel* ⇨Persuadee

Unsuccessful = No Persuadee

Attitude and/or Behavior
Modification

FIG. 3.1.   A persuasive paradigm in which the persuader is the primary
symbolizing agent (Passive Reception Paradigm; from Miller & Burgoon,
1973).

titudes and behaviors, it has largely been treated as a process where
persuaders send messages and persuadees receive and respond to them.
Moreover, as the quotation notes, this paradigm accurately describes the
typical circumstances in persuasive transactions involving large audiences (e.g., speeches to crowds numbering in the thousands or mass
media persuasive messages). Notwithstanding this fact, however, an alternative paradigm exists for involving persuadees more actively in the
symbolizing role, and research evidence indicates it is a valuable persuasive resource. This paradigm is explored in the next section.

It is difficult to imagine a public relations professional (or almost any
persuader, for that matter) who would gamble persuasive success on a
single message. Rather, the impact of most public relations campaigns,
formal or informal, is dependent on transmitting multiple messages.
That the vast majority of persuasion findings are based on responses to a
single message thus poses serious limitations when generalizing to real-
world persuasive situations. Lest I am misunderstood, my intent is not to
argue that such studies are of no value to persuasive practitioners, but
rather to indicate that their results should be interpreted cautiously.
Such caution is additionally justified by the barrage of competing messages people encounter in their daily activities.[2] Even if a solitary message influences a target audience, the effect may be ephemeral because it
is quickly erased by messages advocating opposing viewpoints.

---

[2]This is a particularly thorny problem when the persuasive goal is to change attitudes
and/or behavior, for as students of *selective exposure* (e.g., Freedman & Sears, 1965; Sears &
Freedman, 1967; Zillmann & Bryant, 1985) emphasize, under conditions of voluntary
exposure, individuals who disagree with a viewpoint are likely to avoid messages advocating it. Consequently, the problem is not simply negating the effects of competing messages,
it extends to enticing people to attend to supportive ones.

The limits of attitudinally related verbal behaviors were underscored in the previous section. On some occasions, verbal acquiescence may suffice; at times, it may provide all the evidence persuaders have or need as to whether or not others agree with their evaluative predispositions. Nevertheless, most persuasive practitioners, including public relations professionals, are frequently in search of supportive actions that transcend verbal assent. Time, money, votes, active public advocacy: These and a host of other attitudinally consistent behaviors signal greater commitment to a product, policy, or person than does mere "talk." Because such behaviors are more costly, they are harder to control symbolically. Hence, the fact that almost the entire body of current persuasion research has focused solely on verbal measures of attitude gives little cause for optimism when it comes to generalizing to other attitudinally consistent behaviors. Moreover, the handful of studies that have examined other behaviors (e.g., DeFleur & Westie, 1958; Festinger, 1964) support the pessimistic prognosis that more demanding, costly behaviors—in the language of Campbell (1963), behaviors with a higher response threshold—are harder to come by persuasively than is verbal agreement.

Finally, the extensive reliance on college students as research participants affects the confidence with which findings can be generalized to other populations of persuadees. Unlike some extreme skeptics, I am not suggesting that findings obtained with college respondents are ipso facto relevant *only* to that population. What is needed for intelligent interpretation is careful analysis of whether or not the variables of interest in the study are likely to be influenced markedly by the differing characteristics of other parent populations. In some instances, such analyses warrant confidence in generalizing to other populations of potential persuadees—consider that many of the findings regarding communicator credibility (for a thorough summary of these findings see McGuire, 1985) are probably relevant to persuadees from all walks and stations in life. In other cases, however, generalization is fraught with hazards—for example, results pertaining to the persuasive effectiveness of varying levels of message complexity (again, see McGuire, 1985, for a summary) that are based on responses of college students cannot be confidently generalized to less-educated persuadees.

This formidable list of limitations has not deterred persuasion researchers from going on about their merry research ways. With the possible exception of language, persuasion has been studied more extensively than any other aspect of the communication process. Capturing the flavor of this vast literature is a task transcending the modest scope of this chapter; interested readers are invited to peruse the numerous published review articles (e.g., McGuire, 1969, 1985; Miller, 1987; Miller, Burgoon, & Burgoon, 1984). Moreover, even if such a grand synthetic sweep were possible, many of the findings are of limited value to persuasive practitioners. Consequently, my remaining remarks will center on two problem areas that afford fruitful opportunities for researcher-practitioner collaboration. My choice of these two areas reflects my belief that both have considerable potential for expanding the scientific understanding of persuasion researchers *and* for enhancing the persuasive effectiveness of public relations professionals.

PROFESSING AND PRACTICING PERSUASION: TWO AREAS FOR COLLABORATION

Saying is Believing (Sometimes)

The alternative persuasive paradigm mentioned in the preceding section is depicted in Fig. 3.2. This *active participation* paradigm, which Burgoon and I (1973) labeled *counterattitudinal advocacy*, assigns the primary symbolizing task to the intended persuadee(s). The persuader's major task lies in inducing the persuadees to prepare and to present publicly a belief-discrepant message, (i.e., a message at odds with their prior attitudes). If this step can be achieved, the acts of encoding and transmitting the message are anticipated to involve the persuadees in a process of *self-persuasion: The persuadees become their own persuaders, at least under certain circumstances and situations.* This reversal of persuasive roles accounts for the subtitle of this section, which takes liberties with the venerable

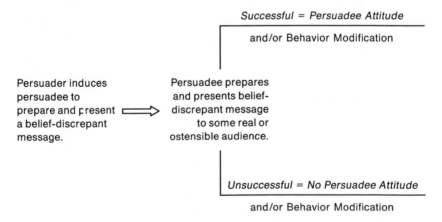

FIG. 3.2. A persuasive paradigm in which the persuadee is the primary symbolizing agent (Active Participation Paradigm; from Miller & Burgoon, 1973).

cliché "Seeing is believing" by suggesting that "saying" also sometimes creates new beliefs and attitudes.

Instances of self-persuasion abound in daily life. Rather than engaging in endless monologues, perceptive parents induce children to talk about the advantages of believing and behaving in particular ways, although factors such as peer pressure may have caused the child to doubt initially the wisdom of these behaviors. Support groups, such as Alcoholics Anonymous, require members to discourse publicly on the perils of alcoholism, and whereas some members have doubtless internalized the belief that they are alcoholics before their maiden speeches, it is highly probable that dubious skepticism or outright hostility concerning this negative dimension of self-concept has been erased by saying, "I am a drunk!" to an audience of sympathetic peers. Finally, returning to a social setting alluded to earlier, students seeking evaluative endorsements from their teachers sometimes offer comments in class or write answers on examinations that coincide with their teachers' interpretations of events but not with their own.

Counterattitudinal advocacy also affords a possible explanation for the findings of several studies that have gained the status of social-scientific classics. Consider the pioneering work of Lewin (1965) and Coch and French (1948) on the problem of overcoming resistance to change. These investigators concluded that group discussion and participative decision-making were more effective in changing attitudes and behaviors than were such passive reception strategies as lecture and managerial edict. Their interpretation of this finding emphasized the superiority of involving, democratic practices over noninvolving, authoritarian techniques. Because specifying the precise causal links is impossible, their explanation may, indeed, hold considerable water. It should also be noted, however, that participating in these discussions placed group members squarely in a situation requiring counterattitudinal advocacy: Members were required to articulate the positive features of personal behaviors and managerial policies to which they were initially opposed. This public advocacy of attitudinally discrepant positions may well have triggered a self-persuasive process culminating in more favorable attitudes toward such activities as eating organ meats (Lewin, 1965) and changing work practices and production methods (Coch & French, 1948).

Notwithstanding the potential persuasive power of the active participation paradigm, things, of course, are never as simple as they could be. For one reason or another, people frequently say things they do not believe without changing their attitudes a whit. In other words, as the preceding section title stresses, *saying is sometimes but not always believing.* The task for persuasion researchers, then, is to identify the circumstances rendering counterattitudinal advocacy an effective persuasive tool as opposed to the circumstances inhibiting its effectiveness. Pursuit of this objective has sparked lively theoretical and empirical controversy.

By far the most controversial issue concerns the role of *justification* in facilitating or inhibiting subsequent self-persuasion.[3] More specifically, *justification* refers to the magnitude of the incentives offered to persuadees for engaging in counterattitudinal advocacy: Put in everyday language, should people be rewarded meagerly or handsomely for advocating belief-discrepant stands? (I have deliberately shunned the more economical term *lying*, because it is sure to raise an immediate ethical red flag for many readers. However, there is nothing inherently unethical about active participation strategies.) Cognitive dissonance theorists (e.g., Aronson, 1968; Festinger, 1957; Festinger & Carlsmith, 1959; Nel, Helmreich, & Aronson, 1969) posit a negative relationship between the two variables: The less the justification, the greater the subsequent attitude change. These theorists reason that awareness of engaging in counterattitudinal advocacy is dissonant with other cognitions (e.g., the cognition, "I believe x" is cognitively dissonant with the cognition, "I am advocating not–x" [Festinger, 1957], or the cognition, "I am a decent, moral individual" is dissonant with the cognition, "I am trying to con this audience into believing something they shouldn't believe" [Aronson, 1968]). A basic premise of cognitive dissonance theory states that people experiencing dissonance will behave *in some way* calculated to restore cognitive consonance. One way to restore consonance is by changing attitudes so they comport more closely to the originally belief-discrepant viewpoint (i.e., the individual reasons, "At first I didn't believe x, but now that I think of it, I'm becoming more favorably inclined toward x").

If there is strong justification for engaging in counterattitudinal advocacy, however, other means of reducing dissonance become more likely. For instance, if the advocate were paid a handsome sum for encoding counterattitudinal messages, or if the task were undertaken at the behest of an attractive source, the advocate could reason, "I don't believe what I'm saying, but it's worth saying because I'm making a lot of money," or, "I'm saying this only because Gerry asked me to, and after all, Gerry's a real nice guy." In short, the persuadee could employ other means of dissonance reduction that permit her or his initial attitudes to escape unscathed.

Another road to the same negative relationship is provided by Bem's

---

[3]Some writers have chosen to label this issue *the psychology of insufficient justification*. This label is confusing and inaccurate, for if justification were insufficient, then by definition persuadees would refuse to engage in counterattitudinal advocacy. What is at issue is a range of justification extending from very high to barely enough to induce counterattitudinal message encoding.

(1965, 1968, 1972) self-perception theory, mentioned briefly in my earlier discussion of the temporal ordering of attitudes and behavior. Bem contended that when substantial justification is offered for engaging in counterattitudinal advocacy, persons are likely to infer that their communicative behaviors represent attempts to mand reinforcement (i.e., reap rewards) from the environment, not expressions of their actual attitudes. By contrast, when cues of reinforcement are absent or ambiguous, advocates are likely to infer, "I must believe x because I'm saying it." Whether one prefers the cognitive dissonance or the self-perception explanation, both theories hypothesize an inverse relationship between justification and self-persuasion.

Incentive theorists (e.g., Elms & Janis, 1965; Janis, 1968; Janis & Gilmore, 1965) arrive at the opposite prediction of a positive relationship between justification and self-persuasion: The greater the justification, the greater the subsequent attitude change. These theorists argue that substantial justification heightens motivation to analyze and to consider belief-discrepant arguments carefully, and in turn, such careful scrutiny ("biased scanning," in incentive theory terms) leads to greater acceptance of the arguments. Not only is this a reasonable alternative, it comports closely with conventional wisdom, which holds that if you reward persons handsomely for counterattitudinal communication, they are more likely to become true believers. Of course, dissonance and self-perception theorists can counter that no actual attitude change has occurred, that the advocate continues to espouse the viewpoint because of the continuing rewards, and that once these rewards cease the advocate will revert to his or her original stance.

Space does not permit an examination of the large body of theoretical and research literature bearing on the justification question (for a summary see Miller, 1973), nor an exploration of other variables thought to bear on the persuasive efficacy of counterattitudinal advocacy. Given this limitation, public relations professionals may feel they have been left with a fine kettle of persuasive fish. After all, how can they hope to employ the active participation paradigm effectively when they are given no inkling of how to resolve the issue of optimal justification? Should they seek to provide persuadees with barely minimal justification for engaging in counterattitudinal advocacy, or should they "sweeten the pot" by providing as much justification as possible?

Fortunately, a definitive answer to this question is not only impossible at this moment, it is also probably unnecessary. As with many issues that receive attention from persuasion researchers, an either—or dichotomy is both oversimplified and misleading: Either minimal or maximal justification may be more effective depending on other communicative and situational factors. Moreover, some evidence suggests that counterattitudinal advocacy exerts a persuasive impact whether the attendant justification is high *or* low. Fifteen years ago, one of my students and I conducted an unpublished field study for an East Coast department store seeking to lure former customers back into the fold. From credit data provided by the store, we drew a sample of former regular charge customers who had not purchased merchandise for the past year. We assumed that most of these former customers had developed negative attitudes about the store, an assumption supported in many cases by written complaints and requests to close charge accounts.

This sample was equally and randomly assigned to three groups: a control condition, a counterattitudinal advocacy/high justification condition, and a counterattitudinal advocacy/low justification condition. Customers assigned to the control condition received no messages from the store. Customers in the two advocacy conditions received letters inviting them to write a short essay (100–200 words) on the topic, "Why I Enjoy Shopping at *(the sponsor's store)*," and indicating that authors of the best essays would receive $25 gift certificates. More than 90% of the customers in both conditions returned essays by the deadline. They next received one of two responses from the store: Customers in the high justification condition received gift certificates along with congratulatory letters, whereas customers in the low justification condition received letters thanking them for participating but indicating they had not won a prize.

The measure of persuasive effectiveness consisted of monitoring the credit data for the next 6 months to ascertain how many customers resumed shopping in the store. This analysis revealed that *both* advocacy groups showed a significantly higher rate of resumed shopping than did the control group, both in terms of the number of customers and the amount of money spent on purchases (excluding, of course, the $25 certificates received by the high justification group). Although these two indices were slightly higher for the high justification than for the low justification customers, the difference was not significant. Thus, engaging in counterattitudinal essay writing resulted in more favorable attitudes toward shopping at the store regardless of the level of justification offered for writing the essays.

These results suggest that perceptive public relations professionals can put counterattitudinal advocacy to good persuasive use even if they are unable to manipulate justification effectively or are uncertain of the level at which it should be pitched. Moreover, in terms of opportunities for collaborative efforts with persuasion researchers, it should be possible to devise field studies that test hypotheses about variables influencing the persuasive efficacy of active participation strategies in natural confines. As with other areas of persuasion research, most prior studies of counterattitudinal advocacy have occurred in laboratory settings. The public relations arena provides a beautiful natural laboratory for broadening and extending cooperative research endeavors.

My optimistic prognosis does not imply that counterattitudinal advocacy provides a persuasive panacea for public relations professionals. Clearly, the active participation paradigm is not well-suited to extremely large audiences; in most cases, it would be prohibitively expensive, if not totally impossible, to involve thousands of people in counterattitudinal message encoding. When addressing such large aggregates, the traditional passive reception paradigm offers the most realistic and economical means of persuasion, although its persuasive impact may not be as great. Counterattitudinal advocacy is particularly attractive when the goal is to persuade a few key opinion leaders, either singly or in small groups, because the benefits to be gained from persuasive success justify the additional time, effort, and ingenuity.

Earlier I remarked that there is nothing inherently unethical about using active participation strategies. Indeed, such strategies have the added virtue of forcing persuadees to weigh the merits of alternative positions, a process they might avoid if left to their own communicative wiles. Nevertheless, ethical questions can arise about the tactics used to induce persuadees to engage in counterattitudinal encoding. Unquestionably, blatant deception and outright coercion should be eschewed. If this dictum of responsible inducement is heeded, the active participation paradigm provides a valuable persuasive resource for public relations professionals seeking to expand their vistas for exercising symbolic control of the environment.

As I Was Saying Earlier . . .

Earlier it was emphasized that most persuasive campaigns rely on multiple messages. Media advertising and political campaigns offer two excellent cases in point: Persuadees are induced to buy certain products and to vote for particular candidates by exposure to carefully orchestrated sequential messages, not by a single persuasive tour de force. It is not uncommon for people to scoff at the possibility that they are affected by such message salvos; to hear them tell it, they turn deaf ears and blind eyes to the repeated persuasive inducements emanating from the media. Bem (1970) offered a commonplace example to counter this claim of persuasive immunity, noting that many of the same persons who assert that media persuasive messages do not influence their behavior can be observed at drugstores purchasing name-brand aspirin when they could buy equally effective generic aspirin for a fraction of the cost.

Despite this widespread reliance on sequential message strategies, persuasion researchers have only recently commenced to spell out the ways such strategies function and to identify variables influencing their persuasive effectiveness. In particular, attention has been directed at sequential strategies that employ initial messages to "set up" persuadees for subsequent appeals. In other words, opening overtures are not expected to yield substantial persuasive returns; instead, it is anticipated they will put persuadees in a frame of mind that makes them more susceptible to later persuasive messages.

An example of one such sequential approach is the *door-in-the-face* or the *reject-then-retreat* strategy (e.g., Cialdini et al., 1975; Even-Chen, Yinon, & Bizman, 1978; Mowen & Cialdini, 1980; Shanab & O'Neill, 1979). This technique directs an initial request at the persuadees that is clearly excessive and all but certain to be refused. After the initial refusal, subsequent messages present sharply scaled-down demands. The key assumption is that refusal to honor the initial outrageous request will predispose persuadees to assent to more modest, later demands that actually are congruent with the persuasive goal. Thus, to return to the familiar example of a teacher–student transaction, suppose a student has received a "D" in an examination but believes a "C" is warranted. To use the door-in-the-face strategy, the student begins the communicative exchange by opining that a grade of "A" would have been appropriate. The teacher quickly indicates that this request is out of the question, but after additional message exchanges, concludes that the "D" was perhaps "a little too harsh" and agrees to raise the exam grade to a "C". The student's sequential message strategy has succeeded. Moreover, although there are disagreements about how to explain the results, several studies conform with this hypothetical outcome, revealing that the door-in-the-face strategy yields persuasive returns (see Dillard, Hunter, & Burgoon, 1984, for a summary; also see Lofthouse, 1986, for a study that supports the persuasive efficacy of the door-in-the-face strategy for the kind of student–teacher transaction described in the hypothetical example).

The other side of the persuasive coin is represented by the *foot-in-the-door* strategy (e.g., Baron, 1973; Foss & Dempsey, 1979; Freedman & Fraser, 1966; Rittle, 1981). Here the psychology is exactly opposite: The persuader begins with a very modest request that is almost sure to be granted, and after the persuadee has complied, the persuader presses forward with more extreme demands. This technique is frequently incorporated into standard selling routines, which perhaps explains its name. The prospective customer is initially presented with some minimal request (e.g., to sacrifice a few minutes to listen to the advantages of the product, to accept some product on a no-cost, trial basis, etc.). On occasion, this technique is even extended to asking questions that are almost certain to produce a "Yes" response (e.g., a reference book salesperson queries, "You want a good education for your children, don't you?"). No matter what the details of the sequential messages, the underlying assumption is the same: By acquiescing to initial small requests, the persuadee becomes highly vulnerable to later more exacting demands. Once again, research demonstrates the persuasive efficacy of the strategy (see Dillard et al., 1984).

Recently, Burgoon and I (Burgoon & Miller, 1985) sketched a *violation of expectations* theory of persuasive effects that illustrates yet another approach to the use of sequential messages. The theory posits that a persuasive message may produce one of three expectational outcomes: It may conform with the persuadees' expectations (e.g., a representative of a tobacco company argues that the case for harmful physical effects from cigarette smoking is inconclusive); it may negatively violate the persuadees' expectations (e.g., a Catholic priest counsels an audience of Catholics on the merits of abortion); or it may positively violate the persuadees' expectations (e.g., the same priest takes the same position with an audience of pro-choicers). The first two kinds of expectational violations are expected to exert minimal persuasive impact (and perhaps even result in boomerang effects) whereas the third is anticipated to enhance persuasive effectiveness.

This same analysis can be applied to a series of messages. Taken alone, a particular message may have little influence on attitudes or behaviors, but by virtue of the fact that it constitutes a positive or a negative violation of audience expectations, it may either pave the way for, or erect barriers to subsequent persuasive success. For instance, during the conference that culminated in this volume, a participant advocated the demise of corporate annual reports because such reports are costly to produce and typically go unread by most stockholders. Although granting the validity of this claim, I argued that if stockholders routinely received these reports, the message, "There will be no annual report this year," could well constitute a negative violation of expectations that would complicate future persuasive endeavors by corporate representatives. At a minimum, then, the decision to abandon annual reports ought to be preceded by considerable communication aimed at informing stockholders of the reasons for the new policy.

Once again, space does not permit a thorough exploration of the many intricacies associated with the use of sequential message strategies. Suffice it to say that public relations professionals rely on such strategies frequently if not almost exclusively. Moreover, as in the case of counterattitudinal advocacy, most research on sequential message strategies has occurred in the cloistered confines of the laboratory. Persuasion researchers and public relations professionals should embark on a cooperative venture aimed at testing the effectiveness and the limits of such strategies in the give-and-take of daily persuasive transactions. For most assuredly, as my title for this section implies, what a persuader has said earlier affects the course of later persuasive exchanges, and many details of this sequential process remain a mystery. Although blessed with deep, stout roots, the two "Ps" in the pod have yet to mature scientifically. If we diligently and cooperatively till the investigational soil, the crop may someday be ripe for harvest.

REFERENCES

Aronson, E. (1968). Dissonance theory: Progress and problems. In R. P. Abelson, E. Aronson, W. J. McGuire, T. M. Newcomb, M. J. Rosenberg, & P. H. Tannenbaum (Eds.), *Theories of cognitive consistency: A sourcebook* (pp. 5–27). Chicago: Rand-McNally.

Baron, R. A. (1973). The "foot-in-the-door" phenomenon: Mediating effects of size of first request and sex of requestor. *Bulletin of the Psychonomic Society, 2,* 113–114.

Becker, S. L. (1963). Research on emotional and logical proofs. *Southern Speech Journal, 28,* 198–207.

Bem, D. J. (1965). An experimental analysis of self-persuasion. *Journal of Experimental Social Psychology, 1,* 199–218.

Bem, D. J. (1968). Attitudes as self-descriptions: Another look at the attitude–behavior link. In A. G. Greenwald, T. C. Brock, & T. M. Ostrom (Eds.), *Psychological foundations of attitudes* (pp. 197–215). New York: Academic Press.

Bem, D. J. (1970). *Beliefs, attitudes, and human affairs.* Belmont, CA: Brooks-Cole.

Bem, D. J. (1972). Self-perception theory. In L. Berkowitz (Ed.), *Advances in experimental social psychology* (Vol. 6, pp. 2–63). New York: Academic Press.

Burgoon, M., & Miller, G. R. (1985). An expectancy interpretation of language and persuasion. In H. Giles & R. N. St. Clair (Eds.), *Recent advances in language, communication, and social psychology* (pp. 199–229). London: Laurence Erlbaum Associates.

Campbell, D. T. (1963). Social attitudes and other acquired behavioral dispositions. In S. Koch (Ed.), *Psychology: A study of a science* (Vol. 6, pp. 94–172). New York: McGraw-Hill.

Cialdini, R. B., Vincent, J. E., Lewis, S. K., Catalan, J., Wheeler, D., & Darby, B. L. (1975). Reciprocal concessions procedure for inducing compliance: The door-in-the-face technique. *Journal of Personality and Social Psychology, 31,* 206–215.

Coch, L., & French, J. R. P., Jr. (1948). Overcoming resistance to change. *Human Relations, 1,* 512–532.

Cushman, D. P., & McPhee, R. D. (Eds.). (1980). *Message-attitude-behavior relationship: Theory, methodology, and application.* New York: Academic Press.

DeFleur, M. L., & Westie, F. R. (1958). Verbal attitudes and overt acts: An experiment on the salience of attitudes. *American Sociological Review, 23,* 667–673.

Dillard, J. P., Hunter, J. E., & Burgoon, M. (1984). Sequential-request persuasive strategies: Meta-analysis of foot-in-the-door and door-in-the-face. *Human Communication Research, 10,* 461–487.

Elms, A. C., & Janis, I. L. (1965). Counter norm attitudes induced by consonant versus dissonant conditions of role playing. *Journal of Experimental Research in Personality, 1,* 50–60.

Even-Chen, M., Yinon, Y., & Bizman, A. (1978). The door-in-the-face technique: Effects of the size of the initial request. *European Journal of Social Psychology, 8,* 135–140.

Festinger, L. (1957). *A theory of cognitive dissonance.* Stanford, CA: Stanford University Press.

Festinger, L. (1964). Behavioral support for opinion change. *Public Opinion Quarterly, 28,* 404–417.

Festinger, L., & Carlsmith, J. M. (1959). Cognitive consequences of forced compliance. *Journal of Abnormal and Social Psychology, 58,* 203–210.

Foss, R. D., & Dempsey, C. B. (1979). Blood donation and the foot-in-the-door technique: A limiting case. *Journal of Personality and Social Psychology, 37,* 580–590.

Freedman, J. L., & Fraser, S. C. (1966). Compliance without pressure: The foot-in-the-door technique. *Journal of Personality and Social Psychology, 4,* 195–203.

Freedman, J. L., & Sears, D. O. (1965). Selective exposure. In L. Berkowitz (Ed.), *Advances in experimental social psychology* (Vol. 2, pp. 57–97). New York: Academic Press.

Janis, I. L. (1968). Attitude change via role playing. In R. P. Abelson, E. Aronson, W. J. McGuire, T. M. Newcomb, M. J. Rosenberg, & P. H. Tannenbaum (Eds.), *Theories of cognitive consistency: A sourcebook* (pp. 810–818). Chicago: Rand-McNally.

Janis, I. L., & Gilmore, J. B. (1965). The influence of incentive conditions on the success of role playing in modifying attitudes. *Journal of Personality and Social Psychology, 1,* 17–27.

Kelman, H. C. (1961). Processes of opinion change. *Public Opinion Quarterly, 25,* 57–78.

Lewin, K. (1965). Group decision and social change. In H. Proshansky & B. Seidenberg (Eds.), *Basic studies in social psychology* (pp. 423–437). New York: Holt, Rinehart & Winston.

Liska, A. E. (Ed.). (1975). *The consistency controversy: Readings on the impact of attitude on behavior.* New York: Schenkman.

Lofthouse, L. J. (1986). *An empirical investigation of individual and situational differences in compliance-gaining.* Unpublished master's thesis, Department of Communication, Arizona State University, Tempe, AZ.

Mcguire, W. J. (1969). The nature of attitudes and attitude change. In G. Lindzey & E. Aronson (Eds.), *Handbook of social psychology* (2nd ed., Vol. 3, pp. 136–314). Reading, MA: Addison-Wesley.

McGuire, W. J. (1985). Attitudes and attitude change. In G. Lindzey & E. Aronson (Eds.), *Handbook of social psychology* (3rd ed., Vol. 2, pp. 233–346). New York: Random House.

Miller, G. R. (1973). Counterattitudinal advocacy: A current appraisal. In C. D. Mortensen & K. K. Sereno (Eds.), *Advances in communication research* (pp. 105–152). New York: Harper & Row.

Miller, G. R. (1980). On being persuaded: Some basic distinctions. In M. E. Roloff & G. R. Miller (Eds.), *Persuasion: New directions in theory and research* (pp. 11–28). Newbury Park, CA: Sage.

Miller, G. R. (1987). Persuasion. In C. R. Berger & S. H. Chaffee (Eds.), *Handbook of communication science* (pp. 446–483). Newbury Park, CA: Sage.

Miller, G. R., & Burgoon, M. (1973). *New techniques of persuasion.* New York: Harper & Row.

Miller, G. R., & Burgoon, M. (1978). Persuasion research: Review and commentary. In B. D. Ruben (Ed.), *Communication yearbook 2* (pp. 29–47). New Brunswick, NJ: Transaction Books.

Miller, G. R., Burgoon, M., & Burgoon, J. K. (1984). The functions of human communication in changing attitudes and gaining compliance. In C. C. Arnold & J. W. Bowers (Eds.), *Handbook of rhetorical and communication theory* (pp. 400–474). Newton, MA: Allyn & Bacon.

Miller, G. R., & Steinberg, M. (1975). *Between people: A new analysis of interpersonal communication.* Chicago: Science Research Associates.

Mowen, J. C., & Cialdini, R. B. (1980). On implementing the door-in-the-face technique in a business context. *Journal of Marketing Research, 22,* 253–258.

Nel, E., Helmreich, R. K., & Aronson, E. (1969). Opinion change in the advocate as a function of the persuasibility of his audience: A clarification of the meaning of dissonance. *Journal of Personality and Social Psychology, 12,* 117–124.

Rittle, R. H. (1981). Changes in helping behavior: Self versus situational perceptions as mediators of the foot-in-the-door effect. *Personality and Social Psychology Bulletin, 7,* 431–437.

Sears, D. O., & Freedman, J. L. (1967). Selective exposure to information: A critical review. *Public Opinion Quarterly, 31,* 194–213.

Shanab, M. E., & O'Neill, P. (1979). The effects of contrast upon compliance with socially undesirable requests in the door-in-the-face paradigm. *Canadian Journal of Behavioral Science, 11,* 236–244.

Simons, H. W. (1974). The carrot and stick as handmaidens of persuasion in conflict situations. In G. R. Miller & H. W. Simons (Eds.), *Perspectives on communication in social conflict* (pp. 172–205). Englewood Cliffs, NJ: Prentice-Hall.

Zillmann, D., & Bryant, J. (Eds.). (1985). *Selective exposure to communication.* Hillsdale, NJ: Laurence Erlbaum Associates.

Four Major Social Scientific Theories and Their Value to the Public Relations Researcher

Marcia Prior-Miller
Iowa State University

ABSTRACT

The process of building a body of theoretically and empirically based knowledge about public relations need not take place in a vacuum. This chapter explores four major sociological perspectives that constitute the frameworks for much of contemporary organizational theory and research. Working from the premise that public relations is an inherently organizational form of communication, the author explores some assumptions and propositions which the symbolic interactionist, exchange, conflict, and structural–functional theories suggest, both for enriching existing theory and building new public relations theory.

The need for theoretically based research as the foundation for the growth of the public relations field has been argued by a number of writers (Cutlip, Center, & Broom, 1985; Dozier, 1985). One logical theoretical tradition for building this foundation is communication theory, because much of the practitioner's work incorporates interpersonal and mediated communication.

However, public relations is inherently organizational. By definition (Cutlip et al., 1985) and by historical precedent, the focus of the field is on the relations that an organization has with its publics, whether those publics be internal, external, or both. Therefore, researchers seeking to enrich existing public relations theory and to build new theory will also want to draw on the body of organization theory and research.

Contemporary organization theory has its roots in a number of social scientific disciplines. A careful review of existing literature on the sociology of organizations highlights this fact. Indeed, such a review will quickly show that "organization theory" does not refer to a single theory that is capable of providing explanations and predictions for the totality of observed organizational phenomena. Rather, it is comprised of a highly complex and diverse group of middle-range theories (Merton, 1967; Wallace, 1971). Each of these middle-range theories strives to explain some aspect of organizations. Champion (1975) called these middle-range theories "partial theories" because of their limited ability to explain the various dimensions of organizations.

Researchers in public relations sometimes use more than one perspective to explain relationships. Several authors, including Cutlip and Center (1982), have noted that research in public relations may draw on as many as 10 or more different research traditions. Some are based in sociology. Others are derived from the work of social psychologists. Still others are rooted in psychology, economics and political science.

Astley and Van de Ven (1983) have given the proliferation of perspectives on organizations a mixed review:

> On the one hand, this theoretical pluralism should be encouraged so that researchers will uncover novel aspects of organizational life and sharpen their critical inquiry. But on the other hand, this pluralism encourages excessive theoretical compartmentalization, and it becomes easy to lose sight of the ways in which various schools of thought are related to each other. (p. 245)

Thus, these authors highlight an important point. Researchers who would build a unified public relations theory by drawing on diverse theoretical traditions need to understand the root theories out of which the various research traditions have grown. Only then can they continually relate new research and emerging theories to those intellectual origins.

Four theoretical frameworks within sociology have provided the roots for a large number of middle-range organization theories: symbolic interactionism, exchange theory, conflict theory, and structural–functional theory. Drawing on these frameworks, researchers have sought to explain behaviors of individuals in organizations, structures of organizations, and networks in and between organizations. In fact, these four perspectives have been so influential in assisting researchers in building middle-range theories, not only in the study of organizations but in all types of human social interaction, that sociologists often refer to these four theories as grand theories. Middle-range theories designed to explain systematically and predict the nature, patterns, and dynamics of public relations will be enriched similarly by contributions from these theoretical frameworks.

Turner (1982) called the four grand theories orientations or perspectives. Thus, Turner casts them into that category of theories described in chapter 1 as metatheory. Each of these metatheories builds on a unique combination of assumptions and propositions about how individuals and groups create and maintain social relations. As a result, each perspective offers different strengths for identifying and explaining the phenomena that can be observed both in and outside of organizations. Each theory offers unique capabilities for sensitizing public relations researchers to different dimensions of organizations and the processes of communication within and between them. Similarly, the interplay among these four theoretical perspectives, and the research that arises from them, can lead to a broader understanding of how organizations work and how public relations practitioners can represent the organizations.

This chapter introduces the four major sociological theories and their importance to public relations. Following a synopsis of each theory and its historical roots, a few assumptions and propositions are selected to (a) capture the primary focus of each theoretical perspective and (b) illustrate how each perspective can assist with the systematic study of public relations and the organizations that it serves.

Although it is beyond the scope of this chapter to do so, it should be noted that an in-depth understanding of these sociological theories could be gained through careful analysis of the grand theories and by tracing middle-range theories to their origins in the grand theories. It is possible, through a careful analysis of the literature on symbolic interactionism, exchange, conflict, and structural–functional theory, to tease out large numbers of assumptions and propositions for each perspective. Turner (1982), for example, suggested some 45 basic assumptions and propositions in five primary areas that could be used to compare the two perspectives on symbolic interactionism known as the Chicago and Iowa Schools. Turner also suggested a total of 17 propositions for each of nine stages of conflict theory. Blau (1979–1980) identified 21 assumptions, 34 theorems, and more than 150 subtheorems for his macrostructural theory.

SYMBOLIC INTERACTIONISM

Symbolic interactionism, with its roots in behaviorism, grew out of some of the earliest efforts of sociologists to understand the interactions among people and the impact those interactions have on society (Turner, 1982). Among the seminal thinkers on the perspective were George

Herbert Mead (1934), Charles Horton Cooley (1964), W. I. Thomas (1978), Herbert Blumer (1969) and Manford Kuhn (Kuhn & McPartland, 1954).

Symbolic interactionism proposes that social reality is what people think it is. That is, meanings of social interactions are determined by the meanings held by the people who are interacting. One of symbolic interactionism's key strengths is its recognition that people use symbols in their interactions and that the meanings of those symbols can be negotiated. Indeed, symbolic interactionism proposes that social phenomena are in a continual state of negotiation.

Viewed from the symbolic interactionist perspective, organizations are what people believe them to be. They are the products of social interactions (Manis & Meltzer, 1978; Rosenberg & Turner, 1981; Turner, 1982; Wilson, 1983).

The articulation of symbolic interactionism by its key writers assumed the individual as the unit of analysis. As a result, the tradition of research on organizations that has grown out of symbolic interactionism is a tradition established largely by social psychologists. In general, social psychologists assume it is easier to understand larger groups by looking first at individuals and how those individuals interact to create the personality of groups or other social structures, such as organizations. In so doing, social psychologists have found symbolic interactionism to be a useful perspective for fully understanding intraorganizational dimensions and processes: how people behave in relation to organizations and the impact that organizational patterns and structures have on individual behaviors.

However, if a researcher assumes that (a) the unit of analysis is the organization, rather than individuals or groups within the organization, and (b) aspects of organizations, like aspects of individual interaction, are capable of having self-identities and of being collectively negotiated, then the assumptions and propositions of symbolic interactionism can be translated from the individual level to the organizational level. In so doing, symbolic interactionism could assist a public relations researcher in exploring not only individuals in relation to public relations and its organizations but also dimensions of organizations in relation to each other. Working from these assumptions and from the symbolic interactionist assumptions that humans are self-determining, have the capacity to think, select objectives, and choose between alternative behaviors, the following assumptions about organizations are suggested.

Because organizations are the products of human interaction, people working through organizations will choose between alternative organizational behaviors, objectives, and symbols to shape and direct organizational interactions both with organizations and with other constituencies. Organizations will play roles in relation to each other. Organizations will act to create their own realities. Organizational structures will be a result of patterning roles.

Organizational communication will be the process of negotiating meanings. Organizational conflict will be a result of discrepancies in meanings. Organizational change will be a result of continually redefining realities. Organizational behaviors will be rational and enacted, not predetermined. Organizational management will be both reactive and proactive.

In essence, then, the symbolic interactionist perspective explains the ways and the extent to which the structures and processes of organizations result from individual and collective efforts to find and define realities. Research would explore the extent to which these propositions of symbolic interactionism can be used to explain and predict organizational phenomena.

To illustrate: A researcher observes that public relations organizations regularly invest significant amounts of time, money and human resources in the development of logotypes and corporate identity packages for marketing the organization and its products. The researcher, then, might use the symbolic interactionist perspective to explore how those symbols become statements of strategic choice, how the symbols are used to establish organizational roles in relation to other organizations or to control organizations' internal and external environments.

Propositions for such a study are suggested by Wilson (1983) and Stryker (1981): The more an organizational symbol is associated with organizational reality, the greater will be the expectation of that reality when the symbol alone is presented. The greater the commitment, the higher the identity salience and the more likely role performances will reflect institutionalized values and norms.

EXCHANGE THEORY

At the heart of exchange theory and its variations posited by key theorists such as Peter M. Blau (1964, 1968), George C. Homans (1974), and Richard M. Emerson (1972) is the basic proposition that social structures result from social exchanges between individuals. The theory further suggests that in those exchanges individuals (or organizations) will seek to balance the ratio of their inputs and outputs (Emerson, 1981; Turner, 1982; Wilson, 1983).

More specifically, the perspective assumes that people form and sustain relationships when they believe the rewards from those relationships will be greater than the costs. Like symbolic interactionism, exchange theory has historical roots in behaviorism. Unlike symbolic interactionism, exchange theory also has roots in micro-economic theory and derives elements from the positivist paradigm.

The key theorists assumed the individual as the unit of analysis (Homans, 1974). Thus, as with symbolic interactionism, the body of research rising from the exchange perspective has concentrated on studying behaviors of individuals within organizations. The equity theory studies of motivation in organizations (Mowday, 1983), for example, are derived from the exchange perspective.

Emerson (1981) has grouped the multiple assumptions upon which the various versions of exchange theory have been based into three basic assumptions: (a) that people will act in ways that produce what are for them beneficial events; (b) every valued event has a variable value that will increase, or decrease, as the need for the event is filled; and (c) the benefits of social interaction are conditional in that they are based on the benefits of what is received in the exchange.

The propositions of exchange theory, as articulated by Homans (1974) and Blau (1964), arise from these assumptions and address the motivations of individuals for choosing actions. Conflict will result when rewards are expected, but punishment is given. The need for rewards will increase when needs are satisfied. Change will occur when inequities in power occur in relationships.

If researchers again choose the organization as the unit of analysis and assume that aspects of organizations, like aspects of individuals' interaction, are capable of being collectively negotiated, the assumptions and propositions of exchange theory can be translated to the organizational level. Zey-Ferrell (1979) and Hall (1982) summarize research in which sociologists have drawn on exchange theory to analyze organizations at the individual, group, and organizational levels. Included in their summaries are studies by Aldrich and Pfeffer (1976) and Pfeffer and Salanick (1978) testing the middle-range resource-dependence theories. These theories are derived from the exchange perspective.

Exchange theory translated to the organizational level proposes that people working through organizations will negotiate decisions about alternative organizational behaviors and objectives. They will collectively shape and direct organizational interactions, both with other organizations and with other constituencies, to maintain equity in power and resource exchanges. Organizational structures will result from the need to maintain balance in exchanges. Organizational communication will occur or fail to occur when relationships are not in balance. Organizational conflict will occur when inputs and outputs are not in balance and one organization or the other refuses to act to restore that balance. Organizational change will result from continually negotiating inputs and outputs. Organizational management will be both reactive and proactive in such negotiations.

As researchers analyze the dimensions of the public relations function in organizations, it is possible to identify multiple points at which such negotiations, or exchanges, are made. Exchange theory might be used to assist with the study of the motivations of organizations in their processes of internal coordination, of socialization, of decision-making and communication. Although Turner (1982) has noted that the theory's definitions of social structure and structural complexity are weak, studying the extent to which organizational exchanges determine structure, context or the level of performance of organizations might prove fruitful.

Sullivan, Dozier, and Hellweg (1984) found that although public relations practitioners perceive differences in the hierarchy of their roles in organizations, more years of professional experience did not necessarily result in practitioners moving into higher order, better paying roles. An exploration of organizational reasons for this failure to reward public relations practitioners might lead researchers to examine the negotiating relationships between the hiring organizations and practitioners. Study of such relationships will determine the bases used for the interactions, who participates, who is dependent on whom in the negotiations and how each finds equity in the relationships.

Propositions from exchange theory (Emerson, 1981; Wilson, 1983) might include the following:

1. The more often hiring organizations find they are able to retain highly experienced practitioners at low salaries and hierarchically low positions, the more likely they are to continue offering low salaries.
2. The more often in the past hiring organizations have received feedback that indicates practitioners will apply for and accept placement in positions without greater rewards, the more likely they are to continue to offer low salaries and hierarchically low positions to experienced individuals.
3. The greater profit hiring organizations receive as a result of their actions, the more likely they are to continue to perform the action.
4. The greater the dependency of practitioners on hiring organizations for job tenure, the greater the hiring organizations' power over practitioners, and the less power practitioners have to require higher pay for their skill and knowledge.

CONFLICT THEORY

The conflict perspective assumes that conflict is the basis of social interchange and the product of social interchange. Conflict theory thus assumes that organizations, rather than being products of the consensus of individuals or organizations interacting with each other as symbolic interactionism and exchange theory suggest, are the products of conflict among actors. Conflict theory arises from the writings of Karl Marx (1969), Georg Simmel (1955), Ralf Dahrendorf (1959), and L. A. Coser (1956). Although conflict theory did not gain a strong following in the United States during the first half of this century, a fact attributed to Marx's deterministic and polemical approach (Turner, 1982), there is a growing recognition that the perspective offers researchers insights into organizational phenomena, which other perspectives do not.

Katz and Kahn (1978), for example, suggest that Marxian theory, separated from its "propagandistic doctrines" and time- and locale-specific aspects, was one of the earliest systematic efforts to move beyond the social-psychological emphasis on personal characteristics to social relationships as determining forces of social structure. Marx's emphasis on the production process as a unit of analysis also suggests an entirely different perspective than that offered by symbolic interactionism, exchange and structural–functional theory.

Conflict theory assumes that conflict is an inevitable part of social interactions because of the incompatible, competing goals and values of individuals and organizations: the dialectics of social phenomena. That is, the perspective assumes that in every reality there is both a positive and a negative aspect. These opposites will play off each other and will affect the direction of any interaction that is related to that reality. Thus, conflict theory assumes there are always differences in power, and resources will always be scarce. The perspective further assumes that people in interaction will fight over the distribution of these resources.

Within the broad perspective are some substantial differences in the assumptions about the nature and value of conflict. Marx (1969; Appelbaum, 1978) assumed conflict as a necessary antecedent to equally necessary change, whereas Simmel (1955) assumed conflict is inevitable, but can be a step toward greater cohesion. In spite of these differences, the propositions of the theory, which derive from the assumptions, are similar. These propositions focus on the manifestations of conflict, the sources of conflict, and the power relationships and exchanges in relation to scarce resources.

In the existing research on complex organizations, conflict theory has retained these two primary thrusts: the dialectical conflict and the functional conflict models (Zey-Ferrell, 1979). The dialectical model assumes that conflict is inherent in the organization and the organization is itself in the process of working out that conflict. The functional model focuses on the usefulness of conflict to the goals and values of special interest groups, and strives to reduce conflict to preserve the organization.

Perhaps the most common focus of research using conflict theory is on the manager–laborer dimensions of industry organizations. However, this is not the only dimension that could appropriately be explained if a broad articulation of the perspective is used. Zey-Ferrell (1979) suggests that the conflict perspective might lead a researcher to look at sources of conflict at every level in an organization: within as well as between individuals, between units or departments in the organization, and between organizations.

Conflict theory suggests that any aspect of an organization is merely a reflection of conflict inherent in the organization. To study the organization or any aspect of it is to focus on the inherent contradictions in the organization, how these lead to conflict, and where and how change occurs as a result. Marxist conflict theory and critical theory, as articulated by the Frankfurt School (Fuhrman & Snizek, 1979–1980), both emphasize historical analysis to determine the extent to which historical values and goals contribute to conflict.

The conflict perspective suggests some different variables of interest to Sullivan et al.'s (1984) question of organizational role hierarchy. To explain why public relations practitioners are unequally rewarded in salary and power within an organization, the functional conflict perspective suggests that researchers look at the differences in the practitioner's and the organization's vested interests. The researcher might also examine the practitioners' conflict: Do unequal rewards motivate practitioners to seek changes of status or positions of greater power with the organization?

The dialectical model suggests that researchers look at the inherent contradictions that lead to the conflict: at how practitioners in organizations become aware that inequalities exist in the resources that they have available and the power they have to make decisions about the products of their work; and then how they bring pressure to bear, both individually and collectively, on the existing power group to effect change.

STRUCTURAL–FUNCTIONAL THEORY

Structural–functional theory is variously regarded as a joint perspective and two distinct theoretical frameworks: structuralism and functionalism (Turner, 1982; Wilson, 1983). The perspective, with roots squarely in the scientific positivist paradigm, is an outgrowth of the writings of Emile Durkheim (1947) and Max Weber (1968). Structuralism–functionalism has been variously articulated by theorists such as Talcott Parsons (1948), Robert Merton (1968), and Peter Blau (1977). The structural–functional perspective suggests that social phenomena occur as a result of the interaction of social structures and the functions that those structures serve.

Thus, rather than viewing organizations as symbols of social interactions, or the products of social exchanges in which actors seek balanced relationships, or the crystallizing of power coalitions, the structural–functional perspective assumes that organizations and relationships exist as part of a larger system, much as any single part of the human body exists to serve the whole. The processes that occur in those organizations, such as cooperation, conflict, or communication, are a result of the different parts of the system influencing and adjusting to each other to maintain the social whole.

Structural–functional theory assumes that society and its structures—such as complex organizations—are more than the sum of their parts. That is, social phenomena are more than an aggregate of individuals as separate entities. Thus, where the symbolic interactionist would look at the individual to understand the whole, the structural–functional perspective would look at the whole to understand its parts.

In this way, the perspective is the antithesis of the symbolic interactionist and exchange perspectives as they are typically interpreted. In structural–functionalism the individual and the values and goals of the individual take second place to the purposes that the individual serves in the larger structure in which the individual is located (Wilson, 1983).

Structural–functional theory assumes that actors' social interactions are determined by the larger social order and that interactions serve to maintain that order, rather than people setting the rules for their social interactions and acting to shape and mold the social order to suit their meanings. Wilson (1983) suggested that when viewed as separate perspectives, the functional perspective sees social structures—such as organizational structures—occurring as a result of the functions they serve; the structural perspective sees functions as a natural result of existing structures. Viewed from the structural–functional perspective, complex organizations are systems. Organizational structures are a result of the functions they serve; the functions served determine the structures.

Because of these assumptions, the structural–functional perspective has been an important sociological perspective for studying complex organizations. Interestingly enough, however, the perspective has been little used in the study of communication in organizations, particularly mass communications. In the early 1970s, Tichenor, Donohue, and Olien (1973) noted the absence of structural variables from mass communication research. They suggested that communication research would benefit from this framework. Public relations research also benefits from looking at structural variables (Grunig & Hickson, 1976).

Researchers seeking to study public relations and its role in organizations might find structural–functionalism useful in teasing out and understanding the underlying structures of organizations and the role that communication and public relations play in the organization as a result of their positioning within the structure.

Given the question of why public relations practitioners' hierarchical roles in organizations are not related to experience or tenure with companies (Sullivan et al., 1984), researchers might look for relationships between practitioners' roles and the functions of public relations in the organizations. Research might attempt to identify relationships between the networks (which include practitioners) in the organizations, the position that the public relations function holds in the organization structure, and the rewards the practitioner receives. Propositions to guide this analysis might include:

1. The more integrated practitioners are in the organizational network, the greater the practitioners' rewards.
2. The higher the position of public relations in the organizational structure, the greater the practitioners' rewards.
3. The greater the professional qualifications required of the practitioner, the greater the rewards.

SUMMARY AND RECOMMENDATIONS FOR FUTURE RESEARCH

In every human social interaction, structures and processes play off each other in a variety of ways. Processes may lead to structures; structures, once in place, may influence the course that processes take. When public relations practitioners seek to fulfill their roles in organizations, these structures and processes come into play. At times, communication processes are effective; sometimes they are not.

In the search for answers to questions posed by these differing situations, researchers who conduct basic and applied research to contribute to the body of knowledge about public relations and to solutions to public relations problems, seek ways to explain why and how public relations processes and structures interact with differing effects. The grand sociological theories: symbolic interactionism, exchange theory, conflict and structural–functional theory, can make contributions to these explanations. Each will do so in different ways.

Whether reviewing existing research on public relations or designing studies to answer new questions, public relations researchers and practitioners should ask which perspective can provide the most insight into the question at hand. Are there meanings that are being negotiated, motivations behind actions to be discerned, sources of conflict to be identified, or relationships of structures and functions at issue? When current research does not appear to provide a sufficient explanation, a different perspective from the original study may provide a more comprehensive explanation. When findings of existing research appear to be contradictory, the reasons for the contradictions may lie in the differing assumptions and propositions of the theoretical frameworks within which the question was asked, even if the perspective was not carefully articulated.

Careful study of these four sociological metatheories and equally careful study of existing research in preparation for new studies of public relations phenomena will enable public relations researchers to build connections between existing middle-range theories and their theoretical roots. This knowledge is the beginning point for the emergence of new theories that are better able to explain and predict public relations phenomena, as public relations researchers contribute to the development of a unified theory of public relations.

ACKNOWLEDGMENTS

The author gratefully acknowledges the contributions to this chapter of Motoko Y. Lee, PhD, and Steven C. Padgitt, PhD, Department of Sociology and Anthropology, Iowa State University, Ames.

REFERENCES

Aldrich, H. E., & Pfeffer, J. (1976). Environments of organizations. In A. Inkeles, J. Coleman, & N. Smelser (Eds.), *Annual review of sociology* (pp. 79–105). Palo Alto, CA: Annual Review.

Appelbaum, R. (1978). Marx's theory of the falling rate of profit: Towards a dialectical analysis of social change. *American Sociological Review, 43,* 47–80.

Astley, W. G., & Van de Ven, A. H. (1983). Central perspectives and debates in organization theory. *Administrative Science Quarterly, 28,* 245–273.

Blau, P. M. (1964). *Exchange and power in social life.* New York: Wiley.

Blau, P. M. (1968). Interaction:Social exchange. In D. L. Sills (Ed.), *International encyclopedia of the social sciences* (Vol. 7, pp. 452–458). New York: Macmillan.

Blau, P. M. (1977). *Inequality and heterogeneity: A primitive theory of social structure.* New York: The Free Press.

Blau, P. M. (1979–1980). Elements of sociological theorizing. *Humbolt Journal of Social Relations, 7,* 105.

Blumer, H. (1969). *Symbolic interactionism: Perspective and method.* Englewood Cliffs, NJ: Prentice-Hall.

Champion, D. J. (1975). *The sociology of organizations.* New York: McGraw-Hill.

Cooley, C. H. (1964). *Human nature and the social order*. New York: Schocken Books.

Coser, L. A. (1956). *The functions of social conflict*. Glencoe, IL: The Free Press.

Cutlip, S. M., & Center, A. H. (1982). *Effective public relations* (rev. 5th ed.). Englewood Cliffs, NJ: Prentice-Hall.

Cutlip, S. M., Center, A. H., & Broom, G. M. (1985). *Effective public relations* (6th ed.). Englewood Cliffs, NJ: Prentice-Hall.

Dahrendorf, R. (1959). *Class and class conflict in an industrial society*. London: Routledge & Kegan Paul.

Dozier, D. M. (1985). Planning and evaluation in PR practice. *Public Relations Review, 11*, 17–25.

Durkehim, E. (1947). *The division of labor in society* (G. Simpson, Trans.). Glencoe, IL: The Free Press.

Emerson, R. M. (1972). Exchange theory, Parts I and II. In J. Berger, M. Zelditch, & B. Anderson (Eds.), *Sociological theories in progress* (Vol. 4). Boston: Houghton-Mifflin.

Emerson, R. M. (1981). Social exchange theory. In M. Rosenberg & R. H. Turner (Eds.), *Social psychology: Sociological perspectives* (pp. 30–65). New York: Basic Books.

Fuhrmann, E. R., & Snizek, W. E. (1979–80). Some observations on the nature and content of critical theory. *Humbolt Journal of Social Relations, 7*, 33–51.

Grunig, J. E. & Hickson, R. H. (1976). An evaluation of academic research in public relations. *Public Relations Review, 2*, 31–43.

Hall, R. H. (1982). *Organizations: Structure and process* (3rd ed.). Englewood Cliffs, NJ: Prentice-Hall.

Homans, G. C. (1974). *Social behavior: Its elementary forms*. New York: Harcourt Brace Jovanovich.

Katz, D., & Kahn, R. L. (1978). *The social psychology of organizations* (2nd ed.). New York: Wiley.

Kuhn, M., & McPartland, T. S. (1954). An empirical investigation of self-attitudes. *American Sociological Review, 19*, 68–76.

Manis, J. B., & Meltzer, B. N. (1978). *Symbolic interaction: A reader in social psychology* (3rd ed.). Boston: Allyn & Bacon.

Marx, K. (1969). *Karl Marx and Frederick Engels: Selected works in three volumes*. Prepared by the Institute of Marxism-Leninism under the Central Committe of the CPSU. Moscow: Progress Publishers.

Mead, G. H. (1934). *Mind, self and society*. Chicago: University of Chicago Press.

Merton, R. K. (1967). *On theoretical sociology*. New York: The Free Press.

Merton, R. K. (1968). *Social theory and social structure* (revised & enlarged ed.). New York: The Free Press.

Mowday, R. T. (1983). Equity theory predictions of behavior in organizations. In R. M. Steers & L. W. Porter (Eds.), *Motivation and work behavior* (3rd ed., pp. 91–112). New York: McGraw-Hill.

Parsons, T. (1948). *The structure of social action* (2nd ed.). Glencoe, IL: The Free Press.

Pfeffer, J., & Salanick, G. R. (1978). *The external control of organizations: A resource-dependence perspective*. New York: Harper & Row.

Rosenberg, M., & Turner, R. H. (Eds.). (1981). *Social psychology: Sociological perspectives*. New York: Basic Books.

Simmel, G. (1955). *Conflict* (K. H. Wolff, Trans.). Glencoe, IL: The Free Press.

Stryker, S. (1981). Symbolic Interactionism: Themes and Variations. In M. Rosenberg & R. H. Turner (Eds.), *Social psychology: Sociological perspectives* (pp. 3–29). New York: Basic Books.

Sullivan, B. A., Dozier, D. M., & Hellweg, S. A. (1984, August). *A test of organizational role hierarchy among public relations practitioners.* Paper presented at the annual meeting of the Association for Education in Journalism and Mass Communication, University of Florida, Gainesville.

Thomas, W. I. (1978). The definition of the situation. In J. G. Manis & B. N. Meltzer (Eds.), *Symbolic interaction: A reader in social psychology* (3rd ed., pp. 254–258). Boston: Allyn & Bacon.

Tichenor, P. J., Donohue, G. A., & Olien, C. N. (1973). Mass communication research: Evolution of a structural model. *Journalism Quarterly, 50*(3), 419–425.

Turner, J. H. (1982). *The structure of sociological theory* (3rd ed.). Homewood, IL: Dorsey Press.

Wallace, W. L. (1971). *The logic of science in sociology.* New York: Aldine.

Weber, M. (1968). *The theory of social and economic organization* (A. M. Henderson & T. Parsons, Trans.; T. Parsons, Ed.). New York: The Free Press.

Wilson, J. (1983). *Social theory.* Englewood Cliffs, NJ: Prentice-Hall.

Zey-Ferrell, M. (1979). *Dimensions of organizations: Environment, context, structure, process, and performance.* Santa Monica, CA: Goodyear Publishing.

SUGGESTED READINGS

General Sociological Theory

Ashley, D., & Orenstein, D. M. (1985). *Sociological theory: Classical statements.* Boston: Allyn & Bacon.

Ritzer, G. (1983). *Contemporary sociological theory.* New York: Alfred A. Knopf.

Symbolic Interactionism

Blumer, H. (1969). *Symbolic interactionism: Perspective and method.* Englewood Cliffs, NJ: Prentice-Hall.

Manis, J. G., & Meltzer, B. N. (1978). *Symbolic interaction: A reader in social psychology* (3rd ed.). Boston: Allyn & Bacon.

Exchange Theory

Blau, P. M. (1964). *Exchange and power in social life.* New York: Wiley.

Homans, G. C. (1974). *Social behavior: Its elementary forms* (rev. ed.). New York: Harcourt Brace Jovanovich.

Conflict Theory

Appelbaum, R. (1978). Marx's theory of the falling rate of profit: towards a dialectical analysis of social change. *American Sociological Review, 43,* 67–80.
Coser, L. A. (1956). *The functions of social conflict.* Glencoe, IL: The Free Press.

Structural Functionalism

Durkheim, E. (1938). *The rules of sociological method* (8th ed.). (S. A. Solovay & J. H. Mueller, Trans., and G. E. Catlin, Ed.). New York: The Free Press.
Merton, R. K. (1968). *Social theory and social structure* (enlarged ed.). New York: The Free Press.

Traditional, Enlightened, and InterpretivePerspectives on Corporate Annual Reporting

Michael Smilowitz
University of North Carolina—Charlotte

Ron Pearson
Mount Saint Vincent University

ABSTRACT

The preparation and dissemination of the corporate annual report is an important communication activity for organizations. Researchers and practitioners have provided an extensive body of literature to better explain the communicative role of the annual report as well as to provide prescriptions for its use. This chapter provides a framework by which to organize and synthesize the theory and prescriptions found in this literature. Through a process of metatheoretical analysis, the chapter illustrates how assumptions about the report's intended purpose, relevant audience, and the nature of language distinguish three perspectives in the study of corporate annual reporting.

Today's annual report is a slick, multicolor document; with sophisticated graphics; portraits of the organization's management; and a carefully worded message from the organization's chief officer(s). The preparation and dissemination of these reports are an important part of corporate communications. Millions of dollars are spent annually by more than 25,000 public companies to produce over 50 million annual reports (Rutchti & Wasserman, 1983). One estimate put the production cost of annual reports for 1987 for American corporations at about $4.3 billion (Byrne, 1987).

The volume of organization resources spent on corporate annual reporting has encouraged researchers and practitioners to develop a considerable body of literature for the purposes of both theoretical explanation and prescription. As it is with any body of literature, it is difficult to organize, synthesize, and critique the various theoretical and prescriptive claims made about the process of corporate annual reporting. In part, the difficulties arise because in any body of literature there is rarely a single, underlying theoretical framework. As chapters 1 and 2 in this volume indicate, theory development, whether descriptive or prescriptive, is influenced by the metatheoretical perspectives its developers bring to bear upon the phenomena of interest.

The term *perspective* is used in this chapter in a fashion similar to Fisher's (1978) usage: the point of view used in the process of observing/interpreting a thing or event. As perception exercises aptly demonstrate, observation and interpretation are interlinked. The understanding we have of the "reality" of some thing or some event develops out of the perceptual set that we are using as we experience the phenomenon.

Theory development is not different in this regard. The claims theorists make come about from the perceptual sets that influence their thinking. That is, their points of view define what they will see, how they will do their analysis, and ultimately, how they reach their conclusions. Fisher's (1978) term for this property of theoretical perspectives is *relevance determining.*

It is helpful when trying to make sense of a body of literature, to have a basis for examining how the perspectives of the different theorists influence their work. Theorists are rarely explicit about their perspectives. It may even be fair to say that many theorists are themselves only tacitly aware of how their perspectives are influencing their work. *Metatheoretical analysis* refers to the analysis of theories. Through such analysis, it is possible to identify a researcher's point of view and describe how those metatheoretical assumptions influence theory generation. The results of the analysis can provide for more critical understanding and evaluation of different theoretical claims.

This chapter illustrates the application of metatheoretical analysis. The purpose is to provide a framework by which to organize and synthesize the theory and prescriptions found in the literature about corporate annual reporting. There were three steps involved in this metatheoretical analysis:

1. Review the available literature.
2. Determine characteristics that appropriately and parsimoniously distinguish different approaches in the study of corporate annual reporting.
3. Develop a classification scheme that will inform on how the perspectives of the various theorists account for the explanations

DISTINGUISHING QUESTIONS

	Intended Purpose?	Relevant Audience?	Nature of Language?	
T H E O R E T I C A L A S S U M P T I O N	To promote favorable perceptions of the firm's financial status.	Investors and the financial community.	Language has determined and predictable effects.	TRADITIONAL
	To depict the firm as socially responsible and ethical.	Legislative and public interest groups.	Language is capable of mirroring reality.	ENLIGHTENED
	To provide for the firm's own sense making regarding its performance.	The firm's management and workers.	Language constructs reality and expresses subjective experience.	INTERPRETIVE

FIG. 5.1. Classification grid for organizing the literature on corporate annual reporting.

and/or prescriptions that they offer about corporate annual reporting.

The result of this process is summarized in Fig. 5.1. Answers to the three questions across the top appeared to account for what the various theorists determined as relevant: (a) What does the theorist conceive to be the intended purpose for the annual report? (b) What types of audiences does the theorist believe to be relevant to the annual report? (c) What ontological and epistemological assumptions does the theorist make about the nature of language? Using these three questions, the literature was classified into three groups. The balance of this chapter describes these three groups as representative of traditional, enlightened, and interpretive perspectives for the theorizing about corporate annual reporting.

THE TRADITIONAL PERSPECTIVE

The first function of annual reports is to meet the requirements of the Securities and Exchange Commission regulations. Firms that offer stock for trade must provide financial disclosure information. If compliance with reporting requirements was the only intent for annual reporting, then the document could easily take the form of a plainly prepared accountant report. The graphic sophistication that has become an expected characteristic of the final documents suggests that the reports are intended for more than auditing purposes.

The earliest of the perspectives, which can be called the *traditional perspective*, regards the annual report as an important communication effort for enhancing perceptions of the firm's fiscal features. As such, in both research and prescription there is an emphasis on those audiences that will most likely affect the firm's financial status. These types of audiences were identified by Grunig and Hunt (1984) as: (a) current shareholders, (b) prospective shareholders, (c) the financial community, (d) the financial media.

The traditional perspective recognizes that organizations that release annual reports are attempting to meet objectives that go beyond the legal mandate for financial reporting. These other objectives were also identified by Grunig and Hunt's (1984) analysis. Elaborating on a study completed by McGrath (1979), Grunig and Hunt indicated at least five objectives:

1. Achieve open communication channels.
2. Build ongoing relationships with financial analysts.
3. Provide for an informed market so that investment worthiness can be judged on merits and not by rumor.
4. Establish credibility so that the firm is regarded as reliable.
5. Accomplish the long-term objectives of favorable stock prices and profit to earning ratios.

Traditional notions about financial reporting assume the meeting of these objectives can be achieved by a process of selecting the right information, casting that information in the most appropriate format, and selecting the most relevant channels for communication. The traditional perspective for annual reports is therefore mechanistic (Fisher, 1978) and effects oriented. The process is mechanistic in that the locus of communication resides in the message and the effects of the channel. Little attention is given to analysis of the particular characteristics of the audiences. Instead, audience characteristics are seen as less relevant than producing documents that conform to the ideal formal characteristics of effective messages. The need for an effects orientation is represented in Marston's (1979) claim that: "Companies need an active market for their securities to improve the corporations' positions in mergers or in acquisitions, to create a market for future stock issues, and to broaden the base of ownership" (p. 73).

The emphasis on formal characteristics of messages remains prevalent in spite of early challenges to the "hypodermic needle" theories of communication. These challenges pointed out the inadequacy of the presumption that messages have predictable and unmediated impact (Bauer, 1971; see also Cox & Willard, 1982).

For example, the traditional perspective's effect orientation is clearly evident in the research and theorizing about the impact of the annual report on stock prices (Chambers, 1974; Findlay, 1977; Foster, Jenkings, & Vickrey, 1986; Verrecchia, 1981). These studies, however, actually do more to discredit the effects assumption. The many failed hypotheses that appear in these studies suggest that the annual report has little, if any, effect on the actual market value of a firm's stock offerings. Hines (1982) offered explanations for the failure to find the predicted relationships. The previous studies may have been too short term because investors may not evaluate annual reports until some time after they are received. Also, the information that most likely triggers stock trading is released through more rapid sources than the annual report. Hines concluded that the auditor's report contained in the report usually does no more than confirm the firms' preliminary profit reports.

Although it has been difficult to identify direct impacts of the annual report on market prices, researchers have continued to assume that the information format of the report must influence perceptions within the financial community. Bell (1985) used a quasi-experimental design to evaluate whether quantitative or qualitative information has a greater impact when annual reports are used to evaluate the firm's performance and growth potential of its stocks. Bell found that financial analysts responded differently to the type of information format depending on the functional type of the firm.

The theory, research, and prescriptions within the traditional perspective assumes that language is able to alter perceptions of reality. In particular, traditionalist perspectives claim that the proper selection and organization of the financial data and a president's message that provides rationalizations for the corporations' performance will result in the relevant financial markets overestimating the value of the firm's stock offerings. Seen from a traditionalist perspective, the purposes for the annual report include persuasion and publicity functions. Research within this perspective is primarily concerned with prescriptions for practice that place heavy emphasis on the form and structure of the messages to gain publicity and to achieve narrow behavior effects with a narrow group of financial publics.

THE ENLIGHTENED PERSPECTIVE

During the 1960s, pressures on large organizations led them to see themselves as more accountable for their ethical and social responsibility (Buchholz, 1985). These forces enlarged the traditional perspective beyond a constrained environment. Financial and legal restrictive factors were extended to include audiences such as legislative and public interest groups. This more "enlightened" view acknowledges the potential of annual reports for achieving a variety of corporate purposes with a variety of publics.

Hill and Knowlton Executives (1975) noted functions of the annual report that go beyond financial concerns. They suggested annuals are useful for: (a) Establishing the credibility of the business so that efforts to explain itself will meet with public acceptance, (b) Communicating activities of business that indicate its wider social involvement, (c) Articulating the position of business on legal and regulatory measures affecting a company or even its industry.

According to Cutlip, Center, and Broom (1985):

> The trend is for reports to do more than reflect and compare a company's current financial results. Some reports show a company's international scope, or its impact on the economy. . . . Some convey the position of management on public issues. The emphasis is on the role of the modern corporation in society, beyond its own immediate survival. (p. 493)

These authors pointed out that copies of annual reports are often used for a variety of publics and purposes, including: suppliers, libraries, trade associations, contract proposals to customers, students, and community and government officials.

The interest in communicating with a wide variety of publics is associated with the considerable interest in the readability of annuals (Heath & Phelps, 1984; Hoskins, 1984; Means, 1981; Soper & Dolphin, 1964). The premise for these studies is that the language of the annual report must be clear and free of jargon if it is to be an effective communication medium for publics with a variety of backgrounds, knowledge and interests. The prescriptions for improving readability, however, appear to have had little effect. Hoskins, as well as Heath and Phelps, has suggested that readability indices of annual reports are not improving.

The necessity for clarity is a major position in the theory and prescriptions within the enlightened perspective. Hill and Knowlton Inc. (1984) expressed the premise as they emphasized the need for management to "tell it like it is." Moreover, Hill and Knowlton have regarded the need for clear and accurate information as crucial for annual report credibility. Kallendorf and Kallendorf's (1985) examination of business communication style also indicates that clarity is a key value motivating research and prescriptive advice for practitioners.

Both the traditional and the enlightened perspectives are characterized by an effects orientation. The difference is that the traditional perspective regards the audience as concerned exclusively with financial performance and the market value of the organization. In the enlightened perspective, the number of audiences are larger, more varied, and more critical of all the aspects of organizational performance. For example, the research of Lentz and Tschirgi (1963) finds that organizations do in fact use the annual report as a forum for reporting noneconomic behaviors. These researchers demonstrated that companies that receive greater social benefits, or are highly regulated, have a greater tendency to report noneconomic behaviors.

Bowman and Haire (1975) provided another insight regarding the reporting of social and ethical responsibility. In their study, they compared profitability to the amount of discussion devoted to corporate responsibility. They found that, up to a point, the amount of discussion devoted to describing the organization's noneconomic efforts increased with profitability.

These studies have clear implications for practice. Seen from an enlightened perspective, the language choices for the annual report need to persuade others of the firm's *ethos,* and do so through the Aristotelian sense of the term: Identify the organization as knowledgeable; indicate the high moral character of the organization; and illustrate how the organization has the public's best interests in mind. Firms should take the opportunity in the annual report to mitigate indictments that profit must be at the expense of others. Strategies such as these are believed to allow the firm to present itself as a noble rather than self-serving organization.

THE INTERPRETIVE PERSPECTIVE

Of the three perspectives, the interpretive perspective is the newest and also the perspective that is least represented in the literature. It should not be presumed that because it is the newest, the interpretive perspective is therefore better than the previous two. Rather than a better or worse approach, the interpretive perspective simply emphasizes different features of language usage because of its differing metatheoretical assumptions. By being more explicit about the epistemological and ontological assumptions about language that characterize the traditional and enlightened perspectives, it will be easier to understand how an interpretive perspective leads to different conclusions about corporate annual reporting.

Both the traditional and enlightened perspectives fit what Astley and Van de Ven (1983) described as the system–structural view. The ontology of a system–structural view assumes the world as objective and behavior as constrained by structural features. Human choice is, at best, adaptive within the possibilities allowed by the environment. Accepting these assumptions makes possible the claim that preparers of annual reports are capable, if properly guided, of making rational choices about their language usage. If the world can be "known" and clearly defined, communicators can discover relevant structures of that world and model their messages on those structures. Meaning can be understood as the conventions shared about the nature of the world. Identification of the commonly shared conventions informs on the practices that are best able to accomplish the intents and objectives of communicators. Practices such as accentuation of positive characteristics and identifying with the concerns of the audience are believed to be instrumental in persuading others to fulfil the firm's interests.

The annual reports that are best understood from the traditional perspective are those with a concern for using symbols, whether expressed mathematically or verbally, to manipulate the perceptions of relevant financial publics. To do so, language is believed to be a powerful tool, capable of having marked cognitive and affective impact. Words and figures speak "literally" rather than metaphorically. However, because it is often assumed necessary to obfuscate rather than enlighten, it becomes subsequently necessary for reports to use symbols strategically.

Two of the possible strategic choices include the "hype and hoopla" approach and the "it will be better next year" approach. In the former, symbols are selected to exaggerate success in the minds of the relevant audiences. In the latter, the objective is to persuade the intended audiences to begin or continue their confidence in the firm's practices in spite of poor performance. The selection of more particular rhetorical strategies is based on the firm's anticipation of how its audience will most favorably respond. For example, when an annual touts efficiency it does so from the recognition that at least some of its audiences—owners and management specifically—value efficiency. When service and value are thought to be the more crucial value in the minds of the intended public—such as the case for non-manufacturing firms—measures of service and product quality are presented as the measures of effectiveness. Implementation of these strategies is made possible because once the minimum legal requirements are met, the firm has full control of its presentation of the "facts."

In contrast, the enlightened view of annuals emphasizes the interests of more diverse publics and therefore believes it necessary to provide clear, useful, factually accurate information to achieve a wide variety of effects with an increasingly diverse group of publics. The enlightened perspective shares the same ontological assumptions as the traditional perspective, but elaborates its epistemology in its efforts to identify how language accurately reflects reality. The enlightened perspective takes the stance that "facts" speak for themselves and, if properly expressed, are able to mirror the financial and social status of the firm. The research imperative of this perspective is to discover how a neutral language can best be used to refer accurately to objects in the real world.

The characteristics of an interpretive perspective have already received considerable attention elsewhere (Burrell & Morgan, 1979; Deetz, 1982; Putnam, 1983) and therefore are sketched here to show their contrasts with the traditional and enlightened perspectives. The foremost distinction of an interpretive perspective is its position that all experience is subjective, resulting from sharing symbols that people actively select and communicate as they interpret their actions and the actions of others. Rather than a reality that is seen as objective and discoverable, an interpretive perspective would regard reality as subjective and enacted (Weick, 1979), in which symbols are used in accomplishing consensually negotiated understandings (Smircich, 1983).

Replacing the ontological and epistemological assumptions of both the traditional and enlightened perspectives with the assumptions of what Astley and Van de Ven (1983) described as a "strategic-choice view" helps to make apparent the metatheoretical basis of an interpretive perspective. Astley and Van de Ven described a strategic-choice view as one in which "people and their relationships are organized and socialized to serve the choices and purposes of people in power" (p. 247).

An interpretive approach to annual report research has an epistemological stance, with respect to language, that is different from the other two perspectives. From this perspective, it becomes more appropriate to speak of "corporate annual interpretation" than of corporate annual reporting. Language is regarded as incapable of reflecting corporate financial or social reality with the impartiality of a mirror. The goal of "telling it like it is" becomes an illusion when language usage is believed to be inescapably affected by motive and intent. What are seen as rational language choices in the first two perspectives are seen from an interpretive perspective as strategic and rhetorical.

A researcher using an interpretive perspective would find that the rhetorical obligations of the annual report are many. Perhaps the foremost of its obligations is to persuade owners of the firm that its managers have a legitimate claim to their positions of power. Because managers are no longer owners, they must justify their positions under the banner of efficiency and rationality (Kanter, 1977) and must present themselves as qualified to make decisions. As such, the report needs to elaborate management's accomplishments in making good decisions and provide accounts that will be interpreted as signs of its capabilities. Pfeffer (1981) made the same point when he argued that "a critical administrative activity involves the construction and maintenance of belief systems which assure continued compliance, commitment, and positive affect on the part of participants, regardless of how they fare in the contest of resources" (p. 1).

A second rhetorical obligation follows from the first. As the evaluation of effectiveness is not based on concrete, objective measures of performance, sales, and profit figures hold less importance. Their importance will be diminished especially when technical progress or social and ethical responsibilities are seen as competing values. For example, General Motors accounts for its recent poor performance with the argument that it is preparing itself for better outcomes through redesign, restructuring, and tightening its belt.

In general, the evaluation of effectiveness is a complex set of subjective attitudes and beliefs that is a product of rhetorical processes. The firm, through its rhetoric, attempts to position and order the criteria that will best cast the firm as effective. Keeley (1984), for example, suggested that the necessary amount of net profit is itself a subjective measure as different constituencies hold different expectations for profit. Keeley dismissed theories of impartiality for the alternative that organization members select and information to further their own interests.

Even the annual's reliance upon financial data cannot be seen as contradicting the notion that the report is fundamentally rhetorical. O'Leary (1985) presented a convincing case that even the most quantitative data does not mirror but rather interprets. O'Leary pointed out that all scientific theories, including theories of accounting, are underdetermined by facts. As a consequence, O'Leary has called for an intellectual honesty that acknowledges this degree of uncertainty, ambiguity, and the role of interpretation, which is characteristic of even the hardest data in an annual report.

Salancik and Meindl (1984) argued that management, having no real control over organizational outcomes, use attributions in the pages of corporate annual reports to foster an illusion of control. Salancik and Meindl pointed out how this strategy can be particularly subtle. Firms will sometimes take responsibility for negative outcomes as a strategy for indicating awareness of problems and a sense of being in control of them. Bettman and Weitz (1983) studied attributions in corporate annual reports and concluded that unfavorable outcomes were attributed more to external and uncontrollable forces than were favorable outcomes. Frazier, Ingram, and Tennyson's (1984) content analysis of annual reports reached similar conclusions. They successfully identified themes that could be linked to management's incentives to misrepresent performance. Studies such as these illustrate the notion that annual report production can be interestingly viewed as acts of interpretation couched within rhetorical strategies.

The diverse obligations faced by the annual report become even more complex when we realize that the process of preparing the report represents a period of sense-making for the organization itself. As important as performing a legitimating function for external publics is the annual report's role of legitimating past actions for management itself. That is, the annual report construction is both a public and a private affair; a time of year when management participates in a collective effort of sense-making vis-à-vis actions in the previous year.

Weick's (1979) model of organizing is appropriate to an interpretive perspective of annual reports. A major assumption made by Weick is that members of organizations do not simply react to an objective world, but rather enact an environment through attempts to reduce equivocality. Weick suggested that organization members test various selection processes until they believe themselves successful in their efforts to reduce equivocality. Those selection processes that are regarded as useful are retained and become part of the organization's intelligence.

As already pointed out, the absence of exact criteria makes the assessment of an organizational performance highly equivocal. For that reason, the process of annual reporting seems ideally suited to the type of analysis suggested by Weick's model. This type of analysis enlarges the notion of audience to include the organization's self-image. Whether the amount and type of participation of organization members varies from complete internal preparation to preparation by an external agency, the final text represents and constrains the subsequent sense-making processes of the organization.

The research that can be characterized as within an interpretive perspective is research that seems to have little prescriptive value for the preparation of annual reports. Bowman's (1976) study illustrates how an interpretive analysis of annual reports reveals much about the organization's culture, information that might be useful to considerations of mergers. Two studies by Bowman (1978, 1984) also illustrate how examination of annual reports can be used to interpret the organization's sense-making processes, especially in terms of their perceptions of their own risk-taking and environmental-coping behaviors.

Examining the interactions involved in annual report preparation should provide excellent examples of what Weick (1979) has called "retrospective sense making." According to Weick, organizations talk to themselves to make sense of their actions. Research may find that the "talk" involved in the preparation and dissemination of annual reports may be a very important antecedent to the organization's strategic decision-making.

CONCLUSIONS

There is no utility in the position that any one of the perspectives is superior to the others. This chapter was intended to demonstrate how metatheoretical analysis helps to identify the impact of theoretical perspectives on theoretical explanations and prescriptions, not that any perspective is superior to another. The metatheoretical approach of this chapter should help public relations researchers to understand the reasons and implications of their own theoretical choices (whether their interests are in corporate annual reporting or some other aspects of the public communication of organizations).

The subsequent development of theory will depend on the attractiveness of the assumptions that characterize the three perspectives. Researchers and theorists who prefer the ontology and epistemology associated with accepting reality as objective and constrained will continue to advance understandings within traditional and enlightened perspectives. Such research will likely continue its attempts to identify effect oriented characteristics of the report. Researchers and theorists interested in the subjective, rhetorical nature of annual reporting will enlarge the literature within the interpretive perspective. One direction for research is to see how the interaction between the organizations' top management and those individuals directly responsible for preparing the report is related to how the organization thinks about itself.

To the extent that practitioners are primarily concerned with meeting the self-interests of the firm, they are better advised to consider all three perspectives as each makes it own convincing arguments within the framework of the perspective. The traditional perspective identifies and elaborates on what probably remains the most sought after objective for an annual report: to improve the firm's financial image. The enlightened perspective recognizes that if the firm desires effects with a variety of publics, it is necessary for it to give attention to the clarity of the report. Examination of interpretive approaches may aid practitioners in understanding their behaviors as they prepare and use annual reports.

REFERENCES

Astley, W. G., & Van de Ven, A. H. (1983). Central perspectives and debates in organizational theory. *Administrative Science Quarterly, 28,* 245–273.

Bauer, R. A. (1971). The obstinate audience: The influence process from the point of view of social communication. In W. Schramm & D. F. Roberts (Eds.), *The process and effects of mass communication* (pp. 326–346). Urbana: University of Illinois Press.

Bell, J. (1985). The effect of presentation form on the use of information in annual reports. *Management Science Review, 30,* 169–85.

Bettman, J. R., & Weitz, B. A. (1983). Attributions in the boardroom: Causal reasoning in corporate annual reports. *Administrative Science Quarterly, 28,* 165–183.

Bowman, E. H. (1976). Strategy and the weather. *Sloan Management Review, 17* (2), 49–62.

Bowman, E. H. (1978). Strategy, annual reports and alchemy. *California Management Review, 20*(3), 64–71.

Bowman, E. H. (1984). Content analysis of annual reports for corporate strategy and risk. *Interfaces, 14*(1), 61–71.

Bowman, E. H., & Haire, M. (1975). A strategic posture toward corporate responsibility. *California Management Review, 18*(2),49–58.

Buchholz, R. (1985). *The essentials of public policy for management.* Englewood Cliffs, NJ: Prentice-Hall.

Burrell, G., & Morgan, G. (1979). *Sociological paradigms and organizational analysis.* London: Heinemann.

Byrne, J. (1987, April 13). This year's annual reports: Show business as usual. *Business Week,* p. 42.

Chambers, R. J. (1974, June). Stock market prices and accounting research. *Abacus,* 39–54.

Cox, R. J., & Willard, C. A. (1982). Introduction: The field of argumentation. In R. J. Cox & C. A. Willard (Eds.), *Advances in argumentation theory and research* (pp. vii–xvii). Carbondale: Southern Illinois University Press.

Cutlip, S. M., Center, A. H., & Broom, G. M. (1985). *Effective public relations* (6th ed.). Englewood Cliffs, NJ: Prentice-Hall.

Deetz, S. (1982). Critical interpretive research in organizational communication. *Western Journal of Speech Communication, 46,* 131–149.

Findlay, M. C. (1977, December). On market efficiency and financial accounting. *Abacus,* 106–122.

Fisher, B. A. (1978). *Perspectives on human communication.* New York: McMillan.

Foster, T. W., Jenkins, D. R., & Vickrey, D. W. (1986). The incremental information content of the annual report. *Accounting and Business Research, 62* 91–98.

Frazier, K. B., Ingram, R. W., & Tennyson, B. M. (1984). A methodology for the analysis of narrative accounting disclosures. *Journal of Accounting Research, 22*(1), 318–331.

Grunig, J., & Hunt, T. (1984). *Managing public relations.* New York: Holt, Rinehart & Winston.

Heath, R. L., & Phelps, G. (1984). Annual reports II: Readability of reports vs. the business press. *The Public Relations Review, 10*(2), 56–62.

Hill and Knowlton Executives (1975). *Critical issues in public relations.* Englewood Cliffs, NJ: Prentice-Hall.

Hill and Knowlton Inc. (1984). Annual report credibility. *Public Relations Journal. 40*(11), 31–34.

Hines, R. D. (1982). The usefulness of annual reports: The anomaly between the efficient market hypothesis and shareholder surveys. *Accounting and Business Research, 12,* 299–309.

Hoskins, R. L. (1984). Annual reports I: Difficult reading and getting more so. *Public Relations Review, 10*(2), 49–55.

Kallendorf, C., & Kallendorf, C. (1985). The figures of speech, ethos, and Aristotle: Notes toward a rhetoric of business communication. *Journal of Business Communication, 22*(1), 35–50.

Kanter, R. B. (1977). *Men and women of the corporation.* New York: Basic Books.

Keeley, M. (1984). Impartiality and participant interest theories of organizational effectiveness. *Administrative Science Quarterly, 29,* 1–25.

Lentz, A., & Tschirgi, H. (1963). The ethical content of annual reports. *The Journal of Business, 36,* 387–393.

Marston, J. E. (1979). *Modern public relations.* New York: McGraw-Hill.

McGrath, P. S. (1979). *Communicating with professional investors.* New York: The Conference Board.

Means, T. L. (1981). Readability: An evaluative criterion of stockholder reaction to annual reports. *Journal of Business Communication, 18*(1), 25–33.

O'Leary, T. (1985). Observations on corporte financial reporting in the name of politics. *Accounting, Organizations and Society, 10*(1), 87–102.

Pfeffer, J. (1981). Management as symbolic action: The creation and maintenance of organizational paradigms. In B. M. Staw & L. L. Cummings (Eds.), *Research in organizational behavior* (Vol. 3, pp. 1–52). Greenwich, CT: JAI Press.

Putnam, L. (1983). The interpretive perspective: An alternative to functionalism. In L. Putman & M. Pacanowsky (Eds.), *Communication and organizations: An interpretive approach* (pp. 31–54). Beverly Hill, CA: Sage.

Ruchti, U., & Wasserman, N. (1983). Public companies have to view themselves as publishers. *Public Relations Quarterly, 27*(4), 2–9.

Salancik, G. R., & Meindl, J. R. (1984). Corporate attributions as strategic illusions of management control. *Administrative Science Quarterly, 29,* 238–254.

Smircich, L. (1983). Concepts of culture and organizational analysis. *Administrative Science Quarterly, 28,* 339–358.

Soper, F. J., & Dolphin, R. (1964). Readability and corporate annual reports. *The Accounting Review, 39,* 358–362.

Verrecchia, R. E. (1981). On the relationship between volume reaction and consensus of investors: Implications for interpreting tests of information content. *Journal of Accounting Research, 19,* 271–283.

Weick, K. (1979). *The social psychology of organizing* (2nd ed.). Reading: Addison-Wesley.

SUGGESTED READINGS

Fisher, B. A. (1978). *Perspectives on human communication.* New York: McMillan.

Grunig, J., & Hunt, T. (1984). *Managing public relations.* New York: Holt, Rinehart & Winston.

Pfeffer, J. (1981). Management as symbolic action: The creation and maintenance of organizational paradigms. In B. M. Staw & L. L. Cummings (Eds.), *Research in organizational behavior* (Vol. 3, pp. 1–52). Greenwich, CT: Jai Press.

Putman, L., & Pacanowsky, M. (Eds.). (1983). *Communication and organizations: An interpretive approach.* Beverly Hill, CA: Sage.

Weick, K. (1979). *The social psychology of organizing* (2nd ed.). Reading: Addison-Wesley.

6

Theory Development in Public Relations

Carl H. Botan
Rutgers University

ABSTRACT

Using a communication centered view of public relations, this chapter addresses theory development in public relations as an instance of theory development in the social sciences. The social scientific theory development process is summarized as it applies to public relations and it is suggested that broader adoption of this process is the key link in increasing the professionalism of public relations. Implications of adopting this process, for practitioners, for scholars, and for ethics are discussed.

We are in an exciting phase in the development of our understanding of public relations, one in which both scholars and practitioners may have to alter existing views on a multitude of questions, including the role of theory. This book addresses one emerging view by examining public relations as an applied social science based in communication. A book that seeks to contribute to a communication-based understanding of public relations takes upon itself some obligation to assess what changes may result.

This chapter attempts such an assessment in three steps. First, public relations is very briefly identified as an applied social science. Second, the social scientific approach to theory development, as it could apply to public relations, is discussed. Finally, with an eye toward encouraging such discussions, a few of the implications of a social science theoretic approach to public relations are discussed.

PUBLIC RELATIONS AS AN APPLIED
SOCIAL SCIENCE

Public relations is concerned with using communication to exchange meanings between organizations and their publics. Public relations is, therefore, an instance of applied communication that can be studied using theoretic and research tools from the communication discipline. In addition, because communication is a social science, public relations may be studied as an applied social science, meaning that some theoretic and research tools of other social sciences may be useful in studying public relations. The chapters in this book are instances of using metatheoretic, theoretic and methodological tools from communication and other social sciences to address public relations.

The First World Assembly of Public Relations Associations, meeting in Mexico City in 1978, also held that public relations is a social science (Simon, 1980). But this does not mean that anyone practicing public relations is an applied social scientist. As Grunig (1983) noted, an important distinction exists between viewing public relations as an applied social science and viewing public relations practitioners as applied social scientists. Practitioners who fail to make use of theories in their practice are not applied social scientists, because an applied social scientist is one who applies theory and, hopefully, uses the insight thus obtained to expand and correct the theory. Applied social scientists are thus a part of the theory development process. Those practitioners who draw from the body of theoretic knowledge to advance their practice and use their practice to contribute to that body are applied social scientists.

With its roots stretching back to the beginning of this century, public relations is not young as social science goes. In spite of this comparatively long history public relations practitioners, and even scholars, have generally limited themselves to questions of how-to-do-it and how-to-do-it-better. With a few notable exceptions, public relations has not systematically addressed the development of theory or the relationship of practice to research and theory building. The result is that, as Toth (1986) said "there are few consistent or theoretical perspectives developing about public affairs" (p. 29). A lack of understanding of the social scientific approach to theory development, and its usefulness to public relations, may partially explain this shortage.

SOCIAL SCIENTIFIC APPROACH
TO THEORY

The social sciences, including communication, have evolved an approach to knowledge and theory development, some of the building blocks of which are discussed at length in chapter 1. For a consistent theoretic perspective to be developed in public relations, the ways of knowing and theory development procedures that social science uses will have to be broadly adopted by scholars and practitioners.

Ways of Knowing

Human beings come to know things by different means. My colleagues and I have provided elsewhere a taxonomy of the ways of knowing (Frey, Botan, Friedman, & Kreps, in press). We said that the primary distinction in the ways humans come to know things is between *everyday knowledge,* which is based on faith and accepting things at face value, and *research,* or scientific knowledge, which is based on disciplined inquiry. Disciplined inquiry means not only studying something in a planned manner, but reporting both the results and the means of study so that others may judge the usefulness and validity of the results.

Everyday knowledge is often based on authority, our faith in the source; intuition, our feeling that something just "makes sense"; or tenacity, the belief that something must be true because it has always been true. We would not be able to practice public relations without depending on these sources because the practitioner or scholar who had to research everything before making any move would be unable to move most of the time. Much public relations knowledge that is based on these sources is quite valid.

But everyday knowledge has several limitations. For example, it is difficult, if not impossible, for practitioners and scholars to compare beliefs based on everyday knowledge, because there is often no standard for evaluating which part should be adopted and which part discarded. Standby terms like *effective* fail as standards precisely because defining the term often requires reliance on one of the everyday ways of knowing, frequently authority. Each authority uses its own criteria to define effectiveness, which is unquestioned by its adherents, but is often quite different from the criteria used by the adherents of other authorities. In another example, everyday knowledge that is based on tenacity may be valid if the original decision was correct. But, if the original decision was in error, tenacity may be very problematic, because it provides no means for rejecting erroneous beliefs.

Research, on the other hand, seeks to understand why and how something happens, thus it requires a systematic approach that affords the opportunity for testing and rejecting each existing bit of knowledge. A readiness to subject findings and opinions to the disciplined and objective scrutiny of others and to reject one's own beliefs based on that scrutiny is the hallmark of the researcher.

Research, although holding some advantages over everyday knowledge, is not perfect. The most disciplined and objective inquiry can produce mistakes because it must be based on existing knowledge and must use existing means of investigating phenomena. For example, picture our forbearers huddled in a cave, using their best and most sophisticated collective analysis to decide that the thunder outside was due to the thunder god's anger and that a different color of face paint would appease him or her and alleviate the problem. Their analysis was not unreasonable, considering the base of knowledge and means of investigation available to them. And, right or wrong, these cave people were at least trying to figure out some systematic interpretation of their environment and some systematic way to deal with it.

Will future generations of public relations researchers look on our efforts with an amused smile? Possibly, because we too must build from today's knowledge using today's tools. But this does not indict the social scientific method; it merely illustrates that, although not perfect, the process is cyclical, with each cycle adding new understanding to the last.

Therefore, although the results of any single piece of research can be just as erroneous as knowledge gained any other way, the cyclical nature of the social scientific method gives us the best chance of correcting our errors. Our confidence in research-based knowledge can, therefore, be greater, and bits of such research-based knowledge can be organized into theories.

Theory

According to Hawes (1975), "the social scientist's primary task is to explain all manner of human behavior. Such explanations are referred to as theories" (p. 2). With such a general definition, it is clear that we are all theory builders. When a practitioner offers an explanation for why a public relations effort succeeded or failed, he or she is taking the first step in propounding a theory. The generally accepted explanations and ways of doing things that have evolved over the years in public relations are therefore rudimentary theories.

Not all theories are useful for an applied social science like public relations, however. When compared with the generally accepted explanations just discussed, social scientific theory is, as Toth (1986) noted, "more formally organized knowledge, more explicit and more abstract knowledge that can provide a framework for coping with reality" (p. 30). Social scientific theory can help deal with reality because, as Littlejohn (1983) said, "theory and experience interact continually for the ultimate improvement of both" (p. 14). So theory is a legitimate concern of public relations practitioners because practitioners can contribute to theory development and the theories developed can then contribute to the work of practitioners.

Theory Development Process

Theories, even more formal ones, can be thought of as fairly developed, but still temporary, explanations. Seeing the theories of today this way helps focus on the fact that theories are not set in stone, but represent transient points between what we understood yesterday and what we will understand tomorrow. New information often forces modification or rejection of existing theory. Such new information can be generated by practitioners just as well as by scholars. As a result, both practitioners and scholars have as one of their legitimate functions, testing, and even rejecting, theory. This task, of course, requires a basic familiarity with the process of theory development.

Theory development is based on research. Theories about how things work or should work are tested, and the results are used to modify the formulations with which the process started. The new product is, in turn, subjected to retesting. Littlejohn (1983) has asserted that, "this testing-retesting process stresses the need for research, which is vital to theory development" (p. 15).

Theory building and theory testing are the two complementary halves of the social scientific theory development process. As represented in Fig. 6.1, each half is a necessary but not sufficient part of the process. The process cannot go forward unless both halves are used.

The inductive, or theory-building, step in theory development was described by Hawes (1975) as one "which carries the scientist from fac-

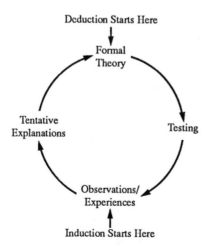

FIG. 6.1. Theory development: The theory-building-research cycle (adapted from Wallace, 1971).

tual observation to the formation of theories" (p. 20) through "educated guesswork" (p. 21). The theorist must use his or her own creative skills to impose order on a jumble of observations of the phenomena under investigation. This requires an inferential leap from having a question and a pile of observations up to a tentative answer. That tentative answer is a theory, but only a temporary or proposed one. Unfortunately, public relations theory development all too frequently stops at this step.

The deductive or theory-testing step in theory development was described by Hawes (1975) as "the derivation of consequences from the proposed theory" (p. 21). In this step the theorist makes predictions based on the logic of the theory, often in the form of research questions or hypotheses. He or she then conducts research to test these predictions. This process is known as hypothesis testing, or theory-driven research.

Hypothesis testing is actually not an attempt to prove a theory is correct, but rather an attempt to disprove or disconfirm it. The logic of hypothesis testing is that if the temporary theory is sound, a test of one of its predictions should prove positive. But a single positive result does not prove that a theory is completely true, because all the other implications of the theory have not been tested. Many tests may be necessary before we can become even relatively confident of the theory in question. On the other hand, if even one prediction of the theory proves not to be sound, its present formulation can be rejected and a new temporary explanation is formulated using the results (with a few exceptions as discussed in chapter 1).

Both steps are necessary for social science theory development. Construction of tentative explanations from experience and observations, a process that draws heavily on the humanistic side of public relations, may appeal to some scholars and practitioners. However, if too much attention is concentrated on this half of the process it might stop at this point, in which case the theory will not be refined and we will not know whether we can have confidence in it. If, the other hand, too much attention is concentrated on the testing half of the model, a process that draws heavily on the scientific side of public relations, we will fail to help build new theory. In particular, we will fail to make use of valuable negative, or disconfirming, results.

Valuable negative results? Yes. Positive results tell us only that a theory works in a particular situation, at a particular time. Negative results, however, can be used to correct temporary theories so that they become more useful. Because of the cyclical nature of theory development in public relations, negative results can sometimes be more valuable than positive ones (although the practitioner working on a budget would no doubt sooner have their first application of a theory work successfully rather than adopt this more long-term perspective).

When practitioners use research to evaluate campaigns, they are taking a potentially valuable step in theory development, because they have applied some level of theory and are now testing the outcome. If the results are not shared and used to rebuild or replace theories the process breaks down, and the field suffers because we miss a chance to help our knowledge base grow.

Ways Theory Develops

According to Kaplan (1964) theories grow incrementally by *extension* or *intension*. Kuhn (1970) identified a third way in which knowledge grows—in sudden leaps called *scientific revolutions*. These three represent the basic ways through which the theory development process can be applied to expand the knowledge base of public relations.

When we develop theory by reaching out for knowledge bit by bit, using each existing bit as a lead to the next bit, we are engaged in theory development by extension. Extension uses current understandings to gain understanding about some new area so it is somewhat analogous to using a telescope to reach outward and see new things.

When we develop theory through a deeper understanding of existing knowledge we are engaged in theory development by intension. Intension examines current areas of understanding in more depth to tease out new insights or understandings so it is somewhat analogous to using a microscope for detailed and minute examination.

In referring to intension and extension Kaplan (1964) said, "both sorts of growth, I believe, are involved in every theoretical advance" (p. 305). Both are therefore legitimate tools for practitioners and scholars alike. Although practitioners may find that, at first, extension appeals most because they can draw new ideas and understanding from the constantly changing situations which the practice of public relations brings them into contact with. Scholars may, at first, feel most comfortable with intension because they may be free to concentrate attention on smaller bits of knowledge to develop new understanding.

After a certain amount of theory development by the "normal" means of extension and intension, a situation develops which requires taking a large leap outside such step-by-step approaches. These leaps are what Kuhn (1970) called scientific revolutions. Einstein's relativity theory is an example of a scientific revolution from the physical sciences.

Such scientific revolutions lead to whole new theoretic approaches which in turn can lead to new practices. For example, Kuhn (1970) said,

Led by a new paradigm [theoretical approach], scientists adopt new instruments and look in new places [and] what were ducks in the scientists world before the revolution are rabbits afterwards. (p. 111)

As we might expect, this process is often not a smooth one. According to Littlejohn (1983):

Often during the years when a new theoretical approach is being formulated, theorists who support the old approach become defensive, protecting their many years or entire lifetimes of work that may be at stake. (p. 15)

Neither Littlejohn nor Kuhn are likely to have had the applied social science of public relations in mind when they wrote. But the parallels with our rapid changes, even leaps, in understanding public relations and the resulting resistance from some established scholars and practitioners is hard to miss.

IMPLICATIONS

Accepting public relations as an applied social science based in communication would have several implications including, for example, impacts on professionalism, on practitioners and scholars, and on ethics.

Professionalism

Pavlik and Salmon (1984) noted that:

[The] lack of a systematic body of knowledge is particularly significant, as it remains a hindrance in the development of public relations from a 'practice' to a profession. One important criterion that distinguishes traditional professions such as law or medicine from practices or pseudo-professions such as journalism and public relations is the lack of an underlying systematized body of theory and knowledge from which practitioners draw their work. (p. 40)

As indicated in the last section of this paper, development of such theory is based on research, but not all research contributes to theory building. Pavlik (1987) summarized the research being conducted in public relations today by saying:

Only a fraction of the past 10 years of PR research has been basic research. Most has dealt with specific, practical problems or issues. It has not been the kind designed to build a general, theoretical body of knowledge. (p. 17)

Pavlik went on to say that:

> Basic research is a special type of research that is especially lacking in the field of public relations. It is research designed to build theory—not to answer specific practical problems. (p. 17)

Theory does not develop automatically out of a large body of practical research. Systematic application of the theory development process is required. The assessments of Toth (1986), Pavlik and Salmon (1984), and Pavlik (1987) result from the fact that public relation has not widely embraced the theory development process rather than from any lack of experience.

If an applied social science approach is taken, public relations can develop a body of theoretic knowledge that meets its needs and distinguishes the practice of public relations from the craft of communication technicians. Such a body of theoretic knowledge (not the issue of licensing) is the foundation stone on which public relations can develop more and more professionalism. As we have seen, practitioners and scholars have complementary roles to play in this undertaking.

Practitioners

Practitioners who put the practice of public relations first are acting appropriately, but they may be able to get double service out of their practice by also using it to make contributions to theory development. Possibly the most immediate contribution that practitioners can make to advancing public relations theory is making broader use of the research currently being conducted. Today, most research by public relations practitioners is restricted to adopting social science methods for campaign planning and campaign evaluations. Using social science methods to help conduct more efficient campaigns is different from using these methods for the purpose of theory development, although, as we have seen, the two uses are not contradictory.

Practitioners could also encourage more theory development and professionalism by giving theoretical education some value in the credentialing process. For example, the qualification to test for Accredited Public Relations (APR) under Article XIII, Section 2, of the Public Relations Society of America's (PRSA) By-Laws is having "devoted a substantial portion of time for a period of not less than 5 years to the paid professional practice [or teaching] of public relations" ("By-Laws", 1987). In an extreme case this requirement might be construed to permit a bright high school graduate who had successfully completed 5 years of practice, and passed the test, to become an APR whereas a person with a 4.0 GPA and a masters degree, but only 4 years of professional experience, would be prohibited from even attempting to gain accreditation.

Scholars

In 1975 the Commission on Public Relations Education (1975) warned that:

> Most PR educators—not having attained the Ph.D. level—have not been required to do such [basic] research, have not learned how to do it, or have not been interested in doing it. Most of them, indeed, are teaching skill courses that have little relationship to basic research. (p. 19)

The situation has no doubt improved with the passage of more than a decade. But even today scholars and teachers sometimes add little of their own, preferring instead to repeat the skills and ethical prescriptions of the practitioner without question or expansion.

Scholars should prepare their students with marketable skills, but we also have an obligation to contribute to the development of social scientific public relations theory by investigating new ideas, including some which may meet with resistance. Scholars have a responsibility to join practitioners in the forefront of developing new public relations theory and techniques.

Ethics

One of the burning issues in public relations is, and has been, the question of ethics. Because public relations has been viewed essentially as a craft or practice, most of the concern for ethics has been appropriately focused on how to practice public relations ethically. Established codes of ethics, such as PRSAs and the International Association of Business Communicator's, are good foundations for the practice of public relations and should be part of the training of every public relations student, practitioner or scholar.

But if public relations is beginning to be viewed as an applied social science, the ethical issues the field faces may be expected to expand in ways that the current codes could not foresee. For example, one such area of expanding ethical concern lies in the distinction between proprietary and public research. Because most current research in public relations is intended to help plan or evaluate campaigns, the data generated are often proprietary (meaning that they are private property). When research is paid for by a client or company, this is appropriate. But public relations research can only contribute to theory development if it is made available in the public domain. Researchers and practitioners may be increasingly faced with questions about when and under what circumstances to release the results of research.

In another example—in the past, public relations education was largely based on the practice of journalism, and persuasion was sometimes seen in a somewhat negative light. Within the bounds of operational definitions, Neff (Chapter 9) has found that communication is now the leading element in public relations education. As demonstrated by some of the chapters in this book, the large persuasive component in public relations may be addressed in new ways by a field that has actively studied persuasion since Aristotle.

Communication can address persuasion in public relations from several perspectives. For example, from a rhetorical perspective, communication can employ all of the ethical thinking from ancient times as well as that addressing current political communication, including the key notion of free will. From scientific persuasion studies and social influence, the body of ethics literature—ranging from treatment of subjects to use of confederates—is available, and so on.

CONCLUSION

This chapter has attempted to identify public relations as an applied social science, to identify several of the major aspects of theory development in the social sciences and what they mean for public relations, and to initiate discussion of some of the implications of a theory-building approach to public relations. The vested interest of public relations practitioners in theory development has been discussed, and the research currently being done to evaluate campaigns has been identified as a potential resource for theory development.

Although the practitioners and scholars who advocate the need for more professionalism and theory in public relations are correct, our current level of understanding in public relations should not be viewed negatively. If the development of knowledge in a subject area is an evolutionary (sometimes revolutionary) process, our current understanding of public relations must be accepted as the foundation on which to build. This chapter has suggested that if such building is desirable, a conscious and systematic approach, based on understanding how theory is developed, may be in the best interest of public relations.

REFERENCES

Broom, G. M. (1982). Comparison of sex roles in public relations. *Public Relations Review, 8,* 17–22.

By-Laws of the Public Relations Society of American, Article XIII, Sec. 2, (1987, June). *Public Relations Journal, 43*(6), Register Issue.

Commission on Public Relations Education (1975). *Design for public relations education.* New York: Foundation for Public Relations Research and Education, Inc.

Frey, L. R., Botan, C. H., Friedman, P., & Kreps, G. (in press). *Investigating communication.* Englewood Cliffs, NJ: Prentice-Hall.

Grunig, J. E. (1983). Basic research provides knowledge that makes evaluation possible. *Public Relations Quarterly, 28,* 28–32.

Hawes, L. C. (1975). *Pragmatics of analoguing: Theory and model construction in communication.* Reading: MA: Addison-Wesley.

Kaplan, A. (1964). *The conduct of inquiry: Methodology for behavioral science.* New York: Chandler Publishing.

Kuhn, T. S. (1970). *The structure of scientific revolutions* (2nd ed. enlarged). Chicago: University of Chicago Press.

Littlejohn, S. W. (1983). *Theories of human communication* (2nd ed.). Belmont, CA: Wadsworth.

Pavlik, J. V. (1987). *Public relations: What research tells us.* Newbury Park, CA: Sage Publications.

Pavlik, J. V., & Salmon, C. T. (1984). Theoretic approaches in public relations research. *Public Relations Research and Education, 1*(2), 39–49.

Simon, R. (1980). *Public relations: Concepts and practices.* (2nd ed.). Columbus, OH: Grid Publishing.

Toth, E. L. (1986). Broadening research in public affairs. *Public Relations Review, XII,* 27–36.

Wallace, W. (1971). The logic of science in sociology. Chicago: Aldine-Atherton.

Business Ethics as Communication Ethics:Public Relations Practice and the Idea of Dialogue

Ron Pearson
Mount Saint Vincent University

ABSTRACT

This chapter is an exercise in model building in public relations. Its purpose is to suggest theoretical statements for a theory of public relations ethics. This model building exercise clarifies how the corporate communication function—sometimes called public relations, public affairs, or issues management—can be seen as playing a critical role in ethical organizational conduct. The model suggests that business ethics can be studied as a series of questions about how a business organization communicates with the individuals, groups, and other organizations with which it has relationships. Business ethics is a question of communication.ethics, and the chapter argues that ethical communication is closely related to the idea of dialogue. Public relations, to the extent it plays the central role in corporate communication, also plays the major role in managing the moral dimension of corporate conduct.

> *What is not realized in communication is not yet, what is not ultimately grounded in it is without adequate foundation. The truth begins with two.*
> —Karl Jaspers (1978), *Way to Wisdom: An Introduction to Philosophy*

According to Hawes (1975), a model is an analogy. The model builder begins with two objects or processes that are *dissimilar* in many ways. One object or process is then taken as an analogue or representation of the second object or process based on some ways in which it can be said that two objects or processes are *similar*: For instance, a busy beehive may be taken as a helpful analogue for a particular human community. The analogue is clearly dissimilar because it is not a human community, but a community of insects. Yet in other ways it may be seen as similar—in the way work is divided, perhaps it is on the basis of such a perceived similarity that the analogue may help describe the human community or increase understanding of it.

Hawes pointed out that a model builder typically knows more about one object or process than about the other. On the basis of the suggested analogy, the model builder tentatively transfers this knowledge from the well known to the less well known. If a good fit exists between the analogue and the material modelled, the model will have heuristic or explanatory power. It will assist the researcher to discover insights, develop theory, and frame testable hypotheses about the less well-known object or process.

This chapter develops an analogy between two processes that are fundamentally different. However, they seem to be similar in ways that increase our understanding of public relations and public relations ethics. One of these processes involves relationships between epistemological concepts, or different approaches to the theory of knowledge. The other process involves relationships between historical concepts that attempt to explain the different ways business organizations have established relationships with their moral environments. According to Hawes (1975), a model has been constructed when the *substance* of one process is projected or mapped onto the *structure* of another process that serves as its analogue. Subsequently, substantive components of an historical process will be mapped onto the structural components of an epistemological process.

First, the chapter defines three epistemological concepts—objectivism, relativism, and intersubjectivism—that figure prominently in what is called post-modern rhetorical theory. The explication of facets of this theory lay the ground work for the analogue. Second, the chapter defines three historical concepts developed by Buchholz (1985) to describe business' approach to its moral environment. Buchholz called these the social responsibility approach, the social responsiveness approach, and the public policy approach. Third, the relationship between these two processes is drawn out. This is a question of detailing the isomorphism between the analogue and the material modelled and of indicating the contribution of knowledge transferred from the analogue. Finally, the chapter outlines theoretical and practical implications of the model for a theory of public relations ethics.

RHETORIC, EPISTEMOLOGY, AND MORAL TRUTH

The problem of the relationship between knowledge and human communication processes has a history as old as ancient Greek philosophy. *Rhetoric* (broadly defined as the use of symbols to achieve agreement, to persuade, or to induce cooperation), and *epistemology* (that branch of philosophy concerned with the theory of knowledge), have always had a stormy relationship. At times the two fields have been incompatible, whereas in other ages they have been closely allied. Rhetoric has always been accorded more respect and served a clearer sense of purpose in ages where important issues were in dispute. Thus, in 5th-century Athens, with traditional aristocratic values crumbling, rhetorical practice and theory possessed a dignity subsequent ages have seldom granted it. During the middle ages, rhetoric was of less value because important issues were already decided, as a result of revelation or by the decree of authority. In modern times, rhetoric has been supplanted by science. Rhetoric, as Aristotle conceived it, was concerned with decision-making in the context of probabilities. When there is certainty, or at least a faith that certainty is achievable, rhetoric plays a superfluous role for the intelligent and educated, an ornamental role for the less gifted. The following sections outline three approaches to epistemology and indicate the role language or rhetoric plays in each. Each section also suggests how these epistemological assumptions are related to different approaches to public relations practice.

Objectivism. Whenever philosophy is given the upper hand in debate with rhetoric it is because philosophy seems to offer a successful path to absolute certainty. Setting aside theology's claims for a revealed certainty, it can be said that this path has presented itself in two distinct ways: rationalism or empiricism. Rationalism and empiricism are often contrasted as ways of doing philosophy, but they have in common a belief Bernstein (1983) has called objectivism. Bernstein described objectivism as follows:

> By "objectivism," I mean the basic conviction that there is or must be some permanent, ahistorical matrix or framework to which we can ultimately appeal in determining the nature of rationality, knowledge, truth, reality, goodness, or rightness. . . . Objectivism is closely related to foundationalism and the search for an Archimedean point. The objectivist maintains that unless we can ground philosophy, knowledge, or language in a rigorous manner we cannot avoid radical scepticism. (p. 8)

Descartes' interior odyssey in search of what could not be doubted is no less an expression of objectivism than were Francis Bacon's or Locke's common concern to ground certainty in the apprehension of empirical objects. Rationalism grounds knowledge in what is self-evident to thought, empiricism in what is self-evident to the senses.

In neither rationalism nor empiricism does language or rhetoric necessarily involve knowledge. Rhetorical activity involves at least two people, a message sender or speaker and a message receiver or listener. Neither Descartes, Bacon, nor Locke needed to communicate with others in their search for certainty. This search was individual and personal. The successful researcher who claims to be in possession of the truth has two communication choices. The researcher can remain silent and retire to contemplative hermitage, or embark on a persuasive campaign to convert or enlighten others. To be sure, this process of enlightenment uses language, but only to give expression to a scientific or moral truth that has been pre-established. The receiver has nothing meaningful to contribute to the process. For the message sender, it's a question of finding effective strategies for getting the other "to see" things as they really are. Public relations practitioners often assume that achieving public support for a policy is a question of "educating" a public. The pioneering practitioner Ivy Lee, for example, believed that once his clients were understood, public support would follow (Heibert, 1966). Similarly, 19th-century railway executives who saw issues only from the perspective of their own industry, and who believed what was good for the railways was also good for the public, operate with objectivist assumptions (Olasky, 1987).

Relativism.   One of the assumptions of objectivism is that everyone's individual search for certainty leads, ultimately, in the same direction. Over the long run, scientists and philosophers will be able to decide when one person's search is misguided. Relativists, on the other hand, are more sceptical about this. According to the relativist position, there are no objective standards for deciding who is misguided and who is going in the right direction. No rational method exists for mediating among competing claims about what is true or right. In the philosophy of science, where the objectivism–relativism debate has raged fiercely in recent decades, the relativist argues that no neutral, objective language exists that scientists can use to decide between alternative scientific theories. Even the most mundane fact is tainted with a theoretical perspective.

The role language or rhetoric plays in relativism can also be approached as a pair of communication options, one of which is silence. But for the relativist, these options have different implications. To choose silence follows from the belief that it is pointless to communicate one's view of scientific or moral truth to another person, because no way exists to show why that view is any better. Relativism can thus breed frustration and quietism. On the other hand, relativist arguments can also lead to a cynical kind of activism where self-interest (or client) interest is the standard for action. For instance, a skillful wordsmith, although he or she believes there is no way to decide between competing points of view, can use carefully crafted arguments to make a particular client's viewpoint seem superior. For this person, language is important, not because it plays an essential role in discovering what is true or right, but because it can make something look true or right when another viewpoint is equally valid. An early critic of the sophists, Plato charged that they used language in this way. The phrase "mere sophistry" remains a pejorative term, and many would argue that public relations is sophistical in this cynical sense. A number of public relations scholars have also suggested that relativism is the moral stance of many practitioners (Olasky, 1985; Ryan & Martinson, 1984; Wright, 1985). Olasky (1985) reported interview data that suggest some practitioners see themselves as unavoidably practicing a cynical kind of sophistry: "There is no such thing as truth. You judge actions depending on whether they're done by someone above you or someone below you" (p. 43). Similarly, Lewis (1984) made it plain that self-interest can drive public relations practice:

> It may be useful to recognize unequivocally that we are being paid to promote the *self-interest* of our client or corporation. . . . Compromise and concession are the very nature of the democratic process, but I believe that public affairs can best be understood by first thinking about it as a "win–lose" situation for the practitioner. Compromise is what we do when all else fails. (p. 32)

Intersubjectivism. Post-modern rhetorical theory rejects objectivism but at the same time does not embrace the sceptical, sometimes cyncial, relativist view described here. Instead, post-modern rhetorical theory argues that language and rhetoric play a fundamental epistemological role, and scientific and moral knowledge is a function of dialogue and intersubjectivity. Audience agreement is seen as a criterion of knowledge, and the way that the contact of minds alters the shape of knowledge is of critical importance for post-modern rhetorical theory (Cherwitz, 1977; Cherwitz & Hikins, 1985; Farrell, 1976; Kneupper, 1980; Leff, 1978; Willard, 1979a, 1979b, 1983). Radical relativism is neatly circumvented by what Scott (1976) has called rhetorical relativism.

Leff (1978) identified a number of ways in which the claim that rhetoric has a constitutive, creative role in the generation of knowledge is made. The weakest claim is that rhetoric "imparts knowledge by clarifying relationships between a problematic particular and a fixed, absolute standard of truth" (p. 78). This knowledge is rhetorical because it is intersubjectively sanctioned. The strongest claim about the epistemic role of rhetoric is that all epistemological endeavor is rhetorical. According to Leff, this view collapses the empirical into the symbolic: We live in a symbolic world, and all knowledge is a function of how communities of knowers construe and manipulate symbols.

A view occupying middle ground asserts that rhetoric plays a decisive role in deciding on first principles in science, philosophy and ethics as well as on the relationship of these principles to particulars. Kuhn (1970) has suggested that competing scientific world views are defended rhetorically. In ethical theory, Perelman (1963) has defended a theory of justice where rhetoric plays the decisive role. Whenever a rule of justice is challenged, according to Perelman, it is incumbent on whomever advances the challenge to show it is consistent with other more general rules. This is the process of justification, and Perelman holds that it leads ultimately to value statements that are unjustifiable in terms of other statements. Like explanation in science, justification in ethics ultimately confronts foundational principles that are provisional and contingent. A discussion about justice will discover no thesis that is absolutely certain, only theses that are accepted or granted by a listener. This emphasis on the agreement of the listener underscores the intersubjective quality of scientific and moral truth.

Toulmin (1958) has also suggested that a theory of argument or rhetoric is central to a theory of ethics. He rejects universalistic or objectivist ethical theories that suggest the value "good" is an objective property that normal people cannot help "seeing" if only they learn to look in the right way. He also rejects the relativism implied in subjectivist ethical theories that suggest people cannot help having different standards of value, as well as the view that ethical statements are merely exhortations or expressions of feeling. For Toulmin, the study of ethics is the study of the communication process of argument.

As statements of the view that rhetoric is epistemic move further from the idea of objectivism, it would seem that they lead inexorably toward a radical relativism. Yet, as noted earlier, no assertion of an epistemic view of rhetoric embraces such a sceptical view. In general, defenders of this view hold up intersubjective agreement among members of a community of discourse as a real possibility and a practical goal that offers an alternative to relativism. Bernstein (1983) has argued that a "communicative" or rhetorical view of truth overcomes and transcends the objectivism/relativism dichotomy. Human rationality is essentially dialogical and based on intersubjective agreement, he said. Such

> A dialogical model of human rationality . . . stresses the practical, communal character of this rationality in which there is choice, deliberation, interpretation, judicious weighing and application of "universal criteria" and . . . rational disagreement about which criteria are relevant and most important. (p. 172)

The idea of communality is critical here, especially because Bernstein has linked it to human rationality in the broadest sense. On the one hand, decision making that is rooted in community resists objectivism: The values, norms, traditions and standards embraced by a community are contingent in that they are conditioned socially and historically. On the other hand, an extreme relativism is avoided because community decisions are not subjective or arbitrary. Rather, they are the result of intersubjective communication and are "out there" in the community. For the researcher who believes scientific and moral truth are sanctioned intersubjectively, silence implies tacit agreement or is a moment in an ongoing conversation. Active communication means to engage oneself or one's organization in dialogue. For the public relations practitioner who holds intersubjectivist assumptions, taking other perspectives into account as valid is a necessary step in the formulation of policy (Culbertson, 1984).

The foregoing discussion of objectivism, relativism and intersubjectivism has presented the material that constitutes the analogue. Following paragraphs sketch the material that is to be modelled, initially by indicating the context of ethical questions relevant to business conduct.

BUSINESS AND ITS MORAL ENVIRONMENT

One usually thinks of ethics in general as having to do with free, intentional human conduct where that conduct affects, or has the potential of affecting, another person or persons. Similarly, business ethics is concerned with free, intentional organizational conduct that affects or has consequences for a public or publics (Grunig & Hunt, 1984). Ethical questions about corporate conduct are raised within the context of corporate/public relationships.

Until very recently, business as a whole took for granted most of these relationships because they were relatively stable and unproblematic. But during the 1960s the environment of business activity, once predominantly legal and economic, became marked by volatile social and political factors. Rapid social change revealed within the environment of business moral, social, and political dimensions that either to had been hidden, non-existent, or taken for granted. These changes added a new dependency and vulnerability to business/environment relationships (Gollner, 1983; Buchholz 1985), and business responded in different ways. The concepts developed in the following paragraphs are based on a discussion by Buchholz (1985) in which he distinguished three stages in business' response to a changing environment: (a) a social responsibility approach, (b) a social responsiveness approach, and (c) a public policy approach. It is important to note at the outset that whereas these approaches are more or less typical of different historical times, they are not mutually exclusive.

The Social Responsibility Approach. Buchholz placed the genesis of this approach in the 1960s. It implied a recognition by business that it had an obligation to serve social needs that were not strictly economic and that were not achieved through the economic mechanism of the free market. However, Buchholz suggested that a key problem with the concept was the lack of clear moral principles to support it. Without clear guidelines for management action, "corporate executives who wanted to be socially responsible were left to follow their own values . . . or . . . vague generalizations about changing social values or new public expectations" (p. 8). The new business environment represented a crumbling of generally held values about business' purpose and about what was right and wrong in corporate conduct, values that had previously been considered universal. The values that were now being questioned were those implicit in free enterprise ideology—a combination of ethical egoism and classical utilitarianism (Beauchamp & Bowie, 1979). This combination asserts the view that if one pursues one's self-interest (ethical egoism) within a market governed by Adam Smith's invisible hand, the result is the greatest happiness—economic well-being—for the greatest number of actors in that market (classical utilitarianism). As a result of the collapse of universal agreement about these views, a plurality of values and a growing uncertainty about how to mediate among them emerged, although not yet a scepticism that such mediation was impossible.

The Social Responsiveness Approach. Perhaps disillusioned by the specter of pluralism where once there had been certainty, business developed a stance Buchholz called the social responsiveness approach. This approach skirts the moral debate over conflicting values and focuses on the effectiveness of corporate response mechanisms. During the 1970s,

as part of this approach, businesses set up public affairs departments, began practicing environmental scanning, and carried out social audits. Buchholz wrote:

> The important questions in this philosophy are not moral, related to whether a corporation should respond to a social problem out of a sense of responsibility, but are more pragmatic and action oriented, dealing with the ability of a corporation to respond and what changes are necessary to enable it to respond more effectively. . . . This places business in a passive role of simply responding to social change. (pp. 13, 16)

The Public Policy Approach. Ultimately, the social response approach is untenable for business because it begs the moral questions by pretending corporations are not active moral agents but merely passive response mechanisms. But the approach was also impractical and unrealistic, as Buchholz pointed out, because during that time government, itself reacting to social pressures articulated in the public policy process, was rewriting the rules of business by introducing new regulations of business activity. Business, during the 1970s and 1980s, thus discovered that it was prudent to understand the public policy process and to try actively to influence it in ways that were congruent with business interests. Thus, a new approach is born, one in which business sees itself as an active political participant in what is essentially a political process and, as is emphasized here, a communication process.

THE DIALECTIC OF CORPORATE CONSCIENCE: A MODEL

This section addresses the task of mapping Buchholz' historical concepts onto the structure of the epistemological concepts just outlined. Hawes (1975, p. 136) called this model a conceptual model. In other words, it is not a scale model nor a formal, mathematical model. It is the "internal structure or web of relationships in the original object or process [i.e., the analogue]" that is important. Hawes discussed the possible structure an analogue might have, but none describe accurately the structure of the analogue used here. The key structural attribute of the process leading from objectivism, to relativism, to intersubjectivism is a dialectical process.

Dialectic is one of those words in philosophy that has many shades of meaning. Here it is taken to mean that process in which a thesis is opposed by an antithesis followed by a synthesis of both points of view. In a genuine dialectical process, the synthesis overcomes, transforms or transcends what seemed at first to be an irreducible dualism or contradiction. Post-modern rhetorical theory can be seen as a moment in a dialectical process in which one of philosophie's oldest dualisms, the objectivism–relativism pair, is challenged and transcended. The task of the following sections is to transfer knowledge about this dialectical process to our understanding of the history of corporate public affairs as Buchholz has described it.

Social Responsibility and Objectivism. The social responsibility approach to the pressures from a business organization's moral environment is best understood as a period in which objective, universal values are challenged. But it is also a time when managers, initially at least, feel some confidence that corporate actions to achieve social goals can be reconciled with business goals and that no absolute or unbridgeable contradiction exists between them. The business manager is, at first, not sceptical about the possibility of moral insights but believes it is possible to discover right courses of action. However, as Buchholz pointed out, managers soon discover it is difficult, if not impossible, to make these discoveries of moral truth. The social responsibility approach has its roots in an objectivist epistemology but also represents the early stages of a process in which these assumptions are challenged by a growing pluralism of values.

Social Responsiveness and Relativism. The social responsiveness approach represents the radical relativism revealed by the failure of the social responsibility approach and the collapse of objectivist epistemological assumptions. It represents the view that says if there are no overarching universal principles that can guide corporate conduct, then there are no meaningful principles at all. Unable to have the comfort of objectivism, the social responsiveness approach withdraws to a passive quietude to avoid the difficult challenges implied by the loss of universal principles.

Public Policy and Intersubjectivity. The public policy approach seems to overcome the radical relativism implied in the social response approach. But this new approach accomplishes this without returning to the assumptions of an objectivist epistomology. Buchholz acknowledged that moral questions are again explicitly raised as soon as business becomes an actor in the public policy process. But the key observation is that these questions can be asked in terms of how business participates in what is fundamentally a communication process.

The public policy approach to business' moral responsibilities as described by Buchholz has the potential for overcoming or synthesizing an earlier opposition in the same way that post-modern rhetorical theory represents a synthesis of competing epistemologies. In the same way that the objectivism–relativism–intersubjectivism triad seems to represent moments in a dialectical process, so does the social responsibility–social responsiveness–public policy triad represent a dialectical process. Both dialectical processes end with a synthesis that emphasizes communication variables that were absent in the theoretical formulations that preceded them. Neither objectivist nor relativist epistemologies require that one mind communicate with another in the discovery of truth. Post-modern rhetorical theory, on the other hand, claims it takes two minds to make truth, whether scientific or moral. Likewise, the public policy approach says business cannot act unilaterally but must consult and communicate with others through public policy mechanisms. The public policy approach implies an emphasis on intersubjective processes, whereas this is not true for either the social responsibility approach or the social responsiveness approach.

It is critical at this point to make clear that it is not necessary to view the relationship between post-modern rhetorical theory and a public policy approach to business ethics as anything but a contingent one. No claim is being made that somehow the universe is unfolding according to some immanent cosmic plan; indeed, the connection between dialogic communication and different kinds of knowledge is as old as ancient Greek philosophy. Yet neither is it necessary to view as wholly unrelated the collapse of traditional universal values, the increasing complexity and interdependence of modern social systems, and the deep concern with communication within and among these social systems. Recent approaches to organizational theory emphasize the symbolic dimension of interorganizational relationships (Levine & White, 1961; Pfeffer, 1981). Others recognize the value of viewing these relationships as dialogic or dialectical, that is, as relationships that never remain static and in which seeming oppositions or contradictions (i.e. between environmental determinism and voluntary, organizational action) are transcended in favor of more complex relationships of mutual dependency (Astley & Van de Ven, 1983; Benson, 1977; Hrebiniak & Joyce, 1985; Zeitz, 1980).

The benefit of interpreting Buchholz' historical concepts in terms of the concepts of different espistemologies is the heightened understanding gained as a result. Post-modern rhetorical theory offers powerful and cogent theory with which to conceptualize public relations theory and business ethics. If it is accepted that the analogue is a good fit for the material modelled, it follows that insights that apply to the analogue apply also to the material modelled. If the view is accepted that moral truths are rhetorical and are grounded in the way we communicate, the study of business ethics is the study of the public communication processes that decide corporate action. For it is in this processes that the moral truths shaping corporate conduct are grounded.

The model developed thus far makes an implicit argument that the focal concept for ethical public relations is dialogue (see Fig. 7.1). Indeed, this concept is the basic theoretical implication of the model. Dialogue represents a transcendence of two other approaches to public relations, both of which are essentially monologic as is shown by the epistemological assumptions underlying each. One approach involves an organization with implicit objectivist views. This organization believes it "knows best" and seeks to educate publics. The other approach involves an organization with relativist views. This organization practices a sophistical public relations; given the lack of standards on which to base its actions, it would be inclined to base them on self-interest.

It is also important to recognize that in practice there is nothing neces-

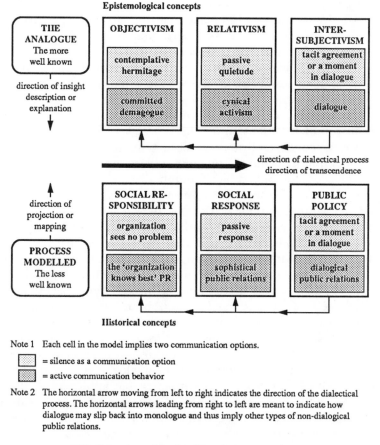

FIG. 7.1.   A model of public relations practice.

sary and inevitable about the structure of the two dialectical processes. Both silence and monologue may be moments in dialogue, but both these communication options may also indicate that a communicator is operating under objectivist or relativist assumptions and has lapsed back into an "organization knows best" or "sophistical" type of public relations. The intersubjective approach to scientific or moral knowledge transcends the objectivism–relativism dualism only when genuine dialogue occurs among decision-makers. Similarly, the public policy approach to public relations transcends the other two approaches only when genuine interorganizational dialogue takes place. The possibility is always present that dialogue will lapse into monologue. A genuine dialogic public policy approach to decision making about issues affecting an organization and its publics always confronts the possibility of becoming a monologic social responsibility or social responsiveness approach. In other words, the communication behavior of an organization can easily become the demagoguery of a committed objectivist, or the sophistical and argumentative posturing of the cynical relativist. The model thus suggests that a key ethical imperative of public relations practice is to transcend the tendency toward monologic communication styles in favor of interorganizational dialogue.

The following sections spell out what this means for the public relations practitioner by clarifying the idea of a genuine dialogue. The discussion begins by looking at the idea of dialogue as a value in communication and then turns to the conditions that enhance the possibility of dialogue. The following sections of the chapter thus continue to draw out the theoretical and practical implications of the model for a theory of public relations ethics.

COMMUNICATION ETHICS AND THE IDEA
OF DIALOGUE

The word "dialogue" designates a host of ideas. Unpacking these is a useful way to focus on the issue of ethics as it relates to communication. Plato placed great emphasis on both dialogue as a method and listener agreement as an essential element of that method. One does not have to accept Plato's version of objectivism (the belief that communicator agreement could coincide ultimately with what was universally true) to appreciate the necessary role played by dialogue. Plato objected to monologic styles of rhetoric that seek to define what appears to be the case although allowing no challenge. Much of the sophistic rhetoric that Plato condemned was concerned to see one view prevail, the view that advanced a client's interests rather than discussing alternative views.

As Weaver's (1953) interpretation of Plato's *Phaedrus* suggests, successful dialogue takes place only when speakers treat each other as ends rather than means. The base communicator fears true dialogue and uses language forms to maintain quiescence and lack of self-awareness among listeners, for listeners in that state do not threaten the status quo. The noble communicator, on the other hand, enters into dialogue for the listener as much as for himself and has no special interests to protect or advance.

The foregoing discussion of Plato introduces a key value in dialogue—the speaker's attitudes toward and relationship with the listener. Others since have sustained this focus. Brockriede (1972) contrasted the rhetorical rapist, seducer and lover. The rapist's attitudes toward listeners are superiority and contempt; listeners are objects and methods are manipulative. The seducer—and this is where Brockriede would likely put much of current public relations practice—is deceptive, insincere, charming, and indifferent to the identity, integrity, and rationality of the audience. On the other hand, attitudes of the rhetorical lover toward an audience include equality, respect, and the desire to promote free choice among audience members envisioned as persons, not objects.

In the public relations literature, Sullivan (1965) distinguished between three values in public relations. One emphasizes technical values—techniques that include writing, audience analysis, publication production, and effects measurement. Another emphasizes partisan values and is characterized by loyalty to employer or client and to the views advocated by an employer or client. Yet a third, called mutual values, places emphasis on the rights of the audience to full information about issues that effect them. Sullivan's third class of values clearly places emphasis on dialogue as opposed to monologue. Grunig and Hunt (1984) and Cutlip, Center, and Broom (1985) likewise place a great deal of emphasis on two-way, symmetrical communication in public relations. Indeed, Grunig and Hunt define organizational public (social) responsibility in dialogic terms as *communication, negotiation,* and *compromise.* Grunig and Hunt developed a model of public relations communication practices that clearly distinguishes monological (asymmetrical) and dialogical (symmetrical) approaches.

CONDITIONS FOR DIALOGUE

Johannesen (1981) observed that much of the writing on dialogue speaks of it as "more of communication spirit or orientation than a specific method, technique, or format" (p. 45), and most of the foregoing discussion supports the idea that dialogue is intimately connected with the attitudes of a speaker toward self, audience, topic, and situation. Johannesen (1974) used a number of words to describe this quality of dialogue: honesty, concern for the other person, genuineness, openmindedness, mutual respect, empathy, lack of pretense, nonmanipulative intent, and encouragement of free expression (p. 96). In contrast, monologue is characterized by deception, superiority, exploitation, dogmatism, insincerity, pretense, personal display, coercion, distrust, and self-defensiveness.

These descriptors may be useful in helping a business manager develop a sense of the rich connotations associated with the idea of dialogue, but the manager's ethical problems are more practical and pressing. If establishing and maintaining dialogical communication between a business organization and its publics is a precondition for ethical business practices affecting those publics, managers also need clear-cut rules and guidelines for bringing about and sustaining those conditions that encourage the attitudinal orientation described by Johannesen. Cherwitz (1977), although affirming that "knowledge exists within man and does not exist in any fixed or absolute state" (p. 216), also holds that not all human discourse operates to generate knowledge. He insisted that certain conditions are needed before dialogue can be expected to yield scientific or moral knowledge:

1. There must be a genuine clash of attitudes—they have to meet and truly challenge each other. It is not enough just to express them, to inject them into the process.
2. Participants must have equal control and initiative in the communication process.
3. Participants must truly risk their own point of view and be prepared to modify it.

Habermas (1970, 1984) offered a formal definition of dialogue based on his theorizing about the different levels of theoretical and practical discourse: dialogue occurs when participants are able to move freely from one level of abstraction to another. Moving to higher levels of abstraction during a public relations interaction would allow participants to raise questions that, in day-to-day communication, are part of a background consensus shared within a community of discourse. What Habermas called discourse takes place at a level of abstraction where participants challenge the validity of one another's statements against more generally accepted norms.

For Habermas, the general structural requirement of a communication situation within which it is possible to achieve a "progressive radicalization" of an argument toward higher levels of abstraction is a symmetrical and balanced relationship between or among participants. Burleson and Kline (1979) spelled out the requirement in this way (p. 423):

1. Participants must have an equal chance to initiate and maintain discourse.
2. Participants must have an equal chance to make challenges, explanations, or interpretations.
3. Interaction among participants must be free of manipulations, domination, or control.
4. Participants must be equal with respect to power.

Additionally, Burleson and Kline pointed out that each of the above requirements is linked in Habermas to specific types of speech acts. Requirement 1 says participants have an equal chance to use *communicatives*—speech acts that involve saying, speaking, asking; requirement 2 says participants have the same chance to use *constatives*—speech acts that involve asserting, describing, explaining; requirement 3 says participants have an equal chance to use *representatives*—speech acts that involve admitting, confessing, concealing, denying; requirement 4 says participants have equal opportunities to use *regulatives*—speech acts that involve commanding, forbidding, allowing, warning.

Habermas' ideas can be made to yield some useful guidelines for public relations practice (Pearson, 1986). Ethical business practice can be analyzed in terms of speech acts where ethical communication is operationalized as the opportunity among communicators both to engage in all types of speech acts and to move the discussion toward levels of increasing abstraction (or concreteness). Indeed, the organizational communication theorists Farace, Monge, and Russell (1977) suggested a way of measuring structural aspects of a communication environment that uses coorientation theory. A communication environment that promotes dialogue and, therefore, legitimate decision outcomes would be marked by mutual agreement among communicators about structural attributes of the environment and mutual satisfaction with those structural attributes. Farace, Monge, and Russell proposed questioning communicators about the following topics: Who initiates interaction? How are delays treated? How frequent is contact? Who selects the topics of discussion? (They suggested this is perhaps the most important question;) How are topic changes handled? How satisfied are communicators with these "communication rules?" Whereas Farace, Monge, and Russell are concerned with the structure of interaction between individuals in organizations, there is no reason why similar measures cannot be applied to communication relationships between organizations (the key area of interest for public relations). Making this application would be an important step toward developing a full blown theory of dialogue for organizations.

CONCLUSION: AN ETHICAL IMPERATIVE FOR PUBLIC RELATIONS

The foregoing discussion of some of the characteristics of dialogue and the conditions that promote, inhibit, or even measure it indicate the ways in which communication can become relevant for business ethics. Indeed, this chapter argues that such a focus should become the central focus of business ethics. If one accepts the conclusions of post-modern rhetorical theory—that communication processes play a fundamental role in the generation of both scientific and moral truth—then ethical business conduct is conduct that is sanctioned within the parameters of a dialogic communication process between a business organization and those organizations, groups or individuals that are affected or potentially affected by its conduct. No other source of ethical standards exists. Conduct that is not sanctioned or legitimized by that process is open to attack on moral grounds.

Day (1961) proposed an argument, similar to the one just advanced, that questions of right and wrong in public policy decisions are relevant only in relation to the process that produced them. Having prefaced his own remarks with Burke's (1957) depiction of democracy as a device for institutionalizing the dialectic process, Day suggested that:

> Democracy as a political philosophy does not specify what the *good life* is, rather it provides a methodological framework within which each individual may seek to fulfill his [sic] own conception of the good life . . . for the person who accepts decision by debate, the ethics of the decision-making process are superior to the ethics of personal conviction on particular subjects. . . . Democracy is a commitment to means, not ends. (pp. 5 & 7)

For Day, the ultimate moral status of an action within the sphere of public policy is not based on its intrinsic quality or on the tenacity with which debaters support the action. Instead, its rightness or wrongness depends on its having been sanctioned by a particular kind of decision-making process.

Questions of communication ethics are questions about the communication rules that govern the decision-making process rather than questions about the moral rectitude of individual interests. By implication, public relations ethics is also very much concerned with communication rules. At issue are the kinds of rules accepted by a community of discourse according to which public policy decisions—those decisions that jointly affect a focal organization and one or more publics—must be made. Scott (1976) emphasized that it is important to determine these rules and standards intersubjectively. Ehling (1985) makes a similar point in the public relations literature.

Probably the most important consideration for ethical communication is the recognition that interorganizational communication systems cannot be structured perfectly, and the need to challenge their efficacy inproducing legitimate outcomes is a constant requirement. The question of whether a communication system does promote dialogue must always be one of the possible questions that can be raised within that system. Structural constraint is unavoidable and necessary for shared meaning, but dialogue requires that these structures are never taken for granted and that their impact on dialogue is constantly monitored. Dialogue requires that these structures are always possible objects of analysis and possible targets for change.

Corporate public relations departments, to the extent that they are concerned with how a corporation communicates with its publics, are charged with the responsibility of managing the moral dimension of corporate conduct. This is because dialogue is a precondition for any legitimate corporate conduct that affects a public of that organization. The prime concern of those departments is the constitution and maintenance of communication systems that link the corporation with its publics—those organizations and groups affected by corporate actions. The goal of public relations is to manage these communication systems such that they come as close as possible to the standards deduced from the idea of dialogue. This is the core ethical responsibility of public relations from which all other obligations follow.

Acceptance of this view implies that future public relations research and practice could profitably focus on the types of interorganizational communication systems that generate agreements characterized by high levels of participant satisfaction. An important empirical question is the kinds of communication rules and behaviors communicants associate with dialogue. It seems important that representatives of an organization and a public should agree on these rules and behaviors. Coorientation theory suggests methods for measuring the degree of mutual understanding of these rules and behaviors, and satisfaction with them.

Future public relations research could examine the rules and behaviors thought to be dialogical and compare these with ideals deduced from theories of dialogical communication and with actual communication behavior. Indeed, this kind of measurement could play a role in the regular program assessment activities of an organization. Another interesting question is whether these rules and behaviors vary situationally, say from a crisis situation to more routine communication. These questions, and others, are suggested by a theory of public relations that emphasizes the centrality of dialogue.

REFERENCES

Astley, W. G., & Van de Ven, A. H. (1983). Central perspectives and debates in organizational theory. *Administrative Science Quarterly, 28,* 245–273.

Beauchamp, T. L., & Bowie, N. E. (Eds.). (1979). *Ethical theory and business.* Englewood Cliffs, NJ: Prentice-Hall.

Benson, J. K. (1977). Organizations: A dialectical view. *Administrative Science Quarterly, 22,* 1–21.

Bernstein, R. J. (1983). *Beyond objectivism and relativism: Science, hermeneutics and praxis.* Philadelphia: University of Pennsylvania Press.

Brockriede, W. (1972). Arguers as lovers. *Philosophy and rhetoric, 5,* 1–11.

Buchholz, R. (1985). *The essentials of public policy for management.* Englewood Cliffs, NJ: Prentice-Hall.

Burke, K. (1957). *The philosophy of literary form.* New York: Vintage Books.

Burleson, B. R., & Kline, S. L. (1979). Habermas' theory of communication: A critical explication. *Quarterly Journal of Speech, 65,* 412–428.

Cherwitz, R. (1977). Rhetoric as a 'way of knowing': An attenuation of the epistemological claims of the 'New Rhetoric.' *Southern Speech Communication Journal, 42,* 219–29.

Cherwitz, R., & Hikins, J. (1985). *Communication and knowledge: An investigation in rhetorical epistemology.* Columbia, SC: University of South Carolina Press.

Culbertson, H. M. (1984, August). *Breadth of perspective: An important concept for public relations.* Paper presented to the Public Relations Division, Association for Education in Journalism and Mass Communication, Gainesville, FL.

Cutlip, S. M., Center, A. H., & Broom, G. M. (1985). *Effective public relations.* Englewood Cliffs, NJ: Prentice-Hall.

Day, D. G. (1961). The ethics of democratic debate. *Central States Speech Journal, 17,* 5–14.

Ehling, W. (1985). Application of decision theory in the construction of a theory of public relations II. *Public Relations Research and Education, 2*(1), 4–22.

Farace, R. V., Monge, P. M., & Russell, H. M. (1977). *Communicating and organizing.* New York: Random House.

Farrell, T. B. (1976). Knowledge, consensus, and rhetorical theory. *Quarterly Journal of Speech, 62,* 1–14.

Gollner, A. B. (1983). *Social change and corporate strategy: The expanding role of public affairs.* Stamford: Issue Action Press.

Grunig, J. E., & Hunt, T. (1984). *Managing public relations.* New York: Holt, Rinehart & Winston.

Habermas, J. (1970). Toward a theory of communication competence. *Inquiry, 13,* 360–375.

Habermas, J. (1984). *The theory of communicative action* (Vol. 1, T. McCarthy, Trans.). Boston: Beacon Press.

Hawes, L. (1975). *Pragmatics of analoguing: Theory and model construction in communication.* Menlo Park, CA: Addison-Wesley.

Heibert, R. (1966). *Courtier to the crowd.* Ames, IA: Iowa State University Press.

Hrebiniak, L. G., & Joyce, W. F. (1985). Organizational adaptation: Strategic choice and environmental determinism. *Administrative Science Quarterly, 30,* 336–349.

Jaspers, K. (1970). *The way to wisdom: An introduction to philosophy* (R. Manheim, Trans.). New Haven, CT: Yale University Press.

Johannesen, R. L. (1974). Attitude of speaker toward audience: A significant concept for contemporary rhetorical theory and criticism. *Central States Speech Journal, 25,* 95–104.

Johannesen, R. L. (1981). *Ethics in human communication.* Prospect Heights, IL: Waveland Press.

Kneupper, C. W. (1980). Rhetoric, argument, and social reality: A social constructivist view. *Journal of the American Forensic Association, 16,* 173–181.

Kuhn, T. S. (1970). *The structure of scientific revolutions.* Chicago: University of Chicago Press.

Leff, M. C. (1978). In search of Ariadne's thread: A review of the recent literature on rhetorical theory. *Central States Speech Journal, 29,* 73–91.

Levine, S., & White, P. E. (1961). Exchange as a conceptual framework for the study of inter-organizational relationships. *Administrative Science Quarterly, 5,* 583–601.

Lewis, M. C. (1984). Policy planning. In C. Burger (Ed.), *Experts in actions: Inside public relations* (pp. 31–56). New York: Longman.

Olasky, M. (1985). Inside the amoral world of public relations: Truth molded for corporate gain. *Business and Society Review, 53,* 52–5.

Olasky, M. (1987). The development of corporate public relations, 1850–1930. *Journalism Monographs, 102.*

Pearson, R. A. (1986, August). *The ideal public relations situation: Alternative criteria for program evaluation.* Paper presented to the Public Relations Division, Association for Education in Journalism and Mass Communication, Norman, OK.

Perelman, C. (1963). *The idea of justice and the problem of argument.* New York: Humanities Press.

Pfeffer, J. (1981). Management as symbolic action. The creation and maintenance of organizational paradigms. In B. M. Staw & L. L. Cummings (Eds.), *Research in organizational behavior* (Vol. 3, pp. 1–51). Greenwich, CT: JAI Press.

Ryan, M., & Martinson, D. L. (1984). Ethical values, the flow of journalistic information and public relations persons. *Journalism Quarterly, 61,* 27–34.

Scott, R. L. (1976). On viewing rhetoric as epistemic: Ten years later. *Central States Speech Journal, 27,* 258–266.

Sullivan, A. J. (1965). Values in public relations. In O. Lerbinger & A. J. Sullivan (Eds.), *Information, influence and communication: A reader in public relations* (pp. 412–439). New York: Basic Books.

Toulmin, S. E. (1958). *An examination of the place of reason in ethics.* Cambridge: Cambridge University Press.

Weaver, R. M. (1953). *The ethics of rhetoric.* Chicago: Regnery Press.

Willard, C. A. (1979b). The epistemic functions of argument: Reasoning and decision-making from a constructivist/interactionist point of view. *Journal of the American Forensic Association, 15,* 169–191.

Willard, C. A. (1979a). The epistemic functions of argument: Reasoning and decision-making from a constructivist/interactionist point of view. Part II. *Journal of the American Forensic Association, 15,* 211–219.

Willard, C. A. (1983). *Argumentation and the social grounds of knowledge.* University: University of Alabama Press.

Wright, D. (1985). Age and moral values of practitioners. *Public Relations Review, 11*(1), 51–60.

Zeitz, G. (1980). Interorganizational dialectics. *Administrative Science Quarterly, 25,* 72–88.

II

ISSUES OF THEORY

Public Relations? No, Relations with Publics: A Rhetorical–Organizational Approach to Contemporary Corporate Communications

George Cheney
University of Colorado

George N. Dionisopoulos
San Diego State University

ABSTRACT

This chapter examines the functions and roles of contemporary corporate communications in light of recent developments in organizational, rhetorical and "critical" theory. The essay is divided into several parts: (a) the necessary convergence of organizational and rhetorical theory, (b) the maturing of the corporate person, (c) the blurring of organizational boundaries, (d) the challenges to "producers" of corporate public discourse, and (e) the challenges to "consumers" of corporate public discourse. We urge both scholars and practitioners to take the growing activities of corporate communications seriously, especially with respect to the values and interests being promoted in/by corporate messages.

We begin with the powerful words of Charles Perrow, from his recent book, *Normal Accidents: Living with High Risk Technologies* (1984):

Organizational theorists have long since given up hope of finding perfect or even exceedingly well-run organizations, even when there is no catastrophic potential. It is an enduring limitation—if it is a limitation—of our human condition. It means that humans do not exist to give their all to organizations run by someone else, and that organizations inevitably will be run, to some degree, contrary to their interests. This is why it is not a problem of "capitalism"; socialist countries, and even the ideal communist system, cannot escape the dilemmas of cooperative, organized effort on any substantial scale and with any substantial complexity and uncertainty. (pp. 338–339)

Not only do Perrow's words inspire, but they also connect with several issues of importance here. First, given the role of persuasion, and more generally of the symbolic, what can rhetorical theory tell us about the "dilemmas of cooperative, organized effort"—specifically the challenges of corporate communications? Second, given the development of organizational theory—which has, itself, taken a decidedly "symbolic turn" of late (as Tompkins, 1987, explained), what can be said about the complexities of the world of corporate public discourse? And, third, given the state of "Organizational America" (as Scott & Hart, 1979, termed it and as Perrow, 1984, so eloquently described it), what kinds of pragmatic and critical recommendations should be made to various corporate actors and to various publics?

These are the questions we address in tracing some implications of contemporary rhetorical theory, organizational theory, and *critical* theory (we use this term broadly) for study and practice in corporate communications. This chapter thus works with issues of metatheory, considers specific theoretical domains, and explores implications for public relations (and related practices).

THE NECESSARY CONVERGENCE
OF ORGANIZATIONAL AND RHETORICAL THEORY

That organizing and communicating are inextricably interwoven dimensions of social life is now an axiom of organizational studies. Indeed, the revival of interest in Chester Barnard's (1938/1968) classic, *The Functions of the Executive,* in which he defined the organization in expressly communicative terms, is one important indication of the "communicative turn" in organizational studies. So is the popularity and widespread usage of Karl Weick's (1979) *The Social Psychology of Organizing,* which its author has openly described in terms readily appreciated by scholars in communication. The organizing-as-communicating equation is supported further by recent attempts to recast "essentially contested" (we derive the term from Gallie, 1955–1956) concepts such as leadership as "the management of meaning" (Smircich & Morgan, 1982).

But how sharp is this communicative turn in the study of organizations, and to what kind of road does it lead? We see the change in course as profound and wide-ranging in its implications, especially when it is seen in conjunction with the rhetorical preoccupations of contemporary philosophy.

As the book title *After Philosophy: End or Transformation?* (Baynes, Bohman, & McCarthy, 1987) suggests, philosophy is now experiencing a severe identity crisis. In the wake of the "linguistic turn" in the middle part of this century and because of the renewed interest in the writings of Heidegger, Dewey, Wittgenstein (his later work), and Nietszche, the very assumptions of philosophical discourse—in particular, the privilege of validating claims to knowledge across all disciplines (i.e., epistemology)—are now being reexamined with respect to the role of the symbolic and the pervasiveness of persuasion.

In fact, a Zeitgeist can be identified here, linking scholars in Europe (e.g., Derrida, Foucault, and Ricoeur) and the United States (e.g., Davidson, MacIntyre, and Rorty). Whereas the perspectives represented by these names may be distinguished sharply on several dimensions, they share a concern with the full power of the symbolic. Richard Rorty has been particularly influential on this count. His *Philosophy and the Mirror of Nature* (1979) offered a systematic deconstruction of the *representational view* of language. Rorty's (1982) follow-up work, *Consequences of Pragmatism,* pursues the argument further, insisting that "all problems, topics and distinctions are language-relative—the results of our having chosen to use a certain vocabulary, to play a certain language-game" (p. 140). In reconstructing the pragmatism of Dewey and William James and placing it in the domain of postmodern (we use this term broadly) philosophy, Rorty is saying that the test of truth in discourse of any kind is how a text or message works for/on a particular audience. This is not to discourage us—in any discursive domain, lay or scholarly—from pursuing Truth, but to remind us of the necessary role of symbolism in defining any truth. We cannot (as laypersons, scholars, or public relations specialists) stand outside the symbolic, says Rorty, although we often try mightily to do this (orthodox logical positivism being perhaps the best case-in-point).

We mention one other major figure here to define more clearly what we see as the rhetorical interest of contemporary philosophy. Michel Foucault (e.g., 1984) helped to catalyze philosophy's identity crisis, although he treated discourse and communication in quite a different manner than did Rorty. Foucault's *critical-social-history* (as we label it) takes a sweeping view of the discourse of history, focusing on breakpoints, exclusions, oppositions, and margins. Foucault exposed the rules underlying the formation of various bodies of discourse, showing how/why some things get talked about and legitimated, others get eschewed, and still others are ignored (being quite literally outside the domain of a particular body of discourse—for example, that produced in the names of powerful institutions).

Foucault's perspective offers an important complement to that of Rorty because Foucault highlighted the political and social practices that have led us to represent phenomena in a particular way. Paul Rabinow (1986) explained:

The problem of representations for Foucault is not, therefore, one that happened to pop up in philosophy and dominate thinking there for three hundred years. It is linked to the wide range of disparate, but interrelated, social and political practices that constitute the modern world. (p. 240)

Thus, whereas Rorty exposed the inadequacies of the philosophy of representation, Foucault revealed the nature of its politics; both pointed us toward the significance of rhetoric.

Now, what are the implications of these views for rhetorical and organizational theory in general, and for corporate communications in particular? First, as Phillip Tompkins (1987) defined it, *symbolism* must be considered as the substance of organization. In fact, "much of what is today called organizational theory . . . is an extension of the classical concerns of rhetorical theory" (Tompkins, 1987, p. 77). This point attends to the rhetorical turn in philosophy and how it was, in fact, anticipated by Kenneth Burke (e.g., 1945/1969, 1950/1969). *The organization is at least words and other symbols,* to deepen the communicative definition offered by Barnard (1938/1968), "a system of consciously coordinated activities or forces of two or more persons" (p. 73). Although we are prone to reify, instantiate, or otherwise make concrete the notion of organization (many public relations articles are clear testimony to this tendency), it is better thought of as a "text" or "intertext" (in the words of Barthes, 1981) than as a thing, an entity, or a monolith. A symbolic, rhetorical, textual conception of organization gives us—individual practitioners, clients, analysts, consumers, and observers—more direct access to the workings of an organization *qua* an organization (see, e.g., Cheney & Tompkins, 1988; Tompkins, Tompkins, & Cheney, in press).

Second, the postmodern impulse directs our critical awareness to the practices and assumptions of organizational actors (in particular) and organized society (in general), many of which *are taken for granted.* Several such assumptions bear mention here. The premise that "what's best for the organization is best for the individual" is subtly persuasive and usually goes unchallenged in American society (as Scott & Hart, 1979, have argued) and, for that matter, in the entire postindustrial world. Second, consider the related and equally pervasive assumption that individual identity is best appropriated from/for organizational sources (see, e.g., Cheney & Tompkins, 1987; Tompkins & Cheney, 1985; cf. Whyte, 1956), with individuals celebrating themselves by highlighting their affiliations (see Burke, 1950/1969). Third, consider the remarkably unquestioned belief that "*the* organization speaks with a unitary voice," perpetuated by both our synecdoches for organizations (e.g., the White House, the Pentagon, "Ma Bell," etc.) and the persistent use of the passive voice by organizational policy makers (e.g., "It has been decided that . . ."; see Sennett, 1980). Fourth, note the "primitive" and prevalent view of power as *a concrete resource* that is possessed by individuals and groups rather than being an immanent dimension of social *relations* (see, e.g., Daudi, 1986); the latter view directs our attention to the *workings* of power (cf. Foucault, 1984; Tompkins & Cheney, 1985). Finally, we must note the assumption that there is really such a thing as "mere symbolism" or "mere rhetoric." This assumption (which is, fortunately, now dispelled in philosophical circles and is being challenged in some sectors of non-academic society) prevents us from appreciating the full power of the symbolic in all our organizational dealings. Even economic factors, often referred to as "the bottom line," are intimately wrapped up with symbolism (see, e.g., McCloskey, 1985). Thus, we must recognize organizational processes (even material ones) for how we know them—*through, with,* and *in* symbols.

All of these assumptions have striking relevance to the study and practice of public relations, corporate image making, organizational advocacy, and related topics that we place collectively under the rubric "corporate communications" (or "corporate public discourse"). Corporate communications specialists are *in the business of producing symbols.* They, much more than others in the organization, tell various publics "what the organization is." They shape identity, manage issues, and powerfully "locate" the organization in the world of public discourse. The identity-based campaign "A Company Called TRW" is a good example, as well as the almost-ubiquitous advertising by AT&T and the full-page "technological advocacy" ads by United Technologies. In persuasive efforts such as these, issues and identities are tightly interwoven; connections between positions on certain issues and corporate images are consistently made in the hope that publics will make them as well (see, e.g., Cheney & Vibbert, 1987; Sethi, 1977).

Thus, by virtue of their very activities, corporate communications specialists should be aware of *the assumptions and the effects* of their symbols in the "marketplace" of corporate discourse. Particularly in today's postindustrial and mass-mediated society, corporate communications specialists help to *make*—not just *announce*—what organizations are. Thus, there is a powerful sense in which organizations are texts (see e.g., Cheney & Tompkins, 1988; Tompkins, Tompkins & Cheney, in press) for certain publics that "consume" corporate public discourse. And corporate communications texts help to locate not only the identities of the organizations to which they refer, but also the identities of individuals who identify with them. Nowhere is this clearer than in the "I'm the NRA" series, sponsored by the National Rifle Association, which depicts Americans in various walks of life, sporting guns, and proclaiming their membership in the powerful lobby organization. Individual and organization, identity and advocacy, all become blended symbolically within the full-page ads.

In summary, corporate communications (in practice and in theory) must be self-conscious about its role in the organizational process (which is fundamentally rhetorical and symbolic) in responding to and in exercising power (in public discourse), and in shaping various identities (corporate and individual).

THE MATURING OF THE CORPORATE PERSON

In order to consider further the implications of the theoretical strands we have woven, we need to ask, "How did we get here?" That is, what can organizational history say to us about the prominent role of contemporary corporate communications? In this (necessarily but unfortunately) brief sketch of the rise of the modern organization, we rely primarily on three theorists: James Coleman (1974), Max Weber (1978) and Richard Edwards (1979). Then we turn specifically to the place of corporate communications on the societal stage.

As Coleman (1974) explained, the "juristic" or corporate "person" was established in the late Middle Ages by natural or corporal persons (individuals) to enhance their power vis-à-vis the institutions most powerful then, the Church and the State. However, Coleman continued, although the *sum total* of power in industrialized society has expanded over the centuries (i.e., new power is created each time a new collectivity is formed), the *proportion* of power by individuals has decreased relative to that enacted by corporate persons (or organizations). This, of course, has important implications for our legal system (in which a corporation *is* a legal person), our economic system (where corporate persons often join or merge) and our society as a whole (where individual identity is in large part derived from associations with corporate persons).

Coupled with this gradual transfer in power and transformation of power relations, is the seemingly unchecked march of bureaucracy. Weber (1978), of course, was profoundly ambivalent about the rise of the bureaucracy that he witnessed and analyzed early in this century. He saw both *benefits* in "rationalizing" the modern organization and *dangers* in the undue concentration of power, threats to individuality (that all might become, in his words, "cogs in a machine"), and the celebration of means over ends (e.g., efficiency for its own sake). What bureaucratic organization has done, in terms explained by Edwards (1979), is to move the locus of control in the organization from direct supervision or technical direction (the latter exemplified by assembly-line technology) to shared values, goals, rules, regulations. The modern bureaucratic organization is held together in just this manner, communicating and "inculcating" (Barnard's, 1938/1968, term) premises for action to employees (internally) and to other publics (externally). When general premises are internalized (for example, those relating to quality, or growth, or efficiency, or cost), organizational members can be *depended on* to act in the best interests of the organization, as they understand them (cf. Cheney, 1983a, 1983b; Tompkins & Cheney, 1983, 1985; Simon, 1976). That is, loyal organizational members will seek to trace out the implications of a premise held by the organization—say, "Growth is good"—by using that premise in their decisions.

It is within this scene of organizational development that corporate communications has arisen and expanded, from its originally "defensive" role (see, e.g., the historical accounts in Hiebert, 1966; Tedlow, 1979) to its contemporary political and proactive role (see e.g., Crable & Vibbert, 1985; Heath & Nelson, 1986; Jones & Chase, 1979). Many organizations, most notably the resource-rich members of the *"Fortune 500,"* along with powerful lobbies, governmental agencies, unions, and religious groups, are now engaged actively in promoting particular value premises "for" their respective publics. Such activity is not new, although it has been noticeably stepped up in the late 1970s and the 1980s. In response to the early 1970s—years in which public confidence in American institutions was at an all-time low—corporations and other organizations began adopting a more aggressive and decidedly political posture in their messages (see the review in Cheney & Vibbert, 1987).

Mobil's "Observations" series in the late 1970s represented a significant effort to shape public opinion in ways favorable to the corporation's relationship with Washington. Particular premises—for example, *freedom* from government regulation—were promoted in the context of American values and "common sense" (Crable & Vibbert, 1983). Encouraged by Mobil's recovery (much of which was attributed—although not conclusively—to the corporation's advocacy), other organizations followed the lead. Thus, today we find numerous and diverse organizations engaged in "packaging" premises, using the best technologies available for reaching their respective publics. In this way, the bureaucratization and rationalization of society have become more complete, more thoroughgoing: organizational control is exercised in powerful yet often unobtrusive ways.

Organizations have "gone public" in the promotion and inculcation of value premises in new and profound ways. For example, Herb Schmertz, Mobil's vice president for public relations, states: "There's a dialogue out there, and you're either in it or you're not. We've decided we want to be in it" ("Mobile Corp. Wants Fair Publicity," 1979, p. 30). Heath and Nelson (1986), among others, describe this situation so:

Our bewildering information environment today offers more than a challenge—it makes possible a new dialogue, in effect demanding that key
social institutions, such as corporations, vigorously speak out if they are to
participate in restructuring the social agenda of the approaching twenty-
first century. (p. 11)

But many critics take a dimmer view. Herbert Schiller, for example,
argues the following:

[O]ne means . . . of the dominant corporate interest to obtain still further
control of the country's informational climate—acknowledging their already preponderant position—is to press for legislative, judicial, or legal
measures that will hold the media still more accountable to the ruling
power centers. (1981, p. 85)

This debate—free speech versus undue privilege—is a critical one in our
consideration of contemporary corporate communications because of
the maturation of corporate persons and organized society as a whole.

The debate came into sharp relief with the 1978 *Bellotti* decision by the
U.S. Supreme Court that supported the right of a corporation to pub-
licize its views in an attempt to try to influence the outcome of a political
referendum. In the court's opinion, the type of advocacy proposed by
the plaintiff, the First National Bank of Boston, was "at the heart of the
First Amendment protection." The court held that corporate public discourse "is the type of speech indispensible to decision-making in a democracy, and this is no less true because the speech comes from a corporation rather than an individual" (*First National Bank v. Bellotti*, 1979, p.
714). Furthermore, in the *Con Ed* decision of 1980, the court ruled in
favor of a "major expansion of the free speech rights of corporations" on
controversial matters of public policy (Greenhouse, 1980, p. 1).

Thus, we find in the 1980s that major corporations and other large
organizations have the resources, the legal rights, the technology, and
the precedents for openly conducting political issue advocacy. Moreover,
the corporation as legal or juristic person is now also the visible "corporate persona." Of course, the term *persona* traces its history to the ancient
use of dramatic masks during social and religious ceremonies (Elliot,
1982, p. 20). Organizations, in essence, select and present their social
masks (or personae) through the use of corporate communications. Dionisopoulos and Vibbert (1983) capture the full significance of this in
terms of "discourses which defend organizational personae against ethically based challenges" (p. 1). For example, Kaiser Aluminum and
Chemical Corporation in 1980 responded to an ABC–TV "20–20"
broadcast about low safety in aluminum wiring with full-page ads in 10

major newspapers around the country (Kaiser, 1980; see also "The Business Campaign Against 'Trial by TV'," 1980). Dionisopoulos & Vibbert (1983) write:

> The basis of that defense [itself] was not only that Kaiser *did* not act unethically, but also that Kaiser *could* not act in such a way, since such acts were not in keeping with their character as a corporate agent (p. 18)

Thus, the corporate persona is shaped, asserted, and even self-referential. The organization becomes powerfully located in a matrix of public messages (cf. McMillan, 1982). In practice, then, an organizational persona is "an organizational image which [is] *created* from the accumulated symbols by which the organization represents itself" (McMillan, 1987, p. 37).

One implication about the power of corporate public discourse is clear: Many public relations and issue advocacy messages are designed to have political influence without allowing their sources to be identified as political actors. This paradoxical situation is vivid in the case of the U.S. Catholic bishops, who have made major political statements in recent years while trying to maintain a status as *non*-political actors (see Goldzwig & Cheney, 1984). As Heath (1980) defined corporate advocacy:

> [It] consists of the research, analysis, design, and mass dissemination of arguments on issues contested in the public dialogue in an attempt to create a favorable, reasonable, and informed public opinion which in turn influences institutions' operating environments (p. 371)

This view, reflective of the institutions engaged in such advocacy, necessitates an indirect model of political involvement: the organizations (corporations and others) "must proclaim political messages *without at the same time being represented as political bodies*" (Cheney & Vibbert, 1987, p. 189).

Nevertheless, many of our largest organizations are involved in the shaping of public thought and public policy in new and powerful ways. Larry Judd (1984) described this new posture as "militancy." Given the corporation's natural interest in controlling its environment (including the government) and the fact that the political system allows for the broad exercise of political influence by corporations, there exists, as Nadel (1976) wrote:

> [a] corporate quest for hegemony—preponderant influence over the economic environment—and exercise by corporations of great political power in the formal institutions of government and society as a whole. (p. 18)

Such hegemony does not refer to simple or outright domination but rather to control over the (value) premises that shape basic and applied policy decisions. In essence, corporate discourse seeks to establish public frames of reference for interpreting information concerning issues deemed important by Corporate America. These interests are undergirded, moreover, by a prevalent attitude that Burke (1935/1984) identified long ago: "business for business' sake." Herein lies the real power of corporate communications: for public relations statements and issue management campaigns not only reflect the society of which they are part, they also help to create and recreate it.

THE BLURRING OF ORGANIZATIONAL BOUNDARIES

We have already seen how the question "What is the organization?" can be answered effectively in communicative-rhetorical terms. But the issue of *organizational boundaries* becomes even more important in light of several recent developments: the growth of extra- and interorganizational relations, the increased influence of the mass media, and the burgeoning power of corporate public discourse.

Traditionally, organizational studies have maintained a rather distinct boundary between the organization and the environment (see, e.g., Aldrich, 1979). However, not only is this distinction becoming increasingly less clear, it is also being questioned as something of a fiction. In analyzing many service organizations, for example, it makes little sense to divide clients completely from the organization; after all, as Mills and Margulies (1980) pointed out, the client–provider *interface* is perhaps the most important identifying characteristic of service organizations.

The complexity of interorganizational relations today makes organizational boundaries difficult to maintain in theory or in practice. Public–private partnerships, the privatization of part of the third sector (e.g., much of health care), the spread of multinationals, the increased dependence of public universities on private monies, and the sheer number of organizational interlockings—these and related developments make it exceedingly problematic to distinguish organizational units (see, e.g., Bozeman, 1987).

Weick (1979) has pointed out that when a large organization *looks* at its *environment*, it often *sees* the consequences of actions the organization itself has taken. Thus, for many of our largest organizations and institutions we can add a second sense in which reality is socially constructed: "As an organization becomes larger it literally becomes more of its own environment and can hardly avoid stumbling into its own enactments" (Weick, 1979, p. 167). Certainly this is true for such large organizations as IBM; the AFL-CIO; the Department of Defense; and for NASA, which continues to cope with, among other problems, the symbolic stress the agency *itself* placed on the ill-fated Challenger mission.

A second factor to consider here is the growth and omnipresence of the mass media. For support on this point, we find a book by Joshua Meyrowitz (1985), *No Sense of Place*, to be particularly provocative and helpful. Meyrowitz argued essentially that the connections between physical and social space have been irrevocably severed by the influence of the electronic media. "As a result, *where* one is has less and less to do with what one knows and experiences. Electronic media have altered the significance of time and space for social interaction" (Meyrowitz, 1985, p. viii). Meyrowitz's book is important for our purposes because of what it says about social *boundaries*. Extending and applying his analysis to the organization, we maintain that the media (in the form of television, computers, teleconferencing, and the plethora of printed publications—all of which are used in corporate communications) have tended to blur even more the organizational–environmental boundary, obliterating (or at least clouding) our collective sense of place with respect to the major institutions of our society. *Where,* for example, is Beatrice? *Where* is the NRA? *Where* is the telephone company? (the latter, a particularly pertinent question, because we are often asked to use the telephone even when visiting an office of a telephone utility). Today, we find the lack of a place-identification for corporate messages to be common occurrence.

Although this line of reasoning should not be followed too far, it is important to realize that the lost sense of place puts all the more emphasis on the intertextual relations among corporate public messages, as the line separating internal and external communications becomes more suspect and corporate messages become more interrelated. General Motors recognized this in their recent attempts to coordinate internal messages to employees with external messages to *the* public (with employees being seen in the very nontraditional role of corporate advocates). Many of these messages flow together, in that, for example, employees who receive internal messages also go home to watch corporate messages to the external public on television (e.g., about safety); thus, the traditional distinction between corporate communications *inside* the organization and public relations *outside* the organization makes little sense (Paonessa, 1983). Another interesting case in point concerns the post-Three Mile Island efforts of the nuclear power industry's main public relations organization, the Committee for Energy Awareness (CEA). In the summer of 1979, the CEA called for an industry-wide effort to generate politically active "citizens' groups" among "employees and wives" of utilities, nuclear suppliers, and large energy users (Hilgartner, Bell, & O'Connor, 1982, p. 82).

In fact, a 1979 Conference Board study found that employees were among the most common target audiences for grassroots lobbying efforts, or corporate communication aimed at generating support within the political environment. According to Grunig and Hunt (1984), these efforts implore employees to "provide political support by writing letters, calling or visiting legislators, or otherwise supporting the organization's position" (p. 293).

Public relations scholars and practitioners alike have recently argued for breaking down the organization–environment boundary. Krippendorff and Eleey (1986), for example, seem to use the term *environment* loosely when they argue the need for organizations to "monitor their symbolic environment" using a variety of strategies that analyze, manifest, and project their specific interests. Furthermore, James Grunig (1984) found that many public relations specialists are beginning to appreciate the creative potential of their activities—for crossing and even redefining organizational boundaries.

Of course, here again, we come to terms with the power of corporate public discourse.

> Public relations officers [and we would add, all other corporate communications specialists] are necessary contributors to the "interface" between ["organization" and "environment"]. As "boundary spanners" whose job is *defined as communication*, [these specialists] are continually involved in making symbolic connections between organization and environment, even as they "say" what each of the linked domains *is*. (Cheney & Vibbert, 1987, p. 178)

The ambiguities of organizations and environments can be and are managed through corporate public communications. A communication campaign by Illinois Power offers a good illustration of this. On November 25, 1979, a story aired on CBS's "60 Minutes" claimed that cost overruns experienced by Illinois Power were due to "the company's inexperience in nuclear construction, and, possibly, to the [mis]management resulting from it" (Goldstein, 1980, p. 7). Within a week of the network broadcast, using videotape made simultaneously with CBS's filming, Illinois Power produced "60 Minutes/Our Reply," a "telling [and] polished counter-program" that included "the entire CBS segment interspersed with company rebuttal" (Graham, 1980, p. 24). The important point for our purpose here is that this program was originally designed for an audience of Illinois Power employees, customers, and the investment community (Goldstein, 1980, p. 7); however, requests for the videotape "poured in from everyone from university professors to major corporations to congressional leaders" (Graham, 1980, p. 24; see also, Aldridge,

1980, p. 12). According to the utility, more than 1,300 copies of the reply tape were distributed, and it has reached a "significant thinking audience," an audience that obviously breaks down lines demarking internal and external communication.

In this and other instances, the power of corporate public discourse is demonstrated in its capacity to locate the organization with respect to certain values, issues, identities and images (see Cheney & Vibbert, 1987). In the maze of symbols that is our society, corporate public discourse performs an architectonic function, helping to shape how various publics see their world. Because of this power, we must consider both the challenges posed to the producers of corporate communications and those faced by consumers of those messages.

THE CHALLENGES TO "PRODUCERS" OF CORPORATE PUBLIC DISCOURSE

The challenges to "producers" are considered in three categories: organizational, rhetorical and ethical. The prominence of corporate communications in many large organizations and the complexities of those activities necessitate a careful look at the very process of organizing.

The Organizational Challenge

As early as 1973—when Watergate was bursting into the news, the United States was pulling troops out of Vietnam, and the nation faced the OPEC oil embargo—it was argued that corporations should "consolidate the communications function" (e.g., Cook, 1973), bringing together various public communications activities such as advertising, public relations, and issue management, into a central organizational function. Certainly this is desirable for financial, legal, and administrative reasons. But it is also important in terms of the various publics reached by large organizations (and here we refer to corporations, unions, governmental agencies, religious groups, universities, hospitals, and so forth). Corporate communications must be managed so as to mesh with the rest of organizational activities and yet direct itself toward wide audiences (many of which are outside what we commonly think of as the organization and its clients). Corporate communications must be responsive to the demands of the organization (there are, after all, publics inside the organization) and to the demands of the environment. One specialist (Anspach, 1982) stressed the importance of these interrelationships in handling such symbols as corporate names and logos. As an organizational activity, corporate communications should be both enriched and kept in check by connections to multiple interests—inside and outside the organization. Thus, a balance between organizational autonomy and interdependence must be achieved.

The Rhetorical Challenge

The rhetorical challenge to producers of corporate public discourse is closely related. Simply put, communications specialists should strive to present a consistent and self-reflective image of the organization, adapting, of course, to various publics. Consistency is especially important when one considers that many publics overlap, that the media are so pervasive, and that *identity*—both corporate and individual—is often at stake. Some corporations, for example, are sensitive to the need to *maintain* symbols from acquired companies, and employees value this (see, e.g., Cheney, 1983).

Self-reflectiveness is a more complex and nuanced matter. What we mean by the application of the term here is this: Organizations, specifically their communications officers, should represent interests in such a way that both persuades and allows for others to persuade. Here we echo Henry Johnstone's, 1981, dictum to maximize persuasiveness and persuasibility for all parties to communication. That is, corporate communications should not *limit* possibilities for understanding, but rather *encourage* them. We offer by way of negative example a recent piece of advocacy advertising by AT&T entitled "The Paradox of Power" (AT&T, 1987). As part of the corporation's series on "Issues of the Information Age," this ad asks the reader to accept a view that technology is problematic *only because it is not powerful enough.* AT&T explains this view through what it calls "the paradox of power": "the more powerful the machine, the less power it exerts over the person using it" (AT&T, 1987, p. 7). Of course, *what the ad expounds is in itself* paradoxical—a vicious circle—yet there is no mention of *that* possibility. Moreover, the ad promotes the primitive and limiting view of power-as-simple-domination we mentioned earlier. Self-reflectiveness in this case would mean offering the possibilities for critique, or at least not presenting the corporate view through such blatantly circular and self-justifying reasoning.

The Ethical Challenge

These concerns push us toward the third challenge for producers of corporate public discourse: ethics. Corporate rhetors, in the forms of communication specialists who do the actual speaking, share the responsibilities of all rhetors for maximizing the possibilities for human dialogue (no matter what their specific arguments or interests may be). (See Habermas, 1973, 1979, on the "ideal speech situation;" cf. McCarthy, 1978.) These responsibilities are, in fact, enlarged for corporate communications specialists because of (a) their access to great resources, (b) the concentration of information control among a relatively small number of organizations and institutions in our society, and (c) the "one-way" nature of most (although not all) corporate communications. These factors combine to produce a significantly privileged position for the corporate rhetor; that privilege (in more than one sense of the word) should be taken seriously.

A recent ruling by the Federal Trade Commission about the advocacy advertising of the R. J. Reynolds Company highlights this need. Specifically the FTC ruled that Reynolds ads that address smoking issues (e.g., effects of passive smoke, smoking in bed, etc.) but do not mention the company's products, are not subject to FTC regulations on "truth and accuracy." By being defined as "corporate opinion," rather than "commercial speech," the Reynolds ad campaign receives protection under the First Amendment (Colford, 1986). Such definitions and distinctions become very important—in what they *include* within (or privilege) and *exclude* from certain categories of discourse. Without debating the appropriateness of this and similar rulings, we wish to stress the enormous ethical responsibility that goes with the advancement of particular economic and political interests.

Some corporations and other organizations have addressed this ethical challenge by paying for or in some way sponsoring *competing* advocacy messages. For example, in an unsuccessful 1979 effort to buy network air time for its advocacy messages, Mobil offered to buy additional time so that those who differed with them could reply at Mobil's expense (see the discussion in Dionisopoulos & Vibbert, 1988). In another case, since 1979 the Committee for Energy Awareness has sponsored debates concerning the role of atomic power in the energy future of the United States. The belief that a legitimate debate has more credibility than a one-sided presentation has often prompted the CEA to recruit and pay the expense of the anti-nuclear speakers.

However, even in instances like these, corporate advocates have an enormous rhetorical advantage that should be used carefully and with attention to individual and societal interests. Practitioners of corporate communications should give testimony through their work to the words of Patrick Jackson (1985), former president of PRSA: "I am convinced public relations is a philosophy more than anything else. It is a belief that human dignity is invaluable, that people are capable of governing themselves, and they are entitled to a voice in decisions that affect their lives" (p. 24). *This* the privileged voices should keep in their speech repertoire.

THE CHALLENGES TO "CONSUMERS" OF CORPORATE PUBLIC DISCOURSE

There are, naturally, corresponding challenges for "consumers" of corporate public discourse (and here we restrict our attention to *individuals*), although they receive little attention in the literature of public relations and related areas. These challenges, as we see them, are individual (vis-à-vis organizational), rhetorical and ethical.

The Individual Challenge

The individual challenge is one of "de-organizing" identity in an age when so much of individual self-hood is derived from work organizations and the mega-institutions of society (see e.g., Cheney & Tompkins, 1987; Goodman, 1984). The proliferation of corporate public discourse heightens this challenge for the member of society.

One of the most effective strategies to de-organize identity is to participate in what Berger and Neuhaus (1977) called "mediating structures" (i.e., neighborhood, family, religious congregation, voluntary association) to (re)gain a sense of community and individual involvement. This not only enables individuals to become identified through more local associations—as contrasted with the diffuse and often overwhelming (even alienating) attachments to government, giant corporations, national unions, large religious structures, and so on—but also *empowers* individuals when mediating structures (or groups) *do their own advocacy.* Greater reliance on local groups can restore to some extent that sense of place and offer individuals a place to stand in coping with corporate public discourse. The philosophy here is probably best represented by the slogan, "Think globally, act locally."

The Rhetorical Challenge

Mediating structures also offer people possibilities for addressing the *rhetorical* challenge, which we pose as "How to converse with a corporate rhetor." The usual imbalance in resources—both material and symbolic—makes this task enormously difficult for the average citizen. Nevertheless, although persuasive parity is often unreachable, individuals can take advantage of existing opportunities to be heard and create some of their own. Employee participation programs, such as quality circles, offer some possibilities for voicing concerns and influencing corporate communications practice (albeit usually within predefined parameters). So do meetings for policy input (which some organizations hold regularly, bringing together employees from across departments and hierarchical levels). Outside the work organization, we find editorial opportunities, citizen action groups, lobbies, and various grassroots groups. Of course, any group runs the risk over time of becoming bureaucratized and alienating, but that tendency should be guarded against.

The Ethical Challenge

The ethical challenge to consumers of corporate public discourse should by now be rather clear—to give a fair and informed reading of corporate messages, being aware of both the sources and the contexts of messages.

The sources of corporate messages, as we have seen, are often difficult to isolate. Nevertheless, individuals should remember that such statements are crafted by people in specific organizational positions. Furthermore, sometimes individuals can "reduce" corporate agents by identifying communications officers and managers party to decisions about public relations and advocacy messages. For example, at the Rocky Flats nuclear weapons manufacturing facility near Denver, specific communications officers came forward recently in the public debate over the proposal by Rockwell International (the manager of the facility) to conduct a controlled burn of radioactive and hazardous materials on a semi-continuous basis. The identifiable role of the Communications Department and its representatives, pointed to by a number of citizen groups, has made possible more direct and manageable exchanges between and among the various parties to the debate, including citizens acting in groups and individually (see, Connolly, 1987).

However, in cases such as this one, while individuals are analyzing corporate messages and locating sources, they should be careful to consider the *context* for the messages—on several levels. First, in terms of corporate decision-making, it should be remembered that many activities of corporate communications do, in fact, represent the interests and wishes of upper management quite directly (see, e.g., Levinson, 1972). After all, "house organs are [usually] relegated to editors who are all well controlled by several administrative layers above them" (Levinson, 1972, p. 223). Thus, consumers should be cautious although determined in making source attributions.

Second, consider the context of the industry or type of organization from which the message comes. That is, Mobil's advocacy ought to be considered and evaluated within the context of the oil industry, AT&T's

in terms of telecommunications, R. J. Reynold's in terms of tobacco, and so forth. (Of course, this is problematic with respect to conglomerates, of which there are many; but even then, clusters of interests can be identified.) In this way the individual consumer can make better sense of messages from individual corporate rhetors, messages that will necessarily have points of contact with those of similar organizations and points of uniqueness. This is especially important when dealing with corporate messages whose sponsors do not readily acknowledge industrial affiliation. A provocative example is the advocacy message by Edward Teller concerning the accident at Three Mile Island. Entitled "I Was the Only Victim of Three Mile Island," the ad was sponsored by Dresser Industries. However, nowhere did the ad indicate that Dresser Industries was the manufacturer of one of the valves that malfunctioned at Three Mile Island or that this conglomerate is even connected with the atomic power industry (Dionisopoulos, 1984).

The third and broadest context is that of the issue itself. The consumer of corporate public discourse needs to be sensitive both to what *is* said about an issue and what is *not* said. As we now know about power, it is often exercised in subtle and unobtrusive ways. The ways discussions are *shaped and defined* are, in general, more powerful than specific arguments that are advanced (see, e.g., Daudi, 1986; Foucault, 1984; cf. Lukes, 1974; Tompkins & Cheney, 1985). As Gunther Kress (1985) explained, following Foucault's (1984) analysis, "Discourses [as organized sets of statements] define, describe and delimit what is possible to say and not possible to say . . . with respect to the area of concern of that institution, whether marginally or centrally" (p. 68).

The ramifications of this observation are well illustrated by the conscious efforts of corporate rhetors to impose definitional limits on discourse concerning issues within the public domain of ideas. For example, a 1975 report by Cambridge Reports, Inc. suggested a context for the campaign to promote nuclear power that, in effect, limited questions concerning safety. They stated; "The nuclear debate should *not* be 'Should we build nuclear power plants?' but rather, 'How do we get the energy/electricity needed for *your* jobs and home?' " (Dionisopoulos, 1984). Of course, the Reagan Administration pursued a parallel strategy in promoting the Strategic Defense Initiative in the mid-1980s, confining much of the public debate to questions of *feasibility*. The current campaign by the R. J. Reynolds Tobacco Company is an attempt to define the problems associated with smoking as "social," thus suggesting that political solutions would be counterproductive. Individual consumers should be sensitive to *the existing range of and the possibilities for* discussion on any particular issue.

CONCLUSION

Our discussion has been intentionally wide-ranging, bridging concerns of organizational theory, rhetorical theory, and critically-oriented theory in an effort to illuminate what we see as important issues in the study and practice of contemporary corporate communications. We have tried to capture both historical influences and current trends. We have treated both philosophy and politics. We have attempted to address both scholars and practitioners. That corporate communications (in the form of public relations, internal communication programs, advocacy advertising, issue management, etc.) *are important* is given decisive testimony by the fact of this volume. What we hope, most of all, is that the discussion proceeds in such a way that keeps the loftiest interests—what's best for all—uppermost in mind. That is one way in which we should serve as advocates for the common good. No organization, after all, is perfect—or even close.

REFERENCES

Aldrich, H. (1979) *Organizations and environments.* Englewood Cliffs, NJ: Prentice-Hall.

Aldridge, R. (1980, May 14) Illinois firm's "Reply" has "60 Minutes" on the defensive. *Chicago Tribune,* sect. 3, p. 12.

Anspach, R. R. (1982) Selling a new identity "inside." *Public Relations Journal, 38,* 12–14.

AT&T. (1987, March) The paradox of power (advertisement). *The Atlantic,* p. 7.

Barnard, C. (1968) *The functions of the executive* (30th anniv. ed.). Cambridge, MA: Harvard University Press. (Originally published, 1938)

Barthes, R. (1981) Theory of the text. In R. Young (Ed.), *Untying the text: A poststructuralist reader* (pp. 31–47). Boston: Routledge & Kegan Paul.

Baynes, K., Bohman, J., & McCarthy, T. (Eds.). (1987) *After philosophy: End or transformation?* Cambridge, MA: MIT Press.

Berger, P. L., & Neuhaus, R. (1977) *To empower people: The role of mediating structures in public policy.* Washington, DC: American Enterprise Institute.

Bozeman, B. (1987) *All organizations are public.* San Francisco: Jossey-Bass.

Burke, K. (1984) *Permanence and change: An anatomy of purpose* (3rd. ed.). Berkeley: University of California Press. (Originally published, 1935)

Burke, K. (1969) *A grammar of motives.* Berkeley: University of California Press. (Originally published, 1945)

Burke, K. (1969) *A rhetoric of motives.* Berkeley: University of California Press. (Originally published, 1950)

The business campaign against "trial by TV". (1980, June 2) *Business Week,* pp. 77, 79.

Cheney, G. (1983a) On the various and changing meanings of organizational membership: A field study of organizational identification. *Communication Monographs, 50,* 342–362.

Cheney, G. (1983b) The rhetoric of identification and the study of organizational communication. *Quarterly Journal of Speech, 69,* 143–158.

Cheney, G. (1985) *Speaking of who "we" are: The development of the U.S. Catholic bishops' pastoral letter* The Challenge of Peace *as a case study in identity, organization, and rhetoric.* Unpublished doctoral dissertation, Purdue University, West Lafayette, IN.

Cheney, G., & Tompkins, P. K. (1987) Coming to terms with organizational identification and commitment. *Central States Speech Journal, 38,* pp. 1–15.

Cheney, G., & Tompkins, P. K. (1988) On the facts of the "text" as the basis of human communication research. In J. A. Anderson (Ed.), *Communication Yearbook 11* (pp. 455–481). Newbury Park, CA: Sage.

Cheney, G., & Vibbert, S. L. (1987) Corporate discourse: Public relations and issue management. In F. M. Jablin, L. L. Putnam, K. H. Roberts, & L. W. Porter (Eds.), *Handbook of organizational communication* (pp. 165–194). Newbury Park, CA: Sage.

Coleman, J. (1974) *Power and the structure of society.* New York: Norton.

Colford, S. W. (1986, August 18) RJR ruling may "open up" issue advertising. *Advertising Age,* pp. 6, 77.

Connolly, M. (1987, March 29) Union, Flats clash over release of safety records. *Daily Camera* (Boulder, CO), p. 1-A. cols. 2–5.

Cook, J. (1973) Consolidating the communications function. *Public Relations Journal, 29,* 6–8, 28.

Crable, R. E., & Vibbert, S. L. (1983) Mobil's epideictic advocacy: "Observations" of Prometheus-bound. *Communication Monographs, 50,* 380–394.

Crable, R. E., & Vibbert, S. L. (1985) Managing issues and influencing public policy. *Public Relations Review, 11,* 3–16.

Daudi, P. (1986) *Power in the organization: The discourse of power in managerial praxis.* Oxford: Basil Blackwell.

Dionisopoulos, G. N. (1984) *Corporate advocacy of the atomic power industry following Three Mile Island.* Unpublished doctoral dissertation, Purdue University, West Lafayette, IN.

Dionisopoulos, G. N., & Vibbert, S. L. (1983, November) *Organizational apologia: "Corporate" public discourse and the genre of self-defense.* Paper presented at the annual meeting of the Speech Communication Association, Washington, DC.

Dionisopoulos, G. N., & Vibbert, S. L. (1988) CBS vs. Mobil Oil: Charges of creative bookkeeping in 1979. In H. R. Ryan (Ed.), *Oratorical encounters: Selected studies and sources of twentieth-century political accusations and apologies* (pp. 241–251). Westport, CT: Greenwood Press.

Edwards, R. (1979) *Contested terrain: The transformation of the workplace in the twentieth century.* New York: Basic Books.

Elliot, R. C. (1982) *The literary persona.* Chicago: University of Chicago Press.

First National Bank of Boston et al. v. Francis X. Bellotti. (1979) *United States Supreme Court Reports, Lawyer's Edition, 55,* San Francisco: Bancroft-Whitney.

Foucault, M. (1984) *The Foucault reader* (P. Rabinow, ed.). New York: Pantheon.

Gallie, W. B. (1955–1956) Essentially contested concepts. In *Proceedings of the Aristotelian Society* (pp. 167–98).

Goldstein, K. K. (1980, May/June) Turning the tables on "60 Minutes". *Columbia Journalism Review,* p. 7, 9.

Goldzwig, S., & Cheney, G. (1984) The U.S. Catholic bishops on nuclear arms: Corporate advocacy, role redefinition, and rhetorical adaptation. *Central States Speech Journal, 35,* 8–23.

Goodman, E. (1984, February 24) Workplace our identity. *Lafayette* (IN) *Journal and Courier,* p. A-10, cols, 1–4.

Graham, S. (1980, June 27) Illinois Power pans "60 Minutes." *Wall Street Journal,* p. 24, cols. 4–6.

Greenhouse, L. (1980, June 21) Two rulings by high court expand corporation's free speech rights. *New York Times,* pp. 1, 26.

Grunig, J. E. (1984) Organization, environments and models of public relations. *Public Relations Review and Education, 1,* 6–29.

Grunig, J. E., & Hunt, T. (1984) *Managing public relations.* New York: Holt, Rinehart & Winston.

Habermas, J. (1973) *Legitimation crisis* (T. McCarthy, Trans.). Boston: Beacon Press.

Habermas, J. (1979) *Communication and the evolution of society* (T. McCarthy, Trans.). Boston: Beacon Press.

Heath, R. L. (1980) Corporate advocacy: An application of speech communication perspectives and skills—and more. *Communication Education, 29,* 370–77.

Heath, R. L., & Nelson, R. A. (1986) *Issues management: Corporate public policymaking in an information society.* Newbury Park, CA: Sage.

Hiebert, R. E. (1966) *Courtier to the crowd: The story of Ivy Lee and the development of public relations.* Ames: Iowa State University Press.

Hilgartner, S., Bell, R. C., & O'Connor, R. (1982) *Nukespeak: Nuclear language, visions, and mindset.* San Francisco: Sierra Club Books.

Jackson, P. (1985) Tomorrow's public relations. *Public Relations Journal, 41,* 24–25.

Johnstone, H. W., Jr. (1981) Toward an ethics of rhetoric. *Communication, 6,* 305–314.

Jones, B. L., & Chase, W. H. (1979) Managing public policy issues. *Public Relations Review, 7,* 3–23.

Judd, L. R. (1984) A new militancy. *Public Relations Journal, 40,* 15–16.

Kaiser Aluminum and Chemical Corp. (1980, October 31) Press release.

Kress, G. (1985) Discourses, texts, readers and the pro-nuclear arguments. In P. Chilton (Ed.), *Language and the nuclear arms debate: Nukespeak today.* London: Frances Pinter.

Krippendorff, K., & Eleey, M. F. (1986) Monitoring and organization's symbolic environment. *Public Relations Review, 12,* 13–36.

Levinson, H. (1972) *Organizational diagnosis.* Cambridge, MA: Harvard University Press.

Lukes, S. (1974) *Power: A radical view.* London: Macmillan.

McCallister, L. (1981) The interpersonal side of internal communications. *Public Relations Journal, 37,* pp. 20–22.

McCarthy, T. (1978) *The critical theory of Jürgen Habermas.* Cambridge, MA: MIT Press.

McCloskey, D. (1985) *The rhetoric of economics.* Madison: University of Wisconsin Press.

McMillan, J. (1987) In search of the organizational persona: A rationale for studying organizations rhetorically. In L. Thayer (Ed.), *Communications—organizations* (Vol. 2, pp. 21–45). Norwood, NJ: Ablex.

McMillan, J. J. (1982) *The rhetoric of the modern organization.* Unpublished doctoral dissertation, University of Texas at Austin.

Meyrowitz, J. (1985) *No sense of place: The impact of electronic media on social behavior.* New York: Oxford University Press.

Mills, P. M., & Margulies, N. (1980) Toward a core typology of service organizations. *Academy of Management Review, 5,* 255–265.

Mobil Corp. want fair publicity. (1979, October 21) *New Orleans Times-Picayune,* p. 30, col. 1.

Nadel, M. V. (1976) *Corporations and political accountability.* Lexington, MA: D. C. Heath.

Paonessa, K. A. (1983) *Corporate advocacy and organizational member identification: A case study of General Motors.* Unpublished master's thesis, Purdue University, West Lafayette, IN.

Perrow, C. (1984) *Normal accidents: Living with high risk technologies.* New York: Basic.

Rabinow, P. (1986) Representations are social facts: Modernity and post-modernity in anthropology. In J. Clifford & G. E. Marcus (Eds.), *Writing culture: The poetics and politics of ethnography* (pp. 234–261). Berkeley: University of California Press.

Rorty, R. (1979) *Philosophy and the mirror of nature.* Princeton, NJ: Princeton University Press.

Rorty, R. (1982) *Consequences of pragmatism.* Minneapolis: University of Minnesota Press.

Schiller, H. I. (1981) *Who knows: Information in the age of the Fortune 500.* Norwood, NJ: Ablex.

Scott, W. G., & Hart, D. K. (1979) *Organizational America.* Boston: Houghton Mifflin.

Sennett, R. L. (1980) *Authority.* New York: Random House.

Sethi, S. P. (1977) *Advocacy advertising and large corporations.* Lexington, MA: D. C. Heath.

Simon, H. A. (1976) *Administrative behavior* (3rd ed.). New York: The Free Press.

Smircich, L., & Morgan, G. (1982) Leadership: The management of meaning. *Journal of Applied Behavioral Science, 18,* 257–73.

Tedlow, R. S. (1979) *Keeping the corporate image: Public relations and business, 1900–1950.* Greenwich, CT: JAI Press.

Tompkins, E. V. B., Tompkins, P. K., & Cheney, G. (in press) Organizations, texts, arguments and premises. In W. T. Page (Ed.), special issue of *Journal of Management Systems.*

Tompkins, P. K. (1987) Translating organizational theory: Symbolism over substance. In F. M. Jablin, L. L. Putnam, K. H. Roberts, & L. W. Porter (Eds.), *Handbook of organizational communication* (pp. 70–96). Newbury Park, CA: Sage.

Tompkins, P. K., & Cheney, G. (1983) Account analysis of organizations: Decision making and identification. In L. L. Putnam & M. E. Pacanowsky (Eds.), *Communication and organizations: An interpretive approach* (pp. 123–146). Newbury Park, CA: Sage.

Tompkins, P. K., & Cheney, G. (1985) Communication and unobtrusive control in contemporary organizations. In R. D. McPhee & P. K. Tompkins (Eds.), *Organizational communication: Traditional themes and new directions* (pp. 179–210. Newbury Park, CA: Sage.

Weber, M. (1978) *Economy and society* (2 vols. G. Roth and C. Wittich, Trans. and Eds.). Berkeley: University of California Press.

Weick, K. E. (1979) *The social psychology of organizing* (2nd ed.). Reading, MA: Addison-Wesley.

Whyte, W. H., Jr. (1956) *The organization man.* New York: Simon & Schuster.

SUGGESTED READINGS

Barnard, C. (1968) *The functions of the executive* (30th anniv. ed.). Cambridge, MA: Harvard University Press. (Originally published, 1938)

Barthes, R. (1981) Theory of the text. In R. Young (Ed.), *Untying the text: A poststructuralist reader* (pp. 31–47). Boston: Routledge & Kegan Paul.

Berger, P. L., & Neuhaus, R. (1977) *To empower people: The role of mediating structures in public policy.* Washington, DC: American Enterprise Institute.

Burke, K. (1969) *A rhetoric of motives.* Berkeley: University of California Press. (Originally published, 1950)

Coleman, J. (1974) *Power and the structure of society.* New York: Norton.

Edwards, R. (1979) *Contested terrain: The transformation of the workplace in the twentieth century.* New York: Basic.

Johnstone, H. W., Jr. (1981) Toward an ethics of rhetoric. *Communication, 6,* 305–314.

Kress, G. (1985) Discourses, texts, readers and the pro-nuclear arguments. In P. Chilton (Ed.), *Language and the nuclear arms debate: Nukespeak today.* London: Francis Pinter.

Rorty, R. (1982) *Consequences of pragmatism.* Minneapolis: University of Minnesota Press.

Weick, K. E. (1979) *The social psychology of organizing* (2nd ed.). Reading, MA: Addison-Wesley.

9

The Emerging Theoretical Perspective in PR: An Opportunity for Communication Departments

Bonita Dostal Neff
Public Communication Associates

ABSTRACT

Public relations offerings in 240 communication departments, of which 21 are graduate programs, suggests that a shift away from journalism is quietly taking place in response to increasing complexity in both the practice and teaching of public relations. This academic redirection suggests that public relations theory may be developing a communication orientation based on the social sciences.

The academic foundation of public relations is rapidly switching from departments of journalism into departments of communication. There are two sources for this change. First, the nature and level of complexity of the practice of public relations is evolving from a simplistic orientation stressing the production of publicity into a more sophisticated processural orientation that emphasizes the role of communication in allowing organizations and publics to interact. Second, the development and expansion of public relations programs in academic communication departments indicate the appropriateness of these departments as sites for developing public relations theory and research. This chapter examines these two trends and discusses some implications for public relations theory development.

STATUS OF PUBLIC RELATIONS:
GROWING DEMANDS ON THE PROFESSION

Sloane (1987) described the conflicts that have arisen in society as a result of the "transformation of an industrially based society to a knowledge or information-based society" (p. 5). During this transformation conflict, risk, and uncertainty are high. Sloan (1987) said that for greater success the public relations professional "will have to excel at explaining, ameliorating, guiding and educating—practices that stand in stark contrast to obfuscating, stonewalling, manipulating and disinforming" (p. 9).

The heightened crises and complexities of public relations functions have resulted in a more complex and specialized role for public relations. Possibly as a result of this role change in public relations, and other changes in the economy, many in-house public relations staff members have been leaving large organizations to join public relations agencies, around 143,000 in 1985 (Kleinman, 1987).

Technology, meanwhile, has impacted heavily on public relations. For example, word processing, satellite transmission, computer graphics, on-line data processing, and teleconferencing contribute additional dimensions to the communication process. Although computers assist communication interaction, a new orientation is required to give public relations professionals insight into the potential contributions of this "electronic renaissance to public relations" (Williams, 1983 p. 245).

At a much broader level, Cantor (1985) described the impact of technology on public relations when he suggested that the various communication mediums are capable of carrying out company objectives, supporting basic values, and planning public relations change. He summarized that "this is public relation's turf" (p. 391). Furthermore, the professional will have to learn this technology, apply this technology, and have an understanding of the potential of these tools to become effective participants in the decision-making process of international organizations.

A professional response to the growth and increased responsibilities of public relations comes from both those working in the field and academia (Seitel, 1987). A survey of professionals in the Public Relations Society of America (PRSA), the Association for Education in Journalism and Mass Communication (AEJMC), the International Communication Association's PR Interest Group (ICA), the International Association of Business Communicator's Educators Academy (IABC), and the Speech Communication Association's PR Commission (SCA) (Hamilton 1986), also indicated such a response.

In summary, the field of public relations has a more international focus, technology has opened up new communication possibilities, and the professional is increasingly involved in major conflicts. These advancements and transformations in public relations are at least partly due to societal forces and technological developments. The increased responsibilities and greater accountability for public relations actions have caused an intense study of curriculum, theory, and professional standards by professional organizations.

Theory Development From a Public Relations Perspective

Theory development in public relations is at a nascent stage. Introductory texts often relegate theory to a way of viewing management such as Theory X or Theory Y or mention Hollander's social exchange theory, which brings in situational variables (Crable and Vibbert, 1986). Other theories, such as the system concept of management, are borrowed from organizational theory and provide constructs useful for viewing the variety of public relations roles found in organizational settings (Grunig & Grunig, 1986). Persuasion theory, the more traditional view from communication, is often held as being the prime technique for implementing public relations efforts. But Grunig & Hunt (1984) suggest in their text, *Managing Public Relations,* that it took many years for a concept of public relations as something other than persuasion to develop.

A more graphic explanation of these roots in literature is available from a historical perspective. The early beginnings of public relations as communication originate from Aristotle, whose 4th-century B.C. work, *Rhetoric,* first formalized the art of speaking. Aristotle dealt extensively with persuasive speaking, a cornerstone of communication up to the 20th century. Crable and Vibbert (1986) argue public relations development in terms of the role of the sophists, the hired arguers in ancient Greece. Public relations managers, like sophists, are considered to be "researching their topics, observing meaningful connections through analysis, and communicating their findings in interesting and useful ways" (Crable & Vibbert, 1986, p. 101).

MODELS USED IN PR: A CLUE TO THE MISSING THEORETICAL PERSPECTIVE IN PUBLIC RELATIONS

A number of useful models are provided in public relations. For example, Crable and Vibbert's (1986) Task Levels, Nager and Allen's (1984) Management by Objectives (MBO), and Grunig and Hunt's (1984) abstractions of the major stages of public relations development models provide clarification of public relations practices and serve as the basis of useful classification systems. The aforementioned models are reviewed to identify clues to missing theoretical perspectives. The analysis is based on the degree to which these approaches meet the level of responsibilities demanded by the profession today.

Task Levels

Crable and Vibbert's (1986) three levels of public relations development established a very useful approach to developing a public relations program. Their categories of performance, analysis, and identification are distinct levels tied closely to human development. Each of these stages serve as a classification system and strongly characterizes activities for ease of program development. One can develop an effective intern placement program, for example, around these skill levels. Additionally, the levels provide a set of standards by which progress is measured.

Essentially, the category system of task levels is a descriptive approach to viewing public relations activity in terms of complexity of task. Whereas useful as a guideline for task development, the means for accomplishing this task are left largely hidden. The transformation process in moving a human being to a higher task level is assumed to be in the domain of tasks. This view of public relations as *task* oriented is not extensively supported by the scenario of public relations practices. For example, the developments in technology are greatly expanding the boundary-spanning capacities of public relations. Boundary spanning occurs at a time when agencies report an increased interest in learning more about interpersonal communication. The management concept of public relations, however, must as Neff (1985) noted, "develop beyond a public relations expert skilled at 'handling' information" to a more expanded role in communication viewing public relations, for example, as networking, including policymaking (pp. 8-10).

Management by Objective

The management by objective (MBO) presentation by Nager and Allen (1984) is a rationalistic model that provides very succinct distinctions for a goal-oriented approach. The goal-orientation concept is easily grasped, and the graphic, step-by-step procedures are much appreciated by students who desire concreteness. Focusing on goal orientation imposes, unfortunately, a rigid grid on the communication process. A skill that may be easy to learn but not necessarily an effective way to work in terms of social interaction. Public relations has evolved into long-range planning. Those in the discipline must be aware of the limitations, or the effect, of the management-by-objectives perspective on the communication process.

Types of Public Relations

Another approach to models comes from Grunig and Hunt's (1984) abstraction of the public relations field's activity from its early beginnings. Their four models trace the development of public relations and provide a very useful distinction between public relations functions, qualifying those that are more research-based. The propaganda technique, for example, was first used as a model for public relations and marks the early years of public relations. The public information type was developed to bring more objectivity to the public relations role and thus enable organizations, like government offices, to have a public relations function. The most popular approach adapted to public relations is more commonly referred to as persuasion, and it reflects the primary contribution of the communication discipline to public relations. The most recent contribution to the literature has been the type of public relations emphasizing two-way symmetrical communication (The goal here being not persuasion but a balanced exchange among people with the outcome being understanding.) Although persuasion functions are clearly established in the public relations field, the two-way symmetrical model of understanding needs further elaboration.

Understanding

The concept of understanding stems from a journalistic goal tied closely to objectivity and ethics. Understanding is sought in quality journalism. A skillful reporter's objectivity is assisted by not resorting to fiction or opinion but presenting the facts with supplemental information or helpful contexts. Reporters, then, are expanding their repertoire to include first, news; second, interpretation; and third, opinion. This expansion of journalism, to include interpretive reporting, is viewed as important but, as Hulteng and Nelson (1983) note, "it must be with the ethic of objectivity, not a substitute for it" (pp. 30–37). Understanding in journalism is strongly developed in the descriptive domain and is grounded in the rationalistic tradition of communication. Reporting is operating in the realm of the known or what can be known.

Imposing journalistic assumptions into interpersonal communication is problematic. The reporting mode is a carefully constructed ethic, an agreed upon behavior subscribed to by professionals. The adaptation of understanding to areas outside of a journalistic application and to situations where a rule or formalized ethic is not established is difficult. In addition, sharing a role with those not subscribing to professional expectations is a tremendous obstacle. Yet the role of understanding outside of journalism has evolved.

Conflict resolution professionals implement a model of understanding under carefully prescribed practical settings. Practitioners (court negotiators, labor arbitrators, community conflict resolutions leaders) in the field espouse the role of understanding in conflict resolution. Here the distinction between persuasion and understanding is stated very clearly. Experienced negotiators and arbitrators have emphatically stated that their role cannot involve persuasion. This recognition by expert arbitrators, including the trainers of arbitrators for the Better Business Bureau, strongly suggests that understanding stands alone as a valuable communication process.

Obviously the essence of public relations, as now practiced, would be vastly different if grounded in the understanding model. Grunig and Hunt (1984) recognize the need for a theoretical framework to solve problems in public relations. Should a similar role for the public relations practitioner be developed or is this best left to the judges, negotiators, and arbitrators? Could public relations develop a similar technical service for PR-related matters? The idea is worth exploring in a volatile world, where bombs can be dropped because a message was not decoded properly and no channel for correcting this impression was possible. The current conflict resolution settings are weighted down by protocol. The importance of having someone in place awaiting such communication breakdowns is obvious. Equally important would be for the trained person to know the limitations of the understanding approach.

The limitations on developing an understanding model in public relations are obvious. Having a highly controlled situation is possible, but certainly not probable in many public relations situations, particularly in international relations. What does one do when understanding fails to bring about desired results? Within the basic set of assumptions available to most people in public relations the response might be: "To explain is not enough; you must persuade" (Executive Strategies, 1987).

Thus, in examining the models operating in public relations, one focuses on the assumptions that are directing the developments in the discipline. One needs to ask if what exists now is enough to meet the demands of the public relations profession, both academically and professionally. As the previous discussion illustrated, current assumptions are in some instances limiting our possibilities, in other instances assumptions are relatively undeveloped, and in some cases assumptions totally blind us to the nature of the communication process.

A Proposal for Developing Public Relations Metatheory

Proposed here are a set of assumptions that characterize the communication process in public relations. These assumptions reflect the premises integral to the public relations environment.

1. Public relations is a discipline closely tied to the applied orientation. Being an action-oriented profession suggests that theories in the descriptive domain would not be the major contributors to public relations. As practiced, public relations is not bound by the assumptions found in the goal of understanding as developed in journalism.

2. Public relations is necessarily based in social interaction and thus intricately tied to the communication process. Public relations is increasingly a boundary-spanning activity, and technology only increases the potential for interaction. The increased opportunities for languaging for action inherent in social interaction increases the responsibilities and potential effect of the public relations role.

3. Public relations, based in the communication process and developed through social interaction, is a process that is not rationalistic. Professionals must be trained to see that people live in their interpretation of experiences and actions (Burke, 1985). Public relations training must illustrate how language structures one's existence and how the languaging, as Flores (1982) wrote, is not a mere "transmission or processing of information" (p. 1).

STATUS OF PUBLIC RELATIONS:
CHANGE IN LOCATION

Although changes in practice are highly visible, less visible but equally important changes are occurring at universities.

Walker's Study

Nearly 7 years have passed since Walker's study on "Status and Trends in Public Relations Education 1981" clearly demonstrated the growth of public relations programs in communication departments ("Public Relation Education," 1982). Walker surveyed colleges and universities in 1981 with a 51.5% response (256 respondents). The results indicated for the first time the movement away from journalism's dominance. Journalism accounted for fewer than half the programs. Another study noted a tendency toward an increased mix of disciplines in a public relations program. The movement toward interdisciplinary programs (business and management as well as advertising) suggested an interest in a more varied background other than journalism ("Public Relation Education," 1982).

Survey

In an effort to find out whether public relations has moved toward communication departments in the United States, over 3,201 higher education catalogs were surveyed (Neff, 1987). The perusal of the catalogs yielded 578 undergraduates and 48 graduate departments offering public relations courses—twice as many universities and colleges offering public relations as found in the 7-year-old Walker study.

The review of college catalogs revealed the direction of the public relations curriculum. Course offerings specifically identifying *public relations* in the title or course description were included. Only the internship course (including laboratory, field, workshop, practicum designations) was counted as a public relations course if the term public relations did not appear in the title.

The results substantiated Walker's findings and indicated that the trend away from journalism was greater than suspected. In addition to journalism, a variety of departments offered public relations courses including: communication(s), business, mass communication(s), interdisciplinary programs with communication and/or journalism combined with other disciplines, public relations, and a small group of departments labelled miscellaneous.

The predominance of communication departments offering public relations suggests the initial trend identified by Walker is accelerating. In fact, there are more communication departments teaching public relations than the total for journalism and mass communication combined. (In spite of the fact that these latter departments are governed by the PRSA-AEJMC Accreditation System.) Figure 9.1 identifies the departmental offerings for undergraduate public relations programs.

The predominance of communication(s) departments teaching public relations may bring into question some of the assumptions in the 1987 *Design for Undergraduate Public Relations Education.* The Commission's statement indicating "the reality is that most public relations programs are associated with schools or departments of journalism or mass communications" is not supported ("Design" p. 3).

The departments offering public relations courses, as defined here, are listed in Table 9.1.

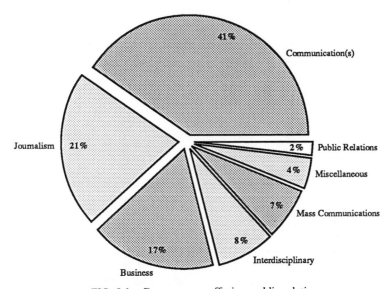

FIG. 9.1.   Departments offering public relations.

TABLE 9.1
Departments Offering PR Courses

Communication(s)—240 Departments Total

Broadcast Communications (1 department)
Communication (51 departments)
Communication and Creative Arts (1 department)
Communication/Fine Arts (1 department)
Communication and Media Studies (1 department)
Communication and Theatre (1 department)
Communication and Theatre Arts (4 departments)
Communication Arts (39 departments)
Communication Arts and Sciences (3 departments)
Communication Processes (1 department)
Communication Studies (7 departments)

Communications (75 departments)
Communications and Broadcasting (1 department)
Communications and Media Arts (2 departments)
Communications and Speech (1 department)
Communications and Theatre (3 departments)
Communications Media (2 departments)

Communicative Arts (2 departments)
English and Communication(s) (3 departments)

(Continued)

TABLE 9.1
(*continued*)

Communication(s)—240 Departments

English and Speech Theatre (1 department)
Media and Communications (1 department)
Public Communication (1 department)
Radio, Television, Film (1 department)
Speech (8 departments)
Speech and Theatre (1 department)
Speech Communication (15 departments)
Speech Communications (3 departments)
Speech Communication(s) and Theatre (Arts) (5 departments)
Speech and Theatre (1 department)
Speech and Drama (2 departments)
Speech, Drama, Communication (1 department)
Theatre Arts and Communication (1 department)

Journalism Departments—123 Departments Total

Journalism (124 departments)

Business—100 Departments Total

Administration and Management (1 department)
Banking (1 department)
Banking and Finance (3 departments)
Business (18 departments)
Business Administration (20 departments)
Business Administration and Economics (1 department)
Business and Commerce (1 department)
Business and Economics (1 department)
Business and Social Sciences (1 department)
Business Management (5 departments)
Business Management/Administration (1 department)
Business/Marketing (1 department)
Business Studies (1 department)
Business Technology (2 departments)
Fashion Merchandising (1 department)
General Business (1 department)
Management (13 departments)
Mangement and Commerce (1 department)
Mangement and Finance (1 department)
Managment and Marketing (1 department)
Management and Supervision Technology (1 department)
Marketing (18 departments)
Marketing and Advertising (1 department)
Marketing and Management (1 department)

TABLE 9.1
(*continued*)

Marketing and Retailing (2 departments)
Marketing and Sales (1 department)
Marketing and Sales Distribution (1 department)

Interdisciplinary—45 Departments Total

Communication(s)/Journalism (1 program)
Communication Arts/Business Administration (1 program)
English/Communication Arts (1 program)
English/Communications (2 programs)
English/Journalism (1 program)
Humanities/Communication (2 programs)
Journalism/Broadcasting (1 program)
Journalism/Communications (1 program)
Journalism/Mass Communication(s) (14 programs)
Journalism/Photography (1 program)
Journalism and Public Communication (1 program)
Journalism/Public Relations (1 program)
Journalism/Radio-TV (4 programs)
Journalism/Telecommunication(s) (3 programs)
Law/Journalism/Management (1 program)
Marketing/Communications (1 program)
Mass Communication/Journalism (1 program)
Mass Communications, Sp Communication, Theatre Arts(1)
Mass Media/Marketing and Management (1 program)
Mass Media and Performing Arts (1 program)
Media and Communication Studies (1 program)
Speech and Mass Communication (1 program)
Speech Communication/Theatre/Journalism (1 program)
Speech/Theatre/Humanities (1 program)
Speech Communication, Mass Communication, and Marketing
  (1 program)

Mass Communication(s)—39 Departments Total

Mass Communication (15 departments)
Mass Communications (21 departments)

Media Arts (2 departments)
Media Studies (1 department)

Miscellaneous—23 Departments Total

English (15 departments)

(*Continued*)

TABLE 9.1
(*continued*)

English, Classics, Philosophy (1 department)
English/Language (1 department)
English/Linguistics (1 department)
Humanities and Social Sciences (1 department)
Language and Literature (2 departments)
Transfer Division (1 department)
Written Communications (1 department)

Public Relations—13 Departments/Programs Total

Advertising and Public Relations (1 department)
No Department (2 programs)
Public Relations (9 departments)
Written Communications (1 department)

Graduate programs are critical aspects to the development of theory in public relations. Presently the potential for theory development in public relations is supported by a significant degree of graduate activity. Graduate programs in public relations are listed in Table 9.2.

Communication departments led, again, in offering public relations programs. Twenty-one departments of communication, in contrast to 12 journalism and 6 mass communications departments, offer graduate public relations courses.

An Opportunity for Communication Departments

The future for public relations theory is clearly in the field of communication for two reasons. First, scholars have identified communication as a site for public relations theory research by the focus of present theory and public relations models, both of which emphasize two-way balanced interaction processes between groups. Second, the predominance of communication has been established by the reality of the number of communication departments offering public relations courses and programs. It should also be noted that departments in fields such as business, although mentioned frequently, usually offer a *single* public relations course focused on some aspect of public relations (banking, fashion, etc.).

Communication departments may therefore be emerging as bodies

TABLE 9.2
Graduate Programs in PR

Graduate Programs in PR—48 Departments
Advertising (1 department)
Broadcast Communications (1 department)
Communication (4 departments)
Communication and Theatre (1 department)
Communication Arts (2 departments)
Communication Education (1 department)
Communication Studies (1 department)
Communications (7 departments)
Journalism (12 departments)
Journalism/Mass Communication (5 departments)
Mass Communications (6 departments)
Nonprofit Management (1 department)
Public Relations (2 departments)
Speech and Mass Communication (1 department)
Speech and Theatre (1 department)
Speech Communications (1 department)
Speech Communication, Theatre/Journalism (1 program)

uniquely qualified to help develop a new body of theory, and resulting practices, for public relations. If a positive and clear identity is developed for public relations, a thrust that both the public and professionals can rally around, the trust and credibility developed will redirect public relations toward becoming a desirable profession (Center, 1987). The public relations professional should have a primary role in the complex social events of our world (Steward, 1987).

REFERENCES

Burke, J. (1985) *The day the universe changed.* Boston: Little, Brown.
Cantor, B. (1985, February) Forecast '85 the year in public relations. *Public Relations Journal,* 22–25.
Center, A. H. (1987, Spring) Is our profession ready to conquer the new challenges? *Public Relations Review,* 10–12.
Joint Commission of the Public Relations Society of America and Association for Education in Journalism and Mass Communication (1987) *Design for undergraduate public relations education.* Chicago: Author.
Crable, R. E., & Vibbert, S. L. (1986) *Public relations as communication management.* Edina, MN.: Bellweather Press.
Executive Strategies: Business Personal. (1987, August). Cover letter. New York: National Institute of Business Management.

Flores, C. F. (1982) *Management and communication in the office of the future* (Dissertation). San Francisco: Hermenet Inc.

Grunig, J. E., & Grunig, L. S. (1986, May) *Application of open systems theory to public relations: Review of a program of research.* Paper presented to the International Communication Association, Chicago.

Grunig, J. E., & Hunt, T. (1984) *Managing public relations.* New York: Holt, Rinehart & Winston.

Hamilton, P. (1986, April) *Communication competence and public relations research.* Paper presented to the Central States Speech Association, Cincinnati, OH.

Hulteng, J. L., & Nelson, R. P. (1983) *The fourth estate: An informal appraisal of the news and opinion media.* New York: Harper & Row.

Kleinmen, C. (1987, February 22) Agencies are landing the leading roles in public relations. *Chicago Tribune,* sec. 8, p. 1.

Nager, N. R., & Allen, T. H. (1984) *Public relations management by objective.* New York: Longman.

Neff, B. D. (1985, May). *State of the art in public relations: An international perspective.* Paper presented to the International Communication Association, San Francisco, CA.

Neff, B. D. (1986, April) *Communication competence in the agency/organization relationship.* Paper presented to the Central States Speech Association, Cincinnati, OH.

Neff, B. D. (1987, April) *Trends impacting the public relations profession: New challenges for educators.* Paper presented to the Southern States Speech Association and Central States Speech Association, St. Louis, MO.

Public Relations Education: Two surveys (1982, February) *Public Relations Journal, 38*(2), 19, 33.

Seitel, F. P. (1987) *The practice of public relations.* Columbus, OH: Merrill Publishing.

Sloan, C. S. (1987) Foundation lecture: Social, economic and political contexts for PR. *Public Relations Review, 13*(1), 3–10.

Steward, H. D. (1987) Is public relations the art of deception for fun and profit? *Public Relations Quarterly,* Spring.

Williams, F. (1983) *The communications revolution.* New York: New American Library.

Game Theory as a Paradigm
for the Public Relations Process

Priscilla Murphy
Drexel University

ABSTRACT

This chapter proposes the theory of games as a model for public relations decision-making, particularly where a compromise must be negotiated between the practitioner and one or more publics. The models and methods of game theory are shown to be useful in testing assumptions, establishing norms, and analyzing outcomes for typical public relations situations involving disclosure of information. News-statement timing is analyzed in terms of a noncooperative zero-sum game, the duel; the process of releasing or withholding information from a reporter is modeled as a non-zero-sum game. The chapter suggests some additional ways to apply game theory models to theoretical areas, practice, empirical research, and teaching.

Most scholars of public relations agree that lack of a theoretical base is a central problem in public relations research today. The problem is especially acute because of the historical conflict between the approaches of theorists, who are usually academics, and practitioners, who generally shun theory for situation-specific "how-to" approaches. In fact, as David Dozier (1984) has pointed out, most practitioners tend to negotiate relationships with their constituencies through a combination of experience, instinct, and interpersonal skills—what Dozier called the "seat-of-the-pants" approach.

Practitioners have traditionally defended these intangible qualities of their craft, resisting attempts to categorize or quantify their decision-making. Still, in recent years scholars of public relations have found ways to systematically predict and measure factors that influence public relations behavior in negotiating situations. The general systems theory advanced by James Grunig (1975a, 1975b, 1976, 1977) has been especially influential here as it formally categorizes, predicts, and measures the outcome of public relations decision-making as a response to environmental pressures.

In disciplines outside of communication—notably in the decision sciences—quantitative measures have also been used to analyze negotiating strategies and determine which of many possible outcomes will satisfy the needs of all the involved parties. Given the substantial body of research and applications provided by decision theory, there is good reason to think that this discipline may prove useful for public relations decision-making as well.

William P. Ehling's decision theory model (1975, 1984, 1985) lays the theoretical groundwork for this. Viewing public relations as a mediating activity that manages conflict between organized groups, Ehling pointed out that in order to resolve a conflict, an individual has to identify a number of possible choices, rate their usefulness and efficiency in achieving a desired outcome, and select the optimal choice accordingly: "this, in turn, means that there is a norm for choice-making. Such a norm specifies what choices the individual *ought* to make under specified conditions" (1975, p. 20).

Furthermore, Ehling (1984) asserted that conceptual tools to define these norms and provide guidelines for making the optimal choice are provided by decision theory. The decision theory paradigm allows mathematical analysis of a situation that involves choice. This in turn opens the way to apply such concepts as probability, utility, and efficiency to public relations strategies. Decision theory thus makes it possible to measure and test what the practitioner calls instinct, experience, craftsmanship, or seat-of-the-pants choices within a scientific, quantitative, objectively developed framework.

Nonetheless, it is useful to make a distinction between Ehling's *decision theory* model and a *game theory* model, which is the subject of this chapter. Strictly speaking, decision theory involves choosing a strategy in isolation, without considering the possible strategies of others.[1] In contrast, game theory uses a different body of analytical techniques that views one

---

[1]Decision theory essentially involves a game against Nature. Unlike the sentient other players in game theory, Nature's strategy is unaffected by the human player's proposed strategy, and the human in turn gives no thought to Nature's alternatives. Clearly this is not as realistic a model as that proposed by the theory of games. For more on decision theory, see Raiffa (1968).

"player's" decision-making as a strategy designed to cope with the diverse strategies of other players. Game theory thereby more closely models the realities of public relations situations in which the practitioner frames strategy *relative to the desires of various publics*.

Based on this key concept, this chapter applies game theory as a paradigm for the public relations process, particularly in situations that require negotiation. In addition to using game theory to model an overall public relations conflict–resolution process, this chapter suggests specific applications in which game theory can be used to analyze a particular negotiation session and select a preferred outcome.

GAME THEORY: AN OVERVIEW

Game theory is a relatively new discipline. Its foundations were laid in 1928 with the publication of John von Neumann's "minimax theorem." In 1944, von Neumann and Oskar Morgenstern published the landmark *Theory of Games and Economic Behavior* in which, Davis (1983) suggested, "it was shown that social events can best be described by models taken from suitable games of strategy. These games in turn are amenable to thorough mathematical analysis" (p. x).

Beginning in the 1950s, hundreds of articles began to appear on game theoretical approaches to social science problems.[2] Sociologists have applied game theoretical techniques to the study of bargaining, negotiation, and social interaction and conflict. Anthropologists have used game theory to model gift-giving, potlatches, and the influence of social norms. Psychologists have developed games to study cooperation, and psychiatrists have used aspects of game theory as models to study addiction and stress. Game theory has proved particularly useful in economics and political science, where it has been used to analyze voting, diplomacy, coalition formation, and power structures. Similar studies have been used in business situations to analyze labor relations, mergers, and cartels, to determine pricing structures and to resolve quality-control problems. Game theory has even been applied to the physical sciences, particularly to the study of evolution. In communication, however, game theory has scarcely been utilized.[3] Indeed, communication scholars have

---

[2]For a summary of social science applications of game theory, see Shubik (1982), chapter 12.

[3]Game theory has also been neglected for historical reasons. Early on it was heralded as a panacea for all sorts of social science problems. Unrealistic expectations were succeeded by disillusionment and rejection in the 1950s and 1960s: "initially there was a naive bandwagon feeling that game theory solved innumerable problems of sociology and economics. . . . This has not turned out to be the case" (see Luce & Raiffa, 1957, p. 10; see also

tended to ignore the theory and have focused instead on gaming exercises in which negotiation patterns are studied through lab simulation—a related but very different field.

Lucas (1972) proposed the following definitions and basic concepts, which will help to establish the usefulness of game theory as a model for the public relations process:

> Game theory is a collection of mathematical models formulated to study decision making in situations involving conflict and cooperation. It recognizes that conflict arises naturally when various participants have different preferences and that such problems can be studied quantitatively rather than as a mere illness or abnormality which should be cured or rectified. Game theory attempts to abstract those elements which are common and essential to many different competitive situations and to study them by means of the scientific method. It is concerned with finding optimal solutions or stable outcomes when various decision makers have conflicting objectives in mind. In brief, a game consists of players who must choose from a list of alternatives which will then bring about expected outcomes over which the participants may have different preferences. The game model describes in detail the potential payoffs which one expects to occur, and it points out how one should act in order to arrive at the best possible outcome in light of the options open to one's opponents. Game theory attempts to provide a normative guide to rational behavior for a group whose members aim for different goals. (p. 19)

Even on the basis of this broad definition, the application of game theory to public relations practice is intuitively clear. First, game theory posits that there are two or more "players." For our purposes, one player is a public relations practitioner and the other is a public, either inside or outside the organization. An opposing player may be one person (e.g., an individual reporter) or many people playing as a unit (e.g., a competing company, a certain group of employees, a citizens' lobby).

Among this group of players, each has certain preferences and dislikes; each has to select "plays" or strategies for reaching a preferred outcome. Each has to gauge how to juggle preferences to achieve the best outcome in relation to the other players—whose strategies may not even be known. To take an example of a simple public relations "game," a company may need to decide exactly when to distribute a news release about its quarterly earnings. In order to get maximum publicity, the

---

Heckathorn, 1986, pp. 206–208). Mathematicians have since developed newly sensitive models that can better handle social science problems. A new wave of publications in the 1980s (e.g., Colman, 1982, Davis, 1983, Raiffa, 1982, and Shubik, 1982) suggests that it is time to reconsider game theory's relevance to the social sciences.

company wants to publish earnings before its chief competitor does; otherwise, it may receive less attention in shared coverage. In game theory terms, this is a classic "duel" situation in which the opponent's strategy is not known. Most practitioners would solve this game by instinct and historical experience. But game theoretical guidelines can suggest which strategy will lead to the best outcome for this dilemma. The next section works through a similar timing "duel" in some detail.

Each outcome for a game is associated with a given payoff, which is designated quantitatively. Sometimes such numerical denotation is easy because the payoff consists of a financial reward—a desired wage level in labor negotiations, a target price for purchasing a commodity. But often a payoff consists of nonmonetary gain: In public relations terms, a payoff could be a favorable news story, access to a target audience, or a negative event that was averted. For such nonmonetary payoffs, game theory does allow players to rank the value of outcomes quantitatively, as we see when we work out applications later.

Overall, the theory of games neatly describes the public relations practitioner's central activity: coping with situations in which the goals and strategies of others—internal and external publics—must somehow be orchestrated with one's own organization's goals and strategies. Thus, the practitioner must not only be able to deduce the strategy of others, but must also have a lucid, systematic way to reach a compromise so that everyone's claims are taken into account. Defining and ranking goals, and developing an optimal strategy, are the essence of game theory.

Game theorists partition games into two broad categories.

Zero-Sum Games.   Simply put, these are games in which the better one player does, the worse the other fares. Player A's win means Player B's loss. Games of survival and ruin are zero-sum. Monopoly is a zero-sum game; so is poker.[4]

At first glance, many public relations situations may appear to be zero-sum. For example, a reporter may obtain some information that would considerably damage a company's reputation if revealed—but publishing it would enhance the reporter's reputation equivalently. Company A's loss is Reporter B's gain. In specific terms, the *New York Times'* publication of the Pentagon Papers might be construed as a zero-sum game.

In fact, the zero-sum approach has real pitfalls. Often what appears on the surface to be a zero-sum game of pure opposition may actually cloak opportunities for cooperation between the parties so that *both* can

---

[4]Zero-sum games are so termed because the sum of the players' payoffs always equals zero: for example, if Player A wins 10 points, Player B loses 10 points (10 − 10 = 0).

benefit—or at least, one will not lose as badly. As we see in the next section, public relations people are well advised not to view situations as zero-sum games, lest they forfeit opportunities to salvage a difficult situation through cooperation. "Stonewalling" is a typical zero-sum public relations game that seldom works out well. The public outcry that followed the 5-hour news blackout after the Challenger explosion of January 1986, for instance, exemplifies the dangers of handling media relations as a zero-sum stalling game. Indeed, one of a public relations practitioner's most useful functions may be to turn apparent zero-sum games into cooperative ventures.

This concept of mutual gain leads to the second major category of games—one that is far more common in public relations.

Non-Zero-Sum Games.   These are games in which opportunities exist for all the players to make the most of the situation by negotiating skillfully so that no one loses and everyone gains an acceptable payoff. Non-zero-sum games are, of course, the essence of public relations practice. They are what seat-of-the-pants practitioners refer to when they talk about experience, craft, and intuition, rather than scientific method, as the tools of their trade.

In fact, game theory can often improve upon experience, craft, and intuition. These intangibles are built into the mathematical tools of game theory and are expressed through its formal procedures. They allow us to analyze a past situation in which a seat-of-the-pants choice led to a given outcome and can show *how* the choice made that outcome inevitable. Often the same analytical tools will also show that a different strategy would have resulted in a better outcome than that prescribed by gut feelings. Or, if a practitioner is in the midst of a current dilemma, analysis through game theory can show him or her what choice to make with the highest probability of an acceptable outcome. In some cases, game theory may show that no outcome can satisfy all the players, and it may therefore help explain why stalemates and public relations "failures" occur despite massive, well-intentioned communication efforts.

In non-zero-sum games, cooperation between players is key because the issue is not "winning" or "losing" per se, but rather negotiating an outcome that will maximally benefit all players. Indeed, a player may actually choose to cede "points" early on to maximize his or her own payoff later. Non-zero-sum games thus build in strong incentives for cooperation. Just as the Pentagon Papers episode is a typical instance of a zero-sum public relations game, Johnson & Johnson's efforts to keep the media informed during the 1982 Tylenol crisis is a typical instance of a non-zero-sum PR game in which cooperation increased payoffs for everyone.

However, such games are not always played cooperatively. For a variety of reasons (such as lack of skill, lack of understanding, or perhaps a rigid management that ties one's hands) a player may not be able to behave cooperatively. In that case, the benefits that accrue from cooperative play will not be fully realized, and all players may suffer.

In fact, playing a noncooperative version of a non-zero-sum game is a frequent experience for many public relations practitioners and helps shed light on the frustration and burnout endemic in the field. In media relations, noncooperative games are legion because corporate players often mistrust the motives of media players. For instance, a reporter may request an interview with a key member of management with potential for a positive story; the risk-averse executive may direct the public relations person to decline the interview; a story opportunity is lost and the public relations person loses face. In other cases, the corporate player may cooperate and the media player may not. We view such games nearly weekly on TV newsmagazine shows. To take a glaring example, the notorious "*60 Minutes*" coverage of Illinois Power's nuclear plant involved a non-zero-sum game in which the corporate player followed a cooperative strategy, and the media player pursued a bad-faith strategy.

Indeed, cooperation in non-zero-sum games is a complicated and highly relativistic concept. Although a non-zero-sum game fosters cooperation, it may in reality be played across a spectrum ranging from complete cooperation to complete noncooperation. For instance, players may conceal information from other players; they may give out misleading information about their goals and motives; they may make *sub rosa* deals with other players—all in the name of maximizing their own gains. Sometimes such strategies work; sometimes they result in unnecessary stalemate or (if exposed) can backfire on the bad-faith player. Frequently they involve questions of ethics.

In any case, the playing of non-zero-sum games is in many respects an apt definition of what it is to practice public relations. Nearly all public relations activities consist of selecting among strategies that involve different degrees of cooperation, different concessions of "points"; most of the time, the practitioner can only guess at the other players' strategies. Here is where practitioners typically call upon instinct, experience, and sometimes luck to see them through.

From the standpoint of game theory, such guesswork is needlessly inefficient—or at least, can be turned into more educated guesswork. In principle, by following game-theoretic guidelines one can not only improve the accuracy of an instinctive response, but also act confidently to ensure that the benefits are maximized and the other players accept the solution.

What are these guidelines and how do they apply?

GAME THEORETIC APPLICATIONS

Thus far we have been concerned with showing how the public relations process fits into a game theory paradigm. As the zero-sum and non-zero-sum models suggest, the analogy between the two disciplines is very close.

However, the game theory paradigm provides much more than an analogy. It provides a model for thinking about problems that can be valuable in collecting information, organizing alternatives, and arriving at a solution. We see this by examining several commonly encountered public relations situations from the standpoint of game theory.

Problems in game theory often deal with the same sorts of variables encountered in public relations situations. Among the commonest in both fields are problems that involve timing and disclosure of information.

Games of Timing. Practitioners frequently must make decisions in which timing plays a critical role. When should the news conference for the new product be scheduled? When should the announcement of the CEO's resignation be released? Should management refrain from answering employees' questions about a rumored layoff until the plan is completed or discuss partial plans now?

Frequently decisions about timing must be made in a state of uncertainty about the other players' moves: one does not know when the competition will issue a release; one does not know when the media will become aware of a problem situation; one does not know what the TV news budget will be on any given day and how that will affect coverage of an event. Faced with such unknowns, practitioners generally turn to instinct and luck to guide decision making—and cross their fingers that they've guessed right.

In all these situations, practitioners are playing a class of games that theorists call *games of timing.* Often such situations can be modelled by a certain subclass of games of timing: the *duel.* By working through a public relations timing dilemma in terms of a duel, we may not be able to assure "winning" every time, but we can optimize our chances of the most favorable timing and the likeliest "hit."

Let us consider the following scenario: the ABC Chemical Company runs a plant in Alphaville that enjoys a good safety record. However, at 6 a.m. one morning the public relations director, Mr. Aye, gets a call about a pipeline break somewhere in the system. Workmen are trying to locate the source of the break, but it will take several hours—maybe much longer—to bring the situation under control. Aye reasons as follows:

- This is an inactive news time: today's morning papers are being distributed; the TV morning news is about to be shown; but radio news coverage and the evening TV news remain worrisome possibilities.

- If the leak is brought under control soon, there will be no impact on the community; there will be no crisis and no news value. But if it lasts until this afternoon, fumes could cause evacuation of homes near the plant.

- The longer Aye waits to issue a statement, the likelier the problem will be resolved. Even if the problem is not resolved soon, he needs to delay in order to assemble adequate information. If he is forced to issue a statement too soon, he (and ABC) will appear misinformed and incompetent.

- If the media hear of the leak through sources other than ABC Company, there will be negative coverage and allegations of a cover-up. And the longer the leak goes uncontrolled, the likelier the media will hear about it.

When should Aye make an announcement to the media—or should he issue a statement at all?

If Aye knew the theory of games, he would model his dilemma as a classic two-person, zero-sum game—a duel in which he is one player and the media are the other player. In this duel, a "hit" for Media is to get a good news story about the crisis. A "hit" for Aye is to have the crisis fully under control before the public hears of it. Aye clearly wins when the pipeline leak is sealed (the crisis is no longer news). But Aye may also win if he can beat Media to the public by announcing that the situation is at least under control. The longer he delays his shot, the likelier the situation will be under control—the surer his chance for a hit, in duel terms. But if he delays too long, he will lose the duel because Media will shoot first by reaching the public with the story.

Game theory has established the minimax principle as a satisfactory solution for this case. That means Aye should pursue whatever strategy minimizes his maximum expected loss by balancing a delayed public statement against the risk of Media reaching the public first. In other words, Aye should quietly sit by, letting the crisis get more under control, until the time when it becomes dangerously likely that Media will raise questions. At that moment, Aye should go for his own "hit" by issuing a statement based on the best knowledge then at hand. That would not be as perfect as waiting until the crisis is resolved—but it would be a lot better than letting Media "shoot" first.

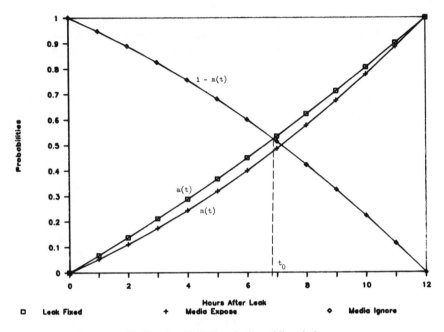

FIG. 10.1.   Timing for ABC Chemical's public relations statement.

This strategy may simply describe what the practitioner would do instinctively, but if Aye were mathematically inclined, he could test out— and probably improve on—instinct by pinpointing the optimum moment to issue a statement. Figure 10.1 shows how he could calculate it.

Let the functions for a public statement or news story ("hit probabilities") be $a(t)$ and $m(t)$, respectively, for Aye and Media. Therefore $1 - m(t)$ is the probability that Media will miss the story altogether. Both $a(t)$ and $m(t)$ functions increase from 0 to 1, where 0 is the time at which the leak occurred and 1 is the time when the pipe is sealed or there is complete information about the leak's consequences.[5] Because both $a(t)$ and $m(t)$ = 0 at time 0, Aye gains no advantage by rushing out with a statement. In fact, as long as $1 - m(t) > a(t)$, then Aye can expect to be

_____

[5]Based on experiential precedent, probabilities were developed by the hour, both for solving the leak and for attracting media attention. The following equations yield a close approximation of these probabilities:

$$a(t) = 1/15x + 1/720x^2$$

$$m(t) = 1/20x + 1/360x^2$$

better off not saying anything. But as soon as $1 - m(t) < a(t)$, Aye would be better off by issuing a public statement. According to the minimax theorem, Aye can hope for no better payoff than

$$1 - m(t), a(t)$$

because the best Aye can do is to minimize his maximum expected loss. This means holding off to issue a statement until $1 - m(t) = a(t) = 1$, which is shown on Fig. 10.1 as time t_0.

In words, as soon as the sum of probabilities for a public relations statement and a news story equals 1, Aye should make a statement. In this case, Aye's best bet is to issue a statement at about 12:45 p.m. This may not be his most preferred timing, but by issuing a statement at time t_0 Aye can assure a probability of beating the media of at least $a(t_0)$ regardless of what the media do. In the less-likely event that Aye falls on the wrong side of the probability and is pre-empted by the media, at least he will have a rational accounting to give his management.

Bargaining Games. In reality, few public relations situations are zero-sum. Most actually work out best if modeled as non-zero-sum games in which there are no clear-cut "winners" and "losers." In these situations, the object of the game is for both players to maximize their own points—and this often means that during the course of play, concessions must be made to improve one's final payoff. The game is thus not a zero-sum duel, but a negotiation in which information becomes a commodity to be traded strategically so that each player can live with the final apportionment. Although this information may be particularly sensitive in a crisis situation,[6] the negotiation model also holds true for day-to-day decisions where the public relations practitioner must trade off the company's needs and desires against those of other stakeholders. As Colman (1982) pointed out, in this respect the theory of games would more accurately be called the "theory of interdependent decisionmaking" (p. 3).

Based on these probability curves, we can compute the optimum time for Aye to issue a statement as follows:

$$\frac{1}{15}x + \frac{1}{720}x^2 = 1 - \frac{1}{20}x - \frac{1}{360}x^2$$

$$\frac{7}{60}x + \frac{3}{720}x^2 = 1\frac{1}{240}x^2 + \frac{7}{60}x - 1 = 0$$

$$t_0 = (-\frac{7}{60} + \sqrt{[\frac{7}{60}]^2 + 4 * \frac{1}{240}} * 1/(2 * \frac{1}{240})$$

$$= 6.878394$$

[6]See earlier version of this chapter, focusing on the application of game theory to crisis communication in *Public Relations Review, 14* (winter 1987), pp. 19–28.

A typical scenario for this type of game is as follows: Mr. Smith is public relations director for the XYZ Company, a large (5,000 employees) corporation in Alphaville, a mid-sized city. The economy has been soft, straining both Alphaville's social services and XYZ's profits. XYZ's senior management has just determined that it will be necessary to cut the company's payroll by about five percent—about 250 employees—during the next six months. However, many decisions still have not been made, including who will be laid off. Mr. Smith is concerned about media coverage of the move, because XYZ's sagging profits have attracted negative media comment, as did a previous layoff. He has therefore prevailed on his company's management to offer laid-off employees a generous outplacement package.

In the meantime, Ms. Jones, a reporter with the Alphaville *Post*, has just received a call from a distraught employee. The employee has heard a rumor that the company is planning to lay off 500 people and is concerned that she will lose her job. The *Post*, a morning newspaper, is about to be put to bed; Ms. Jones has less than 1 hour to get the story written. She realizes that the economic impact of the rumored layoff could affect many readers. She is ambitious and does not want to be scooped. She calls Mr. Smith.

What should Smith's strategy be? And how should Jones negotiate to get a truthful, but responsible, story?

At the outset, both players need to consider the implications of various actions. How will their management react to their strategies? Will they need to maintain goodwill in order to work together in the future? How much is a favorable story worth? How much for an exposé? For example, Jones may be tempted to print a sensationalizing story because such stories sell papers, and she knows this would please her editor. But she will have to weigh this temptation against Smith's probable wrath and its effects on her need for information in the future. For his part, Smith would probably like to stonewall Jones, but should consider what kind of coverage he will receive if he treats her cavalierly.

Having identified the salient issues and their contingent effects, players should assign numerical utilities (or preferences) to each point. Although this can seem arbitrary, it will be a useful index in negotiating an acceptable compromise because it forces people to evaluate their strategies. In fact, most people can work well with preference scales like that used here. For purposes of argument here, seven simplified outcomes and their values are summarized in Table 10.1, showing results that range from completely open discussion to extremely hostile discussion between Smith and Jones. In each case, decision criteria were rated on a scale of -10 to $+10$ where 0 is neutral, -10 is the worst payoff, and $+10$ is the best payoff.

TABLE 10.1
Sample Payoffs for XYZ Company Story Outcomes*

Main Outcome	Contingent Effects	Smith Payoffs	Jones Payoffs
	Outcome #1		
No story: Smith		+10	0
and Jones discuss	Relieved XYZ president	+8	0
potential layoffs;	Disappointed news editor	0	−5
Jones decides material	Smith pleased by Jones' compliance	0	+8
isn't timely enough	Jones disappointed by contact	−2	0
to cover now	TOTAL	+16	+3
	Outcome #2		
No story: Smith		+10	−8
stonewalls and	Relieved XYZ president	+10	0
Jones can't get	News editor angry at Jones	0	−10
material soon	Smith gloats	0	−2
enough to print	Jones feels cheated	−10	0
	TOTAL	+10	−20
	Outcome #3		
Positive story:		+8	+2
Smith uses layoffs	XYZ president pleased	+10	0
to promote XYZ's	News editor wonders about a con	0	−3
progressive	Smith pleased by Jones' compliance	0	+8
outplacement	Jones wonders about a con	−3	0
program	TOTAL	+15	+7
	Outcome #4		
Neutral story:		−2	+8
Smith and Jones	Uneasy XYZ president	−3	0
go over facts; story	Mildly pleased news editor	0	+2
seen as newsworthy	Smith feels treatment was fair	0	+3
but not a major	Jones feels Smith was honest	+8	0
economic blow	TOTAL ...	+3	+13
	Outcome #5		
Neutral-to-negative		−8	−5
story: Smith	XYZ president displeased	−8	0
levels with Jones,	News editor pleased	0	+8
whose story compares	Smith feels betrayed	0	−10
this event with the	Jones feels Smith deserved story	−8	0
previous layoffs	TOTAL	−24	−7

(continued)

TABLE 10.1
(*Continued*)

		Smith	Jones
Main Outcome	*Contingent Effects*	\multicolumn{2}{c}{*Payoffs*}	

		Smith	Jones
	Outcome #6		
Sensationalizing	–10		–10
story: Smith	Angry XYZ president	–10	0
explains facts of	Pleased news editor	0	+5
layoffs; Jones	Smith is furious	0	–10
blows it up into	Jones feels Smith deserved story	–8	0
a major economic	TOTAL	–28	–15
setback			

		Smith	Jones
	Outcome #7		
Sensationalizing	–10		–10
story: Smith	Angry XYZ president	–10	0
stonewalls; Jones	News editor feels vindicated	0	+5
retaliates by	Smith is furious	0	–10
printing exaggerated	Jones feels vindicated	–10	0
rumored numbers	TOTAL	–30	–15

* Payoffs for Smith are based on the story's impact on: public opinion about the company; the probable opinion of his boss about his actions; and Jones's probable opinion of his cooperativeness. Jones's payoffs are based on: the degree to which the story reflected reality; the opinion of her boss about her actions; and Smith's probable opinion of the resulting coverage.

From this array of possible outcomes and values, Smith and Jones could use game theory to extract rational goals and minimize antagonism. Indeed, by applying very basic game theory techniques like utility scales, Smith and Jones could probably arrive at a compromise without resorting to more complicated mathematical solutions. However, the math shows graphically *why* the intuitive solution works.

Non-zero-sum games such as this are considerably more complex than zero-sum games, and their solutions are generally less precise. But as a rule of thumb, in this situation players should aim for the *efficient frontier* —that is, the set of points at which neither player can do better without injuring the other player, and there are no other points where both can do better.

The efficient frontier can be determined quite easily by plotting the paired Smith/Jones utilities on a graph (see Fig. 10.2). Sometimes such analysis will yield a single best solution that dominates all others, represented by one point at the northeastern extreme. That is not the case

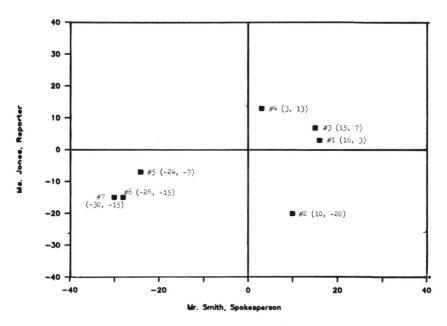

FIG. 10.2.   Outcomes for layoffs story.

here. None of the three acceptable solutions dominates the other two; each gives a slight edge to either Smith or Jones. In such cases it is up to the players to negotiate among acceptable solutions, relying on skill, strategy, or the luck of the draw to attain outcome 1, 3, or 4. As in the ABC Chemical case, these solutions may be arrived at intuitively. What game theory can do is test the instinct—perhaps channel it to a more efficient outcome—and expose the rational laws that underlie each choice.

Although both these scenarios show how game theory can be harnessed as an analytical tool, they present rather schematic and simplified public relations situations, chosen to make the game theoretical applications very clear. Real life, of course, does not often favor us with instances in which the issues are so neatly drawn. A rigid corporate culture, or one risk-averse executive, may become a strategically important factor, so that individual games may be considerably more complicated than these. In addition, there may be more than two major players; there may be possibilities for diverse coalitions; there may be incompatible payoffs or information that can't be divvied up cooperatively. Repeated play may also become a significant strategic factor, as selling out the other player could cause that player to make hostile moves in the next negotiation. Laboratory experiments with similar games have shown that in such repeated play, the best way to win is to cooperate first, then mirror the other player's moves.[7]

These qualifiers do not mean that game theory cannot be applied to achieve helpful insights. But they do mean that in reality game-theoretic models can quickly become highly complex. Game theory, therefore, cannot replace the valuable instinct and experience of practitioners. What it can do is supplement them and channel them toward the best strategies in a qualitative sense. In addition, game theory can make an important contribution to our understanding of *why* things happen the way they do in public relations situations, allowing us to test out our assumptions about negotiating strategies with various publics.

This is a rich area for further work—and much more work needs to be done in extending and refining both theory and applications.

FUTURE DIRECTIONS

The theory of games has particular relevance to three broad areas of public relations studies: public relations theory, empirical applications for scholar and practitioner, and teaching.

In terms of theory, much more work is needed simply to identify and refine different genres of games that could prove theoretically significant when used to structure public relations situations. For example, although this chapter has focused exclusively on game models that describe interpersonal negotiation, very different types of games exist that model the dynamics of group power, the diffusion of information within a system, and the allocation of resources. Currently such concepts have been developed primarily for economic and military contexts, but they have potential within a communication context as well.

On an empirical level, the application of game theory could greatly benefit both scholar and practitioner. Indeed, game theoretic analysis could shed light on any area of public relations that involves influence, negotiation, coalition formation, or allocating information. Thus, a practitioner might use game theory in the future to model and predict the diffusion patterns and impact of information subsidies; to determine

---

[7]For example, Robert Axelrod has done work with the Prisoner's Dilemma game in which each player designed a pure strategy to play against an opponent's unknown strategy, and all the participants were paired off against each other in a computerized round robin. Among all the degrees of cooperation/noncooperation that resulted, a strategy called "Tit for Tat" accumulated the most points in repeated play. "Tit for Tat" cooperated on the first play, and thereafter duplicated whatever its opponent had done on the previous move (see Allman, 1984, and Davis, 1983, pp. 145ff).

how most effectively to divide scarce advertising resources; to identify key groups in lobbying efforts and model the most effective coalitions; and to determine optimum timing and content of key news releases.

For scholars, game theory could usefully supplement existing research methodologies. Applied to empirical research, game theory allows us to establish norms for successful negotiation with various publics and to make predictions about the outcomes that should transpire, given certain strategies. By operationalizing these predictions through gaming situations, we can collect empirical evidence to test and clarify our assumptions. Going beyond such lab situations, we can use game theoretic models for analyzing case histories to examine how certain outcomes transpired and how they might have been improved upon.

Operationalized in the form of classroom gaming sessions, game theory can also provide a powerful pedagogical tool—an advantage long realized by such business schools as Harvard and Carnegie Mellon.[8] Here the pedagogical value is not necessarily to arrive at the "right" answer but rather to show students how the dynamics of a given situation unfold and to test out rules and guidelines: to teach them how to *think* about public relations.

Overall, game theory has some compelling advantages for both theoretician and researcher:[9]

- It imposes formal models that help us to sort out variables, and its rigor and formalism help us to increase our control over the phenomena we are studying.

- Because it is highly formalized, in meeting its requirements we may uncover flaws in the logic of a research design that would have passed unnoticed in less rigorously formulated models.

- It provides new analytical approaches to problems using a variety of different solution concepts. Depending on what solution concepts we apply, we can examine a given problem from the standpoint of

---

[8]Here a distinction must be made between the theory of games and the process of gaming which operationalizes the theory. As Martin Shubik (1972) points out:

> In general, game theoretic reasoning and analysis are of considerable use in constructing and analyzing games and gaming exercises. . . . The solution concepts of theories offered in the theory of games may be regarded as normative or descriptive views of multiperson decisionmaking. When the solution concept is backed up with empirical evidence from gaming experiments or with evidence of behavior from other observations, it may be regarded as having some behavioral justification.(p. 37)

[9]Many of the points made here concerning the advantages and drawbacks of applying game theory to the social sciences are more fully described in Shubik (1982, chapter 12), and Colman (1982, pp. 82–85, 128ff).

cooperation, of maximizing gains, of fairness, of strategic lying, and so forth.

- It provides normative guidelines for behavior and outcomes; these allow us to measure different players' strategies objectively.
- It complements rather than conflicts with less formalized behavioral paradigms, as both approaches study how players respond to factors in their environment.

Still, the very formalism and objectivity that make game theory such a useful paradigm may also carry disadvantages, particularly regarding methodology. For example, game theory requires that players assign numerical values to their preferences. Without such quantification we would have no way of working out mathematical solutions. But often it is difficult to assign numerical values to qualitative preferences, nor do such numbers reflect the *intensities* of players' preferences. Solutions based on such qualified numbers may obscure significant variables. This is not a conclusive objection in all cases, but it does limit some applications.

The extreme formalism of game theoretic rules may in some cases impoverish the theory's realism. For example, game theory requires that any factors not built into the rules do not exist. In many games, the rules acknowledge no communication between players so that players who wish to make deals or otherwise cooperate must express their intentions through their actions during the game itself. In some public relations applications such constraints detract from realism. More often, these constraints provide a useful model for public relations strategy. (For instance, the cases described in the previous section are typical applications where no communication between players could have transpired in reality.)

The rules of game theory also require that all players have *external symmetry*—that is, they are considered homogenous in all respects except those dictated by the rules. Individual personalities, degrees of intelligence and ethical biases are irrelevant unless built into the game guidelines. On the one hand, this may flaw the realism of a solution, given that public relations so often deals with these human quirks and intangibles. On the other hand, any social scientist who selects some variables, rejects others, and targets specific samples for an experiment is asking similar questions as to what the "rules" should be. And, like the social scientist, the game theorist must be sure to select the proper mathematical model to ensure that the results are valid.

Some people may also be bothered by the inconclusiveness of much game theoretical analysis. For example, there is generally no single optimum solution for non-zero-sum games, which describe most public relations situations. Often the best game theory can do is narrow down the set of possible outcomes without pointing conclusively at the "right" one. Different players may choose different models—each mathematically correct—that yield disparate solutions.[10] And game theory cannot predict what *will* happen: It can only suggest a set of possibilities.

For public relations purposes, this inconclusiveness is a strength and not a drawback. It is another way in which game theory adapts closely to the realities of practice, where there are seldom clear-cut winners and losers, and seldom any unequivocal right answers. In the end, game theory helps us to model the *process* of public relations, not to prescribe its results; to formulate a problem and ask the right questions, not to dictate the answers. It does not rule out the intuition and experience of the traditional practitioner. Rather it complements them by setting individual decision making within a larger theoretical framework.

Above all, the discipline and formalism of game theory teach us to *think:* to play out our assumptions to their conclusions; to alert us to false reasoning; to force us to consider alternatives that may have been opaque to us before. By playing according to game theory rules, we may not be able to reach a satisfying conclusion every time. But we will at least understand what all our options are, and why certain outcomes transpire. We will not be operating in the dark, using instinct and gut feeling as our only guides.

REFERENCES

Allman, W. F. (1984, October) Nice guys finish first. *Science 84, 25–32.*

Coleman, A. (1982) *Game theory and experimental games: The study of strategic interaction.* Oxford: Pergamon Press.

Davis, M. D. (1983) *Game theory: A nontechnical introduction* (Rev. Ed.). New York: Basic Books.

Dozier, D. M. (1984) Program evaluation and the roles of practitioners. *Public Relations Review, 10,* 13–21.

Ehling, W. P. (1975) PR administration, management science, and purposive systems. *Public Relations Review, 1*(2), 15–43.

Ehling, W. P. (1984) Application of decision theory in the construction of a theory of public relations management. I. *Public Relations Research and Education, 1*(2), 25–38.

---

[10]For example, Raiffa (1982) gave three disparate and correct solutions for a three-person fair-division game using three different mathematical models, each of which a different player wins (see chapter 19).

Ehling, W. P. (1985) Application of decision theory in the construction of a theory of public relations management. II. *Public Relations Research and Education, 2*(1), 4–22.

Grunig, J. E. (1975a) A multi-systems theory of organizational communication. *Communication Research, 2*, 99–136.

Grunig, J. E. (1975b) Toward a multi-purpose public relations theory. *Public Relations Journal, 31*, 12–15.

Grunig, J. E. (1976) Communication behaviors in decision and nondecision situations. *Journalism Quarterly, 53*, 232–263.

Grunig, J. E. (1977) Developing a probabilistic model for communications decision making. *Communication Research, 4*, 145–168.

Heckathorn, D. D. (1986) Game theory and sociology in the 1980s. *Contemporary Sociology, 15*(2), 206–208.

Lucas, W. F. (1972) An overview of the mathematical theory of games. *Management Science, 18*(5), 3–19.

Luce, R. D., & Raiffa, H. (1957) *Games and decisions: Introduction and critical survey.* New York: Wiley.

Raiffa, H. (1968) *Decision analysis: Introductory lectures on choices under uncertainty.* Reading, MA: Addison-Wesley.

Raiffa, H. (1982) *The art and science of negotiation.* Cambridge: Belknap Press.

Shubik, M. (1972) On gaming and game theory. *Management Science, 18*(5), 37–53.

Shubik, M. (1982) *Game theory in the social sciences: Concepts and solutions.* Cambridge: The MIT Press.

Von Neumann, J., & Morgenstern, O. (1944) *Theory of games and economic behavior.* Princeton, NJ: Princeton University Press.

SUGGESTED READINGS

Colman, A. (1982) *Game theory and experimental games: The study of strategic interaction.* Oxford: Pergamon Press.

Davis, M. D. (1983) *Game theory: A nontechnical introduction* (Rev. Ed.). New York: Basic Books.

Luce, R. D., & Raiffa, H. (1957) *Games and decisions: Introduction and critical survey.* New York: Wiley.

Raiffa, H. (1982) *The art and science of negotiation.* Cambridge: Belknap Press.

Shubik, M. (1982) *Game theory in the social sciences: Concepts and solutions.* Cambridge: The MIT Press.

Theoretical Models for Public Relations Campaigns

James K. VanLeuven
Colorado State University

ABSTRACT

Communication and social science theories serve as frameworks guiding public relations campaign decisions as explained in this chapter.

Each of the five theories suggests a different sequence or hierarchy of effects leading to a campaign's focal objective. Thus, the theoretical models outlined here may be utilized to help set campaign objectives and to determine strategy including message design and channel use.

Much of what passes for theory in public relations comprises a loose collection of professional axioms that pull together divergent perspectives in public relations practice to further establish public relations as a necessary management function.

Nowhere is this more apparent than with public relations campaign planning where practitioners and academics hold up the four-step public relations process as an appropriate underpinning for campaigns. To be sure, the public relations process is a viable outline of the steps undertaken in a campaign although it is not a broad conceptual framework for applying established theory and relevant research findings to the critical decisions required for coherent campaign formulation.

Some argue that campaigns are as much art as science so that any further conceptual specification might mask a campaign's creative opportunities and unique circumstances. A much different argument is advanced here. That is, the public relations body of knowledge will not advance quickly if each campaign plan is considered as an isolated case whose circumstances are unique and nontransferable.

The purpose of this chapter, therefore, is to consider the suitability of five generally accepted communication and social science models as orienting frameworks to undergird campaign design. The five models selected for review here include (a) persuasion/learning effects, (b) social learning, (c) low involvement, (d) cognitive consistency, and (e) value change. Others might have been included but these five were chosen to represent well-established social science orientations.

Underpinning these applications of social science and communication theory to public relations campaigns are three assumptions discussed in chapter 1. First, each of the models serves as a conceptual representation of how communication effects develop from different sets of conditions. That is, each model suggests a different sequence or hierarchy of effects leading to the focal effect(s) because the conditions under which each model operates are different.

Attitude change is the principal effect or outcome of the persuasion approaches, cognitive consistency, and value-change theories. The social learning theory emphasizes behavioral modification whereas the low-involvement model considers conditions under which behavioral change does not require prior cognitive and attitudinal change.

Second, these five communication and social science models focus and clarify how different emphasis given to the elements in the communication process prompts different communication and behavioral effects. For example, the persuasion model explicated by the Yale Communication Program advances particular guidelines for message construction whereas explication of the social learning theory suggests how mass media and interpersonal communication channels must be synchronized to achieve behavioral effects. The low involvement model, in contrast, makes fundamental assumptions about receivers or audiences that influence the campaign planner's selection of sources, message formats, and channel types.

And third, these five models were selected for their general appeal. That is, each offers a certain amount of intuitive appeal relating to decisions about public relations campaign objectives and strategy. In particular, the models serve as useful guidelines in designing campaign evaluation measures.

Each theory offers a different focal point that public relations planners might equate with the campaign's key objective. As well, campaign planners may want to use the varying sequences or hierarchies of effects as justification for establishing particular campaign objectives, determining general action and communication strategies, message design, and channel use plans. In all cases, the varying sequences of effect need to be weighed against overall organizational goals and situational constraints facing different publics.

PERSUASION/LEARNING EFFECTS

The first two models are grounded in social psychology's learning effects tradition. Typically, public relations planners follow the persuasion model derived from instrumental learning and holding that knowledge, attitude, and behavior change take place in a more-or-less stepwise manner.

The central notion behind instrumental learning is that an opinion or attitude becomes habitual because its overt expressions or internal rehearsal is followed by the experience or anticipation of positive reinforcement. This process, as developed in Hovland's Yale Communication Program, progresses in four stages from awareness to comprehension, to acceptance, and finally, retention (Hovland, Janis, & Kelly 1953). Thus, this cognitive-attitudinal-behavioral effects hierarchy is the basis for examining how communication factors influence each stage.

The model's proponents, Hovland and his Yale Communication Program associates, were most concerned with source, message, and audience factors. An extensive list of postulates developed from tests of persuasive effect (Zimbardo, Ebbeson, & Maslach, 1977). For example, with respect to social influences, attitude change is more likely when the credibility of the communicator is high rather than low.

The amount of attitude change increases with the amount advocated when the communicator's credibility is high.

With respect to message factors, conclusion drawing is more appropriate when issues are complex and audiences are not likely to draw the desired conclusion. Two-sided arguments are preferred to one-sided ones when the audience is likely to hear the other side.

The Yale Communication Program is not the only one to adhere to the hierarchy of effects pattern presumed by the persuasion/learning effects model. McGuire's approach (1981) to persuasion and campaign planning follows a similar orientation. The diffusion of innovations research tradition also follows a general persuasion/learning effects orientation although the impact steps are labelled somewhat differently (awareness-interest-evaluation-trial-adoption). Like the Yale program, diffusion research findings suggest guidelines for message and channel strategy.

Research findings from marketing and advertising indicate that the general pattern of effects for persuasion/learning effects models typify situations in which (a) the audience is involved in the topic, (b) that the position advocated by the campaign is clearly distinguishable from others, and (c) when new ideas, services, or products are being promoted (Ray, 1973).

Implications For Campaign Objectives

Implicit in the persuasion/learning effects model and many public relations campaigns is the assumption that the likelihood of attaining an array of campaign objectives tapers off quickly following awareness. Perhaps 70 percent of the audience will achieve awareness, but progressively fewer will gain specific knowledge, change opinions, etc.

Implications for Campaign Strategies

Strategies geared to the persuasion/learning effects model focus on conditions for optimizing impacts in the early stages of a change process. Strategy and programming decisions emphasize techniques for creating awareness and enhancing knowledge gain.

SOCIAL LEARNING MODEL

The social learning model offers a more complex and variegated approach pegged to sustained behavioral change based on careful synchronization of media publicity and interpersonal support programs. It is geared more to education and training than to persuasion.

The theory holds that there is a continuous, reciprocal interaction among a persons's behavior, events going on inside the person (thoughts, emotional reactions, expectations), and the environmental consequences of that behavior. The likelihood that a specific behavior will occur is determined by the consequences the person expects will follow the performance of that behavior. The more positive and rewarding the consequences, the more likely the behavior is to occur (McAlister, 1981).

The sequence or hierarchy of effects at work here is one that brings behavioral change into the process sooner. In fact, attitudinal effects may follow rather than precede behavioral ones because the emphasis here is on shaping social support and other conditions that facilitate and induce behavioral change. Because behavior is selectively rewarded at each step toward the desired goal, attitude change is thought to follow in tandem. Behavioral reinforcement is brought about by (a) direct reinforcement of desired behavior, (b) eliminating the consequences of undesired behavior, (c) vicarious reinforcement and vicarious extinction, and (d) instructions, rules, and communication.

This more focused emphasis on behavior change requires utilizing the mass media up to and including the modelling of recommended new behavior, whereas mass media were utilized in the persuasion/learning effects model to generate awareness and interest. Social learning also includes a well-structured set of interpersonal communication strategies that operate almost in tandem with mass media to give target audience members support for trying the recommended behavior and further reinforcement for maintaining the behavior.

Perhaps the most clearcut explication of the social learning model is the Stanford Heart Disease Prevention Program involving a large-scale community media blitz coupled with a carefully orchestrated system of small group instruction: This program was based on predetermined, individualized behavior change prescriptions adapted to each target audience member's heart disease risk factors (Maccoby & Farquhar, 1975; Maccoby & Solomon, 1981).

The Stanford program and others like it show the campaign planner that complex behavioral change involves breaking down the desired behavior into a series of steps or "hoops." The number of steps varies depending on how susceptible audience members or groups are to the conditions prompting change. By carefully delineating publics in terms of heart disease risk factors and their competencies in following through with the recommended change strategies, campaign planners were able to provide different target audiences with varying amounts of programming to bring each group up to optimal behavioral performance levels.

On balance, the campaign design complexities required by the social learning model support Grunig and Hunt's (1984) contention that campaign planners reserve behavioral change objectives for situations such as fund-raising, where the payoff is more likely to match the campaign programming investment.

Implications for Campaign Objectives

Campaign planners guided by social learning theory generally set separate objectives for each target audience. Those objectives include everything from awareness through sustained behavioral change, although the emphasis given each objective is calibrated to the ease with which particular groups or target audience members may attain each objective.

Implications for Campaign Strategies

The complexities of social learning theory require separate overall strategies and often completely distinct message designs and channel uses for each target audience.

LOW-INVOLVEMENT MODEL

The low-involvement model developed from the advertising and marketing literature and is well suited to short-term promotions and awareness campaigns. It holds that the media may induce action-taking without necessarily affecting parallel cognitive and attitudinal change. This happens because relatively inconsequential behaviors are not dependent on great amounts of knowledge or reconciliation with existing attitudes.

As explained by Krugman (1965), the low-involvement model is premised on the contention that people really do not care about the content of most advertising. Thus, with low perceptual defenses, a single message will have little effect, although the cumulative effect of short, but direct, messages may be noticeably greater. The low-involvement model, unlike others considered here, focuses almost exclusively on response to persuasive messages.

Flay (1986) wrote that the low-involvement model is most likely to be successful when there is little objective difference between the alternative or when the audience does not care about the magnitude of difference between alternatives. He cited the National Safety Council's "If you drink, don't drive—if you drive, don't drink" campaign as one in which media advertising alone could lead directly to behavioral effects since the message was crisp and there were no viable alternatives.

Clearly, the low-involvement sequence of effects fits situations not requiring audience members to stop and think about the issue. The sequence of effects presumed by the model moves from simple awareness to behavioral change, and then, perhaps, to attitudinal change.

Implications for Campaign Objectives

The low-involvement model moves from awareness to behavior change by minimizing the number of steps in between. However, it is often necessary to have at least one intermediate objective (e.g., knowledge gain) in order to provide reason or justification for immediate action.

198

Implications for Campaign Strategies

By relying on awareness to induce behavior, the low-involvement strategy almost always means a short, but memorable, message repeated very often through mass media channels.

COGNITIVE CONSISTENCY MODEL

The cognitive consistency model is a particularly useful framework when dealing with tension reduction situations including crisis communication, certain issue management problems, negotiations and other conditions where imposed behaviors and decisions demand new knowledge and attitude change before they can be generally accepted. It is also a useful planning framework in situations where new knowledge counters existing beliefs and attitudes.

Similar to other consistency theories, Leon Festinger's (1957) cognitive dissonance theory assumes a need for consistent knowledge. Dissonance, or a state of inconsistent knowledge, may stem from many sources, and this happens routinely in public life when an organization advocates a specific policy to the exclusion of alternative ones. That is, the decision in favor of the chosen policy is at odds with beliefs supporting the alternatives.

The sequence or hierarchy of effects portended by the model begins with a behavior and then employs cognitive strategies to adapt to that change and, in turn, to alter attitudes. Typically, campaigns following the consistency model are characterized by high cognitive involvement and issues of great personal relevance.

Cognitive strategies for reconciling inconsistencies include: (a) revoking or attempting to revoke the decision or behavior, (b) lowering the importance of the decision, (c) increasing the ambiguity or cognitive overlap between the discrepant ideas, and (d) adding supportive beliefs to change the ratio of dissonant to consonant elements.

Implications for Campaign Objectives

Focal objectives for campaigns based on the consistency model involve increasing the salience or certain target beliefs along with adding specific new beliefs.

Implications for Campaign Strategy

Message style may be just as important as actual message construction in situations where consistency is being restored. That is, the imposed behavior must be made to appear compatible with existing attitudes, values, and lifestyles. This means that more attention must go to the social context in which the message is presented.

VALUE CHANGE

A more recent campaign planning model builds on Rokeach's (1979) theory of value change and is adaptable to relatively personal and intense issues that challenge the self-esteem of those affected by the issue (such as drug and alcohol abusers).

Value change takes place in at least two ways. The first, following consistency logic, holds that value change occurs when an inconsistency is invoked between a high-ranking personal value and other knowledge, attitudes, values, or behavior. Once made known, the value inconsistency is resolved by first increasing the salience of a target value and then by readjusting knowledge, attitudes, and behaviors in line with the target value. Thus, the sequence of effects moves from value inducement (a cognitive restructuring process) to attitudinal and related behavioral change.

Value strengthening is a closely related but more general change process appropriate to public relations campaign planning. Following Rosenberg's value-attitude instrumentality logic, value strengthening involves defining a specific attitude in terms of a more general value (e.g., linking an issue stand to an important personal value held by members of the target audience [VanLeuven, 1980]).

Implications for Campaign Objectives

Because value change is a generalized cognitive restructuring process, the scope of its effects span to cognitive, attitudinal, and behavior change. Emphasis, however, is on making specific beliefs or issue stands consistent with more generalized values or ideals.

Implications for Campaign Strategies

The value change process suggests several message strategies. Beliefs may be added to provide a new context for a particular value in question. Or, planners might strengthen the instrumental relationship between a strongly held value and its application to the present situation. As well, attitudes held by diverse target publics are often mobilized when the consequences of a problem are cast in terms of a more universally accepted value. A new value may also be injected into a situation to hedge existing values. When a new value is placed alongside an existing one, audience members may be forced to consider both (thereby at least partially neutralizing their previously entrenched positions).

CONCLUSIONS AND IMPLICATIONS

The theoretical models considered here serve as conceptual frameworks for understanding campaigns and their effects. The models should be considered as theoretical ideal-types, or representations of reality. In practice, there is every reason to believe that the complexities of campaign issues will require fusing several models in order to achieve appropriate objectives for different publics who range in their degree of involvement and likely communication behavior.

Each model suggests a different hierarchy or sequence of effects, and these sequences may vary by target public as well. This was evidenced clearly in the recent evaluation of the nationwide "Take A Bite Out Of Crime" campaign (O'Keefe, 1985). This campaign and others suggest that the hierarchies help acknowledge the scope or range of communication and behavioral effects present in different situations.

As well, the sequences of effect provide a basis for setting objectives and in suggesting campaign strategy, particularly message design and channel selection. Thus, the models provide a theoretical framework for campaign decision making that may lead to more universal principles of public relations campaign management.

REFERENCES

Festinger, L. (1957) *A theory of cognitive dissonance.* Stanford, CA: Stanford University Press.

Flay, B. R. (1986, May) *Mass media and smoking cessation.* Paper presented to International Communication Association, Chicago, IL.

Grunig, J., & Hunt, T. (1984) *Managing public relations.* New York: Holt, Rinehart & Winston.

Hovland, C., Janis, I., & Kelley H. (1953) *Communication and persuasion: Psychological studies of opinion change.* New Haven, CT: Yale University Press.

Krugman, H. (1965) The impact of television advertising: Learning without involvement. *Public Opinion Quarterly, 29,* 348–356.

Maccoby, N., & Farquhar, J. (1975) Communication for health: Unselling heart disease. *Journal of Communication, 25,* 114–126.

Maccoby, N., & Solomon, D. (1981) Heart disease prevention: Community studies. In R. Rice & W. Paisley (Eds.), *Public communication campaigns* (pp. 105–125). Beverly Hills, CA: Sage.

McAlister, A. (1981) Anti-smoking campaigns: Progress in developing effective communications. In R. Rice & W. Paisley (Eds.), *Public communication campaigns* (pp. 91–103). Beverly Hills, CA: Sage.

McGuire, W. (1981) Theoretical foundations of campaigns. In R. Rice & W. Paisley (Eds.), *Public communication campaigns* (pp. 41–70). Beverly Hills, CA: Sage.

O'Keefe, G. (1985) Take a bite out of crime: The impact of a public information campaign. *Communication Research, 12*(2), 147–178.

Ray, M. (1973) Marketing communication and the hierarchy of effects. In P. Clarke (Ed.), *New models for communication research* (pp. 147–176). Beverly Hills, CA: Sage Annual Reviews of Communication Research.

Rokeach, M. (1979) *Understanding human values: Individual and societal.* New York: The Free Press.

VanLeuven, J. (1980) Measuring values in public participation programs. *Public Relations Review, 6*(1), 51–56.

Zimbardo, P., Ebbeson, E., & Maslach, C. (1977) *Influencing attitudes and changing behavior.* Reading, MA: Addison-Wesley.

Expanding Psychographic Concepts in Public Relations: The Composite Audience Profile

Joseph C. Scott, III
University of Oklahoma

Dan O'Hair
Texas Tech University

ABSTRACT

The intent of this chapter is to suggest a confluent treatment of independent audience analysis theories by proposing specific techniques of pre-message analysis vis-à-vis creative psychographic strategies. That is, this chapter demonstrates that combining demographic characteristics, creative psychographic information such as values and lifestyle, and adding emotional characteristics will provide a most comprehensive model of audience analysis, what we term the *composite audience profile* (CAP). This approach, garnered from public relations, communication, and advertising theory offers a great deal of utility for the public relations practitioner in that communication strategies can be constructed more effectively. In the following review, demographic characteristics, psychographic concepts, and emotional or affective characteristics of an audience are discussed, culminating in a strategy for comprehensive audience analysis. By utilizing this technique, public relations and communication specialists will have a better understanding of what their audience wants, who they are, and how emotional appeals can focus attention on the message.

The fields of public relations, communication, and advertising are often considered discrete disciplines of theory and practice, yet it is ironic that these three disciplines focus on the same phenomenon—messages. Conceiving and creating the message, deciding where the message is to be sent and to whom it will be sent are communication objectives used by public relations and advertising firms (Newsom & Scott, 1985) as well as individuals and groups. As independent disciplines, each has much to offer the other in those elements of message construction and analysis where overlap occurs.

Perhaps one of the most salient and often studied concerns to each of these disciplines involves the pre-analysis of the situation. Communication scholars refer to pre-message investigation as audience analysis, public relations label the phenomenon as examining their publics (Crable & Vibbert, 1986), and the advertising field is concerned with predicting reactions and effects of the advertising message (Alwitt & Mitchell, 1985). Although each discipline has employed distinct research paradigms in their study of public or audience analysis processes, the fundamental objective remains common: Obtain the most predictive and reliable composite of the message target (audience). It should be noted here that not all areas of this chapter are covered in equal depth because of the variety and vast amounts of research information available. For this reason this chapter re-familiarizes the reader with demographic characteristics, while devoting more emphasis to psychographic information and emotions and the role these phenomenon play in developing an audience profile.

ANALYSIS OF AUDIENCES

There is a definite need to broaden and further refine our ability to predict audience reaction to messages. Public relations, advertising, and communication references are replete with approaches designed to reach desired target markets (Bovee & Arens, 1982; Conrad, 1985; Hafer & White, 1982; MacLachlan, 1983; Murdock & Janus, 1983; Newsom & Scott, 1985; Scissors & Surmanek, 1982; Wells, 1974; Woodruff, Cadotte & Jenkins, 1983; Zikmund & d'Amico, 1986). To express the desired message, to be concise, and to fulfill marketing objectives all involve the need to better conceptualize the target audience.

Whether planning a public relations campaign, or an advertisement for a product/service, or speaking in front of a group, you must consider the audience you are trying to reach. Newsom and Scott (1985) suggested that a public relations practitioner carefully define each public or target audience pertinent to a particular project and determine other publics that might be affected. The use of psychographic information in advertising is the basis for most advertising decisions (Alwitt & Mitchell, 1985). Who? What? When? Why? and How? often are all questions that must be decided upon before a message is sent to the target market.

The rationale for developing the most precise description of a targeted audience is obvious for several public relations reasons. First, economic and human resources can be made more efficient by spending additional effort in determining the salient characteristics of audience members that are likely to affect a favorable reaction to the message. Second, undesired and unintended publics may also be privy to messages intended only for the targeted public or audience. These publics can influence the effectiveness of the communication campaign if both analysis and selection of targeted audiences are not made carefully (Crable & Vibbert, 1986). Third, exacting a comprehensive audience analysis will help to identify opinion leaders who can become assets in a persuasive public relations campaign. Although econometric models have yet to emerge that indicate the comparative advantages of resource expenditure toward a broad-based communication campaign, such models would be welcome. There is little doubt that cost/benefit analysis would suggest that more comprehensive models of audience analysis are warranted.

Audience analysis should involve three fundamental characteristics: (a) an accurate description of the demographic make-up of the audience in question, (b) using psychographic information to focus on the individual's values and lifestyle, and (c) determining the emotional reaction of audience members. Upon fulfillment of these assessment criteria a complete audience profile can be determined.

DEMOGRAPHIC CHARACTERISTICS

Most individuals designing a communication strategy or campaign automatically consider demographic information as a basic staple of any audience analysis. Furthermore, demography is a necessary first step toward establishing more specific and complex analyses of a target audience. Such variables as age, social class, education, sex, cultural background, and occupational status are the primary categories of demographic speculation. Such variables can provide particular utility in assessing audience type—casual, passive, selected, concerted, organized, as well as determining the composition of unintended and undesirable publics exposures to a message.

The development of a composite demographic profile of the targeted audience begins the process of refining how best to predict reactions and behaviors associated with public relations messages. A number of social and economic issues can be preliminarily addressed by a demographic analysis. Social issues such as AIDS, sexism, and surrogate motherhood as well as employment concerns such as budget deficits, unions, unemployment and job discrimination can begin to be understood as a result of demographic categorizing. By analyzing, and therefore, understanding the demographic contour of the audience in question, more specific and less tangible audience qualities can be understood in subsequent steps.

PSYCHOGRAPHIC ATTRIBUTES

Having established a demographic profile of a public or audience, psychographic variables can be applied to further develop the audience profile. According to Bovee and Arens (1982), *psychographics* is defined as the classification of consumers into market segments on the basis of psychological make-up—namely personality, attitude, and lifestyle. Jamieson and Campbell (1983) described psychographics as a self-described self-concept that may include the adjectives: trustworthy, affectionate, kind, intelligent, broadminded, sociable, frank, efficient, self-assured, funny, and creative.

In general, psychographics seek to describe the human characteristics that may have an impact on an audience's responses to messages. Psychographic variables span a spectrum of self-concept, values, attitudes, opinions and individual perceptions (Alwitt & Mitchell, 1985; Wells, 1974). For some time, marketers have considered an understanding of the total human being as he or she makes purchasing decisions to be important (Demby, 1974). Additionally, psychographic research holds great promise as a public relations strategy due to an ability to identify with more predictibility the behavior of an increasingly fragmented society (Zotti, 1985). Psychographic research is composed of two related behavioral concepts: values and lifestyle.

Values

Much of psychographic research is focused on the relationship between values and behavior. Since the pioneering work by Rokeach (1973), a number of research paradigms spanning a multitude of research disciplines have emerged in an attempt to understand attitudes, perceptions, and opinions, as well as behavior based on expressed values (Beatty, Kahle, Homer, & Misra, 1985; Feather, 1975; Kahle 1983, 1985; Mitchell, 1983; Reynolds & Jolly, 1980; Rokeach, 1973; Vinson, Scott, & Lamont, 1977). The basic assumption behind most value research involves having subjects rate or rank a list of values presumably indicating deep-seated feelings and intentions, and subsequently manipulating those scores as either predictive or criterion variables. The number of values employed in any one project depends more on the research objective and ultimate design than on other factors.

A fairly comprehensive list of values was utilized by Becker and Conner (1979), who identified two types of personal values of the heavy user of mass media. They divide values into the categories of terminal values and instrumental values (see Table 12.1).

Of the 37 terminal and instrumental values identified and tested in their study most could be cross-labeled as psychographic information. These values were useful in identifying the potential reactions of media consumers toward targeted message content. Subsequent research particularly by consumer behaviorists has produced even more sophisticated methodologies of values profiling that are discussed in the following sections.

VALS. Zikmund and d'Amico (1986) described one of the most popular psychographic models—the VALS program, a popular psychographic classification scheme that separates consumers according to lifestyle-based segments. This technique was developed at SRI International by Mitchell (1983). Mitchell utilized both Maslow's (1954) hierarchy of needs and Reisman, Glazer, and Denny's (1950) concept of social character to formulate nine different lifestyles (Kahle, Beatty, & Homer, 1986). Each segment describes an essential segment that can be reached

TABLE 12.1
Terminal and Instrumental Values
(adopted from Becker & Conner, 1979)

Terminal Values	Instrumental Values
A comforable life	Ambitious
An exciting life	Broad-minded
Accomplishment	Capable
A world at peace	Cheerful
A world of beauty	Clean
Equality	Courageous
Family security	Forgiving
Freedom	Helpful
Happiness	Honest
Inner harmony	Imaginative
Mature love	Independent
National security	Logical
Pleasure	Loving
Salvation	Obedient
Self-respect	Polite
Social recognition	Responsible
True friendship	Self-controlled
Wisdom	

through different marketing approaches. The four categories are: outer-directed, inner-directed, need-driven and integrated.

An outer-directed individual is described as a *belonger,* one who wants to have affiliations and wants to preserve the status quo; an *emulator,* socially upward and concerned with appearances; or an *achiever,* one who is hard-working and success-oriented. An *inner-directed* consumer is described as an *"I am me"* person (narcissistic and liberal), an *experimenter* (liberal, adventurous) of a *socially conscious* individual (politically active, seeks issues, causes) who is "intent on self-expression." The need driven person is thought to be motivated by necessity. They are the *survivors* who are elderly and poorly educated, and the *sustainers.* Survivors tend to make decisions based on cost, safety and convenience, and are more fearful than the average consumer. The sustainers are described as re-sentful and lacking sufficient financial resources. Need driven indi-viduals have a tendency to purchase only when there is a specific need to be fulfilled. Finally, the integrated consumer has a balanced focus of both the outer-directed and inner-directed qualities. Individuals in this category are affluent, tolerant, and self-assured (Zotti, 1985).

Table 12.2 graphically classifies the VALS system and provides a per-centage breakdown in parentheses of the number of people in the popu-lation who have been characterized to belong in each category (Kahle et al., 1986; Zotti, 1985).

LOV.   Research concerned with values and reaction to messages have been advancing in other circles outside of public relations. Kahle and associates at the University of Michigan Survey Research Center (Beatty et al., 1985; Kahle, 1983, 1986; Kahle et al., 1986; Veroff, Douvan & Kulka, 1981) have developed and refined the List of Values (LOV). This survey includes a list of nine values that subjects can respond to in a

TABLE 12.2
Values and Lifestyle (VALS)
(adapted from Zikmund & d'Amico, 1986)

Outer Directed	*Inner Directed*
Belongers (37%)	"I am me" (3%)
Emulators (8%)	Experimental (6%)
Achievers (22%)	Socially conscious (12%)
Need-Driven	*Integrated*
Survivors (4%)	Combination of outer-directed
Sustainers (7%)	and inner directed (2%)

number of methodological ways. The values included self-respect, security, warm relationships with others, sense of accomplishment, self-fulfillment, sense of belonging, being well respected, and fun and enjoyment in life and excitement. Members of the Michigan group have argued the utility and superiority of LOV over other value methodologies such as VALS. For example, Kahle et al. (1986) suggest that the LOV survey is more contextual in nature and less stereotypical in its assigned categories (i.e., older people are poorer and less educated). A direct comparison was conducted between LOV and VALS as to the predictive utility in assessing consumer behavior, with LOV claiming a greater proportion of the variance in such predictions (Kahle et al., 1986). Furthermore, it was suggested that an additional advantage of the LOV methodology involves the separate attainment of demographic predictions, whereas the VALS approach builds in these characteristics. Additionally, LOV provides flexibility in its level of data. VALS is a nominal level survey restricting data manipulation to nonparametric tests. LOV on the other hand can be adapted to nominal, ordinal, or interval level data collection allowing a wide range of parametric multivariate statistical manipulations. Obviously, additional comparisons between these popular approaches to value research are warranted.

Lifestyles

In addition to consideration of values, psychographics also include lifestyle assessment. In contrast to values, which is more of a cognitive predisposition, lifestyle analysis reflects an individual's behavior. These behaviors may be identified from a broad cultural perspective (Alpert, 1972; Lazer, 1963; Lazer & Smallwood, 1972; Wells, 1974) or from a more specific consumer behavior mode (Hustad & Pessemier, 1974; Plummer 1971–1972;, 1972). It has been especially useful in helping the marketer realize the audience's time allocation, purchasing behavior, leisure activities and in turn provides information for future predictions and communication objectives (Wells, 1974).

Specific application of lifestyle research has focused on questionnaire items that ask subjects about their normal behavior. Some approaches have employed fairly general behavioral tendencies as a basis for making predictions about individuals' reactions to products or advertising messages (Wells, 1970; Wells & Tigert, 1971), whereas others have utilized more specific treatments of behavioral prediction (Heller, 1970). Taken from the more general mode of lifestyle research (Wells & Tigert, 1971), Table 12.3 provides examples of questions posed to potential audience members in an attempt to better understand their lifestyle behavior.

TABLE 12.3
Examples from Lifestyle Questionnaires
(taken from Hustad & Pessemier, 1974)

Price Conscious	Art Enthusiast
I shop a lot of specials	I enjoy going to concerts
I usually watch the advertisements for announcements of sales	I enjoy going through art galleries
A person can save a lot of money by shopping around for bargains	I like ballet

Child Oriented	Fashion Conscious
I take a lot of time and effort to teach my children good habits	I usually have one or more outfits that are of the very latest fashion
My children are the most important thing in my life	When I must choose between the two I usually dress for fashion, not for comfort
I try to arrange my home for my children's convenience	I often try the latest hairdo styles when they change

Lifestyle assessment is a worthwhile complement to value research in a psychographic approach to audience analysis. Together, these two conceptual methodologies can provide information about publics or audience members that demographic techniques could never accomplish independently. As a composite model, demographics combined with psychographics allow in-depth information for making decisions about message content and style. Public relations practitioners are in a much better position to predict audience reaction to communication strategies with this type of strategy, particularly in segmented and specialized campaigns. However, an additional element of audience analysis is still available that would further expand the ability to predict message reaction: emotionality.

EMOTIONALITY

Obtaining a comprehensive profile of a potential audience requires a consideration of the target's emotional state of mind and predicted emotional responses to a message. Emotions are not as easily assessed as demographic characteristics, values, and lifestyle behavior, yet they are intrinsic components in the process of completing the audience profile. Obviously, everyone emotionally reacts to various stimuli differently, and categorizing an aggregate audience according to an emotional state is a risky undertaking. However, by uncovering a trend of both superficial and deep-seated emotions associated with issues, ideas, concepts and messages; message construction can be facilitated in a public relations campaign.

Emotional considerations of audience analysis are techniques unique from previous strategies discussed because different phenomenon are present. Titchner (1908) believed elements of emotion differed from the elements of thought explaining that our experiences of hunger, dizziness, or tiredness represent a stage or level from which we ascend to emotions; that emotions again represent a stage or level from which we descend to secondary feelings. According to Zikmund and d'Amico (1986) emotions are generally considered motivational factors and do not explicitly fall under the categories specified by the psychographic profile.

Emotions and Cognition

The controversy surrounding the relationship between affect (emotion) and cognition has continued for some time. Notable scholars have lined up on both sides of the issue and the arguments made are worth considering from a public relations perspective. The debate involves supporters of two perspectives: those who believe that all affect and emotion are mediated or related to cognition or at least awareness and those who believe affect and cognition are independent. Zajonc and his colleagues (Zajonc, 1978, 1984, 1985; Zajonc & Markus, 1982a, 1982b) as well as (Flynn, Edwards & Bandler, 1971), have been active in pursuing research leading to a theoretical supposition that affect and cognitive processes can be independent. In the other camp are those who challenge the assumption that affect can occur without some cognitive experience (Gorden & Holyoak, 1983; Tsal, 1985; Watts, 1983).

Such a scholarly discussion is important to public relations for two reasons. First, if affect can be independent of cognition; that is, emotion that can guide decision-making can occur without awareness, then basic theories of logical appeal (cognitive strategies) should be modified. Second, if emotions and cognition are independent in certain circumstances; measurement of audience analysis affect toward ideas and issues becomes more problematic requiring more specialized assessment procedures. For example, the Nisbitt and Wilson (1977) song can be played at full volume in the context of this phenomenon (emotion cannot be recalled if cognition was present).

The perceived quagmire associated with emotional assessment has probably affected the utilization of emotions as a pre-message analysis strategy. It is apparent that the identification of emotions has assumed a secondary role behind cognitive processes, values, vividness, norms and motivational attributes as the primary foci of communication research (Becker & Connor, 1979; Boote, 1981; Kisielius & Sternthal, 1984; Mitchell & Olsen, 1981; Woodruff et al., 1983). The paucity of emotional assessment in public relations is also probably due to a general assumption that emotions are fleeting; they can change rapidly from second to second depending on the stimuli being mentally processed. The psychological concept of emotions is rather arbitrary and elusive with no clear agreement on how emotions should actually be classified (Brandstatter, 1983).

Categories of Emotions

To achieve an acceptable description of what emotions are and how they relate to the concept of audience analysis in public relations requires both contextual and taxonomic treatments of the concept. First, emotions can be defined as psychological transmission of an event into personal attitudinal adjustments which may be classified into various feeling states (Brandstatter, 1983; Titchner, 1908). These feeling states have been typologized into categories of emotions (see Table 12.4). A recent treatment of such typology was provided by Batra and Ray (1986) based on their review of Izard (1977), Ekman, Freisen, and Ellsworth, (1982), Frijda (1970) and Osgood (1966).

While other typologies of emotional categories have been advanced, the present one has more potential utility for public relation theorists and practitioners. The explanatory power of this typology is appealing and measurements of these categories can be constructed depending on the level of data desired and the purpose of the research.

Measurement of Emotion

Efforts to determine the role of emotion and how to use it in audience analysis first require discriminating measures of audiences' emotional response (Stout & Leckenby, 1985). A number of empirical attempts have explicitly dealt with the measurement of emotional response toward messages. For example, Brandstatter (1983) has conducted several studies to measure emotional responses in everyday situations employing diary records. Subjects in these studies kept diaries on their emotional attitudes or emotional responses at a prearranged time of the day with the time of the day being different for every day over a 30-day period. Respondents described their present mood state and sometimes

TABLE 12.4
Emotional Categories
(taken from Batra & Ray, 1986)

Interest/expectancy:	A feeling of being engaged, caught up, curious and anticipative
Surprise:	A feeling of uncertainty, astonishment or even confusion
Disgust/scorn:	A desire to distance oneself from that which is "spoiled" (revulsion, contempt, feeling superior)
Anger:	A state of being annoyed or not being able to do what one desires to do
Fear/anxiety:	A feeling of apprehension, uncertainty, insecurity, and perceived danger
Shame:	A heightened degree of incompetence, inadequacy, self-contempt and self-ridicule
Guilt:	A feeling of being wrong
Sadness:	A state of being downhearted, discouraged, miserable, lonely, and helpless
Surgency, elation, vigor, activation (SEVAL):	A feeling of intense joy combined with feelings of confidence and vigor
Deactivation:	A self-indulgent relaxed state
Social/affection:	A feeling of being loved, of engendering trust, and of being accepted in the surrounding world
Drives:	States brought by tissue changes or tissue deficits such as hunger, thirst, and fatigue

described their emotional response through a variety of adjectives that were in turn rated as positive or negative by the researcher. Last, the respondents were also instructed to explain their moods by identifying goals (motives) that could also account for the mood.

Thus, Brandstatter (1983) had three measures of why respondents felt they were in a particular mood: mood score, adjective value, and goal satisfaction. Brandstatter concluded from his analysis that many situations cannot be avoided and when there is a choice they are approached or avoided not so much according to present mood state but according to expected satisfaction that is perceived as a possible amelioration or deterioration of the present state. He also suggests that powerless and uncomfortable surroundings may also cause mood alternations. The adjectives by which subjects described their mood states also gives some further information on the complex qualities of emotions. In Bradstatter's study over 600 adjectives were used to describe emotions.

Other methods of measuring emotions have proven to have a certain degree of reliability and validity. For example, Batra and Ray (1986) employed an open-ended response technique where subjects ranked stimuli and subsequently wrote down and orally responded according to their felt emotion. Researchers code these responses according to a category system. Obviously, intercoder reliability is a paramount issue as is the integrity of the a priori taxonomy utilized for classification.

Another method of emotional evaluation involves a rating technique. One such procedure has been suggested by Zeitlan and Westwood (1986). With this technique, subjects are exposed to a stimuli and asked to rate what they saw or heard across a battery of items relating to emotional responses. Items such as happy, disgust, exciting, and anxiety are posed with accompanying evaluations such as "does not describe the stimuli at all" to "very strongly describes the stimuli." Close-ended methods such as those described by Zeitlan and Westwood avail researchers the opportunity to employ higher level interval data and make data manipulation less of a coding chore. On the other hand, this type of data is less rich because it forces subjects into choosing a pre-determined emotional category.

In other material related to the use of emotions in the communication process, Knapp (1978) and Ekman et al. (1982) have addressed the use of verbal and nonverbal expressive behavior such as facial expressions and vocal cues to express emotions. A glance at the area round the eyes is sometimes enough to determine what emotion is being felt by a person. For instance, eyelids that are raised, curved and the lower lid drawn down is an expression of the emotion surprise. Another example is when the upper eyelids inner corner is raised and the skin below the eye is triangulated is an expression of sadness. As far as facial expressions are concerned, a frown may represent anger, sadness, or depression. A smile may represent happiness, surprise, or pleasure.

RECOMMENDATIONS AND IMPLICATIONS

The utilization of demographic and psychographic information in conjunction with emotional assessment would provide public relations specialists with what we call a Composite Audience Profile (CAP; see Fig. 12.1). Such a technique would allow for a more comprehensive analysis of potential reaction to communication messages. Adhering to such a technique prior to a communication campaign would reveal how a targeted audience feels about a certain subject and indicate how best to trigger those cognitive and emotional aspects favorably associated with a message

The CAP model holds important implications for existing advertising and public relations audience procedures. For instance, the Personal

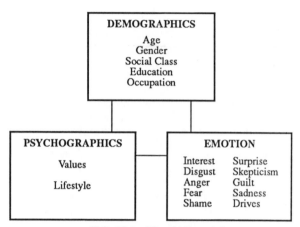

FIG. 12.1   The CAP model.

Profile model (Hafer & White, 1982) could be used more effectively when utilizing a procedure such as CAP. Using psychographic profiles of audiences can make statistical and demographic information more useful (Domzal & Kernan, 1983). Hafer and White define a personal profile as the creation of an ideal person through the use of psychographics and a review of marketing and statistical information plus human insights and a little bit of imagination. The person could be real because he or she is created out of imagination and demographic statistics of the target market.

It is difficult to argue with the theory that a writer can communicate more naturally and more effectively when speaking to just one audience member than to an entire mass audience (Hafer & White, 1982). Instead of developing a conglomeration of the entire audience it would behoove professionals to develop the personal profile of just one audience member to better meet the needs of the entire audience. The guidelines in Table 12.5 may help clarify how the CAP model can be integrated into communication theory.

The personal profile method is but one suggestion of how demographics, psychographics, and emotionality can be effectively utilized for a comprehensive audience analysis. Other methods utilizing group or segment analysis could be appropriately enacted depending upon purposes and resources. The purpose of this chapter was to provide the necessary background information to help better understand how to implement a comprehensive audience analysis technique. If an organization can better judge how their messages will affect their target markets/audiences they can provide audiences with the stimuli and achieve

TABLE 12.5
Guidelines for Integrating CAP Model into Communication Theory

---

1. Create an individual. Give the individual a name. Use your imagination on what they look like.
2. Examine demographic data: age, income, occupation etc.
3. Examine psychographical data: interests, attitudes, values, lifestyle etc.
4. Determine the emotional response desired of the target market and incorporate these into the message that will be delivered to the target market or audience.
5. Tailor the message to meet the characteristics of the individual created.
6. Deliver the message as if talking to that one individual.
7. Develop a response mechanism to determine if the message was accurately received and the appeals or emotional characteristics were achieved (i.e., response rate of direct mail pieces, number of letters received etc.).
8. Change the message if desired outcome was not achieved.
9. Return to step one if needed.

---

the emotional response needed to better fulfill organizational, communication, and relational objectives, and to help produce growth within their own industry.

REFERENCES

Aaker, D. A., Stayman, D. M., & Hagerty M. R. (1986) Warmth in advertising: Measurement, impact, and sequence effects. *Journal of Consumer Research, 12,* 365–381.

Alpert, M. (1972) Personality and the determinants of product choice. *Journal of Marketing Research, 9,* 89–92.

Alwitt, L. F., & Mitchell, A. A. (1985) *Psychographical processes and advertising effects: Theory, research, and applications.* Hillsdale, NJ: Lawrence Erlbaum Associates.

Batra, R., & Ray, M. (1986) Affective responses mediating acceptance of advertising. *Journal of Consumer Research, 13,* 234–249.

Beatty, S., Kahle, L., Homer, P., & Misra, S. (1985) Alternative measurement approaches to consumer values: The list of values and the rokeach value survey. *Psychology and Marketing, 2,* 181–200.

Becker, B. W., & Connor, P. E. (1979) Personal values of the heavy user of mass media. *Journal of Advertising Research, 21,* 37–43.

Boote, A. (1981) Market segmentation by personal values and salient product attributes. *Journal of Advertising Research, 21,* 29–35.

Bovee, C. L., & Arens, W. F. (1982) *Contemporary advertising.* Homewood, IL: Irwin.

Brandstatter, H. (1983) Emotional responses to other person's in everyday life situations. *Journal of Personality and Social Psychology, 45,* 871–883.

Conrad, C. (1985) *Strategic organizational communication: Cultures, situations, and adaption.* New York: CBS College Publishing.
Crable, R., & Vibbert, S. (1986) *Public relations as communication management.* New York: Longman.
Demby, E. (1974) Psychographics and from whence it came. In W. Wells (Ed.) *Life style and psychographics* (pp. 11–30). Chicago: American Marketing Association.
Domzal, T., & Kernan, J. (1983) Television audience segmentation according to need gratification. *Journal of Advertising Research, 23,* 37–48.
Ekman, P., Freisen, W., & Ellsworth, P. (1982) What emotion categories or dimensions can judge facial behavior? In P. Ekman (Ed.), *Emotion in the human face* (pp. 39–55). Cambridge, England: Cambridge University Press.
Feather, N. (1975) *Values in education and society.* New York: The Free Press.
Flynn, J., Edwards, S., & Bandler, Jr., R. (1971) Changes in sensory and motor systems during centrally elicited attack. *Behavioral Science, 16,* 1–19.
Frijda, N. (1970) Emotion and recognition of emotion. In M. Arnold (Ed.), *Feelings and emotions: The Loyola symposium* (pp. 215–251). New York: Academic Press.
Gorden, P., & Holyoak, K. (1983) Implicit learning and generalization of the 'mere exposure' effect. *Journal of Personality and Social Psychology, 45,* 492–500.
Hafer, W., & White, G. (1982) *Advertising writing: Putting creative strategy to work* (2nd ed.). New York: West Publishing.
Heller, H. (1970) Defining target markets by their attitude profile. IN L. Adler & I. Crespi (Eds.), *Attitude research on the rocks* (pp. 45–57). Chicago: American Marketing Association.
Hustad, T., & Pessemier, E. (1974) The development and application of psychographic, life style, and associated activity and attitude measures. In W. Wells (Ed.), *Life style and psychographics* (pp. 33–67). Chicago: American Marketing Association.
Izard, C. (1977) *Human emotions.* New York: Plenum Press.
Jamieson, K., & Campbell, K. (1983) *The interplay of influence: Mass media & their publics in news, advertising, and politics.* Belmont, CA: Wadsworth.
Kahle, L. (1983) *Social values and social change: Adaption to life in America.* New York: Praeger.
Kahle, L. (1984) *Attitudes and social adaption: A person-situation interaction approach.* Oxford, U.K.: Pergamon.
Kahle, L. (1985) Social values in the eighties: A special issue. *Psychology and Marketing, 2,* 231–237.
Kahle, L. (1986) The nine nations of North America and the value basis of geographic segmentation. *Journal of Marketing, 50,* 37–47.
Kahle, L., Beatty, S., & Homer, P. (1986) Alternative measurement approaches to consumer values: The list of values (LOV) and values and lifestyle (VALS). *Journal of Consumer Research 13,* 405–409.
Kisielius, J., & Sternthal, B. (1984) Detecting and explaining vividness effects in attitudinal judgements. *Journal of Marketing Research, 21,* 54–64.
Knapp, M. (1978) *Nonverbal communication in human interaction* (2nd Ed.). New York: Holt, Rinehart & Winston.

Lazer, W. (1963) Life style concepts and marketing. Toward scientific market-
ing. *Proceedings of the American Marketing Association,* 130–139.
Lazer, W., & Smallwood, J. (1972) Consumer environments and life styles of the
seventies. *Business Topics,* 5–17.
MacLaclan, J. (1983) Making a message memorable and persuasive. *Journal of
Advertising Research, 23,* 51–59.
Maslow, A. (1954) *Motivation and personality.* New York: Warner.
Mitchell, A. (1983) *The nine American life styles.* New York: Warner.
Mitchell, A. A., & Olsen, J. C. (1981) Are product attributes beliefs the only
mediator of advertising effects on brand attitudes? *Journal of Marketing Re-
search, 18,* 318–332.
Murdock, G., & Janus, N. (1983) *Mass communications and the advertising industry.*
Paris, France: United Nations Educational Scientific and Cultural Organiza-
tion.
Newsom, D., & Scott, A. (1985) *This is pr: The realities of public relations* (3rd ed.).
Belmont, CA: Wadsworth.
Nisbitt, R., & Wilson, T. (1977) Telling more than we know: Verbal reports on
mental processes. *Psychological Review, 84,* 231–259.
Osgood, C. (1966) Dimensionality of the sematic space for communication via
facial expressions. *Scandinavian Journal of Psychology, 7,* 1–30.
Plummer, J. (1971–1972) Life style patterns: A new constraint for mass com-
munications research. *Journal of Broadcasting, 16,* 78–89.
Plummer, J. (1972) Life style patterns and commercial bank credit card usage.
Journal of Marketing, 35, 35–41.
Reisman, D., Glazer, N., & Denny, R. (1950) *The lonely crowd.* New Haven, CT:
Yale University Press.
Reynolds, T. J., & Jolly, J. (1980) Measuring personal values: An evaluation of
alternative methods. *Journal of Marketing Research, 17,* 531–536.
Rokeach, M. (1973) *The nature of human values.* New York: The Free Press.
Scissors, J., & Surmanek, J. (1982) *Advertising media planning* (2nd ed.). Chicago,
IL; Crain Books.
Stout, P., & Leckenby, J. (1985) *A typology for identifying emotional response to
advertising.* Unpublished manuscript, University of Texas at Austin.
Tsal, Y. (1985) On the relationship between cognitive and affective processes: A
critique of Zajonc and Markus. *Journal of Consumer Research, 12,* 358–362.
Titchner, E. (1908) *Lifestyle and psychographics.* Chicago: American Marketing
Association.
Vernoff, J., Douvan, E., & Kulka, R. (1981) *The inner American.* New York: Basic
Books.
Vinson, D., Scott, J. E., & Lamont, L. (1977) The role of personal values in
marketing and consumer behavior. *Journal of Marketing, 41,* 44–50.
Watts, F. (1983) Affective cognition: A sequel to Zajonc and Rachman. *Behavior
Research and Therapy, 21,* 89–90.
Wells, W. (1970) It's a Wyeth, not a Warhol World. *Harvard Business Review, 46,*
26–32.
Wells, W. (1974) *Lifestyle and psychographics.* Chicago: American Marketing
Association.

Wells, W., & Tigert, D. (1971) Activities, interests, and opinions. *Journal of Advertising Research, 11,* 27–35.

Woodruff, R., Cadotte, E., & Jenkins, R. (1983) Modeling consumer satisfaction using experience based norms. *Journal of Marketing Research, 20,* 296–304.

Zajonc, R. (1978) Feeling and thinking preferences need no inferences. *American Psychologist, 35,* 151–175.

Zajonc, R. (1984) On the primary of affect. *American Psychologist, 39,* 117–123.

Zajonc, R. (1985) Emotion and facial expression: A theory reclaimed. *Science, 228,* 15–21.

Zajonc, R., & Markus, H. (1982a) Affective and cognitive factors in preferences. *Journal of Consumer Research, 9,* 123–131.

Zajonc, R., & Markus, H. (1982b) Must all affect be mediated by cognition? *Journal of Consumer Research, 12,* 363–364.

Zikmund, W., & d'Amico, M. (1986) *Marketing* (2nd ed.), New York: Wiley.

Zotti, E. (1985) Thinking psychographically. *Public Relations Journal, 41,* 26–30.

Zeitlin, D., & Westwood, R. (1986) Measuring emotional response. *Journal of Advertising Research, 25,* 34–44.

The Theory of Psychological Type Congruence in Public Relations and Persuasion

Carolyn Garrett Cline
Michael H. McBride
Southwest Texas State University

Randy E. Miller
University of Texas at Austin

ABSTRACT

This chapter builds on the ideas postulated by Carl Jung that individuals vary in the way they prefer to use certain functions and that these preferences combine into distinct, innate personality types. The authors contend that these types, as described by psychologist David Keirsey, offer a well-tested, reliable, and valid method of segmenting audience motivations and personality.

The theory of type congruence proposes that messages and products or services can also be organized by type; applying cognitive stability theories and categorization theory, the authors propose a model for improving communication reception and retention by achieving a congruence between perceived type of the message and perceived type of the object.

Public relations takes a view of persuasion that is, at best, ambivalent. The roots of modern public relations are solidly planted in persuasion theory based on Freudian psychology, an understandable situation because pioneer Edward Bernays was a double nephew of Sigmund Freud and often consulted with psychologists in planning campaigns. Although Grunig and Hunt (1984) deal with "scientific persuasion" as one of the four major models of public relations practice, most texts dismiss the role of persuasion in public relations either by citing Cantrill's dated "laws" of public opinion and propaganda techniques (Cutlip, Center, & Broom, 1985; Newsom & Scott, 1981), by describing practical applications of accepted conventions (Wilcox, Ault, & Agee, 1986), or by considering public opinion and persuasion theory virtually interchangeable (Seitel, 1984).

Psychological theory is even less visible in public relations, perhaps in a rejection of the attempts to apply to a mass audience Freudian theory that is so strongly rooted in what Jung (1933) called the individual choice of neurosis. The complexity of understanding human motivation based on intensive classic psychoanalysis makes such theories difficult to apply on a practical level.

On the other hand, researchers in interpersonal and organizational communication have sustained a clearly defined body of work attempting to analyze precisely what public relations strives to accomplish: an understanding of human cognition and motivation leading to what Bernays termed "the creation of consent." According to McGuire (1981), about 5% of the 25,000 books and articles summarized in *Psychological Abstracts* each year deal directly with communication effects on attitudes and audiences. McGuire (1981) wrote that "recently we published an annotated bibliography of the persuasion literature (Lipstein & McGuire, 1978) that lists over 7,000 books and articles even though it is restricted largely to recent and applied studies" (p. 43). Yet, McGuire (1981) noted that the social and behavioral sciences:

> are still at a rather primitive stage of theorizing, slouching toward Bethlehem to give birth to simple descriptive categorical theories rather than the axiomatic systems theories; that is, we are still working on our periodic tables rather than on our Euclidean geometries. (p. 43)

This chapter proposes a return to both psychology and the study of persuasion, adopting recent persuasive theories and the older concept of personality types proposed by Carl Jung (1923) in an attempt to take a simple categorization of the human cognitive process and examine it as a potential model for improving public relations.

COGNITIVE STABILITY THEORIES

Much of the recent research into persuasion theory (Reardon, 1981; Zajonc, 1960; Zajonc, 1968) has in common "the notion that thoughts, beliefs, attitudes, and behavior tend to organize themselves in meaningful and sensible ways" (Zajonc 1960, p. 280).

McGuire (1981) segmented cognitive stability theory into four "families," two of which are relevant to this study: consistency theory and categorization theory. Consistency theory, extremely popular in the 1960s, is based on the concept of the individual's necessity to maintain an equilibrium based on thought rather than feeling. The earliest theories of Heider (1946, 1958) and others (Cartwright & Harary, 1956; Newcomb, 1953) were fairly simple models of balance or imbalance. A second approach, the congruence theory as proposed by Osgood and Tannenbaum (1955), was concerned with moving away from stability toward resolution in order to restore equilibrium and was explained as a principle of cognitive interaction by others (Rokeach and Rothman, 1965). Osgood & Tannenbaum (1955) explained that "changes in evaluation are always in the direction of increased congruity with the existing frame of reference" (p. 43).

McGuire's (1981) own explanation for the second family, categorization theory, is clear enough to warrant a full citation here:

> This second class of dynamic theories depicts the person, submerged in a sea of stimuli from the internal and external environments, as acting like a filing clerk striving desperately to cope with the stimulation overload by sorting the incoming information among existing cognitive categories. This concept of the person has been popular from the turn of the century Wuerzberg school to current structuralists like Levi-Strauss and Piaget. It was a particularly popular form of persuasive communication theorizing during the pre-World War II decade when Muzafer Sherif, Luchins, and Asch used it to investigate the importance of first impressions in providing a frame of reference for experiencing subsequent events. Woefel et al. . . . present a recent variant. These theories suggest that persuasion involves not so much changing one's attitude or behavior toward a given stimulus object but rather changing one's perception of what is the stimulus object about which one is expressing one's attitude. (p. 57)

This chapter proposes a theory combining both of these cognitive stability approaches; that is, basic in this theory is the need of the human mind for cognitive stability, as well as the drive of the individual to categorize experiences. The intention of the authors is to introduce into the cognitive stability theories the categorization model of Carl Jung.

PERSONALITY AND NEEDS THEORY

Advertising and marketing research seems to have rejected the cognitive stability approach in favor of the affective theories, most notably those psychological approaches used in the affective growth approaches made popular by Maslow (1954) and Packard (1964). The impact of both Gestalt and Freudian-dominated psychology is clear in the use by marketing researchers of such classic psychological tools as the Minnesota Multiphasic Personality Inventory or the Thematic Apperception Test, which are used on potential consumers, as well as in-depth interviews that at times approach classic Freudian analysis. Behind this approach, according to Larson (1986), lay three assumptions:

> First, they assumed that people don't always know what they want when they make a purchase. Second, they assumed that you cannot rely on what people say they like and dislike. Finally, they assumed that people do not act logically or rationally. (p. 119)

However, mass persuaders are not able to accept a totally illogical audience, for then there would be no consistent way to predict behavior. Thus, marketing researchers have attempted to establish categories for consumers based on wants and needs, and many public relations campaigns have been based on these theories. Researchers have used personality variables in attempting to explain consumer differences and to link human traits with product appeals (e.g., Martin, 1977; Patti & Mizerski, 1978; Van Auken, 1978). Although some researchers acknowledge limited success with gaining broad-based agreement on defining personality (Plummer, 1984/1985; Stanton, 1978) and with establishing strong relationships between personality and purchase behavior (Cravens, 1987; Harrell, 1986; Stanton, 1978), many admit that personality is an important marketing variable in buyer behavior (Britt, 1978; Churchill, 1987; Cravens, 1987; Kassarjian, 1978; Rachman, 1985; Runyon, 1981).

Although there is a strong feeling that personality can provide insight into lifestyle elements (Harrell, 1986), and could prove a useful variable in analyzing behavior (Kotler, 1986), it has proven far more difficult to categorize personality than lifestyle. However, the former would seem the more critical factor, for personality itself as Assael (1984) noted "is more deep-seated than lifestyle since personality variables reflect consistent, enduring patterns of behavior" (p. 266). In fact, Shimp (1978) wrote "The prevalent view . . . is that [personality research] may provide some insight into how consumers differ in their . . . response to advertising appeals" (p. 78). Britt (1978) carried this view still further:

> While personality characteristics differ considerably among individuals, if a communicator is aware of the personality similarities among members of his [sic] target audience, he [sic] can design his [sic] messages for maximum perceiving. The personality of the individual always will be a larger determinant of his [sic] actions than any other aspect. (p. 179)

Although not all attempts to segment markets on the basis of personality similarities and differences have been successful (Plummer, 1984/1985), there are instances where such analyses have helped to exploit the development of products and devise appeals for a variety of products that tend to play on personality differences in prospects. For example, in the 1950s, efforts were made to segment automobile buyers on the basis of personality differences (Evans, 1959), but more successful segmentation strategies were later developed (based on personality traits) for categories like women's cosmetics, liquor, cigarettes and insurance (Young, 1972). Traits such as sociability, autonomy, self-confidence, dominance, order, adaptability, affiliation and others (Horton, 1979) commonly have been used. A classic case from the 1970s is the profiling of four personality types of beer drinkers by drinking pattern and age group (Ackoff & Emshoff, 1975).

Defined, for instance, as "the dynamic organization within the individual of those psychophysical systems that determine his characteristic behavior and thought" (Allport, 1967, p. 28) and as "characteristics that make the person what he or she is and distinguish each individual from every other individual" (Donelson, 1973, p. 3), personality remains a valid realm of investigation for persuaders.

This chapter examines Carl Jung's theory, virtually an untapped research arena for persuaders, and one that offers promise for predicting the best match of message to audience and predicting responses to various appeals. Although Jungian personality theory has found wide acceptance in certain fields, including education, counseling, business consulting and religion, it has been applied only recently to advertising, marketing or public relations (Brock & Shavitt, 1985; Cline, 1985; Cline, McBride, & Miller, 1987a, 1987b; Cline, McBride, Miller, & Hammond, 1987; Jewler & Hunter, 1986; McBride, Cline, & Miller, 1987a, 1987b, 1987c, 1987d).

JUNGIAN TYPOLOGY THEORY

Jung (1923) posited that people are different in fundamental ways, although they all have similar internal instincts. (None is more important than another, but the preference for how we function is of considerable importance.) Preference for a given "function" is characteristic; thus, people may be "typed" by this preference, resulting in Jung's function or psychological types. Jung's typology is often misunderstood and oversimplified, although Jung (1933) himself valued his type theory "for the objective reason that it offers a system of comparison and orientation" (p. 94).

The personality differences concern the way individuals *prefer* to use their minds, specifically in the way they perceive and make judgments

(Myers, 1980; Roberts, 1977; Roberts, no date). There are four functions, which combine into 4 major personality types and 16 more specific individual types. The functions, as Myers described, are:

Extraversion (E)/Introversion (I)—the relative interest in the outer and inner worlds. The introvert's main interests are in the inner world of concepts and ideas, whereas the extravert is more involved with the outer world of people and things.

Sensing(S)/Intuition (N)—the preferred way of perceiving. Sensing is the method of becoming aware of things directly through our five senses. Intuition is indirect perception by way of the unconscious, incorporating ideas or associations that the unconscious tacks onto perceptions coming from outside.

Thinking (T)/Feeling (F)—the preferred way of coming to conclusions. Thinking is a logical process aimed at an impersonal finding. Feeling is process by way of appreciation—equally reasonable in its fashion—bestowing on things a personal, subjective value.

Judgment (J)/Perception (P)—the method of dealing with the world around us. An individual will use the judgment function to shut off perception, to achieve closure, and end a situation. Perception is used to maintain an input of ideas or information or retain an open mind.

Jung said neither that a person is one or the other of each of the four type pairs nor that a person does not change in the extent of preference for one or the other of the four preferences over time. Rather, one generally is a type to some degree, but the preference for that function may strengthen or weaken.

Partly because of the dominance of Freudian theory in the mid-20th-century, Jungian type theory was rather neglected until the work of Katharine C. Briggs and her daughter, Isabel Briggs Myers, who developed a measuring instrument for type by testing more than 5,000 medical students and 10,000 nurses. The result of their years of research is the Myers-Briggs Type Indicator or MBTI (Myers, 1962a, 1962b, 1970, 1980), a tool for identifying 16 different patterns of action, and whose type categories appear to be adequately reliable for adult samples (Carlyn, 1977). The MBTI appeared in the 1950s and has been so widely used that it has created a renewed international interest in the theory of personality types and a growing acceptance of the validity of the MBTI and similar measuring instruments as useful research. Such research, Roberts, Fox, and Branch (1974) noted, has "expanded and clarified Jung's theory that seemingly random variation in human behavior is not really due to chance; it is, in fact, the logical result of basic observable and even measurable differences in mental functioning" (p. 216).

KEIRSEY TEMPERAMENT SORTER

Psychologists David Keirsey and Marilyn Bates (1984) have supported Jung's theory of psychological type and the MBTI, but they proposed a different interpretation of the manner in which the preferred functions operate together to effect behavior.

Because they support the concept that people are different and that being different is positive, Keirsey and Bates say that human growth occurs by differentiation rather than by integration, thereby subordinating the concept of "function type" to the concept of "temperament." Keirsey and Bates (1984) asserted that temperament, determined by consistency in personal actions theoretically observable from an early age, "determines behavior because behavior is the instrument for getting us what we must have" (p. 30). Furthermore, temperament "places a signature or thumbprint on each of one's actions, making it recognizably one's own" (Keirsey & Bates, 1984, p. 27).

For the most part, recent research supports the Keirsey and Bates approach (Hoffman & Betkouski, 1981; McCarley & Carskadon, 1986) suggesting that the instrument is not only reliable but also appears to have considerable validity in the eyes of the respondents themselves (Ware & Yokomoto, 1985).

Symbolized by figures in Greek mythology, the four temperaments are listed here and illustrated in Fig. 13.1.

Dionysians (SP: Sensing Perceivers)—approximately 38% of the population, these are motivated by freedom and action. They value joy and release. They live for and enjoy the present. They lead energetic, spontaneous lifestyles and may become easily bored with routine. They may seem restless and impulsive to other temperaments, but they operate well in high-risk, emergency situations. They tend to be super-realists.

Epimetheans (SJ: Sensing Judgers)—also approximately 38% of the population, they are motivated by duty and responsibility. They value belonging and usefulness. They need to work and feel obligated to social and other units (family, church, company, community, etc.). They may be considered conservative by some and serious by others, but they tend to be stabilizing influences, taking care of unnecessary details ignored by other temperaments.

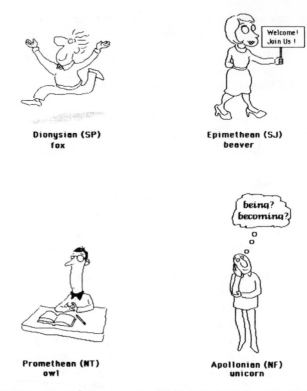

Dionysian (SP)
fox

Epimethean (SJ)
beaver

Promethean (NT)
owl

Apollonian (NF)
unicorn

FIG.13.1.   Four temperaments by Cline and McBride, based on Keirsey's temperaments (1987).

Prometheans (NT: Intuitive Thinkers)—approximately 12% of the population, motivated by power and knowledge. They value science and theory. They seek to understand, control, predict and explain phenomena. They want to know everything; they covet intelligence, and they can be perfectionists. Logical communicators, they demand high standards and may be considered tense, compulsive, arrogant, and oblivious to others' emotions.

Apollonians (NF: Intuitive Feelers)—also 12% of the population, they desire spirit and unity. They value ethics and relationships. They seek the possibilities, peace, beauty and important causes. They strongly believe in people and purpose in life; thus, they can help others communicate honestly and openly. They tend to be dramatic and romantic and may seem naive and unrealistic, but they keep searching for deeper meanings, new insights and personal identity.

THEORY OF TYPE CONGRUENCE

This chapter proposes a theory of congruence not unlike much of the earlier work on cognitive stability and categorization, but we suggest that one of the chief methods by which the individual categorizes many objects is linked to the Jungian theory of type. In other words, a subject may consider object X not only from a purely evaluative stance as negative/positive, or favorable/unfavorable, but also as belonging to a personality type, whether from some intrinsic characteristic or from the way the object has been positioned in the subject's mind. For instance, a sports car carries the image of the exciting SP; the IBM-PC suggests the scientific NT; the United Way the dutiful SJ, and a guru or self-actualization movement the spirit-driven NF.

The theory of type congruence proposes that a conflict between the receiver's perception of an object's intrinsic or positioned type and a persuader's portrayal of the object as a different type creates an imbalance in the receiver. Stated more succinctly, the receiver will prefer a presentation where the type of the object is congruent with the receiver's perception of the object's type.

PILOT STUDY

Implicit in this theory is the concept that many products, services and organizations either intrinsically possess a type or can be positioned by the persuader to be representative of the type. In assigning one or more type characteristics to a product or advertisement, the following keyword descriptors of type were chosen from Keirsey and Bates (1984):

Dionysian Type (SP):
Freedom; action; enjoyment; live for now; impulsive; restless; urge to take off; exciting; compulsive; lust for action; crisis-oriented; endurance; strength; boldness; optimism; cheerful; charming; witty; colorful; spontaneous; little motivation toward goal; play ethic

Epimethean Type (SJ):
Useful; dutiful; must belong; responsible; giver; caretaker; nurturer; parental; obligated; work ethic; desire for hierarchy; pessimism; membership hunger; establishes and maintains institutions; conservative; heritage important; resistant to swift change; concerned with title and entitlement; traditional; stress on home, safety, family.

Promethean Type (NT):
Need to understand and control nature; intelligent; need for competence; self-critical; exacting; demanding; perfectionist; fear of failure; schedules "play"; uses recreation for self-improvement; can become isolated; verbally parsimonious; drawn toward science, technology; work-driven; focus on future; resistant to emotion

Apollonian Type (NF):
Intuitive, feeling; goal of "becoming"; hunger for utility and uniqueness; self-actualization drive; actions must have meaning; integrity; significance; search for subtleties and metaphors; drawn to writing, persuasion, inspiration; sense of mission; sees good in others; hard to know; visionary; passion for creativity; emphasis on what might be; drawn to romance, fantasy; spirit-driven

Organizations and products can either possess a type by their very nature or by their positioning—cigarettes have variously been portrayed as SP (the Marlboro Man), SJ (Catch the Salem Spirit), NT (a millimeter longer), or even NF ("You've Come a Long Way, Baby.") In the case of cigarettes, however, the current perception of the product, combined with the surgeon general's warning, suggests that smoking has become more clearly an SP (i.e., danger-filled) action.

Methodology

The utility of this Psychological Type Congruence Theory was tested first on a series of advertisements. The theory's direct application to public relations is discussed later in the chapter. Ads were used because the restrictions of space and design offer fewer elements to confound the coding and because it was possible to measure the appeal and potential effectiveness of the ads as related to type congruence.

Students in public relations and advertising classes at two universities were trained in the theory of types and were asked to classify 50 advertisements, chosen at random from magazines, as to their dominant type. Forty percent of the ads demonstrated a single dominant type (using an intercoder agreement of 70% as the cut-off), 30% showed a moderately strong primary type with a secondary type, whereas the remainder were classified as "mixed types" meaning, for example, that the headline was a different type from the body copy. A mixed type would be the Polaroid advertisement with the headline that urged readers to "Give a great Polaroid gift this Christmas" (an SJ message, replete with tradition, giving, sentiment) and with body copy that stressed the technological advantages of the "high-surge Polapulse."

The authors assumed that each major part of a message delivers a "cue" as to the type of the product as it is portrayed; in some cases, the art is the dominant cue, in others the headline, but rarely is it the body copy. The "cue" enters the cognitive system of the receiver and reacts with a previous categorization; if there is no categorization, the receiver must create one based on the cue.

When conflict occurs (if, for example, the dominant cue is NT but the pre-existent category is SP), the receiver is faced with the problem of reducing dissonance (Festinger, 1957). The receiver faces three choices: (a) to examine other elements of the ad for cues more consistent with the categorization and consider any later, congruent cue as dominant; (b) to change the categorization of the product, or (c) to reject the message outright or to use selective perception or selective retention.

This led to our research questions:

1. Would the congruence of the types of an ad and the product increase recall of ads?
2. Would the dominance of the congruent cue increase recall?

Again, the questions were first tested on advertisements, and the specific public relations applications were examined later.

Panels were selected from graduate students in public relations and persuasion classes who had received extensive training in the background and applications of type theory. They were given 15 advertisements selected from two editions of *Which Ad Pulled Best?* (Burton, 1981; Burton & Purvis, 1985) that feature matched pairs of ads for the same product and the results of selected research methods to measure recall, awareness, persuasion and amount of copy read. (The various tests had been conducted by Gallup and Robinson Magazine Impact Research Service [MIRS], Starch or Readex, Inc.)

Using descriptors from Keirsey and Bates, students were asked to determine what type or types they perceived the product in each advertisement to be and then to determine the type of each ad as a whole. They then voted on which ad did pull best.

Results

The theory of congruence was supported in every case, although the sample size was too small to demonstrate significance. The following example illustrates the process. The advertisement in question was for a car stereo system. The intrinsic type for car stereo speakers was not immediately obvious, so the panel examined the two possible positionings for a car stereo: the linkage of car speakers with fun, speed, excitement and racing down the highway (all SP concepts) or the linkage to the technology involved and the scientific innovations (NT). To decide what the audience perception of the product might be, the panel considered the placement: Ad A ran in *Cosmopolitan* and Ad B ran in *People*. Neither magazine is aimed at NTs, and it was assumed that the SP concept of the stereo would be more logical in magazines that featured glamour, sex, the fast track and pacesetters.

Advertisement A portrayed a wealthy, beautiful woman walking away from a Rolls, saying to her waiting chauffeur, "Bring around the Nova, Peter. It has the Jensen."

Advertisement B showed a drafting table with complex designs and drafting materials, a stereo speaker placed on top of them, tagged "150 watts peak power/digital ready." The headline was: "Designed to be the car stereo classic."

The panel agreed that the copy was clearly NT for both ads, although version B featured some very "hot" words to describe comparatively mundane attributes: "150 sizzling watts . . . torrid 80 watts. . ." But the panel reported that the lengthy copy was not a major cue for them; rather, it was a combination of the headline and the art. The rich woman rejecting the Rolls, exerting power and exuding sex, cued them to code this SP. The drafting table, the careful plans with the cue words of "design" and "digital ready," fit easily into the NT category.

The panel saw a clearer fit of type appeals with ad A, demonstrating the congruence of the Dionysian SP woman with the SP attributes of the stereo; they were less attracted to the NT elements of ad B and the stereo. Apparently, typical readers agreed: Ad A scored a 16% recall PNR score, compared with ad B's 6%.

The process was repeated for each ad. The panel was overloaded with intuitive types, which resulted in a curious phenomenon. In every case except one, at least one individual (occasionally the majority) would reject the model and select the ad where the elements were not in congruence, simply because of a "feeling" that their choice was better for some reason they could not define. Each time they were confident that, in this case, the theory would not hold. They were also wrong.

The occasional failure of the panel's intuition and the success of the theory as a predictive model is heartening, but this pilot study is, of course, not significant. The authors intend to pursue the theory with more testing and experimentation but contend that the concept of type congruence is solid enough to be considered when designing public information campaigns.

TYPE CONGRUENCE IN PUBLIC RELATIONS CASES

The following cases examine the application of type theory to two typical public service communication campaigns. Although the analysis was done after the cases were reported, they present examples of how the theory might be applied in designing public relations campaigns and predicting their probable impact.

Teen-Age Alcohol Abuse

An advertising federation in 1984 (IABC, 1985) selected teenage alcohol abuse as the subject of its 1984 public service campaign. The campaign was essentially an information-based one designed to increase information about alcohol awareness of the problems and increase responsible decision-making about driving and drinking. In addition, the campaign was planned to influence attitudes about drinking to change attitudes and behavior about alcohol abuse (especially concerning drinking and driving) and to raise the consciousness of adults regarding the problem.

Several themes and messages were tested in a focus group, and a slogan, "Think. Don't just drink," was decided upon, "since it better enabled us to meet our awareness and educational objectives" (IABC, 1985, p. 10). (The case report did not indicate what the other proposed themes were.)

The slogan was used in ads, psa's, bumper stickers, t-shirts and general promotional material with a three-part message: (a) you don't have to drink; (b) if you do drink, be a thinking drinker; (c) don't, in any case, drink and drive.

Focus groups conducted by the authors suggest a basic flaw in the design of this public service campaign. Adults, drinkers and non-drinkers alike, reported that drinking is a somewhat logical activity; drinking was seen as adventurous (SP), social (SJ) or logical (NT). Rarely was it reported as a self-actualizing activity, although the decision *not* to drink was occasionally seen as NF. However, for teenagers, drinking was reported to be an adventure in rebellion (SP) or strongly conformist (SJ) and was only very rarely expressed in terms of logic (NT). Without exception, panel members classified the slogan, "Think. Don't just drink," as NT.

Thus, one could follow the model (see Fig. 13.2) and determine the probable outcome of such a slogan (unsupported by other messages as it was in this campaign). The sole cue was NT, which was congruent with adult classifications of drinking. However, it did not fit into the student concept of drinking as an SP or SJ activity. Hence, the slogan created

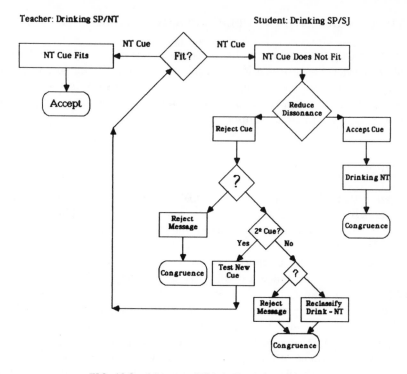

FIG. 13.2.   Message: "Think: Don't just drink."

dissonance, which the teen-aged receiver was forced to reduce. The first branching of the model is the most critical and remains an area for further examination—why do some receivers accept the cue and reclassify drinking, whereas others reject the cue and either reject the message or keep seeking for secondary cues? This decision point appears to be the most critical in the model, for it takes psychological energy, and thus some commitment, to construct a new categorization system. In this case, no strong secondary cue was sent, so the receiver was forced either to reject the message or to reclassify.

The results reported in this case study support the validity of the model. Pre- and posttest surveys were conducted, and the consultant reported "a high level of responsiveness" to the campaign and "measurable increase of knowledge of two alcohol-related facts" (IABC, 1985, p. 12). The case reported no change in attitude, opinion or behavior.

The authors contend that, for those students able to accept drinking as an NT action (as it was presented in the campaign), the predictable response would have been the increase in knowledge reported in the case. Were increased knowledge the goal of the campaign, it could be considered successful. However, because of the dissonance for most adolescents who do not classify drinking as a logical issue, little of the desired attitudinal or behavioral change could be reported.

Blood Drive

A second example is the Red Cross appeal for blood, as reported by Zimbardo and Ebbesen (1970). However, Zimbardo and Ebbesen (1970) noted that, after the end of World War II, patriotic appeals for blood were no longer successful but that "using the skillful techniques of motivation research, it was determined that giving blood arouses many unconscious anxieties, especially with men, by whom it is equated with giving away part of their virility and strength" (p. 109). Thus, Zimbardo and Ebbesen suggested that the Red Cross blood drives reject logic and patriotism and use male-oriented appeals that "make him feel more masculine . . . prove that he has so much virility he can afford to give away a little, and made . . . him feel personally proud of any suffering" (p. 110). They report that using such appeals resulted in a sudden, dramatic increase in blood donations.

The authors contend that the effectiveness of this appeal lay in type congruence as much as in reducing the Freudian castration anxiety. Our focus group research identified type-linked reasons for donating blood: The SPs responded to the image of the Red Cross as disaster-fighters (remembering pictures from floods, hurricanes, etc.); the SJs, as the belongers and natural helpers, were predisposed to donate blood to help others; the NTs reacted to the logical requests for specific numbers of pints; the only motivation that seemed to appeal to the NFs was the personal approach (i.e., donating blood for a specific, identifiable individual).

Skillful positioning by the Red Cross has created campaigns that appeal to all four types. Radio stations in 1986 ran a prototypical Dionysian campaign, challenging the SPs to face the needle without fear. Recent psa's have taken the NF approach: "I need blood. My brother is dying. Only you can help him." Traditional drives still rely on the NT and SJ motivations.

The case reported in Zimbardo and Ebbesen (1970) succeeded in part because it reached the large group of SPs (about 38% of the population) with an adventuresome, macho appeal.

CONCLUSIONS

Simply switching an appeal of a product or cause will only prove effective if the organization has already been perceived as belonging to the type in question. Just changing a campaign to appeal to a different type may not be enough to improve recall or achieve a campaign goal. The type of the message must relate to the perceived type of the object as it is positioned to the public.

The concept of positioning has helped organizations define their image, or how the public views them, and this can be of use in solving problems of congruence. One major health association had positioned itself as a research and educational agency (NT) but discovered that the public perceived them as a fund-raising, helping association (SJ). Their current promotional campaign stresses the SJ aspects, thus resolving the dissonance, and they have reported increased success in audience attention and recall of their educational material by positioning themselves within the "we want to help you" (SJ) mode.

Type congruence offers the communicator a new method by which to segment the audience and its perceptions of the organization or product. More than 30 years of research has defined occupations, life styles, media habits and other variables that are related to psychological type, and the data offer public relations practitioners a new, non-judgmental and fairly easy way of refining persuasive approaches.

REFERENCES

Ackoff, R. L., & Emshoff, J. R. (1975) Advertising research at Anheuser-Busch, Inc., (1968–1974). *Sloan Management Review, 16,* 1–15.

Allport, G. W. (1967) *Pattern and growth in personality.* New York: Rinehart & Winston.

Assael, H. (1984) *Consumer behavior and marketing action* (2nd ed.). Boston: Kent.

Britt, S. H. (1978) *Psychological principles of marketing and consumer behavior.* Lexington, MA: D. C. Heath.

Brock, T., & Shavitt, S. (1985) Personal values affect consumers' behavior. *Contemporary Psychology, 30,* 968–969.

Burton, P. W. (1981) *Which ad pulled best?* (4th ed.). Chicago: Crain.

Burton, P. W., & Purvis, S. C. (1985) *Which ad pulled best?* (5th ed.). Chicago: Crain.

Carlyn, M. (1977) An assessment of the Myers–Briggs Type Indicator. *Journal of Personality Assessment, 41,* 461–473.

Cartwright, D., & Harary, F. (1956) Structural balance: A generalization of Heider's theory. *Psychological Review, 63,* 227–293.

Churchill, G. A., Jr. (1987) *Marketing research: Methodological foundations* (4th ed.). Chicago: Dryden.

Cline, C. G. (1985, November) *Toward a theory of multiple motivations.* Paper presented at the meeting of The Public Relations Society of America. Detroit, MI.

Cline, C. G., McBride, M. H., & Miller, R. E. (1987a, August) *Trying to get human feelings right: Psychological type theory in public relations.* Paper presented at the meeting of the Association for Education in Journalism and Mass Communication. San Antonio, TX.

Cline, C. G., McBride, M. H., & Miller, R. E. (1987b) Using the theory of psychological type congruence to improve advertising recall. In S. G. Green & R. L. Coulter (Eds.), *Marketing: Issues and trends. Proceedings of the Atlantic Marketing Association Annual Conference* (pp. 428–435). Springfield, MO: Atlantic Marketing Association.

Cline, C. G., McBride, M. H., Miller, R. E., & Hammond, V. (1987, August) *Gender, psychological type and roles: Can public relations survive in the 'Information Age'?* Paper presented at the meeting of the Association for Education in Journalism and Mass Communication, San Antonio, TX.

Cravens, D. W. (1987) *Strategic marketing* (2nd ed.). Homewood, IL: Irwin.

Cutlip, S. M., Center, A. A., & Broom, G. M. (1985) *Effective public relations* (6th ed.). Englewood Cliffs, NJ: Prentice-Hall.

Donelson, E. (1973) *Personality: A scientific approach.* Pacific Palisades, CA: Goodyear.

Evans, F. B. (1959, October) Psychological and objective factors in the prediction of brand choice: Ford versus Chevrolet. *Journal of Business,* pp. 340–369.

Festinger, L. A. (1957) *A theory of cognitive dissonance.* Evanston, IL: Row Peterson.

Grunig, J. E., & Hunt, T. (1984) *Managing public relations.* New York: Holt, Rinehart & Winston.

Harrell, G. D. (1986) *Consumer behavior.* San Diego: Harcourt Brace Jovanovich.

Heider, F. (1946) Attitudes and cognitive organization. *Journal of Psychology, 21,* 107–112.

Heider, F. (1958) *The psychology of interpersonal relations.* New York: Wiley.

Hoffman, J. L., & Betkouski, M. (1981) A summary of Myers–Briggs Type Indicator research applications in education. *Research in Psychological Type, 3,* 3–41.

Horton, R. L. (1979, May) Some relationships between personality and consumer decision-making. *Journal of Marketing Research,* pp. 244–245.

International Association of Business Communicators. (1985) *No secrets.* San Francisco: Author.

Jewler, A. J., & Hunter, M. S. (1986) *Targeting advertising audiences in the third dimension through the Myers-Briggs Type Indicator.* Paper presented at the meeting of the American Academy of Advertising, Baton Rouge, LA.

Jung, C. (1923) *Psychological types.* New York: Harcourt Brace.

Jung, C. (1933) *Modern man in search of a soul.* New York: Harcourt Brace Jovanovich.

Kassarjian, H. H. (1978) Personality and consumer behavior. *Journal of Consumer Behavior, 5,* 159–162.

Keirsey, D., & Bates, M. (1984) *Please understand me: Character and temperament types.* Del Mar, CA.: Prometheus Nemesis.

Kotler, P. (1986) *Principles of marketing* (3rd ed.). Englewood Cliffs, NJ: Prentice-Hall.

Larson, C. U. (1986) *Persuasion: Reception and responsibility* (4th ed.). Belmont, CA: Wadsworth.

Lipstein, B., & McGuire, W. J. (1978) *Evaluating advertising.* New York: Advertising Research Foundation.

Martin, C. H. (1977) How major factors of advertising messages correlate with basic personality dimensions: An information-processing approach. *Proceedings of the Annual Conference of the American Academy of Advertising* (pp. 141–144).

Maslow, A. H. (1954) *Motivation and personality.* New York: Harper & Row.

McBride, M. H., Cline, C. G., & Miller, R. E. (1987a) Implications of the Keirsey-Bates temperaments for marketers and advertisers. In S. G. Green & R. L. Coulter (Eds.). *Marketing: Issues and trends. Proceedings of the Atlantic Marketing Association Annual Conference* (pp. 9–16). Springfield, MO: Atlantic Marketing Association.

McBride, M. H., Cline, C. G., & Miller, R. E. (1987b, August). *Toward a theory of psychological type congruence for advertisers.* Paper presented at the meeting of the Association for Education in Journalism and Mass Communication, San Antonio, TX.

McBride, M. H., Cline, C. G., & Miller, R. E. (1987c, July) To live in harmony: Using the theory of psychological type in business communication and public relations. *Conference Highlights: London 1987.* San Francisco, CA: International Association of Business Communicators.

McBride, M. H., Cline, C. G., & Miller, R. E. (1987d, June). *'Infographic' implications of the Keirsey Temperaments: Can advertisements be typed?* Paper presented at the meeting of the Association for Psychological Type, Gainesville, FL.

McCarley, N. G., & Carskadon, T. C. (1986) The perceived accuracy of elements of the 16 type descriptions of Myers and Keirsey among men and women: Which elements are most accurate, should the type descriptions be different for men and women and do the type descriptions stereotype sensing types?" *Journal of Psychological Type, 11,* 2–29.

McGuire, W. J. (1981) Theoretical foundations of campaigns. In R. E. Rice & W. J. Paisley (Eds.), *Public communication campaigns* (pp. 15–40). Beverly Hills, CA: Sage.

Myers, I. B. (1962a) *The Myers-Briggs Type Indicator.* Palo Alto, CA: Consulting Psychologists Press.

Myers, I. B. (1962b) *The Myers-Briggs Type Indicator manual.* Princeton, NJ: Educational Testing Service.

Myers, I. B. (1970) *Introduction to type.* Gainesville, FL: Center for the Applications of Psychological Type.

Myers, I. B. (1980) *Gifts differing.* Palo Alto, CA: Consulting Psychologists Press.

Newcomb, T. M. (1953) An approach to the study of communicative acts. *Psychological Review, 60,* 393–404.

Newsom, D., & Scott, A. (1981) *This is PR: The realities of public relations.* Belmont, CA: Wadsworth.

Osgood, C., & Tannenbaum, P. (1955) The principle of congruity in the prediction of attitude change. *Psychological Review, 62,* 42–55.

Packard, V. (1964) *The hidden persuaders.* New York: Pocket Books.

Patti, C. H., & Mizerski, R. W. (1978) Personality and the use of advertising.

Proceedings of the Annual Conference of the American Academy of Advertising (pp. 86–90).

Plummer, J. T. (1984–1985) How personality makes a difference. *Journal of Advertising Research, 24,* 27–31.

Rachman, D. J. (1985) *Marketing today.* Chicago: Dryden.

Reardon, K. K. (1981) *Persuasion: Theory and context.* Beverly Hills, CA: Sage.

Roberts, D. Y., Fox, C. F., & Branch, C. V. (1974) *Investigating the riddle of man: A modular learning program.* Englewood Cliffs, NJ: Prentice-Hall.

Roberts, D. Y. (1977) Personalizing learning processes. *Revista/Review Interamericana, 7,* 139–143.

Roberts, D. Y. (no date) *Identifying your Jungian psychological traits (i.e., your personality).* Lubbock, TX: Texas Tech University Center for the Improvement of Teaching Effectiveness, Southwest Typology Center.

Rokeach, M., & Rothman, G. (1965) The principle of congruence and the conguity principle as models of cognitive interaction. *Psychological Review, 72,* 129–156.

Runyon, K. E. (1981) *Advertising* (2nd ed.). Columbus, OH: Merrill.

Seitel, F. P. (1984) *The practice of public relations* (2nd ed.). Columbus, OH: Merrill.

Shimp, T. A. (1978) Application of the personality construct in advertising research. In *Proceedings of the Annual Conference of the American Academy of Advertising* (p. 78).

Stanton, W. J. (1978) *Fundamentals of marketing* (5th ed.). New York: McGraw-Hill.

Van Auken, S. (1978) Coupling life style and personality. In *Proceedings of the Annual Conference of the American Academy of Advertising* (pp. 95–96).

Ware, R., & Yokomoto, C. (1985) Perceived accuracy of Myers–Briggs Type Indicator descriptions using Keirsey profiles. *Journal of Psychological Type, 10,* 27–31.

Wilcox, D. L., Ault, P. H., & Agee, W. K. (1986) *Public relations: Strategies and tactics.* New York: Harper & Row.

Young, S. (1972) The dynamics of measuring unchange. In R. I. Haley (Ed.), *Attitude research in transition* (pp. 61–82). Chicago: American Marketing Association.

Zajonc, R. B. (1960) The process of cognitive tuning in communication. *Journal of Abnormal and Social Psychology, 61,* 159–164.

Zajonc, R. B. (1968) Cognitive theories in social psychology. In G. Lindzey & E. Aronson (Eds.), *Cognitive theories in social psychology* (Vol. 1, pp. 320–441). Reading, MA: Addison-Wesley.

Zimbardo, P., & Ebbesen, E. B. (1970) *Influence attitudes and changing behavior.* Reading, MA: Addison-Wesley.

III

ISSUES OF APPLICATION

The Coorientation Model and Consultant Roles

Donald J. Johnson
University of Wisconsin—Madison

ABSTRACT

A typology of four public relations roles currently in use is considered from a combination of coorientation and classic role perspectives. The author argues that current public relations role definitions may not be complete, because they depend on only one point of view—the practitioner's. According to role theory, two necessary perspectives combine to create such roles—that of a role sender (the client) and a role receiver (the practitioner or consultant). A proposed research program uses coorientation variables to combine these perspectives. It focuses primarily on the client–consultant dyad as the unit of analysis and the public relations practitioner role as the object of coorientation. To better understand whether adopted roles result from consultant choice or client prescription, a longitudinal design would allow causal inferences.

> *Consensus should have an importance in social science comparable to that of energy in physics—namely, as a unifying concept, an abstraction that will include and relate more specific concepts and data. Light, heat, sound, and electromagnetism are forms of energy; so, I think, role, norm, symbol, culture, and so on, should be treated as forms of consensus.*
> —Klapp (1957, pp. 340–341)

Of all the research topics in public relations theory, perhaps one of the most important would be that which addresses the consensus-building process affecting the consultant–client relationship. This chapter focuses on a current typology of public relations practitioner roles, and it proposes a research program on the potential causal connections between the construction of consensus (treated here as coorientation) and the essential processes in role taking.

As discussed by Hazleton and Botan in chapter 1, this research fits into an application of Type III theories. It focuses primarily on how we might achieve prediction as a guidepost toward explanation and addresses both conceptual and empirical problems in the present research. Unlike many of the other chapters in this book, however, this one does not *end* with what we should do next, but rather *begins* with that advice. Indeed, this entire chapter concentrates on what public relations research should do in investigating professional roles. It may also have implications beyond the public relations setting to other managerial relationships.

RECENT HISTORY OF ROLES
IN PUBLIC RELATIONS THEORY

Current research on public relations has sought to define the primary functions of the practitioner. Typologies of public relations practitioner role behaviors based on the activities in which they engage have been drawn conceptually (Broom & Smith, 1979; Cutlip, Center, & Brown, 1985) and empirically (Ferguson, 1979; Dozier & Gottesman, 1982). Based on the available consulting literature, Broom and Smith theorized a public relations role typology. Ferguson and also Dozier and Gottesman generated definitions of practitioner roles, which were based on empirical evidence. They drew these, however, via self-reports from one perspective—that of the practitioners themselves.

Additional research has investigated the Broom and Smith roles in relation to organizational decision making (Johnson & Acharya, 1982), in reference to environmental uncertainty (Acharya, 1983), and in connection with gender (Cutlip, Center, & Broom, 1985). Nevertheless, all of these studies have depended on similar self-report data without corresponding client perceptions and expectations.

The implicit assumption made in these studies is that roles reside *within* the individual. The role approach, on the other hand, proposes that roles are a function of a social system made up of role *senders* and role *receivers* (Biddle, 1979; Katz & Kahn, 1978). In other words, the role performed, at least in part, depends on others' expectations. Descriptions of roles from only one side of the role set may not be entirely accurate.

For example, in assessing communication behaviors, Sypher and

Sypher (1984) discovered an impressive lack of agreement between self-reports and those of superiors, subordinates, and peers. Smircich and Chesser (1981) also found that subordinates consistently reported their superiors' perspectives inaccurately. These results suggest that the role occupant's view taken alone may not be an entirely valid picture and that an accurate description of role behaviors must include the role sender's perspective. Further inquiry into the consultant–client relationship logically should focus on establishing stronger construct validity for these self-reported role definitions. It should also investigate the antecedent variables that may determine the roles practitioners play in relation to their clients.

RESEARCH QUESTIONS

The purpose here is to propose testing existing role definitions by following more closely the basic assumptions about roles, in essence, allowing theoretical presuppositions to guide the research and its design.

For the sake of this discussion, we assume the primary role sender is the client or higher level manager, and the role receiver is the public relations practitioner or consultant. This constitutes a role set that can be considered a social unit or system (of two) in and of itself commonly referred to as a dyad. As already suggested, practitioner roles are based in these social relationships. Therefore, to study differences between role sets, the unit of analysis must be the patterned relations between each individual in the dyad, in other words the relationship itself.

It may be useful to point out that such research is considered level-specific to the dyad (Dansereau & Markham, 1987; Jablin & Krone, 1987). In other words, the individual as a unit of analysis can no longer be considered relevant because each person becomes interdependent with another. This research also excludes the larger group as a level of analysis. Although individual networking may extend well beyond the dyad, the dynamics within a given dyad have a specific locus.

Questions related to these small social systems include:

1. How do coordinated perceptions vary *across dyads at the same point in time?* And how is this variation associated with the role performed by the practitioner? Examples include multiple-client situations, various types of organizations, and different organizational environments. This addresses distributional characteristics, such as frequency and location.

2. Because we are discussing a small social system, we must also consider its evolution and how it responds to tension introduced to the system. Essentially, how does the practitioner role vary *within a given dyad*

over time? For example, how might the role vary with changes in understanding or agreement, such as when environmental conditions change or when one member of a relatively stable dyad (say within an organizational setting) exits the relationship and is replaced by a new member, one with entirely new expectations and perceptions? In essence, this question addresses the relation of the parts to the whole.

The second question addresses perceptual patterns in a transaction over time, or in other words, a process. Such research requires sampling from at least two time points in a longitudinal analysis (Warwick & Lininger, 1975).[1] Both of these questions relate to a very basic investigation into the conditions that might determine role performance. For example, is the role definition the result of practitioner choice or client prescription? Such an inquiry is nested in what Jablin (1979) described as research on semantic information distance. Cappella (1987) called this a first-order question, one which is concerned with how intrapersonal cognitive status (such as interpretations and understandings) might affect interpersonal communication and, potentially, behavior. When we assemble these individual behaviors into roles, we may also begin to address Cappella's third-order questions related to patterns and contingencies.

What has been alluded to is an approach to the study of public relations roles that focuses on coorientation, later defined in this chapter as simultaneous orientations or cognitions. As will be shown, coorientation and role approaches are highly compatible: although independent, they are mutually supportive. Both approaches assume social interaction as the link in a causal chain (Katz & Kahn, 1978; McLeod & Chaffee, 1973). In fact, coorientation and roles are each defined as social artifacts dependent on shared meanings. In addition, any coorienting dyad will generate roles as part of the mutual definition of the relationship (Wilmot, 1979). A function of such a research program would be to establish the construct validity for the current typology of roles. The findings, in fact, may produce a synthesis of concepts. The ultimate goal, however, is a causal model of public relations role behaviors, a model that may have implications for the study of other dyads.

This approach also has significance for public relations practice. By exploring the coordination of both practitioner and client (or management) perceptions, we may find out more about role prescriptions and their associated behaviors. At issue as well is to what extent and under

---

[1]Monge, Farace, Eisenberg, Miller, and White (1984) provide a complete discussion of process research in organizational communication, including philosophical, historical, and methodological issues.

what conditions does the public relations consultant influence the adoption of public relations models such as those discussed by Grunig in chapter 2 of this volume. An intriguing question in itself is whether higher level management perceives the same role for the public relations practitioner as the practitioner does.

INDEPENDENT VARIABLES: COORIENTATION

Coorientation variables have been suggested or applied to various objects of coorientation, such as communication rules (Eisenberg, Monge, & Farace, 1984) and public relations programs (Whitcomb, 1976). A strong case for their use in causal analyses has also been made (Brown, Becker, & McLeod, 1976). Logically, the role of the public relations practitioner could be treated as a similar object of coorientation.

The notion of coorientation is one of two traditions in the study of consensus, according to Scheff (1967). The other is the "individual agreement" definition for consensus: the similarity of aggregated individual opinions or values. This agreement definition is characterized by most public opinion polling. In Broom's (1977) words, it is represented by a simple summation of responses "without taking into account the respondent's expectations of relevant others in the social milieu" (p. 41).

A coorientation definition for consensus, on the other hand, considers the perceptions of others' opinions, an approach that on its face seems more valid for the social sciences. Chaffee (1973) as well noted that societal phenomena are largely based on microsocial, not individual, events, and he proposes a metaphor with chemistry. He suggested that society is not composed of many persons (atoms), but of interpersonal relationships (molecules). Similar arguments for this approach were made by McLeod and Chaffee (1973).

This perspective, of course, dates to Newcomb's (1953) original A–B–X paradigm (see Fig. 14.1). He described coorientation as "perceived consensus" in a system "straining toward symmetry" (p. 393). This falls into a larger social psychological tradition of cognitive consistency theories (Shaw & Costanzo, 1982).

The term *coorientation* is an abbreviation from "simultaneous orientations," which refers to the interdependence of A's attitudes toward B and toward X (Newcomb, 1953). If, for example, person A feels negatively toward B and positively toward X, but discovers B feels positively toward X as well, then the system can be said to be imbalanced, or asymmetrical (see Fig. 14.2). This introduces stress to move toward balance. In fact, any time the product of the signs (positive vs. negative orientations) equals a negative, there is perceived asymmetry.

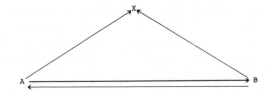

FIG. 14.1. Theoretical model of coorientation (Newcomb, 1953).

O'Keefe (1973) observed that there are two basic assumptions underlying these cognitions: (a) each person knows what he or she thinks about
an object and (b) each person has some notion of how the other person
perceives the same thing. The model becomes a cognitive system in
which communication is the link between the elements. Newcomb (1953)
wrote:

> Communication among humans performs the essential function of ena-
> bling two or more individuals to maintain simultaneous orientation toward
> one another as communicators and toward objects of communication. (p.
> 393)

Thus, *coorientation* is a relational term, and communication is the process
by which it is achieved. From this perspective consensus must be studied

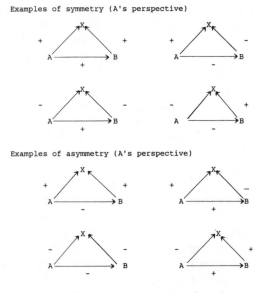

FIG. 14.2. Examples of symmetry and asymmetry.

as an interaction between people rather than as a property of a single individual.

Derived from Newcomb's model are those of McLeod and Chaffee (1972, 1973), Laing, Phillipson, and Lee (1966), and Scheff (1967). Figure 14.3 diagrams these developments in the coorientation approach. Implicit in all of these models is a closed causal loop that connects the constructs of communication, consensus, and social coordination (Scheff, 1967).

Central to McLeod and Chaffee's model is the concept of social reality (McLeod & Chaffee, 1972), which they consider equivalent to consensus, consensual validation, and common value system. According to the authors, this construct represents that part of the person's frame of reference that can be attributed to the interacting social group. Laing et al. (1966) and Scheff (1967) propose a parallel construct: "collective representations." Scheff defined degree of consensus as degree of coordination between members of groups. Both he and Laing et al. offer similar

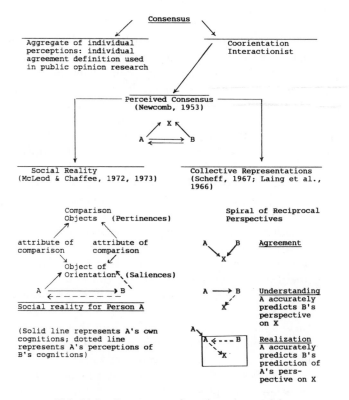

FIG. 14.3.   Consensus and coorientation models.

models of a spiral of reciprocal perspectives. A direct perspective is
"what I think"; a metaperspective, "what I think you think"; a meta-
metaperspective, "what I think you think I think"; and so on. Complete
consensus occurs when there is "an infinite series of reciprocating understandings between members of the group concerning the issue" (McLeod
& Chaffee, 1973, p. 478).

Here, the coorientation definition of consensus is used, meaning the
simultaneous and interacting cognitions between persons regarding
some object (person, thing, idea, process, or behavior).

As seen in Fig. 14.3, these models describe a system and suggest a
process. The variables are neither the objects compared nor the persons
in each system; they are the relationships between these. Those processes provide the independent variables in this research program. The
coorientation literature overwhelmingly refers to these variables as
accuracy, agreement (and understanding), and congruency. Table 14.1 shows
some of these terms and the definitions authors have assigned to each.

As can be seen, there are strong similarities across the definitions for
each term. Major variations only appear in the number of dimensions
applied to each.

In defining these concepts, Stamm and Pearce (1971) suggested distinguishing between the monadic and dyadic perspectives that can be
taken by the actors. For example, one actor's view of an object is a
monadic perspective, a property of that individual. The relation between
his or her own cognitions and those of the other actor, however, is
dyadic, a relational term that requires measurements from both actors.

Stamm and Pearce (1971) pointed out in their explication of accuracy
that it "is really defined as Person A's perception of Person B's view of
some object (as reported to the observer) compared to the observer's
perception (via measurement) of Person B's actual view" (p. 209). Accuracy requires separate measures for each person. This description
shows that accuracy is truly dyadic, a relational term—that it is not experienced solely by A or B. For our purposes, accuracy may be considered
the degree to which one person's perception of another's cognitions
indeed matches the other's actual cognitions. In other words, generating
a valid assessment of what each other actually thinks indicates accuracy.
For example, how well does the consultant gauge his or her client's
expectations?

Like accuracy, agreement is also relational, in that its measurement
depends on comparing reported cognitions to determine the extent to
which the content of A's cognitions are similar to B's.

McLeod and Chaffee (1973) described this similarity as "cognitive
overlap" in the orientations of A and B. Agreement might be thought of
as the degree to which each person holds the same summary evaluations
about an object. Agreement, however, may not represent a single dimen-

TABLE 14.1
Conceptual Definitions in Coorientation Literature
for Commonly Recurring Variables

Source	Agreement	Congruency	Accuracy
Tagiuri et al. (1958)	*Mutuality*: similarity of feelings between two persons	*Congruency*: similarity between perceptions of other person's feeling and your own	*Accuracy*: the correctness of your perception of the other person's feelings as compared with his/her actual feelings about you
Laing et al. (1966)	*Agreement*: comparison between one person's view and another's on the same issue	*Being understood*: comparing a person's meta-metaperspective with his/her own direct perspective, i.e. perceived congruency *Realization*: of being understood by comparing one's meta-metaperspective and the other's metaperspective	*Understanding*: comparing one person's metaperspective with the other person's direct perspective
Scheff (1967)	Three dimensions of consensus— *agreement*: both parties endorse statement X; *understands; realization* (See Laing et al.)		
Wackman (1973)	*Cognitive overlap*: similarity between two person's cognitions about an object	*Perceived agreement*: similarity between one person's cognitions about an object and his/her estimate of the other person's cognitions about an object	*Accuracy*: similarity between one person's estimate of another's cognitions about an object and that other person's actual cognitions about the object
McLeod & Chaffee (1973)	*Agreement*: the same summary evaluations (saliences) *Understanding*: similar object-by-attribute systems for comparison (pertinences)	*Congruency*: degree of similarity between the person's own cognitions and his/her perception of the other person's congitions	*Accuracy*: extent to which one person's estimate of another's cognitions matches what the other person really does think

sion. McLeod and Chaffee (1973) consider "understanding" a prior condition to agreement.

> To the extent that A and B have the same summary evaluations (saliences) of objects, there is agreement. To the extent that their individual orientations comprise similar object-by-attribute systems (pertinencies), there is understanding. (p. 485)

Essentially, understanding represents the degree to which persons share a common definition of the situation regardless of their evaluations of it (Carter, 1962; Carter, Ruggels, & Olson, 1966; Chaffee & McLeod, 1968; McLeod & Chaffee, 1973). For example, coorienting parties generally may recognize the same elements in a public relations problem, in which case there is understanding, but they may not agree on their respective roles and the appropriate responses.

Another coorientation variable—congruency—has been identified, however, by Chaffee and McLeod (1968) as monadic, not really a true coorientation concept, but a construct that exists in the private cognitions for each person in a coorientation setting:

> (It) is of interest in that it only exists in a coorientation context; *it is a perception of one person of a relation between his* [sic] *cognitions and the other person's,* based on his [sic] relationships with the other person. As a 'within-the-person' variable, it also varies with many internal-cognitive processes—rationalization, projection, selective perception. (p. 662)

In essence, congruence represents the degree of similarity between the person's cognitions and his or her perception of the other person's cognitions. For example, the client may have certain beliefs about the functions of a public relations consultant. How closely the client thinks those attitudes match those held by the consultant represents the degree of congruency for the client.

McLeod and Chaffee (1973) propose a coorientation measurement model, as shown in Fig. 14.4, that shows the points from which data would be drawn to generate measures for each variable. According to this model, five measures generate the three basic coorientation variables discussed here.

Although discussed in global terms as coorientation variables, a "collective" or combined measure of these variables, however, may not be possible because they are not independent. Accuracy, agreement, and congruency are each based on measures that also form the basis of the other two. Chaffee and McLeod (1968) provided an apt description of their relationship.

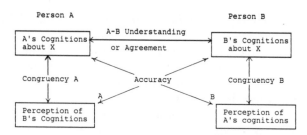

FIG. 14.4. Coorientation measurement model (McLeod & Chaffee, 1973). Note: The boxes indicate measurements on each individual. Arrows connecting the boxes are labeled to indicate measures that are compared to construct each coorientation index.

If agreement is low and congruency high, accuracy is necessarily low; if agreement and congruency are both high (or both low), accuracy is high. A change in one of these variables will affect change in another, if the third is held constant. For example, if agreement is held constant and high, as accuracy increases there will be an increase in congruency; if agreement is held constant and low, as accuracy increases there will be a decrease in congruency. (p. 663)

The specific relations among the coorientation variables themselves appear to be linear. Their relationships to other variables, such as attraction, information seeking, and sending may be curvilinear (Pavitt & Cappella, 1979). The statement by McLeod and Chaffee, however, indicates that taken together they will not provide an index of coorientation that has internal consistency. The effects of each coorientation variable must be measured and analyzed separately.

These provide the independent variables. Since this represents an evolving process of social coordination, it is assumed that these variables and their effects will not only vary for different systems, but will vary across time for a given system. Another basic assumption adopted here is that variances in behavior are a function of variances in perceptions. What, then, are the effects of these coorientation variables both *between* and *within* dyads?

ROLE RESEARCH AND COORIENTATION

Katz and Kahn (1978) proposed the role concept as a major link between individual and organizational levels of theory. This perspective holds that an individual's, or actor's, behavior may best be understood as a function of role (Getzels & Guba, 1954; Katz & Kahn, 1978; Parsons, 1977).

Harre and Secord (1972) defined role as a "subset of rules followed by a particular category of individual" (p. 13). In an organizational setting, the concept of role refers to the standardized patterns of behavior required of individuals in given functional relationships (Katz & Kahn, 1978). As pointed out by the authors, the concept carries with it normative expectations. This role approach is central in Katz and Kahn's definition of organizations, which they see as made up of these patterned individual behaviors. In essence, the organization is simply a system of roles.

The roles themselves may vary across relationships, according to Parsons (1977), leading to involvement in more than one activity or system. In fact, Katz and Kahn have argued that each "office" or role is linked directly or indirectly to many others. These links, in total, become the entire role set. As a result, the role set may extend beyond the supervisor–employee dyad to a larger social network.

The likelihood of such multiple role involvement increases with rank in the organization, according to Katz and Kahn. They have described multiple activities and multiple subsystem involvements that become increasingly evident as one moves up in the organizational hierarchy. Nevertheless, they suggest these may no longer be separate roles occupied by the same individual but a fusion into a single new role such as public relations.

Getzels and Guba (1954) provided some of the original support for this view and noted that each individual occupies a number of roles defined by one's group. He or she, however, must make a commitment to a predominant role to decide on action at choice points.

As shown in Fig. 14.5, the role episode involves four lower order concepts (Katz & Kahn, 1978). Role sending includes *role expectations,* the expected activities and evaluative standards applied to the role occupant's behavior, and *role sent,* any communication attempting to influence the focal person. Role receiving includes *received role,* the focal person's perception of the role sender's expectations, and *role behavior,* which is the focal person's behavioral response. The resulting role behavior is evaluated by the role set according to its expectations, needs, and norms, and the process begins anew.

The parallels between role concepts and the dimensions in coorientation may be readily apparent, especially the relational nature of roles and their dependence on accuracy, agreement, and congruence for their performance.

The communication link in each approach, however, may appear to

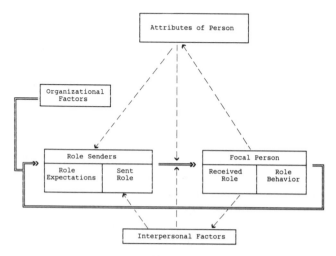

FIG. 14.5.   Model of factors involved in organizational roles (from Katz
& Kahn, 1978).

differ. Coorientation suggests a transactional, horizontal process; role
sending, particularly in an organizational setting, implies a directive,
vertical one. Nevertheless, some authors argue that the role approach
actually fits a transactional perspective better. Jablin (1982) gave special
emphasis to reciprocal communication and negotiation between senders
and receivers, which he refers to as assimilation. Graen (1976) took a
similar perspective described as "role-making" in which the role receiver
actively participates in defining the role, especially during the early
stages of a dyadic relationship. Similar conceptions for dyadic roles come
from an exchange process involving investments and returns (Dansereau, Alutto, & Yammarino, 1984) and of "negotiating latitude" (Dansereau, Graen, & Haga, 1975). Although Fairhurst, Rogers, and Sarr
(1987) focus on control patterns in manager–subordinate interactions,
they discuss these in a context of relational communication that suggests
mutual influence.

    Given the transactional nature of both coorientation and role-making,
these approaches could be linked as a form/content or as a process/con-
struction relationship. Although coorientation variables may serve as the
structure or process for social interaction between the consultant and
client, the constructed role serves as the substance. In essence, the practitioner's role may be seen as an object of orientation for both the client
(Person A) and the public relations professional or consultant (Person
B).

DEPENDENT VARIABLE: PUBLIC RELATIONS ROLE

Based on a synthesis of research on public relations roles (Broom & Smith, 1979; Dozier & Gottesman, 1982), four dominant roles emerge based on reports by the practitioners themselves. These include the expert prescriber, the communication technician, the communication facilitator, and the problem-solving process facilitator (Cutlip, Center, & Broom, 1985).

Drawing on Blake and Mouton (1976), Broom and Smith (1979) describe the *expert prescriber* as an authority on both the public relations problem and the solution. This professional diagnoses the problem and prescribes the solution. He or she also feels a strong sense of responsibility for the program and its results.

On the other hand, the *communication technician* rarely defines the problem or the solution, but only executes other managers' prescribed solutions (Cutlip, Center, & Broom, 1985). Generally, the technician is hired for his or her communication skills, such as writing, editing, photography, or publications design and production.

The *communication facilitator* serves as a mediator or information broker. These practitioners provide a link between the organization and its various publics. Essentially, they focus on the communication exchange (Broom & Smith, 1979; Cutlip, Center, & Broom, 1985).

Finally, the *problem solving process facilitator* engages more frequently in organizational decision making than those in the other roles (Johnson & Acharya, 1982), probably because he/she collaborates with other managers in the organization to define and solve problems (Cutlip, Center, & Broom, 1985). This practitioner acts as a guide in the public relations problem-solving process and may be considered part of the organization's management.

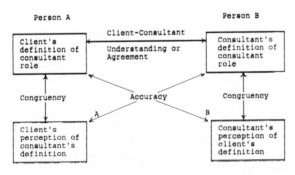

FIG. 14.6. Coorientation measurement model for public relations consultant roles.

Whether these roles, or others emerge, in the clients' cognitions remains an empirical question that deserves investigation. One can adapt McLeod and Chaffee's measurement model (Fig. 14.4) to role behaviors. Figure 14.6 shows a coorientation model of the client–consultant relationship. Each of the central role variables, expectation, sending, receiving, and behavior (Fig. 14.5), could be analyzed in the same coorientation context.

THEORETICAL RELATIONSHIPS

Some theoretical statements are readily apparent. Since the power relationship within the dyad is asymmetrical, the consultant or practitioner may have a tendency to be more accurate in his or her assessment of the client's perceptions of the public relations role than the client would be of the consultant's perceptions. The effects of accuracy and changes in accuracy on how the role actually evolves provides one interesting avenue of inquiry.

Inaccuracy, for example, may encourage members of a dyad to initiate more information exchanges (Stamm & Pearce, 1971), especially when participants are not faced with a unilateral decision (Pearce & Stamm, 1973). A corollary of this relationship, that high accuracy leads to less time in information exchange, also has support (Papa & Pood, 1988).

The level of accuracy also has other effects besides influencing the likelihood and frequency of communication. Papa and Pood (1988) reported that dyads in a high-accuracy situation used friendliness and bargaining as tactics in conflict resolution more frequently than did low-accuracy dyads. Low-accuracy dyads, on the other hand, were more likely to use assertiveness.

Accuracy, however, may not necessarily increase over time. In a longitudinal study, college students' perceptions of other students' views did not grow more accurate during the college years (Brown, Becker, & McLeod, 1976), an intriguing finding because most communication research would predict increasing accuracy from more information over time. This finding, however, may not apply to a social unit as small as a dyad. Nevertheless, it does suggest that some explanation may be necessary to account for possible *decreases* in accuracy.

Another coorientation variable, agreement, may provide additional insights. For example, what effects does agreement have on role variations across dyads? It may be expected that high agreement will lead to more clearly defined public relations roles. For example, high agreement suggests a preceding high level of understanding on policy, leaving more energy available to negotiate procedures. The link to roles may depend, however, on other situational variables. Data from Hatfield and Huseman (1982) suggest that high agreement has a positive linear association with various dimensions of job satisfaction.

Interestingly, some research suggests that a desire to communicate is not a function of disagreement. For example, when individuals who must make a unilateral decision discover they disagree, that disagreement tends to inhibit communication (Pearce & Stamm, 1973). That finding runs counter to earlier studies that showed a positive link between disagreement and information exchange (Festinger & Thibaut, 1951; Schachter, 1951). The association between these variables may also depend on situational constraints (Pavitt & Cappella, 1979), such as perceived uncertainty in a decision-making situation (Pavitt, 1982).

Congruency (perceived agreement), in turn, may have effects on actual agreement. In fact, Brown, Becker, and McLeod (1976) concluded that congruency is causally prior to agreement in large social systems. This may greatly determine the extent to which actual agreement is ever reached and a clear role definition is ever achieved.

Even at the level of the dyad, the effects of congruency may override agreement. In their study of communication rules in managerial dyads, Eisenberg, Monge, and Farace (1984) found that perceived agreement (congruency) and accuracy had positive effects on the manager's evaluations of the employee. Agreement, on the other hand, was negatively associated with evaluations, contradicting intuitive expectations that managers would be more satisfied with high levels of actual agreement.

Possibly, high levels of congruency may lead to rapid, open negotiation and settlement on the role performed, which might account for these findings. Incongruence, on the other hand, would logically introduce uncertainty and extend the period of negotiation. In fact, Brown, Becker, and McLeod (1976) found that incongruence leads to opinion seeking and opinion giving—in essence more communicative acts that would logically extend over a longer period of time.

As such a balance model suggests, tension in the system also may be resolved by responses other than information seeking, such as discounting the other's orientation, changing one's own orientation, or attempting to negotiate a consensus based on an altogether new relationship.

CONCLUSION

The interest here is in validating the role typology currently in use by identifying the role senders' perceptions, an essential but neglected perspective in the study of public relations roles. In addition, this approach could: identify essential differences between public relations role sets; assess coorientational relationships within a given role set and their effects on the roles performed; and examine how these roles may evolve over time. Essentially, these topics address social reality and its construction (McLeod & Chaffee, 1972). This suggests analyses not only of the differences between dyads but the dynamic processes that operate within them as well.

ACKNOWLEDGMENTS

Special acknowledgment is made to Lalit Acharya, California State University-Fullerton, for his suggestions on this topic and to Byron Reeves, Stanford University, and Jack McLeod, University of Wisconsin—Madison, for their comments on earlier versions of this chapter.

REFERENCES

Acharya, L. (1983, August). *Practitioner representations of environmental uncertainty: An application of discriminant analysis.* Paper presented to the Public Relations Division, Association for Education in Journalism and Mass Communication Annual Convention, Corvallis, OR.

Bales, R. F. (1950). *Interaction process analysis: Method for the study of small groups.* Reading, MA: Addison-Wesley.

Biddle, B. J. (1979). *Role theory: Expectations, identities, and behavior.* New York: Academic Press.

Biddle, B. J., & Thomas, E. J. (Eds.). (1966). *Role theory: Concepts and research.* New York: Wiley.

Blake, R. R., & Mouton, J. S. (1976). *Consultation.* Reading, MA: Addison-Wesley.

Broom, G. M. (1977). *Community consensus building: A communication experiment in two rural Wisconsin communities.* Unpublished doctoral dissertation, University of Wisconsin—Madison.

Broom, G. M., & Smith, G. D. (1979). Testing the practitioner's impact on clients. *Public Relations Review, 5,* 47–59.

Brown, J. D., Becker, L., & McLeod, J. M. (1976, August). *A causal analysis of coorientation variables using a non-experimental, longitudinal design.* Paper presented to the Theory and Methodology Division of the Association for Education in Journalism, College Park, MD.

Cappella, J. N. (1987). Interpersonal communication: Definitions and fundamental questions. In C. R. Berger & S. H. Chaffee (Eds.), *Handbook of communication science* (pp. 184–238). Newbury Park, CA: Sage.

Carter, R. F. (1962). Communication, understanding, and support for public education. In W. Schramm (Ed.), *Paris-Stanford Studies in Communication* (pp.

89–106). Stanford, CA: Institute for Communication Research, Stanford University.

Carter, R. F. (1965). Communication and affective relations. *Journalism Quarterly, 42,* 203–212.

Carter, R. F., Ruggels, L., & Olson, R. F. (1966). General introduction. In R. F. Carter, L. Ruggels, & R. F. Olson (Eds.), *The structure and process of school-community relations* (Tech. Rep., Research Project No. 1039, Vol. 3, pp. 1–14). Stanford, CA: Stanford University, School of Education.

Chaffee, S. H. (1973). Applying the interpersonal perception model to the real world. *American Behavioral Scientist, 16,* 465–468.

Chaffee, S. H., & McLeod, J. M. (1968). Sensitization in panel design: A coorientational experiment. *Journalism Quarterly, 45,* 661–669.

Cutlip, S. M., Center, A. H., & Broom, G. (1985). *Effective public relations* (6th ed.). Englewood Cliffs, NJ: Prentice-Hall.

Dansereau, F., Alutto, J. A., & Yammarino, F. J. (1984). *Theory testing in organizational behavior: The varient approach.* Englewood Cliffs, NJ: Prentice-Hall.

Dansereau, F., Graen, G., & Haga, W. J. (1975). A vertical dyad linkage approach to leadership within formal organizations: A longitudinal investigation of the role making process. *Organizational Behavior, 13,* 46–78.

Dansereau, F., & Markham, S. E. (1987). Superior–subordinate communication: Multiple levels of analysis. In F. M. Jablin, L. L. Putnam, K. H. Roberts, & L. W. Porter (Eds.), *Handbook of organizational communication: An interdisciplinary perspective* (pp. 343–388). Newbury Park, CA: Sage.

Dozier, D. M., & Gottesman, M. (1982, July). *Subjective dimensions of organizational roles among public relations practitioners.* Paper presented to the Public Relations Division, Association for Education in Journalism and Mass Communication, Athens, OH.

Eisenberg, E. M., Monge, P. R., & Farace, R. V. (1984). Coorientation on communication rules in managerial dyads. *Human Communication Research, 11,* 261–271.

Fairhurst, G. T., Rogers, L. E., & Sarr, R. A. (1987). Manager–subordinate control patterns and judgments about the relationship. In M. L. McLaughlin (Ed.), *Communication yearbook 10* (pp. 395–415). Newbury Park, CA: Sage.

Ferguson, M. A. (1979). *Role norms, implicit relationship attributions and organizational communication: A study of public relations practitioners.* Unpublished master's thesis, University of Wisconsin—Madison.

Festinger, L. (1950). Informal social communication. In *Theory and experiment in social communication* (pp. 3–17). Ann Arbor, MI: Institute for Social Research, University of Michigan.

Festinger, L., & Thibaut, J. (1951). Interpersonal communications in small groups. *Journal of Abnormal Social Psychology, 46,* 92–99.

Getzels, J. W., & Guba, E. G. (1954). Role, role conflict, and effectiveness. *American Sociological Review, 19,* 164–175.

Graen, G. (1976). Role-making processes within complex organizations. In M. D. Dunnette (Ed.), *Handbook of industrial and organizational psychology* (pp. 1201–1245). Chicago: Rand McNally.

Groot, H. C. (1970). *Coorientation and technical change: Communication variables in perceptions of miracle rice in the Philippines.* Unpublished doctoral dissertation, University of Wisconsin—Madison.

Grunig, J. E. (1978, August). *The status of public relations research.* Paper presented to the Public Relations Division of the Association for Education in Journalism, Annual Convention, Seattle, WA.

Grunig, J. E., & Stamm, K. R. (1973). Communication and coorientation of collectivities. *American Behavioral Scientist, 16,* 567–591.

Hage, J. (1972). *Techniques and problems of theory construction in sociology.* New York: Wiley.

Harre, R., & Secord, P. F. (1972). *The explanation of social behaviour.* Oxford: Basil Blackwell.

Hatfield, J. D., & Huseman, R. C. (1982). Perceptual congruence about communication as related to satisfaction: Moderating effects of individual characteristics. *Academy of Management Journal, 25,* 349–358.

Homans, G. C. (1950). *The human group.* New York: Harcourt, Brace, & World.

Jablin, F. M. (1979). Superior–subordinate communication: The state of the art. *Psychological Bulletin, 86,* 1201–1222.

Jablin, F. M. (1982). Organizational communication: An assimilation approach. In M. E. Roloff & C. R. Berger (Eds.), *Social cognition and communication* (pp. 255–286). Beverly Hills: Sage.

Jablin, F. M., & Krone, K. J. (1987). Organizational assimilation. In C. R. Berger & S. H. Chaffee (Eds.), *Handbook of communication science* (pp. 711–746). Newbury Park, CA: Sage.

Johnson, D. (1987, May). *Coorientation between client and consultant on public relations practitioner roles.* Paper presented to Conference on Applications of Communication Theory: Public Relations, Illinois State University.

Johnson, D., & Acharya, L. (1982, July). *Organizational decision making and public relations roles.* Paper presented to the Public Relations Division, Association for Education in Journalism and Mass Communication Conference, Athens, OH.

Katz, D., & Kahn, R. L. (1978). *The social psychology of organizations* (2nd ed.). New York: Wiley.

Kerlinger, F. N. (1973). *Foundations of behavioral research* (2nd ed.). New York: Holt, Rinehart & Winston.

Klapp, O. E. (1957). The concept of consensus and its importance. *Sociology and Social Research, 41,* 336–42.

Laing, R. D., Phillipson, H., & Lee, A. R. (1966). *Interpersonal perception: A theory and method of research.* New York: Springer.

McLeod, J. M., & Chaffee, S. H. (1972). The construction of social reality. In J. T. Tedeschi (Ed.), *Social influence process* (pp. 50–99). Chicago: Aldine Atherton.

McLeod, J. M., & Chaffee, S. H. (1973). Interpersonal approaches to communications research. *American Behavioral Scientist, 16,* 469–500.

Meiller, L. R. (1977). *A coorientation approach to consensus building in Wisconsin communities.* Unpublished doctoral dissertation, University of Wisconsin—Madison.

Monge, P. R., Farace, R. V., Eisenberg, E. M., Miller, K. I., and White, L. L. (1984). The process of studying process in organizational communication. *Journal of Communication, 34,* 22–43.

Newcomb, T. M. (1953). An approach to the study of communicative acts. *Psychological Review, 40,* 393–404.

O'Keefe, G. J. (1973). Coorientation variables in a family study. *American Behavioral Scientist, 16,* 513–536.

Papa, M. J., & Pood, E. A. (1988). Coorientational accuracy and organizational conflict: An examination of tactic selection and discussion satisfaction. *Communication Research, 15,* 3–28.

Parsons, T. (1977). *Social systems and the evolution of action theory.* New York: Macmillan.

Pavitt, C. (1982). A test of six models of coorientation: The effect of task and disagreement level on judgments of uncertainty, utility, and desired communicative behavior. In M. Burgoon (Ed.), *Communication Yearbook, 5,* (pp. 303–330). New Brunswick, NJ: Transaction Books.

Pavitt, C., & Cappella, J. N. (1979). Coorientational accuracy in interpersonal and small group discussions: A literature review, model, and simulation. In D. Nimmo (Ed.), *Communication Yearbook, 3,* (pp. 123–156). New Brunswick, NJ: Transaction Books.

Pavlik, J. V. (1987). *Public relations: What research tells us.* Newbury Park: Sage.

Pearce, W. B., & Stamm, K. R. (1973). Coorientational states and interpersonal communication. In P. Clarke (Ed.), *New models for mass communication research* (pp. 177–203). Beverly Hills: Sage.

Schachter, S. (1951). Deviation, rejection and communication. *Journal of Abnormal and Social Psychology, 46,* 190–207.

Scheff, T. J. (1967). Toward a sociological model of consensus. *American Sociological Review, 32,* 32–46.

Schein, E. H. (1969). *Process consultation: Its role in organization development.* Reading, MA: Addison-Wesley.

Shaw, M. E., & Costanzo, P. R. (1982). *Theories of social psychology.* New York: McGraw-Hill.

Smircich, L., & Chesser, R. J. (1981). Superiors' and subordinates' perceptions of performance: Beyond disagreement. *Academy of Management Journal, 24,* 198–205.

Stamm, K. R., & Pearce, W. B. (1971). Communication behavior and coorientational relations. *Journal of Communication, 21,* 208–220.

Sypher, B. D., & Sypher, H. E. (1984). Seeing ourselves as others see us: Convergence and divergence in assessments of communication behavior. *Communication Research, 11,* 97–115.

Tagiuri, R., Bruner, J. S., & Blake, R. R. (1958). On the relation between feelings and perception of feelings among members of small groups. In E. E. Maccoby, T. M. Newcomb, & E. L. Hartley (Eds.), *Readings in social psychology* (pp. 110–116). New York: Holt.

Wackman, D. B. (1973). Interpersonal communication and coorientation. *American Behavioral Scientist, 16,* 537–550.

Warwick, D. P., & Lininger, C. A. (1975). *The sample survey: Theory and practice.* New York: McGraw-Hill.

Whitcomb, D. (1976, July–August). *A general paradigm for public relations research.* Paper presented to the Public Relations Division, Annual Convention, Association for Education in Journalism, College Park, MD.

Wilmot, W. W. (1979). *Dyadic communication* (2nd ed.). Reading, MA: Addison-Wesley.

SUGGESTED READINGS

Blake, R. R., & Mouton, J. S. (1976). *Consultation.* Reading, MA: Addison-Wesley.

Chaffee, S. H. (1973). Applying the interpersonal perception model to the real world. *American Behavioral Scientist, 16,* 465–468.

Chaffee, S. H., & McLeod, J. M. (1968). Sensitization in panel design: A coorientational experiment. *Journalism Quarterly, 45,* 661–669.

Hage, J. (1972). *Techniques and problems of theory construction in sociology.* New York: Wiley.

Katz, D., & Kahn, R. L. (1978). *The social psychology of organizations* (2nd ed.). New York: Wiley.

McLeod, J. M., & Chaffee, S. H. (1973). Interpersonal approaches to communications research. *American Behavioral Scientist, 16,* 469–500.

Monge, P. R., Farace, R. V., Eisenberg, E. M., Miller, K. I., and White, L. L. (1984). The process of studying process in organizational communication. *Journal of Communication, 34,* 22–43.

Newcomb, T. M. (1953). An approach to the study of communicative acts. *Psychological Review, 40,* 393–404.

Wilmot, W. W. (1979). *Dyadic communication.* Reading, MA: Addison-Wesley.

Reflexivity and Internal Public Relations:The Role of Information in Directing Organizational Development

Gary L. Kreps
Northern Illinois University

ABSTRACT

Public relations efforts can provide organizational change agents with reflexive information about the relative effectiveness of important organizational activities. Such information is prerequisite to the development and implementation of relevant innovations to accomplish system-wide organizational development. To demonstrate the powerful role of information and reflexivity in directing organizational development, a case study of an action research field study of nursing turnover and retention in a large urban hospital is reported. In the field study, nurses were identified as a key internal public. Nurses' organizational grievances were identified through public relations communication efforts to assess specific issues behind excessive turnover and used to develop an ongoing retention program. The retention program was designed as an internal public relations communication system to gather relevant information from nursing staff, channel information from nursing staff to hospital administration to direct ongoing organizational innovation, and provide feedback to hospital staff about innovations being implemented within the organization.

REFLEXIVITY AND PUBLIC RELATIONS

Leaders need information about organizational activities to direct successful innovation and accomplish system-wide organizational development (Nadler, 1977; Rowe & Boise, 1973). Public relations efforts can provide leaders with relevant information about environmental constraints and internal organizational issues for use in guiding organizational adaptation. All too often public relations efforts are viewed as merely external organizational communication activities, whereas gathering information from and providing information to internal organizational audiences are major elements of effective public relations (D'Aprix, 1984; Grunig & Hunt, 1984; Kreps, 1986). This chapter expands traditional external communication-oriented theoretical perspectives on public relations to include the role of internal communication in providing change agents with relevant information for directing organizational development.

Organization members are an important audience for internal public relations efforts. Information gathered through internal public relations efforts enables organization leaders to clearly see the current state of the organization from the point of view of the organization's membership, promoting increased organizational reflexivity (or the organization's ability to see itself) (Kreps, 1983a, 1985, 1986a). Reflexive information helps leaders identify current and potential problems, as well as identify directions for organizational change. Berrien (1976) contended that "no problem is more important to organizational theory than the management of change, both internal and external," (p. 47). Many external public relations communication activities such as lobbying and government relations, as well as market and public opinion research, are designed to gather relevant information from the environment (Grunig & Hunt, 1984; Kreps, 1986a; Nager & Allen, 1984). Such external information also increases organizational reflexivity by helping leaders see their organization as members of the relevant environment see it and enabling leaders to assess the adequacy of organizing activities for directing organizational innovation and ongoing development.

Increased reflexivity enables leaders to recognize important performance gaps, "discrepancies between an organization's expectations and its actual performance" (Rogers & Agarwala-Rogers, 1976, p. 70). Performance gaps occur in situations where organizational goals are not fully accomplished. The further the organization is from the accomplishment of established organizational goals the wider the performance gap is. Public relations efforts can be used to gather information about the nature and seriousness of organizational performance gaps. In fact, Greenbaum (1974) asserted it is crucial to conduct regular internal organizational communication audits to diagnose performance gaps and direct strategies for narrowing these gaps.

Organizations in which relevant performance gaps are identified are better informed about directions for organizational innovation. Yet, merely having relevant information about needed changes and improvements does not mean that organizations are able to actually develop and implement relevant innovations. Slack resources are needed to energize organizational innovation, "resources that are not already committed to other purposes" (Rogers & Agarwala-Rogers, 1976, p. 161). Slack resources can be personnel that are free to work on solving performance gaps, or equipment that is available, or computer time that can be used, or money that is not earmarked for other purposes. Organizations generally have some slack resources available. To direct and implement innovations that will result in organizational development, slack resources have to be identified and mobilized.

PUBLIC RELATIONS AND ORGANIZATIONAL DEVELOPMENT

The recognition of performance gaps are key steps in accomplishing organizational development (OD) (French & Bell, 1973; French, Bell, & Zawacki, 1978; Pavlock, 1982). Beckhard (1969, p. 4) defines OD as a renewal and change effort that is (a) planned, (b) organization-wide, and (c) managed from the top, to (d) increase organization effectiveness and health through (e) planned interventions in the organization's processes using behavioral-science knowledge. An OD effort involves a systematic diagnosis of the organization, the development of a strategic plan for change, and the mobilization of resources to carry out the effort. By identifying important performance gaps an organizational development specialist can identify and diagnose specific organizational problems and difficulties and design adaptive strategies for organizational innovation that effectively meet an organization's current and future goals.

To direct organizational innovation, OD specialists depend on public relations communication to diagnose performance gap. Public relations communication is an essential tool leaders utilize to gather information from organization members and other relevant publics. They recognize the need for innovation and gather the slack resources necessary for accomplishing organizational development (Axley, 1980). Public relations efforts are used to: (a) gather the information and feedback needed from internal and external sources to identify performance gaps and plan organizational development efforts (Nadler, 1977); (b) gain support for OD efforts from organization leaders (Schein, 1969); (c) mobilize slack resources (Kreps, 1986); (d) implement intervention strategies and plans into organizational operations (Beckhard, 1969; Nadler, 1977); and (e) build long-term commitment to organizational innovations (Axley, 1980; Conner & Patterson, 1982).

DEVELOPING PROACTIVE ORGANIZATIONS

The better organization members are at gathering relevant information from internal and external information sources the better they will be at recognizing important performance gaps. Recognition of performance gaps enables organization members to diagnose current and potential organizational problems. Recognition of performance gaps is a first step in planning innovative OD strategies. The more effective leaders are at identifying and acting on performance gaps the more proactive their organization will be. Proactive organizations do not wait to react to environmental influences. In proactive organizations leaders direct innovative activities to meet upcoming problems before they hit, trying to stay one step ahead of performance gaps. Proactive organization often involves influencing the relevant environment before the environment constrains organizational activities (Rogers & Agarwala-Rogers, 1976).

To develop proactive organization leaders must be trained to establish effective communication relationships with knowledgeable individuals both internal and external to the organization. By seeking relevant information and feedback from key sources leaders can stay on top of changing environmental and internal organizational conditions. With this important information in hand leaders can proactively plan innovative courses for organizational operations.

REFLEXIVITY AND THE NURSE RETENTION
ORGANIZATIONAL DEVELOPMENT PROGRAM

To illustrate the relationships between internal public relations efforts and organizational development, a case study of a nurse retention research program implemented at a large urban Midwestern hospital over the last six years will be described (Kreps, 1983a, 1986b). This program was designed to examine the phenomenon of high turnover of nursing staff at the hospital by identifying the specific problems (performance gaps) nurses encounter in performing their jobs. Information gathered from nursing staff was utilized to enhance organizational reflexivity to direct the implementation of organizational interventions and promote system-wide organizational development. The data gathered from the nurses about performance gaps were used to develop formal feedback channels between nursing staff and hospital administration by providing nurses with organizationally approved communication channels for expressing their concerns. Feedback loops were designed to help the hospital administration make informed choices (based on the expertise of nursing staff), to direct the development and introduction of organizational innovations needed to increase retention of nursing staff, and transform the flow of relevant information within the organization to preserve and utilize organizational intelligence (Kreps, 1986a).

High turnover rates of nursing staff in hospitals across the nation have caused many problems (Filoromo & Ziff, 1980; Wandelt, Pierce, & Widdowson, 1981; Wolf, 1981). Excessive employee turnover has been linked to several organizational problems including: increased costs (recruiting, hiring, assimilation, training, replacement, out-processing), disruption of social and communication structures, productivity loss, loss of high performers, decreased satisfaction among those who stay, increase of undifferentiated turnover control strategies, and negative public relations from those who leave (Mobley, 1977, 1982). High nurse turnover can frustrate remaining organization members and lead to; disruption of work flow, increased work load during and immediately after search for replacement, decreased cohesion, and decreased commitment, in addition to the loss of functionally valued co-workers (Mobley, 1982).

Organizations, like human beings, must be able to adapt to survive (French, Bell, & Zawacki, 1978; Lippitt, 1973). Effective organizations gather information about their performance through public relations efforts from within their boundaries, as well as from their relevant external environments to determine what aspects of their organization need to be developed to promote successful adaptation (Knight & McDaniel, 1979; Rogers & Agarwala-Rogers, 1978). Members are an important source of information in organizations, especially those members who have contact with the public. Yarrington (1983) suggested that employees who have contact with the public serve as ambassadors for the organization and are crucial public relations contact points for gathering and disseminating relevant information. Such members have the potential to provide their organization with information from the internal environment, of which they are a part, and the external environment, with which they have daily contact.

In this study nurses were identified as important sources of relevant information in hospitals (Salem & Williams, 1984). Not only do nurses play key roles in accomplishing hospital activities, but they also have a great deal of contact with consumers and others who comprise an important part of hospitals' relevant external public. This study was designed to elicit relevant operational information from nurses and use the information to develop a nurse retention communication program to help improve organizational activities by making the hospital administration more aware of organizational problems (thus increasing the reflexiveness of the health-care organization).

Nurses who leave hospitals take with them valuable information about how to get things done in their organizations, something Weick (1979) refers to as "organizational intelligence." Hospitals lose additional organizational intelligence when nurses are taken off their jobs to train newly recruited nurses. Newly recruited nurses are often put in jobs that are difficult for them to accomplish because they do not have the organizational intelligence that comes with experience in that hospital (Kreps, 1983, 1986b). Mistakes made by newly recruited nurses can make the work life of other nurses at the hospital frustrating, decrease their job satisfaction, and lead to increased turnover. Reacting to nurse turnover by merely recruiting replacement nurses does not help solve the problems underlying turnover. In fact, recruitment efforts may exacerbate underlying organizational problems because they ignore the organizational intelligence about organizational difficulties and strategies for solving problems possessed by key organization members.

GATHERING INFORMATION ABOUT KEY ISSUES LEADING TO TURNOVER

A field study investigating nurses perceptions about organizational climate and job satisfaction/dissatisfaction was conducted and used to develop an ongoing nurse retention intervention program at Wishard Memorial Hospital of Indianapolis.[1] The hospital was experiencing a high rate of nurse turnover—approximately 35%. The study attempted to interpret the reasons for turnover and use that information to develop procedures for nurse retention.

Three different research phases were used as internal public relations assessment tools in this study to identify the issues underlying high nurse turnover: questionnaires examining nurses' perceptions of organizational climate (Hunter, 1976, 1978) and job satisfaction (Smith, Kendall, & Hulin, 1969), in-depth interviews, and focus group discussions (Calder, 1980; Szybillo & Berger, 1979; Wells, 1974). These three research phases combined quantitative and qualitative methods of analysis, providing a means of "method triangulation" to interpret organizational reality through the eyes of organization members (Albrecht & Ropp, 1982; Jick, 1979). The questionnaires were used to identify general issues of concern to nursing staff members and provide a baseline for examining changes in nurses' interpretations about organizational life, whereas the interviews and focus groups were used to provide in-depth

[1]This research was supported by grants from Wishard Memorial County Hospital of Indianapolis, Indiana. Sincere thanks for help in collecting the data in this study go to Helene Cross, Jeff Golc, and Jim L. Query, Jr.

information about issues facing nurses and recommendations for relieving the problems identified.

The questionnaire was presented to the total population of Wishard nurses ($n = 535$) at their work locations. The interviews were conducted with a selective sample ($n = 49$) of nurses who were identified as "key communicators" (knowledgeable and active members of the hospital's organizational culture) by administrators and staff nurses. The interviews expanded upon the primary topics of climate and job satisfaction identified in the questionnaire, asking respondents to evaluate their work lives, identify specific areas of satisfaction and dissatisfaction, and suggest areas for potential improvement within the hospital. Eight groups of nurses were randomly selected from the total population of nurses for participation in the focus groups, with seven to eight nurses in each group ($n = 62$). Each group evaluated one of six areas for improvement, change, and innovation in the hospital that had been identified in the interviews. Q–sort methodology was used by group members to individually rank suggestions for change within the hospital (Kerlinger, 1973). The top suggestions for change were discussed by the group, and strategies for implementing these changes were examined.

The questionnaire administration generated a response rate of 76% ($n = 408$). The data generated by the climate scale represented the overall hospital climate as being unexceptional, neither highly positive nor negative. The job satisfaction portion of the questionnaire generated data indicating a slightly above average overall level of satisfaction among nurses at the hospital (mean score of 30.1 out of a possible score of 48, and 26.6 being the set neutral point).[2]

The interview research phase further elaborated upon the data generated by the questionnaire, with interviewers using open-ended questions, probing for in-depth answers to questions about the strengths and weaknesses of work-life at the hospital, and urging the respondents to suggest areas for improvement within the organization. The 49 in-depth interviews generated 875 specific suggestions for improving the hospital and the quality of work life, which were then grouped topically into 6 general areas for change: benefits, supply and equipment, organizational structure, education, environment, and communication. Each of these 6 topic areas were composed of between 8 and 13 recommendation headings. Within each heading, on each of the 6 topic areas, specific recommendations (from the 875 suggestions) were listed.

---

[2]The neutral points for the Job Descriptive Index were calculated by Smith, Kendall, & Hulin, 1969, pp. 80–81, based on data collected from large samples of men and women pooled across a broad range of organizations studied.

In the focus group discussions research phase results from the interviews were examined, evaluated, and clarified by groups of nurses. The rankings for the recommendation headings were tabulated for each of the six topic areas, and the twenty highest rated recommendation headings overall were compiled. (These recommendations dealt with problems specific to the hospital under investigation, are not intended to be generalized to other hospitals, and are not pertinent to the purposes of this report.)

USING INFORMATION TO DIRECT
ORGANIZATIONAL DEVELOPMENT

The goal of this research was to collect interpretive organizational data to be used in developing intervention strategies for relieving the problem of excessive nurse turnover facing the hospital. The three research phases were used to find out what problems and concerns the nurses had, and an ongoing retention program was developed to help solve these problems and encourage nurses to stay at their jobs. The administrative philosophy behind the retention program is a radical departure from recruitment responses to nurse turnover (Kreps, 1986b). According to the recruitment approach, as nurse turnover increases hospitals seek new nurses to replace those who leave. The retention program rejects this philosophy, and suggests hospitals should spend more energy on keeping their nurses satisfied and productive than they spend on replacing nurses. The retention philosophy argues that the more a hospital replaces nurses the more problems are created for the organization and its administration through loss of organizational intelligence.

A retention committee was formed composed of representatives from different areas and levels within nursing service at the hospital. The retention committee was essentially an internal communication system whose primary goals were to examine specific problem areas, concerns, and organizational suggestions generated through the research; seek additional information about the issues identified; provide information to hospital decision-makers to initiate informed change; and ultimately increase nurse retention at the hospital. The retention committee was designed to perform an important public relations role within the organization by providing a two-way information link between nursing staff and hospital administration.

Some of the specific public relations roles of retention committee members were to bring information to the committee to act on, identify and report on concerns of nurses; circulate information from the committee to their co-workers at the hospital; and report on personalized information about nursing staff (such as births, marriages, graduations, etc.) to the committee to be published in the retention newsletter, "Dialogue." The newsletter was used as an in-house public relations vehicle to provide nursing staff and other hospital members with information about the activities of the retention committee, including issues under consideration and innovations being implemented, as well as to provide a vehicle for nurses to express their ideas, frustrations, and suggestions about the hospital to other members of the hospital staff. Personal news about nursing staff is also reported in "Dialogue" as a means of sharing interesting information among nurses and helping them feel a sense of hospital identification.

The retention program created a structural change in the hospital and transformed the flow of information within the organization to facilitate a process of on-going identification and implementation of relevant organizational innovations. The program was designed to identify recurring problems facing nurses that lead to job dissatisfaction and turnover. The data generated through the research phases of the study were used to develop strategies and implement plans to resolve recurring problems. The retention committee and newsletter were introduced to initiate action on the problems identified and serve as a public relations feedback channel between nursing staff and hospital administration. The retention committee represented all of the nurses at the hospital as an on-going information clearinghouse, helping to preserve organizational intelligence possessed by nurses and utilize that information for directing organizational innovation. The retention program established formal communication channels for nurses to provide administration with information about specific organizational problems and how they can be solved. It also empowered nurses to air their gripes and suggest directions for developing new hospital policies and procedures.

EVALUATION OF THE RETENTION PROGRAM

The retention program was implemented at the beginning of 1982. The retention program was a permanent structural innovation in the hospital, and the full benefits of this program may not be apparent for many years. Measurable changes in employee attitudes and behaviors due to such an intervention in a large complex organization will take time to emerge. Additionally, socio-economic environmental constraints that affect hospitals (e.g., inflation, budget allocations, work load, management changes, etc.) undoubtedly affect nurse turnover at the hospital. Nevertheless, interesting changes in hospital retention patterns have been observed.

Archival measures of institutional records of the rate of turnover among members of nursing staff have been "unobtrusively" monitored before and after introduction of the retention program (Webb, Campbell, Schwartz, & Sechrest, 1966). These data indicate the retention program may indeed be having a positive influence on nurse retention at the hospital. During 1981 (the year before the retention program was implemented) the nurse turnover rate was 35%, during 1982 (the first year of the program) it dropped 2% to 33%, during 1983 (the second year of the program) the turnover rate dropped 4% more to 29%, and during 1984 (the third year of the program) it dropped 2% more to 27% (Golc, 1984, personal communication, July, 1985). Nurse retention improved by 8% during the first 3 years of the retention program.

These retention figures must be evaluated cautiously. There may be unexplained variance influencing this reduction in nurse turnover at the hospital. To control for some of the environmental factors influencing turnover rates at the hospital during the four year period, 1981 through 1984, unobtrusive archival measures of nurse turnover were examined at four comparable Indianapolis hospitals and compared with the change in turnover at Wishard Community Hospital, St. Francis Hospital, St. Vincent Hospital, and Winona Hospital made available their institutional records of turnover for 1981, 1982, 1983, and 1984. None of the four hospitals experienced as high a reduction in nurse turnover between 1981 and 1985 as Wishard had. The highest four year reduction in turnover among any of these four hospitals was 2.6% as compared to Wishard's turnover reduction of 8% during the same time period. Overall, the four hospitals averaged a reduction of turnover of .8% compared to 2% for Wishard between 1981 and 1982, a reduction of 1.3% compared to 4% for Wishard between 1982 and 1983, and an increase in turnover of 1.3% compared to a decrease of 2% for Wishard between 1983 and 1984 (see Table 15.1). These data indicate that, controlling for similar environmental influences, Wishard Hospital experienced higher reductions of turnover than these other four area hospitals. This adds strength to the contention that the retention program, which was imple-

TABLE 15.1
Comparison of Changes in Turnover Between Wishard Hospital
and Four Area Hospitals from 1981 to 1984

	1981–1982	1982–1983	1983–1984	Total
Wishard Hospital	−2%	−4%	−2%	−8%
Average of four area hospitals	−.8%	−1.3%	+1.3%	−.8%

mented only at Wishard Hospital, did help the hospital reduce turnover and increase retention of nursing staff.

Formal study of changes in nurse satisfaction and organizational climate before and after the implementation of the retention program have been less helpful in evaluating the impact of the retention program on the hospital. Two follow-up administrations of the climate and satisfaction questionnaire were conducted at the hospital 6 months and 12 months after introduction of the retention program to identify any changes in nurses' perceptions of organizational climate and job satisfaction. No significant differences in overall levels of satisfaction and climate between the three questionnaire administrations were generated, indicating that job-satisfaction and climate are relatively stable organizational characteristics that have not at this time been influenced by the retention program.

Unstructured interviews with selected members of the nursing staff and hospital administration ($n = 27$; 24 nurses and 3 administrators) asking for reactions to the retention program have been conducted. The reactions from respondents have strongly indicated members of the hospital organization perceive the retention program as a productive innovation in the hospital. Virtually all nurses reported they felt better about the hospital and their jobs because of the opportunity provided them by the retention program to voice their concerns about the hospital and participate in the hospital's organizational decision-making. These responses indicate the retention program had served to legitimize the relevant information nurses' possess about hospital functioning and use this information to help improve the organization. Those hospital administrators who were interviewed reported that meaningful dialogue among nurses, as well as between nurses and administrators, had increased as a result of the retention program. In addition, respondents indicated that the retention program had been influential in initiating several problem-solving innovations at the hospital including: new in-service education programs, a clinical nursing career ladder, interdepartmental and interprofessional training programs, improvement of child-care facilities for nurses, and introduction of exit interviews.

IMPLICATIONS FOR PUBLIC RELATIONS AND ORGANIZATIONAL DEVELOPMENT

In the field study, nurses' expertise about organizational operations (organizational intelligence) was identified through internal public relations efforts as a relevant slack resource that could be used to direct organizational innovation and improvement. The nurses' organizational intel-

ligence was used to highlight performance gaps in the hospital and develop intervention strategies to narrow those gaps. Revising the communication structure of the hospital by implementing the retention program served to redirect information flow within the hospital, helping the
organization to preserve and employ nurses' organizational intelligence
to proactively improve organizational operations through informed decision making, as well as to increase retention of nursing staff. The retention program process of identifying performance gaps and proposing
different intervention strategies for the organization should have a per-
petual influence on the activities of all areas of the organization resulting
in system-wide innovation and on-going development.

The retention study underscores the need for developing information
reflexivity in organizations. The ability of leaders (and other change
agents) to use internal public relations activities to see the organization as
members do can help leaders recognize and resolve organizational problems. Additionally, such internal public relations efforts can legitimize
employees' interpretations of organizational life and utilize the information they possess to increase these individuals' involvement with the organization and their jobs. Organization members can be given more say
in organizational decision making, and the feedback they provide can
help solve problems they face on their jobs. In the retention study, the
communication structure and activities of the hospital were redesigned
to promote enhanced organizational reflexivity. Information gathered
through public relations efforts were used to identify performance gaps
and direct the development and implementation of relevant organizational innovations to help reduce nurse turnover and promote system-
wide organizational development.

An important aspect of this study is that there was no set formula for
solving the problem of nurse turnover. Rather than introducing pre-
determined innovations into the hospital, the retention program was
designed to seek information from nurses to identify and guide changes
warranted by the conditions existing within the hospital. This implies
that there is no set solution to nurse turnover; for that matter, predetermined solutions to most complex organizational problems are not likely
to be effective. The principle of "requisite variety" suggests that complex
issues are rarely suited to simplistic, rule-governed solutions and are
generally best suited to complex solutions developed out of interactive
processes (Weick, 1979). Each organization must independently develop
internal public relations strategies for gathering and disseminating relevant information to identify performance gaps and develop appropriate
innovations to facilitate organizational development.

REFERENCES

Albrecht, T. L., & Ropp, V. A. (1982). The study of network structuring in organizations through the use of method triangulation. *Western Journal of Speech Communication, 46,* 162–178.

Axley, S. R. (1980, May). *Communication's role in organizational change: A review of the literature.* Paper presented to the International Communication Association conference, Acapulco, Mexico.

Beckhard, R. (1969). *Organization development: Strategies and models.* Reading, MA: Addison-Wesley.

Berrien, F. K. (1976). A general systems approach to organizations. In M. Dunnette (Ed.), *Handbook of industrial and organizational psychology* (pp. 41–62). Chicago: Rand McNally.

Calder, B. (1980). Focus group interviews and qualitative research in organizations. In E. Lawler, D. Nadler, & C. Cammann (Eds.), *Organizational assessment: Perspectives on the measurement of organizational behavior and the quality of work life* (pp. 399–417). New York: Wiley.

Conner, D. R., & Patterson, R. W. (1982). Building commitment to organizational change. *Training and Development Journal, 36,* 18–30.

D'Aprix, R. (1984). Employee communication. In B. Cantor (Ed.), *Experts in action: Inside public relations* (pp. 102–110). New York: Longman.

Filoromo, T., & Ziff, D. (1980). *Nurse recruitment: Strategies for success.* Rockville, MD: Aspen Systems Corp.

French, W., & Bell, C. (Eds.). (1973). *Organization development: Behavioral science interventions for organization improvement.* Englewood Cliffs, NJ: Prentice-Hall.

French, W., Bell, C., & Zawacki, R. (1978). *Organizational development: Theory, practice, and research.* Dallas, TX: Business Publications.

Golc, J. L. (1984). *Recruitment and retention report with goals and objectives for 1984.* Unpublished in-house report, Department of Nursing Services, Wishard Memorial Hospital, Indianapolis, IN.

Greenbaum, H. H. (1974). The audit of organizational communication. *Academy of Management Journal, 17,* 750–752.

Grunig, J., & Hunt, T. (1984). *Managing public relations.* New York: Holt, Rinehart & Winston.

Hunter, R. E. (1976). *The development and evaluation of an organizational climate questionnaire for mental health centers.* Unpublished doctoral dissertation, Ohio University, Athens, OH.

Hunter, R. E. (1978, May). *The mental health center climate questionnaire.* Paper presented to the ICA conference, Chicago, IL.

Jick, T. (1979). Mixing qualitative and quantitative methods: Triangulation in action. *Administrative Science Quarterly* (1979), 602–611.

Kerlinger, F. N. (1973). *Foundations of behavioral research* (2nd ed.). New York: Holt, Rinehart & Winston.

Knight, K. E., & McDaniel, R. R. (1979). *Organizations: An information systems perspective.* Belmont, CA: Wadsworth.

Kreps, G. L. (1983a, August). *Nurse retention and organizational reflexivity.* Paper presented to the Academy of Management conference, Dallas, TX.

Kreps, G. L. (1983b, August). *Organizational communication and organizational culture: A Weickian perspective.* Paper presented to the Academy of Management conference, Dallas, TX.

Kreps, G. L. (1985). Organizational communication and organizational effectiveness. *World Communication, 14,* 109–119.

Kreps, G. L. (1986a). *Organizational communication: Theory and practice.* White Plains, NY: Longman.

Kreps, G. L. (1986b). Description and evaluation of a nurse retention organizational development research program. In H. Guetal & M. Kavanagh (Eds.), *Fifty years of excellence in management research and practice: Proceedings of the Third Annual Meeting of the Eastern Academy of Management,* 18–22, Eastern Academy of Management.

Lippit, G. (1973). *Visualizing change.* Fairfax, VA: NTL Learning Resources Corp.

Mobley, W. (1977). Intermediate linkages in the relationship between job satisfaction and employee turnover. *Journal of Applied Psychology, 67,* 237–240.

Mobley, W. (1982). Some unanswered questions in turnover and withdrawal research. *Academy of Management Review, 7,* 111–116.

Nadler, D. R. (1977). *Feedback and organization development: Using data based methods.* Reading, MA: Addison-Wesley.

Nager, N. R., & Allen, T. H. (1984). *Public relations: Management by objectives.* New York: Longman.

Pavlock, E. J. (Ed.). (1982). *Organization development: Managing transitions.* Washington, DC: ASTD.

Rogers, E. M., & Agarwala-Rogers, R. (1976). *Communication in organizations.* New York: The Free Press.

Rowe, L., & Boise, W. (Eds.). (1973). *Organizational and managerial innovation.* Pacific Palisades, CA: Goodyear Publishing.

Salem, P., & Williams, M. L. (1984). Uncertainty and satisfaction: The importance of information in hospital communication. *Journal of Applied Communication Research 12,* 75–89.

Schein, E. H. (1969). *Process consultation: Its role in organization development.* Reading, MA: Addison-Wesley.

Smith, P. C., Kendall, L. M., & Hulin, C. L. (1969). *The measurement of satisfaction in work and retirement: A strategy for the study of attitudes.* Chicago: Rand McNally.

Szybillo, G. J., & Berger, R. (1979). What advertising agencies think of focus groups. *Journal of Advertising Research, 19,* 29–33.

Wandelt, M. A., Pierce, P. M., & Widdowson, R. R. (1981). Why nurses leave nursing and what can be done about it. *American Journal of Nursing, 81,* 72–77.

Webb, E. J., Campbell, D. T., Schwartz, R. D., & Sechrest, L. (1966). Unobtrusive measures: Nonreactive research in the social sciences. Chicago: Rand McNally.

Weick, K. E. (1979). *The social psychology of organizing* (2nd ed.). Reading, MA: Addison-Wesley.

Wells, W. D. (1974). Group interviewing. In R. Ferber (Ed.), *Handbook of marketing research* (pp. 2–133–2–146). New York: McGraw Hill.
Wolf, G. A. (1981, April). Nursing turnover: Some causes and solutions. *Nursing Outlook*, 233–236.
Yarrington, R. (1983). *Community relations handbook*. New York: Longman.

SUGGESTED READINGS

Cantor, B. (Ed.). (1984). *Experts in action: Inside public relations*. New York: Longman.
Grunig, J., & Hunt, T. (1984). *Managing public relations*. New York: Holt, Rinehart & Winston.
Kreps, G. L. (1986a). *Organizational communication: Theory and practice*. White Plains, NY: Longman.
Kreps, G. L., & Thornton, B. C. (1984). *Health communication: Theory and practice*. White Plains, NY: Longman.
Nadler, D. R. (1977). *Feedback and organization development: Using data based methods*. Reading, MA: Addison-Wesley.
Nager, N. R., & Allen, T. H. (1984). *Public relations: Management by objectives*. White Plains, NY: Longman.
Rogers, E. M., & Agarwala-Rogers, R. (1978). *Communication in organizations*. New York: The Free Press.
Schein, E. H. (1969). *Process consultation: Its role in organization development*. Reading, MA: Addison-Wesley.
Weick, K. E. (1979). *The social psychology of organizing* (2nd ed.). Reading, MA: Addison-Wesley.
Yarrington, R. (1983). *Community relations handbook*. White Plains, NY: Longman.

Educator and Practitioner Differences on the Role of Theory in Public Relations

Keith E. Terry
Kearney State College

ABSTRACT

A major issue in the field of public relations is the existence of public relations theory and to what extent practitioners use theory in their campaigns. The purpose of this study was to investigate those subjects. Specifically, this study examined: the existence of a public relations theory; and the degree of awareness, perceived validity, and practical utility of human behavior; and communication theories by public relations educators and practitioners. The background research laid the groundwork for the formation of a national survey administered to public relations educators and practitioners.

This chapter is divided into four major areas. The first reviews the literature on theory definition, concept, and development; the next presents the survey design created to empirically investigate the research questions; the third section describes the data, results, and methods of analysis; the last offers conclusions based on the research and suggestions for further positive development of the field.

The notion that public relations is emerging as a social science discipline was discussed in chapter 1. In order for a social science to advance, there should be a strong communication link, with mutual understanding, between theorists and those employing the theory. The existence of such a link between public relations theorists and practitioners has been questioned, however. This chapter discusses a national survey that seeks to quantify the perceived validity and practical utility [of 20 popular theories and models] to public relations faculty and practitioners.

THE ROLE OF THEORY
IN THE BEHAVIORAL SCIENCES

The foundation of scientific research is the formulation of theory that explains past behavior and/or predicts future behavior. Research is given direction and purpose by building on this theoretic foundation. But what is theory?

Several definitions of theory are offered by authors in the behavioral science literature. Although differing in form, they are similar in concept. For example, consider how the following authors define theory:

> A theory is a set of interrelated constructs (concepts), definitions, and propositions that present a systematic view of phenomena by specifying relations among variables, with the purpose of explaining and predicting the phenomena. (Kerlinger, 1973, p. 9)

> A theory is a systematic explanation for the observed facts and laws that relate to a particular aspect of life. (Babbie, 1986, p. 37)

> A theory refers to a set of logically interrelated 'propositions' or 'statements' that are 'empirically meaningful,' as well as to the assumptions the researcher makes about his [sic] method and his [sic] data. (Runkel & McGrath, 1972, p. 23)

> Theory. 1) In a general sense, any more or less formalized conceptualization of the relationship of variables. (Marx, 1963, p. 43)

These definitions suggest important characteristics and functions of a theory:

1. A theory presents a systematic view of the observed phenomena.
2. A theory specifies relations among variables.
3. A theory specifies *how* variables are related.
4. A theory explains past and/or present behavior.
5. A reliable theory predicts, with a high degree of probability, future behavior.

The last function may be the most important because it encompasses the previous four. For the proposed theory to predict reliably there is at least some understanding of how the "pieces" (identification of variables and relations) make up the whole (explanation and prediction). "If by using theory we are able to predict successfully, then the theory is confirmed" (Kerlinger, 1973, p. 10).

Trenholm (1986) offered a figurative example of theory: "if X, then Y, under conditions C1, C2, C3" (p. 45). A literal example would be: if children are exposed to televised violence [X], they are likely to demonstrate increased aggression [Y] if aggressive tendencies [C1] are already present.

In summary, scientific research begins with the formulation of a theory. The more general a theory is, the more useful it is in subsequent research because of its potential applications (Kerlinger, 1973, p. 10). A theory serves distinct purposes, and it should possess a number of characteristics, the most important of which is its predictive ability.

THE ROLE OF THEORY IN THE DEVELOPMENT
OF THE BEHAVIORAL SCIENCES

The development of the sciences has progressed through three stages: the theological, the metaphysical, and into the present stage of positivism. It is during the positivistic state that the behavioral sciences have evolved.

These three stages are sequential according to Levy-Bruhl (1973) who cited August Comte:

> The human mind by its nature, in each of its researches makes use successively of three methods of philosophizing, essentially different and even opposed to each other. . . . The first is the necessary starting point of human intelligence, the third, its fixed and final state; the second is solely destined to serve as transition. (p. 36)

The theological state has no religious undertones. Instead, the early theories used by people are anthropomorphic; natural phenomena are seen to occur as a result of the supernatural or will. This theological reasoning has also been called fictitious, mythological, and imaginary.

Thompson (1975) explains that the metaphysical or abstract state was marked by the "gradual decline of the one [theological] and the preparatory rise of the other [positivism], so as to spare our dislike of abrupt change and to afford us a transition almost imperceptible" (p. 64).

The third stage, positivism, "regards all phenomena as subjected to invariable natural laws" (Thompson, 1975, p. 43). It is during positivism that the behavioral sciences moved from post hoc observation to a priori examination and prediction of phenomena.

Each of these three stages has played an important part in the development of scientific thought, inquiry and theory testing as we have moved from the simple to the complex—in much the same way we do as individuals, according to Thompson (1975):

> Now each of us is aware, if [sic] he looks back upon [sic] his own history, that [sic] he was a theologian in [sic] his childhood, a metaphysician in [sic] his youth, and a natural philosopher in [sic] his manhood. (p. 41)

In summary, the abstract sciences and scientific theory have developed concurrently from the simple to the complex. Both science and scientific theory have made use of fictitious, abstract, and scientific explanation at some time during their histories. This evolution of knowledge and thought mirrors the human learning process from the uncomplicated to the composite.

THE ROLE OF THEORY IN THE DEVELOPMENT OF THE FIELD OF COMMUNICATION

Rhetoric, or the post hoc analysis of a speaker's intent, oration, and environment, was the major focus of communication study throughout the western world until the nineteenth century.

During the late 1800s, there was disagreement among rhetoricians concerning their purposes as scholars and teachers in the field. A portion of the group, the Elocutionists, put exceeding importance on "the study of voice, articulation, and gesture" (Bormann, 1980, p. 5). Others as Bormann (1980) wrote, "who were dissatisfied with the emphasis on delivery in the elocution movement, with the position of oral communication in English departments, and with the philological research that was influential in these departments" (p. 5) formed their own national organizations, including the Speech Communication Association. By forming their own professional organizations and departments separate from English, many of those who split off from the main body of rhetoreticians could pursue their individual research concerns. These individuals modified the aim of their investigations. These new communications scholars sought to discover what effect the message had on the audience and the method used by the speaker. They viewed communications as being receiver-oriented rather than speaker-oriented. Bormann (1980) noted "From these beginnings came a tradition . . . that formed the backdrop for the emergence of communication theory" (p. 6).

In summary, communication research has evolved out of the study of ancient rhetoric. As the understanding of human behavior and the human communication process grew, theory formation in the discipline became more complex.

THE ROLE OF THEORY IN THE APPLIED
DISCIPLINE OF PUBLIC RELATIONS

A review of current public relations texts indicate that the field of public relations continues to look to other disciplines for its theory base. These texts describe the utility of various communication, psychology, and social psychology theories such as cognitive dissonance, information processing, cognitive response, attribution, social learning, and congruity. However, except for Grunig and Hunt (1984), no exclusive theory of public relations could be found. The following segment describes the evolution of public relations and borrows from the Grunig and Hunt text extensively.

According to Seitel (1984), public relations faced a period of reform during the 1970s and 1980s. This reformation came about as the result of:

> The growth of large institutions and their sense of responsibility to the public, the increased conflicts and confrontations between interest groups in society, and the heightened awareness of people everywhere brought about by increasingly sophisticated communications technology. (p. 36)

This caused many corporations to discard strategies based on one-way communication and to become more open and receptive to public opinion in order to survive in the marketplace. Research was performed to identify target audiences and to determine which communication channels would best reach those individuals. Research-based strategies and a transactional style of communication emerged as increasingly advanced sources of information were made available to an awakened public.

Grunig and Hunt (1984) offer an excellent description of four historic models of public relations practice. These models are still in use in one form or another today.

The first model, press agentry publicity, finds its roots in the work of press agents or publicists prior to the 1900s. One such individual, a propagandist, was Phineas T. Barnum. He believed that truth was not an essential element of his communications with his publics.

Press agentry publicity is theological in that it was "the necessary starting point" of the discipline and that it relied on fictitious or imaginary means in influencing behavior.

The second model, public information, developed about 1900. Feedback is not an essential element in this public relations model. Public information practitioners believe that the transmission of truth is the most important aspect in any communication.

Public information is situated in the metaphysical state of public relations because it is serving as a transition between the simple and the complex.

The third level in the development of public relations is the two-way asymmetric model that emerged in the 1920's. The two-way asymmetric model has its faults. The communication obtained from the receivers is used to tell management what their publics will accept. Grunig and Hunt (1984) noted: "The organization does not change as a result of public relations; it attempts to change public attitudes and behavior" (p. 23).

The two-way asymmetric model is included in the early formation of the positive state of public relations because of the introduction of market research in discovering the wants and needs of the audience.

The two-way symmetric model completes the development of public relations as we know it. Bernays is considered by Grunig and Hunt to be the leading historical figure in the development of this model because of the groundwork he laid in introducing scientific research to the field in the 1920s.

Bernays (1952) reiterated concepts that he had previously offered in another of his works, *Crystallizing Public Opinion*. He defined his notion of public relations in this way:

> Public Relations is not a one-way street in which leadership manipulates the public and public opinion. It is a two-way street in which leadership and public find integration with each other and in which objectives and goals are predicated on a coincidence of public and private interest. (p. 83)

The two-way symmetric model is marked by its interactive characteristic. No longer are communications with publics asymmetric: instead, they are truly two-sided.

In summary, the physical sciences quickly adapt theories formulated in the laboratory and apply them in real world situations. However, public relations, a behavioral science, is slow to put into practice theories taught by academicians. Theories in the physical sciences pass from the general to the specific, whereas theories in public relations must pass from the specific to the general. Public relations has evolved from the simple to the complex in much the same way that science and scientific theory have. Although the two-way symmetric model is the ideal form of public relations, Grunig and Hunt (1984) estimate that only about 15% of current practice operates at this level. Until theory assumes a more prominent role and more practitioners adopt a two-way symmetric approach, public relations will remain in a metaphysical state. To begin to assess how the field is progressing in this process, the following survey, which measures familiarity with theoretic concepts, was conducted.

RESEARCH DESIGN

This section describes the procedures used in creating the questionnaire, selecting the sample, and coding the results.

Creating the Questionnaire

A search of current texts and journals in public relations, advertising, communications, psychology, social psychology, business, and mass media produced a preliminary list of 90 popular theories, models, and procedures. This list was used to construct the first instrument. The first instrument was mailed to selected scholars and practitioners ($N = 60$), who were asked to rate each theory on a five-point, Likert-type scale in three different areas: degree of familiarity, degree of validity, and degree of practical utility. If a respondent was not familiar with the theory, model, or procedure, he/she was asked to indicate so by marking an "X." In addition, a demographic section was included, and space was provided for the respondents to include any theories not listed.

A mean was calculated for each item on each of the three dimensions. This resulted in three ratings for each theory/model/procedure. The three ratings were then added together and divided by the total number of respondents to arrive at an overall rating.

Thirty-two surveys were returned—a return rate of 53.3%. The mean analysis indicated that 15 theories were rated higher than the others. Table 16.1 describes the results.

Many respondents indicated that four theories; stimulus—response, cognitive consistency, congruity, and diffusion were listed twice but under more popular names; classical conditioning, balance, and multi-step flow. Multi-step flow and two-step flow were combined and treated as one single theory. As a result, the four duplications were deleted and replaced by the three next highest rated theories; expectancy-value, multi-step two-step flow, and self-attribution. Others felt that learning theory was too broad, thus it was changed to social learning. Other respondents listed theories or models that they felt were useful. Subsequently, six additional theories or models were selected: constructivism, coorientation, models of public relations, organizational sociology, public relations roles, and uses and gratification.

Based on the results of the data collected from the first questionnaire a second instrument containing 20 theories/models, including a brief description of each, was constructed.

TABLE 16.1
The 15 Highest Rated Theories on a 5 Point Scale:
Preliminary Survey

| | Mean Response | | | |
Theory	Familiarity	Validity	Practical Utility	Overall Rating
Cognitive dissonance	4.67	3.93	3.78	12.37
Operant conditioning	4.40	4.22	3.44	12.11
Balance	4.41	3.44	3.33	11.19
Classical conditioning	4.37	3.59	3.19	10.78
Systems theory	4.11	3.04	3.41	10.56
Agenda setting	3.56	3.19	3.74	10.48
Hierarchy of needs	4.52	2.70	3.19	10.41
Attribution	3.67	3.48	3.11	10.26
Learning	3.88	3.04	3.19	10.11
Stimulus–response	4.19	3.11	2.81	10.11
Social judgment	3.85	3.00	2.74	9.59
Cognitive consistency	3.74	2.93	2.88	9.55
Congruity	3.85	2.85	2.81	9.52
Diffusion	3.56	2.96	3.00	9.52
Inoculation	3.74	2.85	2.88	9.48

Selecting the Sample

This project was designed to assess the attitudes of public relations academicians and practitioners. In order to sample public relations academicians, 400 individuals were randomly selected from directories of the Public Relations interest group and the organizational communication division of ICA, the educators section of PRSA, and the public relations section in AEJ MC. In order to sample public relations practitioners, 400 individuals, excluding educators, were randomly chosen from the 1986–87 PRSA Directory. Surveys were limited to persons having mailing addresses within the continental United States.

The overall response rate from the instrument was 22.5%. The response rate among the academicians ($N = 400$) was 24.5% and among the practitioners ($N = 400$) was 13.25%. A demographic analysis revealed that there was a third group of individuals who responded, those who teach and consult in some capacity. This third group was labeled "combination": 27 respondents fit into the combination category.

Coding the Results

Respondents were asked to assign a value from 1 to 5 for each of the three variables for each theory/model: degree of familiarity, degree of validity, and degree of practical utility. A "1" indicated a very low level of familiarity, validity, and practical utility, whereas a "5" indicated a very high level in terms of the three variables. If a respondent was not familiar with a theory/model, he/she was asked to indicate so by marking an "X." Means were calculated for each of the three variables.

RESULTS

This section describes the research questions and the data procedures used to analyze the results.

Question 1: Is (Are) there a (any) theory (theories) of public relations?

The data indicated that a majority of respondents (50.6%) believed that practitioners seldom used public relations (communication) theories in their work. However, a large number of individuals qualified their response by noting that practitioners seldom use theories consciously, but unconsciously use them most of the time or extensively.

The data from the open-ended question indicate that many respondents feel that public relations theories are actually drawn from other fields. There was also disagreement among respondents concerning the extent to which public relations theories exist.

Question 2: To what extent are public relations practitioners and faculty aware of relevant human behavior theories, and do they perceive them to be valid and useful in real world situations?

In order to investigate this research question, an overall mean was calculated for each theory/model in regard to familiarity, validity, and practical utility. Only respondents who provided an evaluation were included. The percent of respondents providing a rating is also listed. Table 16.2 describes the results.

The data in Table 16.2 indicate that the highest rated theories/models in terms of awareness were hierarchy of needs (4.67), classical condition-

TABLE 16.2
Awareness, Validity, Practical Utility, and Theories/Models:
Mean Ratings and Percent Responding

Theories/Models	Awareness		Validity		Practical Utility	
	Mean	Percent	Mean	Percent	Mean	Percent
Agenda setting	3.96	91.9	3.75	89.0	3.75	88.4
Attribution	3.56	82.1	3.69	75.7	3.39	74.6
Balance	3.89	83.2	3.61	79.2	3.35	78.6
Classical conditioning	4.59	98.3	3.94	96.5	2.99	96.0
Constructivism	3.00	55.5	3.00	49.1	2.60	49.1
Coorientation	3.44	75.7	3.33	68.8	3.10	68.2
Dissonance	4.20	86.7	3.88	83.2	3.60	83.2
Expectancy–value	3.62	76.9	3.60	68.8	3.29	68.2
Hierarchy of needs	4.67	95.4	3.88	94.2	3.69	93.6
Inoculation	3.85	82.7	3.49	78.6	3.45	79.2
Models of Public Relations	3.85	74.0	3.43	68.2	3.36	68.2
Multi-step/Two-step flow	4.54	90.8	3.57	89.0	3.64	89.0
Operant conditioning	4.26	94.2	3.78	90.2	3.23	90.2
Organizational sociology	3.17	62.4	3.09	52.0	3.00	51.4
Public relations roles	3.74	76.3	3.32	71.1	3.22	69.9
Self-attribution	3.45	64.7	3.31	57.2	2.95	57.2
Social judgment	3.56	59.0	3.29	53.8	3.06	55.5
Social learning	3.33	63.0	3.28	59.5	2.91	59.0
Systems theory	4.15	91.0	4.16	87.9	3.97	89.0
Uses and gratification	3.86	75.1	3.42	71.1	3.33	71.1

Mean = mean rating on a 5-point scale
Percent = Percentage of total subjects who assigned the item a rating score.

ing (4.59), multi-step/two-step flow (4.54), operant conditioning (4.26), dissonance (4.20), and systems theory (4.15). The highest rated theories/models in terms of validity were systems theory (4.16), classical conditioning (3.94), dissonance (3.88), hierarchy of needs (3.88), operant conditioning (3.78), and agenda setting (3.75). The highest rated theories/models in terms of practical utility were systems theory (3.97), agenda setting (3.75), hierarchy of needs (3.69), multi-step/two-step flow (3.64), and dissonance (3.60).

Question 3: To what extent are there differences, if any, between public relations practitioners and faculty regarding awareness of relevant human behavior theories?

In order to investigate this research question, a series of chi-square tests were performed on the proportion of respondents who rated each item. Results indicated that significant differences in rating proportions occurred on all but two items. Table 16.3 describes the results of the chi-squares.

The data in Table 16.3 indicate that practitioners had the lowest response rate concerning all of the 20 theories/models. It may be concluded that, of the three groups, practitioners were the least informed, familiar, or knowledgeable regarding these items.

In order to further investigate this research question, a series of One-Way ANOVAs were performed on the mean responses provided by the respondents. Only respondents who rated an item were included. Results indicated that significant differences in mean responses occurred on 11 items. Table 16.4 describes the results of the ANOVAs.

TABLE 16.3
Awareness of Theories/Models:
Percent of Faculty, Practitioners, and Combination* Rating Items

| Theory/Model | Percent Rating | | | Chi-Square Significance |
	Fac.	Prac.	Comb.	
Attribution	91.8	62.7	84.0	0.000
Balance	90.7	68.6	84.0	0.003
Constructivism	66.0	25.5	76.0	0.000
Coorientation	89.7	41.2	92.0	0.000
Dissonance	95.9	66.7	92.0	0.000
Expectancy–value	84.5	58.8	84.0	0.001
Hierarchy of needs	97.9	88.2	100.0	0.01
Inoculation	91.8	62.7	88.0	0.000
Models of Public relations	83.5	51.0	84.0	0.000
Multi-step/Two-step flow	95.9	76.5	100.0	0.000
Operant conditioning	96.9	86.3	100.0	0.01
Organizational sociology	71.1	39.2	76.0	0.000
Public relations roles	85.6	54.9	84.0	0.000
Self-attribution	76.3	41.2	68.0	0.000
Social judgment	76.3	23.5	64.0	0.000
Social learning	82.5	33.3	48.0	0.000
Uses and gratification	89.7	41.2	88.0	0.000

* (Comb. = Individuals who indicated that they teach and consult).

TABLE 16.4
Awareness of Theories/Models:
Ratings by Faculty, Practitioner, and Combination

Theory	Mean Response			F-Value Significance
	Faculty	Practitioners	Comb.	
Agenda setting	4.27	3.07	4.27	0.0000
Balance	4.10	3.29	4.05	0.006
Dissonance	4.54	3.48	4.00	0.0000
Expectancy–value	3.84	3.21	3.33	0.03
Inoculation	4.11	3.27	3.59	0.001
Models of public relations	4.02	2.92	4.29	0.0004
Multi-step/Two-step flow	4.66	4.27	4.56	0.04
Social judgment	3.77	2.92	3.06	0.02
Social learning	3.55	2.56	3.08	0.01
Systems theory	4.32	3.61	4.35	0.002
Uses and gratification	4.13	3.40	3.41	0.01

The data in Table 16.4 indicate that on all significant items, practitioners assigned the lowest ratings in terms of awareness. However, it does appear that practitioners and combination held the same level of awareness on some items. It may be concluded that faculty felt they were very aware of these theories/models, combination were moderately aware, and practitioners were the least aware.

Question 4: To what extent are there differences, if any, between public relations practitioners and faculty, who received their last educational degree in the 1980s, 1970s, or 1960s and earlier, regarding awareness of relevant human behavior theories?

In order to investigate this research question, a series of chi-square tests were performed on the proportion of respondents who could assign a rating to each item, categorized by date of last educational degree. Results indicate that significant differences in rating proportions by date of last educational degree occurred on 12 items. Table 16.5 describes the results of the chi-squares.

The data in Table 16.5 indicate that on all significant items, lower percentages of individuals responded who received their last educational degree prior to 1970. It may be concluded that length of time since last

TABLE 16.5
Awareness of Theories/Models:
Percent Ratings Items by Date of Last Educational Degree

| | Percent Rating | | | |
Theory/Model	1980s	1970s	1960s & Earlier	Chi Square Significance
Balance	86.5	89.2	73.2	0.04
Classical conditioning	100.0	100.0	94.6	0.04
Constructivism	65.4	60.0	41.1	0.02
Coorientation	80.0	83.1	62.5	0.01
Dissonance	92.3	90.8	76.8	0.02
Expectancy–value	88.5	84.6	57.1	0.000
Hierarchy of needs	98.1	98.5	89.3	0.03
Inoculation	80.8	92.3	73.2	0.02
Operant conditioning	98.1	96.9	87.5	0.03
Self-attribution	71.2	73.8	48.2	0.007
Social judgment	55.8	75.4	42.9	0.001
Social learning	63.5	75.4	48.2	0.009

educational degree did significantly effect the level of familiarity with the theories/models.

Question 5: To what extent are there differences, if any, between public relations practitioners and faculty regarding perceived validity of relevant human behavior theories?

The data in Table 16.6 indicate that practitioners had the lowest responding percentages on all 14 significant items regarding validity. It may be concluded that the practitioner group was less able to evaluate the validity of the items as compared to faculty and combination.

Question 6: To what extent are there differences, if any, between public relations practitioners and faculty, who received their last educational degree in the 1980s, 1970s, or 1960s and earlier, regarding perceived validity of relevant human behavior theories?

In order to investigate this research question, a series of chi-square tests were performed on the proportion of respondents categorized by date of last educational degree. Results indicated that significant differences in rating proportions occurred on 9 items. Table 16.7 describes the results of the chi-squares.

TABLE 16.6
Validity of Theories/Models:
Percent of Faculty, Practitioners, and Combination Rating Items

Theory/Model	Percent Rating			Chi-Square Significance
	Fac.	Prac.	Comb.	
Attribution	83.5	60.8	76.0	0.009
Balance	87.6	66.7	72.0	0.007
Constructivism	57.7	23.5	68.0	0.000
Coorientation	80.4	39.2	84.0	0.000
Dissonance	93.8	60.8	88.0	0.000
Hierarchy of needs	96.9	86.3	100.0	0.01
Inoculation	86.6	60.8	84.0	0.001
Models of public relations	79.4	41.2	80.0	0.000
Multi-step/Two-step flow	93.8	74.5	100.0	0.000
Organizational sociology	58.8	33.3	64.0	0.006
Self-attribution	64.9	39.2	64.0	0.008
Social judgment	72.2	19.6	52.0	0.000
Social learning	78.4	31.4	44.0	0.000
Uses and gratification	86.6	39.2	76.0	0.000

The data in Table 16.7 indicate that on all significant items a lower percentage of individuals responded who received their last educational degree prior to 1970. It may be concluded that date of last educational degree did significantly effect the number of individuals responding.

Question 7: To what extent are there differences, if any, between public relations practitioners and faculty regarding perceived practical utility of relevant human behavior theories?

In order to investigate this research question, a series of chi-square tests were performed on the proportion of respondents who rated each item. Results indicate that significant differences in rating proportions, occurred on 16 items. Table 16.8 describes the results of the chi-squares.

The data in Table 16.8 indicate that on all significant items the lowest percentage of respondents was among the practitioners. It may be concluded that many practitioners did not know how to apply the items in real world situations.

TABLE 16.7
Validity of Theories/Models:
Percent Rating Items by Date of Last Educational Degree

Theory/Model	Percent Rating			Chi Square Significance
	1980s	1970s	1960s & Earlier	
Balance	86.5	83.1	67.9	0.03
Constructivism	61.5	49.2	37.5	0.04
Coorientation	73.1	76.9	55.4	0.02
Dissonance	90.4	87.7	71.4	0.01
Expectancy–value	82.7	70.8	53.6	0.004
Hierarchy of needs	98.1	98.5	85.7	0.004
Self-attribution	65.4	64.6	41.1	0.01
Social judgment	55.8	64.6	39.3	0.01
Social learning	63.5	67.7	46.4	0.04

TABLE 16.8
Practical Utility of Theories/Models:
Responding Percentages of Faculty, Practitioner, and Combination

Theory/Model	Percent Rating			Chi-Square Significance
	Fac.	Prac.	Comb.	
Attribution	81.4	60.8	76.0	0.02
Balance	85.6	66.7	76.0	0.02
Constructivism	57.7	23.5	68.0	0.000
Coorientation	80.4	39.2	80.0	0.000
Dissonance	92.8	62.7	88.0	0.000
Expectancy–value	77.3	51.0	68.0	0.005
Hierarchy of needs	95.9	86.3	100.0	0.02
Inoculation	87.6	60.8	84.0	0.001
Models of public relations	78.4	43.1	80.0	0.000
Multi-step/Two-step flow	93.8	74.5	100.0	0.000
Organizational sociology	57.7	33.3	64.0	0.007
Public relations roles	76.3	52.9	80.0	0.007
Self-attribution	64.9	39.2	64.0	0.008
Social judgment	74.2	21.6	52.0	0.000
Social learning	78.4	29.4	44.0	0.000
Uses and Gratification	86.6	39.2	76.0	0.000

TABLE 16.9
Practical Utility of Theories/Models:
Percent Rating Items by Date of Last Educational Degree

	Percent Rating			
Theory/Model	1980s	1970s	1960s & Earlier	Chi Square Significance
Balance	82.7	84.6	67.9	0.05
Coorientation	73.1	75.4	55.4	0.04
Dissonance	88.5	89.2	71.4	0.01
Expectancy–value	80.8	72.3	51.8	0.004
Hierarchy of needs	96.2	98.5	85.7	0.01
Self-attribution	65.4	64.6	41.1	0.01
Social judgment	55.8	69.2	39.3	0.004

Question 8: To what extent are there differences, if any, between public relations practitioners and faculty, who received their last educational degree in the 1980s, 1970s, or 1960s, and earlier, regarding perceived practical utility of relevant human behavior theories?

In order to investigate this research question, a series of chi-square tests were performed on the proportion of respondents categorized by date of last educational degree. Results indicated that significant differences in rating proportions by date of last educational degree occurred on 7 items. Table 16.9 describes the results of the chi-squares.

The data in Table 16.9 indicate that on all significant items the lowest percentage of respondents were those who received their last educational degree prior to the 1970s. It may be concluded that length of time since last educational degree was a significant factor in terms of the percentage of respondents.

CONCLUSIONS

This section offers conclusions and suggestions based on the quantitative and qualitative data.

It appears that of the three groups, the practitioners were least able to rate the 20 theories/models in terms of familiarity, validity, and practical utility. This may be because they lack: relevant knowledge, useful information, interest in the topic, or application skills.

Another group, those who received their last educational degree prior to 1970, were also significantly less able to rate the 20 theories/models on each of the three dimensions. This may be due to little or no instruction regarding human behavior/communication theories or the inability to recall the previously learned material.

It might be noted that mean ratings gradually became lower when advancing from familiarity through practical utility. This indicates that respondents were highly aware of the items but assigned lower ratings to validity and practical utility, respectively. As such, respondents may not have felt that the theories/models were valid or useful in real world applications.

The data also suggest that faculty were more capable of rating those items developed in their own field than they were of theories/models from other fields. This indicates that there may be a lack of diffusion of information between departments. It could be that the items are limited, in terms of being applicable, to other disciplines or that such theories/models have not appeared, to any great extent, in the journals and texts of other academic areas.

A few respondents specified that "theories are not useful in practical public relations," or "take too much time to implement," or are "hogwash," "claptrap," and "ivory tower concepts."

SUGGESTIONS

What we have to do next, for public relations to fully enter a positive stage of development, is to eliminate the misconceptions among those in the field and integrate theory into practice to a greater extent. To do this, theoretical applications should be taught in more small college and university public relations programs. Also, practitioners need to be persuaded or introduced to the utility of theory. Workshops or continuing education classes would be an important supplement to the learning and retention process because behavior that is quickly learned is quickly forgotten, unless reinforced.

ACKNOWLEDGMENT

The author conducted this investigation as a graduate student at Pittsburg State University, Pittsburg, Kansas. He wishes to acknowledge those in the Department of Communication at P.S.U. who assisted with this project.

REFERENCES

Babbie, E. (1986). *The practice of social research* (4th ed.). Belmont, CA: Wadsworth.

Bernays, E. L. (1952). *Public relations.* Norman, OK: University of Oklahoma Press.

Bormann, E. G. (1980). *Communication theory.* New York: Holt, Rinehart & Winston.

Grunig, J. E., & Hunt, T. T. (1984). *Managing public relations.* New York: CBS College Publishing.

Kerlinger, F. N. (1973). *Foundations of behavioral research* (2nd ed.). New York: Holt, Rinehart & Winston.

Levy-Bruhl, L. (1973). *The philosophy of August Comte.* Clifton, NJ: Augustus M. Kelley.

Marx, M. H. (1963). *Theories in contemporary psychology.* New York: Macmillan.

Runkel, P. J., & McGrath, J. E. (1972). *Research on human behavior: A systematic guide to method.* New York: Holt, Rinehart & Winston.

Seitel, F. P. (1984). *The practice of public relations* (2nd ed.). Columbus, OH: Charles E. Merrill.

Thompson, K. (1975). *August Comte: The foundations of sociology.* New York: Halsted Press.

Trenholm, S. (1986). *Human communication theory.* Englewood Cliffs, NJ: Prentice-Hall.

"If You Knew What I Knew, You'd Make the Same Decision": A Common Misperception Underlying Public Relations Campaigns?

James L. Gaudino
Speech Communication Association Of America

Joe Fritsch
Bruce Haynes
Michigan State University

ABSTRACT

This chapter presents a summary of findings of interviews with the public relations officers in 27 utilities across the country. The interviews were an effort to validate the suggestion by Grunig and Hunt (1984) that the two-way symmetric model fit the public relations programs of regulated industries. The conclusion reached is that the two-way model does fit environments faced by utility companies and most of their actual public relations programs.

The interviews also showed that most of the public relations programs managed by the public relations practitioners interviewed stressed dissemination of rational, objective information. The assumption made by many of the executives operating two-way symmetric programs is the public needs only to be educated for them to come to agreement with the organization. This assumption suggests that these practitioners may not be aware of or appreciative of the literature on receiver involvement or rationality.

This chapter therefore has two goals. First, it summarizes the interviews with the public relations executives concerning the fit of their programs within the Grunig and Hunt typology. Then, it presents some initial thoughts of the authors concerning the value of the constructs of involvement and rationality to the success of such public relations programs.

THE FOUR MODELS OF PUBLIC RELATIONS

Grunig and Hunt (1984) offer four theoretical models of public relations that are based on the direction of the flow of communication between an organization and its publics and the nature of and the potential for influence. More specifically, they suggest public relations practices can be categorized into groups that are primarily press agentry/publicity, public information, two-way asymmetric, or two-way symmetric.

The press agentry/publicity and the public information models both stress information via outgoing information from the organization to the public and the relative absence of feedback. They are distinguished from one another primarily based on the former's willingness to advocate a position at the expense of complete truth and objectivity.

The two-way asymmetric and two-way symmetric differ from the above models by permitting a two-way flow of communication. In the case of the two-way asymmetric, Grunig and Hunt have suggested the purpose is still persuasive, but in this case it is scientific persuasion. That is, the two-way asymmetric uses available social science knowledge and audience research to construct a persuasive campaign. The feedback is used primarily to help construct a better message.

In the two-way symmetric model, both the flow of communication and influence between the organization and its publics is more balanced. Grunig and Hunt refer to a desired state of mutual understanding that is quite similar to what other authors (Cutlip, Center, & Broom, 1985; Simon, 1984) have referred to as social responsibility. Essentially, the publics have as much potential for influence over the organization as the latter has over the publics. The role of the public relations practitioner is therefore to act as the agent for creation of the mutual understanding.

Finally, Grunig and Hunt have suggested that the two-way symmetric model is most likely practiced in regulated business. This appears logical because the publics do, in reality, have a potential for influence over the organization via the regulatory process.

METHODOLOGY

In October 1985, the senior author conducted 27 telephone interviews with utility companies across the nation. In most cases, the interview was with the top public relations officer, although the label given to the position differed considerably. In about a fourth of the cases, the initial call was made to the head of the public relations department whereas the interview was with a division head who had primary responsibility for the program of interest. In three instances the interview was with the head of the government affairs department, who was a lobbyist or government relations officer. In one instance the interview was with the chief executive officer.

The interviews were conducted in conjunction with a project sponsored by a utility interested in obtaining insights into the public relations programs of similar companies. The utilities selected in the study represented a convenience sample suggested by the sponsoring organization. Because of a special interest in obtaining organizations facing similar problems, many of the interviews were with organizations in the midwest. The sample did, however, include large and small organizations from 10 states across the country.

The conversations were of an informal-interview style. More specifically, the author had a specific set of questions that were asked of each respondent, but the order and wording were altered to fit the flow of the conversation. The questions of interest to this study concerned the nature of the communication exchange between the organization and its publics.

The author found the utility executives quite willing to discuss the subject matter. Most interviews lasted approximately 1 hour.

FINDINGS

The use of the two-way symmetric model of public relations was by no means uniform within the utility companies included in the sample. In general, however, the utility executives described public relations programs that did fit the two-way symmetric pattern.

Before discussing the public relations programs, it is useful to briefly describe the regulatory environment faced by utility companies. In all cases covered by this investigation, the utilities are regulated by a state body that has approval authority over most of the major programs conducted by company. For example, the utilities cannot set their own rates, construct additional production facilities or make extensive modification of existing facilities without approval from the regulatory body. In many cases, the regulatory body also oversees the utilities' marketing and other consumer-oriented programs. The regulatory agency is therefore a public with considerable influence.

The utilities have at least two other significant publics. The most commonly discussed was what most public relations practitioners called "intervener groups." These are activist organizations who generally oppose the utility company because of their special interest in consumer protection, environmental protection, or a general dislike or distrust of big business. In most cases, the interveners are a readily identifiable, cohesive group that are generally highly involved in the regulatory process.

The third public or concern to the utilities are the customers. Customers are generally divided into large industrial customers and residential or small business customers. These publics tend to be less organized and less involved than the interveners. although they sometimes approach the utilities' issues with more diverse interests, rates tend to be of primary concern to this public.

The regulatory process is quite similar across the states surveyed. In general, the approval authority rests with the regulatory agency, which itself is housed in a variety of state agencies and is comprised of either elected or appointed officials. The individual regulators may or may not have any special expertise in the area of concern.

There is generally some form of public participation in issues of importance. This varies in style, but provides an opportunity for the publics to have access to information processed by the utility and to offer additional information and concerns to the regulatory body. Most public relations officials claim that most of the participation is exercised by the intervening groups and a few customers who may be directly affected by the plans of the utility.

It appears, therefore, that the environment faced by the utilities surveyed does fit the two-way symmetric flow suggested by Grunig and Hunt. That is, there is a legal requirement for the two-way flow of information and a system that provides for mutual influence. The goal of the regulatory agency is apparently to achieve a mutual understanding and therefore utility programs that meet social needs and expectations.

However, about a third of the utilities surveyed had public relations programs that placed the regulatory agency and the intervening groups in direct opposition to the utility. That is, about a third resisted any significant public participation and said they attempted to influence the regulators. The regulator's attitude is summarized by a respondent comment that "they [regulators] are dealing and they have marked all the cards."

These public relations executives see their roles as essentially that of resisting efforts of the publics to force the utility into programs that are counter to its basic goals of service to the customer and profitability for stock holders. As one said, "We supply them with information but make them work for it. I remember delivering a truck load of documents when asked for our [plan]."

In terms of the Grunig and Hunt models, there is a two-way flow of communication because of the regulatory process. The attempt by the utility, however, is to influence the regulatory body and intervening groups, without permitting a similar influence on the utility. The public relations programs therefore are close to the two-way asymmetrical model. Respondents who discussed their programs within this adversarial context tended to also express the least satisfaction with their regulatory agency, with their intervening groups and with their public relations programs.

A few of the respondents described public relations programs that placed the regulators between the utilities and interveners. Respondents described the commission as being a "shield" or as "taking on the burden of decision making." Respondents using these metaphors suggested a political ordering: the interveners on the left, the commission in the middle, and the utility on the right. These same respondents complained of changes in regulatory decisions based on shifts in public opinion and changes in ruling political parties. Like those discussed above, these utilities were often dissatisfied with their programs.

Such public relations programs do not fit neatly into any of the Grunig and Hunt models. This is perhaps because of the passivity of the programs. That is, these respondents framed their programs as reacting to pressures created by the interveners. The bulk of the communication program was therefore in response to problems, and the general reaction was resistance. Although there are still systems for two-way communication and mutual influence, these utilities using the regulatory bodies as shields generally transfer the responsibility for the communication and mutual understanding to that body.

A third perspective conceptualized by a little more than half of the utility executives is based on cooperation and an interdependence of goals, needs and responsibilities. These utilities see themselves as working with the regulatory body and interveners rather than against them or behind them. They have the best fit with the two-way symmetric model and also expressed the greatest satisfaction with their public relations programs and with the regulators and interveners. They also tended to express the most confidence that regulators and interveners would not intentionally harm the organization by blocking important projects and programs.

These organizations realize the power the customer and intervener publics can exercise via influence on the regulatory process. They therefore understand that it is in the best interest of the utility to establish goals and programs that meet social needs. The confidence they express in their programs is based on the knowledge that decisions of regulators are the result of sound planning models and mutual understanding. As one executive put it,

> Because just about everything a utility does or is planning to do is subjected to public comment and regulatory approval, many decisions and actions that other companies make internally are for us held up for public view. . . . Communication to all publics is key. A good communication

program installed at the beginning will save millions, if not billions, of dollars.

DISCUSSION

The interviews with the 27 utility executives tend to support the Grunig and Hunt suggestion that the two-way symmetric model is used by regulated industries. The finding that the use of the two-way symmetric model of communication is not uniform within the utility industries investigated in this study is not surprising nor does it suggest a problem with the Grunig and Hunt typology. The model does fit the actual situations faced by the utilities and is also supported, at least verbally, by more than half of the executives interviewed.

Yet, in discussing the actual public relations programs with those executives espousing a two-way symmetric model, it soon became evident that the bulk of their effort was in providing rational arguments containing objective information. The resulting public relations program is therefore one of supplying such information via traditional channels, often publicity. As one executive summarized:

> Understanding is the key here and education is the key to understanding. People will make right decisions if they understand the situation. It's our job to educate them. We supply them with the information so they can understand the problem. If we don't educate them, how can we complain that they don't understand.

These executives seem to be making the assumption that the only reason the publics do not agree with the organization is because of a lack of information. Therefore, supplying the groups with the information will result in agreement. One of the public relations executives stated the motto that guided all their programs was, "If you know what I knew, you'd make the same decision."

It would seem that such a stress on objective information might be the result of overconfidence in one's stance on the issue. It might also be that the public relations planners are assuming the public is approaching the situation with the same level of involvement and are making decisions with the same rational processes as are being used by the utility executives.

As suggested earlier, this is not likely the case. In most cases, the utilities have multiple goals of providing quality service to customers and in maintaining profitability. Because the supply of services is their primary business, they are generally highly involved in it. Interveners are also usually highly involved, but their decisions are often based on a single issue or on a different view of the situation. The public may not be involved at all, and if they do consider the situation, their decision may be based primarily on the impact on rates or health of the local economy.

It would seem therefore that many of the public relations programs, although corresponding to the two-way symmetric model, are based on an improper conceptualization of the publics' involvement and rational process.

The concept of involvement has been used within the framework of advertising for some 20 years. In early studies of involvement, Krugman (1962, 1967, 1972) defined the construct as the number of "bridging experiences" or personal references between the message and the receiver's personal life experiences. The more the personal references, the higher the involvement.

Since his early work, the construct of involvement has been frequently studied as a variable mediating the effect of an advertising or marketing message. The role of involvement in mediating attitude change has received considerable research attention (see Petty & Cacioppo, 1979; Petty, Cacioppo, & Goldman, 1981; Zaichkowsky, 1986, for reviews).

Although a single definition of involvement has not emerged from this body of literature, the notion of personal relevance seems to be common in most research. That is, a topic, issue, or object is considered involving if it or the message addressing it is relevant to the receiver.

Grunig and Hunt (1984) included involvement as one of three independent variables in their "situational theory" in identifying publics and how they will react to a given public relations-relevant situation. They argued that level of involvement is determined by the degree to which people perceive themselves to be connected to the problem or situation. Level of involvement will, in turn, determine whether a person will actively seek information (high involvement) or passively receive it (low involvement).

Recent research provides strong support for the assertion that high and low involvement receivers react to messages differently. Petty, Cacioppo and Goldman (1981) presented evidence that involvement is a determinant of whether attitude change is a result of a *central route* in which messages are cognitively evaluated and weighed against other issue relevant arguments or is instead the result of a *peripheral route,* in which the message is associated with other secondary cues such as source credibility, attractiveness, or power.

Krugman's research also supports this low involvement notion. His research indicates that individuals with low involvement with the topic were not affected by rational message content. Krugman's research suggests the application of passive learning that stresses repetition of simple messages that the receiver will not likely actively evaluate.

Rationality has also not been clearly defined in the literature, but is generally meant to refer to the varying use of objective information on which to base a decision. A rational decision-making process is a linear, information-based cognitive activity. On the other hand, an irrational decision is one based more on image and feelings.

Vaughn (1979) and others argued that early conceptualizations of high involvement decision-making tended to emphasize rational thinking (see for example, Engle, Blackwell, & Kollat, 1978; Howard & Sheth, 1969; Lavidge & Steiner, 1961). Within the advertising field, this high involvement sequence became known as the Learn–Feel–Do model.

Vaughn (1979) suggested that advertising planners need to relate the rationality and involvement constructs for advertising effects by crossing them to produce the four conditions of consumer involvement and rationality: high-involvement thinking, high-involvement feeling, low-involvement thinking, and low-involvement feeling. Vaughn suggested the quadrants have implications for the strategic planning of advertising programs because they approximate the four traditional consumer theories (economic, psychological, responsive, social).

The high-involvement thinking quadrant suggests the economic theory of consumer behavior in which the individual attempts to maximize reward and minimize cost via reasoned decisions. Communication campaigns aimed at audiences within this quadrant should stress objective information: long, print-oriented messages and distribution channels that emphasize reflective thought.

The high-involvement feeling quadrant is similar to the psychological perspective on consumer behavior in which relevant decision making is the result of non-rational forces. Such campaigns should focus on arousal of affective reactions because emotions and holistic impressions are important. Images are likely more powerful than long objective messages. The execution of the message takes on increasing importance and the delivery vehicle ought to be able to arouse emotions.

The low-involvement thinking quadrant is similar to the passive learning theory suggested by Krugman. These consumers are doers in Vaughn's terms because they act on minimal thought and often form buying habits. The important communication objective is to provide brief information that permits the consumer to differentiate the product from others. Once a habit is formed, reminders become key. Although information is more important than image, repetition of messages outweighs the rational content. Short, simple messages on easily processed channels are likely to be most effective.

Vaughn has labeled the consumers falling into the low-involvement feeling quadrant as reactors and has suggested the model is most like the social theories of consumer behavior. These consumers are interested in satisfaction of more immediate needs on products that often have social significance. He has suggested large billboard advertisements and point of purchase might be most effective.

Vaughn had cautioned that his quadrants are speculative and should be used as a starting point for advertising planning. The framework he has suggested also overlooks some important research findings, is quite liberal in application of various theoretical perspectives, and is developed with a strong consumer orientation. Yet, if considered with caution and in conjunction with the growing body of research in involvement and rationality, it provides an interesting starting point for future research and for current planning of public relations campaigns.

For example, the conclusion reached in the interviews with the utility public relations executives suggests their campaigns tend to be conceptualized from a high-involvement thinking perspective. Recall the typical comment from the public relations practitioners that "People will make right decisions if they understand the situation. It's our job to educate them" and "If [they] know what I knew, [they'd] make the same decision."

Although objective research is not available concerning the rationality and involvement levels of the utility companies' publics, the comments of the executives interviewed suggested the residential consumers are generally uninvolved, larger industrial consumers are more involved, and the interveners are highly involved.

The executives' responses also suggest that the decisions of the publics are often irrational (at least from the utilities' perspectives). The executives claimed that the decisions of interveners, for example, are often based on a single issue or simplified view of the situation. Whereas this single-issue perspective does not exactly fit into Vaughn's high-involvement feeling quadrant, it does suggest the interveners are not likely to be persuaded by simply educating them to all the facts.

CONCLUSIONS

This investigation and resulting discussion represents the initial thinking of the authors concerning the applicability of the Grunig and Hunt typology and the appropriateness of the public relations programs of utilities. The conclusions drawn are, therefore, tentative.

In general, it appears that the utilities do face a public relations environment that parallels the two-way symmetric model and that most of them perceive their goals to be achieved by mutual understanding between the organization, regulators, interveners, and the customer publics. Their actual programs, however, seem to be based on the strategic assumption that dissemination of objective, rational information will achieve not only mutual understanding, but also agreement.

The research on involvement and rationality suggests that is not necessarily the case. Although this chapter has not attempted to thoroughly review such research, it has been indicated here that involvement and rationality likely play a mediating role on the effect of communication.

The question that remains is whether the frameworks used in advertising, such as that presented by Vaughn, or the more theoretical work offered by authors such as Petty and Cacioppo, can be meaningfully translated into public relations programs. At this point, the authors do not see why such a goal cannot be achieved. It is, in fact, a direction they feel should be undertaken by the academic and practitioner communities.

REFERENCES

Cutlip, S. M., Center, A. H., & Broom, G. M. (1985). *Effective public relations.* Englewood Cliffs, NJ: Prentice-Hall.

Engle, J. F., Blackwell, R. D., & Kollat, D. T. (1978). *Consumer behavior* (3rd ed.). Hinsdale, IL: Dryden Press.

Grunig, J. E., & Hunt, T. (1984). *Managing public relations.* New York: Holt, Rinehart & Winston.

Howard, J. A., & Sheth, J. (1969). *The theory of buyer behavior.* New York: Wiley.

Krugman, H. E. (1962). An application of television advertising: Learning without involvement. *Public Opinion Quarterly, 29,* 349–56.

Krugman, H. E. (1967). The measurement of advertising involvement. *Public Opinion Quarterly, 30,* 583–96.

Krugman, H. E. (1972). Memory without recall, exposure without perception. *Journal of Advertising Research, 17,* 7–12.

Lavidge, R., & Steiner, G. A. (1961). A model for predictive measurements of advertising effectiveness. *Journal of Marketing, 25,* 29–62.

Petty, R. E., & Cacioppo, J. T. (1979). Issue involvement can increase or decrease message relevant cognitive responses. *Journal of Personality and Social Psychology, 37,* 1915–26.

Petty, R. E., Cacioppo, J. T., & Goldman, R. (1981). Personal involvement as a determinant of argument-based persuasion. *Journal of Personality and Social Psychology, 41,* 847–53.

Simon, R. (1984). *Public relations: Concepts and practices.* New York: Wiley.

Vaughn, R. (1979). How advertising works: A planning model. *Journal of Advertising Research, 20,* 27–33.

Zaichkowsky, J. L. (1986). Conceptualizing involvement. *Journal of Advertising, 15,* 4–14.

Reassessing the Odds Against Finding Meaningful Behavioral Change in Mass Media Health Promotion Campaigns

Ronald B. Anderson
University of Texas at Austin

ABSTRACT

This chapter discusses theoretical strategies for improving the odds of finding behavioral change in mass media health promotion campaigns. The discussion focuses primarily on those variables in Flay's (1981) extended information-processing model that are predicted to affect health behavior. Of these, Bandura's (1977b) notion of self-efficacy is presented as an important concept in planning campaigns to teach audiences the skills to change unhealthy lifestyles. An amended version of Flay's extended model is proposed to explain and predict the process by which self-efficacy influences health behavior. Implications for the use of this concept in designing campaigns to prevent drunken driving are explored.

Public-information specialists play an important role in the dissemination of health information to audiences with diverse health needs. The importance of their function in the nation's health-care delivery system is underscored by the fact that most premature death is largely the result of what people do to themselves—or unhealthy lifestyles. Indeed, the Surgeon General's 1979 report stated that of the 10 leading causes of death in the United States, 7 could be radically reduced if people at risk would only change their behaviors (cited in Brehony, Frederiksen, & Solomon, 1984).

Although most public-information campaigns have behavior change as their ultimate goal (Grunig & Hunt, 1984), few mediated health promotion programs actually succeed in altering negative health practices (e.g., Atkin, 1979, 1981; Blane & Hewitt, 1980; Flay, 1981; Grunig & Ipes, 1983; Wallack, 1981; Wallack & Barrows, 1981). However, evidence from the Stanford Heart Disease Prevention Program (Maccoby, Farquhar, Wood, & Alexander, 1977; Maccoby & Solomon, 1981) suggests that cardiovascular risk factors can be reduced significantly when audiences are *taught* how to stop smoking, improve their diets, manage stress, and exercise regularly—in short, change their lifestyles.

This chapter discusses theoretical strategies for improving the chances of finding behavioral change in mass media health promotion programs—commonly referred to as public-information campaigns. The discussion focuses primarily on those variables in Flay's (1981) extended information-processing model that either hold the potential for or have been demonstrated to increase the odds of bringing about and sustaining health behavior change. Finally, an amended version of Flay's extended model is proposed, and its usefulness for designing campaigns to prevent drunken driving is discussed.

FLAY'S INTEGRATIVE MODEL
OF ATTITUDE AND BEHAVIOR CHANGE

Noting that only a few mediated health promotion campaigns have succeeded in changing attitudes and behavior, Flay proposed an extended information-processing model that incorporates theory and evidence from the literature on communication effects to improve the odds of finding these higher order changes (see Fig. 18.1). Flay argued that failure can be attributed to an overreliance by program planners on a model of the behavior change process that assumes cognitive change is necessary and sufficient to bring about changes in attitudes and behavior, what Grunig and Hunt (1984, p. 124) have called the "domino model of communication effects." Flay agreed with the core assumption of this traditional approach to persuasive communication: that changes in awareness, knowledge, and beliefs usually precede changes in attitudes and behavior (as long as there is high involvement with the health topic). However, he disagreed that these cognitive factors are sufficient to induce such changes by themselves—as the classic information-processing model predicts.

Flay has stated that a comprehensive explanation of the health behavior change process would address factors not usually found in the traditional model. His extended model is just such an attempt. The model consists primarily of three parts: the traditional information-processing model developed by Hovland and his associates (1953) at Yale, and later refined by McGuire (1981) into his persuasion matrix; Ajzen and Fish-

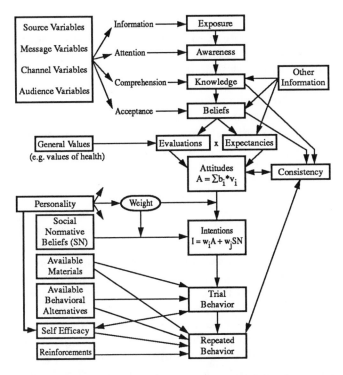

FIG. 18.1. Extended information-processing model that incorporates theory and evidence from literature on communication effects (from Flay, 1981. Copyright © 1981 by K. G. Saur).

bein's (1980) theory of reasoned action; and Bandura's (1977a) social-learning theory.

Flay has posited that in order to facilitate attitude change, a general value-expectancy approach should be followed, as suggested by Ajzen and Fishbein (1980) in their theory. Value-expectancy theories assume that people form beliefs (i.e., expectancies in the model) about the consequences of certain behaviors (such as excessive drinking), and they are more likely to hold positive attitudes toward those behaviors whose consequences are evaluated favorably. For example, many adolescents drink to intoxication simply because they believe there are numerous positive consequences (i.e., perceived benefits) associated with this behavior. Many drive drunk because they believe the probability of an accident is low.

Intervening between attitudes and trial behavior are behavioral intentions (i.e., one's estimate of the probability of performing a given behavior), social normative beliefs (i.e., the expectations of significant others), and personality factors. According to Ajzen and Fishbein, behavioral intentions is the immediate determinant (and strongest predictor) of trial behavior, although an understanding of the audience's health actions can be gained only by assessing the attitudinal and belief components of the model.

The bottom part of the model depicts those variables from Bandura's social learning theory that have been demonstrated to improve the chances of inducing trial behavior and maintaining repeated behavior. This part of the model assumes that changing a person's behavioral intentions will not necessarily lead to trial behavior unless at least one of three conditions exist: (a) *appropriate resources* are available to guide the behavior change attempt (i.e., available materials, such as a self-help guide), (b) the individual possesses *skills* necessary to consummate his or her intention (i.e., available behavioral alternatives), and/or (c) the individual believes he or she is *capable* of performing the behavior (i.e., self-efficacy). Of course, the more conditions that are addressed, the greater the likelihood of trial behavior. Finally, newly acquired skills must be practiced and reinforced if they are to last. For example, the Stanford Heart Disease Prevention Program used the mass media to teach audiences the skills to reduce their risk of cardiovascular disease and supplemented this instruction with hands-on practice in small group settings where subjects received positive reinforcement for their efforts.

To stack the odds in favor of behavior change, Flay has stated that a full assessment of the model's variables is necessary, because breaks in any of the causal links can negate campaign effects. For example, many health programs fail to achieve their behavioral objectives simply because audiences are never *exposed* to message stimuli or fail to *comprehend* behavioral recommendations. This points to the critical role of *formative research* (i.e., precampaign research to improve message design and placement) in planning campaigns. Pretesting messages on small samples of intended target publics can provide program planners with this information (Cutlip, Center, & Broom, 1985; Grunig & Hunt, 1984).

THE HEALTH THREAT CONTROL MODEL

Another useful value-expectancy approach to understanding health behavior is Beck and Frankel's (1981) health threat control model, discussed only briefly here. This formulation differs from the traditional approach to persuasive communication in that cognitive, rather than emotional, factors are thought to intervene between message and subsequent response. Beck and Frankel (1981, pp. 212–213) identify two beliefs as comprising perceived threat control: *response efficacy* and *personal efficacy.* These beliefs combine to form *perceived threat control.* Response efficacy is the belief that a recommended health behavior can prevent, or reduce considerably, the health threat (e.g., recommendations on how to quit smoking can reduce one's chances of getting cancer). Personal efficacy is the belief that one is capable of performing successfully the recommended response. Of the two, personal efficacy is the stronger predictor of protective health behavior (Beck & Lund, 1981).

BANDURA'S THEORY OF SELF-EFFICACY

Bandura's (1977b) theory of self-efficacy proposes that changes in avoidant behavior can be induced psychologically through exposure to different types of efficacy information. Exposure is said to increase one's confidence to cope with subjectively threatening situations by instilling expectations of personal mastery (i.e., self-efficacy beliefs) through the learning of skills and successful performance of dreaded activities. It is predicted that self-efficacy determines whether coping behavior will be initiated, the amount of effort expended, and how long people will persist in their efforts to overcome stressful situations.

Four principle types of efficacy information are identified: (a) performance accomplishments, predicted to be the strongest source of efficacy expectations because it is based on personal mastery experience, or direct evidence of performance capabilities; (b) vicarious experience, which relies on either live or symbolic modeling of successful performance of feared activities; (c) verbal persuasion, which uses suggestion to convince people they can cope with their fears; and (d) emotional arousal, which strengthens expectations of personal competence by extinguishing anxiety-arousing thoughts and feelings.

Performance accomplishments (i.e., guided participation or participant modeling) is predicted to be the strongest type of efficacy information because subjects learn firsthand how to cope with stressful situations. According to Bandura (1977b, p. 196), "Participant modeling provides additional opportunities for translating behavioral conceptions to appropriate actions and for making corrective refinements toward the perfection of skills".

Vicarious experience utilizes live and symbolic modeling to extinguish avoidance behavior. Observation of the successful performance of feared activities (whether live or mediated) can induce efficacy expectations. Vicarious experience is thought to affect self-efficacy beliefs in the following way:

> Seeing others perform threatening activities without adverse consequences can generate expectations in observers that they too will improve if they

intensify and persist in their efforts. They persuade themselves that if others can do it, they should be able to achieve at least some improvement in performance. Vicarious experience, relying as it does on inferences from social comparison, is a less dependable source of information about one's capabilities than is direct evidence of personal accomplishments. (p. 197)

Verbal persuasion relies upon suggestion to convince people that they are capable of handling threatening situations. Social persuasion is a less dependable type of efficacy information than is performance accomplishments, because it does not "provide an authentic experiential base" for one's efficacy expectations (Bandura, 1977b, p. 198).

Emotional arousal is the fourth type of efficacy information identified by Bandura. People rely on information about physiological states to assess their abilities to cope with anxiety-arousing situations. Bandura has argued that a strong sense of personal efficacy can reduce one's susceptibility to generating fear-provoking thoughts, thereby enhancing performance capabilities.

According to Bandura (1977b, p. 194), there are three dimensions of efficacy expectations: (a) magnitude, (b) strength, and (c) generality. Magnitude refers to the likelihood of task performance based on perceived capability. Strength of efficacy expectations refers to how certain one is that he or she will perform the task. Generality of efficacy expectations refers to the extension of one's capability to the performance of similar tasks, as well as to dissimilar tasks and situations. In order to perform an adequate expectancy analysis, all three dimensions should be measured.

Because performance accomplishments is based on personal mastery experience, Bandura has posited that it is the strongest source of efficacy expectations. Indeed, in a study designed to create differential levels of efficacy expectations within severe adult snake phobics, Bandura, Adams, and Beyer (1977) found the performance-based treatment produced higher, stronger, and more generalized expectations of coping behavior (i.e., self-efficacy) with the reptile than did the treatment based on live modeling, or vicarous experience, which in turn surpassed the no-treatment control group.

Early applications of social-learning theory attest to the appropriateness of this conceptual scheme for explaining and predicting changes in avoidant behavior. Virtually all of this research is summarized by Bandura (1977b) in the latest refinement of his theory. One persistent finding is that, like performance accomplishments and live modeling, *symbolic* modeling of how to deal with stressful situations also increases efficacy expectations. However, as Bandura (1977b) noted:

The research completed thus far has tested the predictive power of the conceptual scheme for efficacy expectations developed through enactive, vicarious, and emotive-based procedures. Additional tests of the generality of this approach need to be extended to efficacy expectations arising from *verbal persuasion* (italics added) and from other types of treatments aimed at reducing emotional arousal. (p. 212)

CONCEPTUAL INTEGRATION

This section proposes an amended version of Flay's integrative model to explain the process by which efficacy information is thought to affect self-efficacy beliefs. The amended model (see Fig. 18.2) should prove useful in those situations where campaign audiences need to learn how to overcome their intimidation of stressful situations, such as losing weight, quitting smoking, and preventing a friend from driving drunk.

There are three fundamental differences between the amended model and Flay's. In the amended model, efficacy information is shown to affect self-efficacy beliefs through the intervening influence of knowledge of skills. Flay (1981, p. 76), however, posited that self-efficacy is a function of trial behavior and personality factors. Although Flay did not

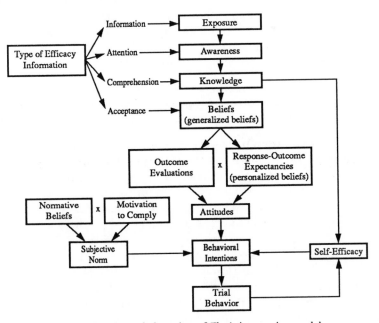

FIG. 18.2.   Amended version of Flay's integrative model.

refer to specific factors, he did note that the behavioral intentions of individuals who are "internally controlled" are determined more by their attitudes than by social normative influences. The opposite holds for "externally controlled" individuals. Bandura (1977b) argued that self-efficacy is based on a person's perception of *successful performance*, rather than on "global personality traits" (p. 203). Instead of being a function of one's personality, Bandura maintained that self-efficacy beliefs are derived from diverse types of efficacy information (i.e., vicarious experience, verbal persuasion, etc.).

A second difference concerns the nature of the relationship between self-efficacy and trial behavior. Flay has postulated a reciprocal relationship between self-efficacy and trial behavior. In the amended model, self-efficacy is predicted to affect trial behavior through the mediating influence of behavioral intentions. This linkage is based on tests of the health threat control model by Beck and Lund (1981), who found a positive association between personal efficacy (i.e., self-efficacy) and behavioral intentions. It seems reasonable to assume that if people are convinced they lack the skills necessary to cope with stressful situations their behavioral intentions will be guided by this lack of confidence.

Self-efficacy theory predicts that past successful performance of a behavior strengthens efficacy expectations. This relationship is depicted in the amended model by the arrow running from trial behavior to self-efficacy. The question, then, is not whether efficacy expectations affect trial behavior, but, rather, how. The amended model hypothesizes that self-efficacy affects trial behavior through the mediating influence of behavioral intentions. According to Bandura (1977b):

> Those who persist in subjectively threatening activities that are in fact relatively safe will gain corrective experiences that reinforce their sense of efficacy, thereby eventually eliminating their defensive behavior. (p. 194)

Thus, people who are initially overwhelmed by inhibitory thoughts and feelings can eventually learn to cope with their fears and stressful situations through successful performance of dreaded activities.

The third difference between the two approaches concerns the process by which behavioral skills are acquired. Flay has included skills (available behavior alternatives) as one of several predictors of trial behavior; yet, his model does not explain how skills are learned. The amended version shows how exposure to efficacy information sets off a causal chain of events where knowledge of skills affects behavioral intentions through the intervening influence of self-efficacy beliefs. Expectations of personal mastery, then, are engendered by the learning of skills and the successful performance of dreaded activities.

There also are several similarities between these two approaches to health-behavior change. In Flay's model *expectancies* is conceptually similar to *response efficacy* in the health threat control model and *response-outcome expectations,* as defined by Bandura and as depicted in the amended model. All refer to *personalized beliefs* about the probability of occurrence of a behavioral consequence for an individual (e.g., a moderate drinker's belief that confronting his or her friends about their drunken driving could get them to think about the consequences of their behavior). These beliefs are multiplied by their evaluations and summed to determine a person's attitude toward the recommended health response.

Flay has stated that *generalized beliefs* also must be considered in health behavior change programs. These beliefs represent a person's probability estimate that a given behavior is associated with a certain outcome (e.g., the belief that moderate drinkers should intervene to prevent their heavy-drinking friends from driving drunk). The difference between the two types of beliefs is that a moderate drinker can believe that dissuading a friend from driving drunk is a socially responsible behavior (generalized belief), but also believe that his or her friend's drinking behavior is none of his or her business (personalized belief) and therefore fail to act.

Another shared concept is, of course, self-efficacy referred to as personal efficacy in the health threat control model. Both Bandura (1977b) and Beck and Frankel (1981) draw important conceptual distinctions between efficacy expectations and response–outcome expectancies. They are differentiated because people can believe that the performance of a given behavior will lead to certain favorable outcomes, but they will not necessarily intend to try the behavior unless they believe they are capable of performing it with some success. According to Bandura (1977b):

> Outcome and efficacy expectations are differentiated because individuals can believe that a particular course of action will produce certain outcomes, but if they entertain serious doubts about whether they can perform the necessary activities such information does not influence their behavior. (p. 193)

IMPLICATIONS FOR DESIGNING DRUNKEN-DRIVING CAMPAIGNS

Most campaigns to prevent drunken driving are targeted at heavy drinkers, which usually are young adult males. These campaigns attempt to dissuade heavy drinkers from driving drunk through use of fear appeals (i.e., public-service announcements that depict the grim consequences of alcohol-related accidents). Despite the frequency with which these spots are aired, the problem persists, claiming the lives of more than 26,000 persons a year (more lives than all other forms of violence), many of whom are between the ages of 18 and 20. It is estimated that drunken-driving accidents cost American society $5.14 billion a year (National Institute on Alcohol Abuse and Alcoholism, 1981).

Better ways need to be found to combat this problem through the mass media, given the disappointing outcomes of past campaigns. The amended version of Flay's extended information-processing model suggests one possible strategy: teach young adult moderate drinkers the *skills* to persuade their heavy-drinking friends not to drive drunk. Instead of targeting heavy drinkers, moderate drinkers could be taught via the mass media how to approach and what to say to their heavy-drinking friends, those who are most likely to drive drunk. Spot announcements also could teach moderate drinkers the appropriate counter arguments to the predictable responses of their friends.

Grunig and Ipes (1983) reached a similar conclusion in their study of the types of publics created by a drunken-driving campaign in Maryland. They recommended that future efforts concentrate on overcoming audience inertia by utilizing interpersonal support to remove the *behavioral constraints* that prevent audiences from doing anything about the drunken-driving problem.

It is quite likely that although many moderate drinkers would favor such a strategy, some might be *reluctant* to act out of fear of offending their heavy-drinking friends and because this is not a common practice among young adults. However, the *modeling* of these skills during televised public service announcements could help to legitimize this approach by creating a supportive social environment for moderate drinkers' persuasive efforts. Demonstration of proper intervention techniques and ease of performance is likely to raise levels of *self-efficacy* among this target public. Spot announcements of this type would convey the message that moderate drinkers can succeed if they apply what they have learned and persist in their efforts. Finally, a controlled study of this type would provide basic researchers with data missing from the literature on the effects of persuasive efficacy information on self-efficacy beliefs and formative researchers with data on message-design factors that enhance beliefs about personal competency. As Kleinot and Rogers (1982) concluded in their study of the effects of fear-arousing communications on intentions to moderate alcohol consumption ". . . the role of self-efficacy in alcohol education programs remains an open empirical question" (p. 810).

CONCLUSION

The odds are that public-information campaigns can teach audiences how to change harmful health practices if they are properly conceptualized and carried out. Campaign effectiveness will be enhanced at the behavioral level if program planners focus their attention on those factors in Flay's model that predict trial behavior and repeated behavior (i.e., self-help materials, skills, self-efficacy beliefs, and positive reinforcement of the behavior-change effort). In all likelihood, the reason so many health campaigns have failed to achieve their behavioral goals is because so few have concentrated on these factors, relying instead on the conventional wisdom of the traditional information-processing approach. For example, surveys indicate that the majority of smokers are aware of the health risks associated with smoking, and many even desire to quit but are unable to because they lack the skills and confidence in their abilities. Yet smoking-cessation campaigns have sought to tell smokers what they already know and encouraged them to do what they want to but can't. Within the last few years, quit-smoking campaigns have begun to address this problem by offering self-help guides that provide specific behavior change strategies and direct smokers to clinics where they receive the social support (i.e., positive reinforcement) often needed to kick the habit.

The crucial role of formative research in campaign planning cannot be overemphasized. Each part of the extended model should be thoroughly researched prior to program implementation to locate target publics within the hierarchy of effects. The same holds for the amended version when the campaign is intended to raise expectations of personal competency and teach skills. Once target publics have been analyzed according to their levels of knowledge, attitudes toward the health behavior, beliefs about their abilities to carry out message recommendations, etc., campaign goals can be set and message strategies developed and pretested. Messages that cannot hold attention, are difficult to understand, lack personal relevance, and are at variance with audience predispositions have little chance of influencing health behavior. Only after the audience understands the nature of the health problem, believes in the effectiveness of message recommendations, and believes it is capable of performing the advocated behavior should behavior change become a campaign goal. Formative research can provide this information.

REFERENCES

Ajzen, I., & Fishbein, M. (1980). *Understanding attitudes and predicting social behavior*. Englewood Cliffs, NJ: Prentice-Hall.

Atkin, C. K. (1979). Research evidence on mass mediated health communication campaigns. In D. Nimmo (Eds.), *Communication yearbook 3* (pp. 655–668). New Brunswick, NJ: Transaction Press.

Atkin, C. K. (1981). Mass media information campaign effectiveness. In R. E.

Rice & W. J. Paisley (Eds.), *Public communication campaigns* (pp. 265–280). Beverly Hills: Sage.

Bandura, A. (1977a). *Social learning theory.* Englewood Cliffs, NJ: Prentice-Hall.

Bandura, A. (1977b). Self-efficacy: Toward a unifying theory of behavioral change. *Psychological Review, 84*(2), 191–215.

Bandura, A., Adams, N., & Beyer, J. (1977). Cognitive processes mediating behavioral change. *Journal of Personality and Social Psychology, 35*(3), 125–139.

Beck, K. H., & Frankel, A. (1981). A conceptualization of threat communications and protective health behavior. *Social Psychology Quarterly, 44*(3), 204–217.

Beck, K. H., & Lund, A. (1981). The effects of health threat seriousness and personal efficacy upon intentions and behavior, *Journal of Applied Social Psychology, 11*(5), 401–415.

Blane, H. T., & Hewitt, L. E. (1980). Alcohol, public education, and mass media: An overview. *Alcohol Health and Research World, 5*(1), 2–16.

Brehony, K. A., Frederiksen, L. W., & Solomon, L. J. (1984). Marketing principles and behavioral medicine. In L. W. Frederiksen, L. J. Solomon, & K. A. Brehony (Eds.), *Marketing health behavior: Principles, techniques, and applications* (pp. 3–22). New York: Plenum.

Cutlip, S. M., Center, A. H., & Broom, G. M. (1985). *Effective public relations* (6th ed.). Englewood Cliffs, NJ: Prentice-Hall.

Flay, B. R. (1981). On improving the chances of mass media health promotion programs causing meaningful changes in behavior. In M. Meyer (Ed.), *Health education by television and radio* (pp. 56–91). Munich: Saur.

Grunig, J. E., & Hunt, T. (1984). *Managing public relations.* New York: Holt, Rinehart & Winston.

Grunig, J. E., & Ipes, D. A. (1983). The anatomy of a campaign against drunk driving. *Public Relations Review, 9*(2), 36–52.

Hovland, C. I., Janis, L., & Kelley, H. H. (1953). *Communication and persuasion.* New Haven: Yale University Press.

Kleinot, M., & Rogers, R. (1982). Identifying effective components of alcohol misuse prevention programs. *Journal of Studies on Alcohol, 43*(7), 802–811.

Maccoby, N., Farquhar, J., Wood, P., & Alexander, J. (1977). Reducing the risk of cardiovascular disease: Effects of a community-based campaign on knowledge and behavior. *Journal of Community Health, 3*(2), 100–114.

Maccoby, N., & Solomon, D. (1981). Heart disease prevention: Community studies. In R. E. Rice & W. J. Paisley (Eds.), *Public communication campaigns* (pp. 105–125). Beverly Hills: Sage.

McGuire, W. (1981). Theoretical foundations of campaigns. In R. E. Rice & W. J. Paisley (Eds.), *Public communication campaigns* (pp. 41–70). Beverly Hills: Sage.

National Institute on Alcohol Abuse and Alcoholism. (1981). *Fourth special report to the U.S. Congress on alcohol and health from the Secretary of Health and Human Services, January 1981.* Washington, DC: U.S. Government Printing Office.

Wallack, L. M. (1981). Mass media campaigns: The odds against finding behavior change. *Health Education Quarterly, 8*(3), 209–260.

Wallack, L. M., & Barrows, D. C. (1981). *Preventing alcohol problems in California:*

Evaluation of the three year "Winners" program. Berkeley: University of California, School of Public Health.

SUGGESTED READINGS

Albert, W. G. (1981). General models of persuasive influence for health education. In D. S. Leathar, G. B. Hastings, & J. K. Davies (Eds.), *Health education and the media* (pp. 169–185). Elmsford, NY: Pergamon Press.

Atkin, C. K., Garramone, G. M., & Anderson, R. B. (1985, May). *Formative evaluation research in health campaign planning: The case of drunk driving prevention.* Paper presented at the meeting of the International Communication Association, Chicago.

Bractic, E., Greenberg, R., & Peterson, P. (1980). HMTS: Improving the quality of public service announcements through standardized pretesting. *Journal of the Academy of Marketing Science, 9*(1), 40–51.

Dervin, B. (1981). Mass communicating: Changing conceptions of the audience. In R. E. Rice & W. J. Paisley (Eds.), *Public communication campaigns* (pp. 71–87). Beverly Hills: Sage.

LaRose, R. (1980). Formative evaluation of children's television as mass communication research. In B. Dervin & M. Voigt (Eds.), *Progress in communication sciences* (Vol. 2, pp. 275–297). Norwood, NJ: Ablex.

Maiman, L. A., & Becker, M. H. (1974). The health belief model: Origins and correlates in psychological theory. In M. H. Becker (Ed.), *The health belief model and personal health behavior* (pp. 9–26). Thorofare, NJ: Charles B. Slack.

Palmer, E. (1981). Shaping persuasive messages with formative research. In R. E. Rice & W. J. Paisley (Eds.), *Public communication campaigns* (pp. 227–238). Beverly Hills: Sage.

Ray, M. L. (1973). Marketing communication and the hierarchy-of-effects. In P. Clarke (Ed.), *New models for mass communication research* (pp. 147–176). Beverly Hills: Sage.

Simpkins, J. D., & Brenner, D. J. (1984). Mass media communication and health. In B. Dervin & M. Voigt (Eds.), *Progress in communication sciences* (Vol. 5, pp. 275–297). Norwood, NJ: Ablex.

Solomon, D. S. (1981). A social marketing perspective on campaigns. In R. E. Rice & W. J. Paisley (Eds.), *Public communication campaigns* (pp. 281–292). Beverly Hills: Sage.

Winett, R. A. (1986). *Information and behavior: Systems of influence.* Hillsdale, NJ: Lawrence Erlbaum, Associates.

Application of a Generalized Persuasion Model to Public Relations Research

Peter K. Hamilton
Pittsburg State University

ABSTRACT

The principle issue addressed in this chapter is the application of communication theory to public relations research. The chapter describes a generalized persuasion model based on cognitive and behavioral theories of human behavior. This model is used as a basis for the development of a public relations research questionnaire that has been used with five field studies. The chapter concludes with a description of additional refinements that are needed to extend this work.

This book, in part, investigates the role of theory in the practice of public relations. One area often overlooked in the application process is the use of theory in building research designs. Chapter 1 described public relations as a social science and as a site for developing and applying communication/social science theory. This chapter links these concepts to public relations research.

The chapter describes the development of a research instrument based on a generalized persuasion model. The instrument was designed to be used in hospital public relations/marketing programs. The chapter also provides a summary of the results of five research projects in which the model based instrument was used.

The "bottom line" of any public relations/advertising campaign is the extent to which the project effects the behavior(s) of the target public. Ultimately, the actions of the target public produce the pay-off for the client and/or company.

Recent reviews of public relations practice (Hamilton, 1986) indicate that public relations practitioners are attempting to use research to assess their communication problems and use the results of the research to structure their campaigns. However, many of these research advocates provide little, if any, theoretical structure to tie the research to a persuasion and/or communication model. Research, in order to be effective, must be purposeful and designed to provide data that will be used in the ensuing campaign.

COMMUNICATION/PUBLIC RELATIONS THEORY AND THE GENERALIZED MODEL

The persuasion model used in this study does not adhere to any one persuasion theory for three reasons. First, whereas some theories have produced limited empirical support, no single theory has emerged as a dominant predictor of human action. Second, the assumption is made that no single theory can adequately provide direction for communication campaigns in all situations. Third, a multiple measurement approach provides a degree of validity for each section in the study and, at the same time, produces multiple measures of the target public. The multiple measure technique is consistent with the ICA communication audit procedure developed to analyze internal organizational communication.

The persuasion model used in this project combined the basic behavioral and cognitive approaches that attempt to predict human behavior. The model has four major elements: (a) a past experience—or behavioral component; (b) a two cognitive component—belief/awareness factor and an evaluative/affective factor; (c) a propensity to act, or intentions factor; and (d) an involvement factor.

The first element combines elementary operant conditioning and portions of Hullian theory. The assumption is that a positive experience with a hospital will not only produce a reinforced trial, but also establish a "habit" of using a given medical institution. The notion of early reinforced trials was seen by Hull (1952) to produce greater increase in habit than reinforced trials later in the experience. The measurement instrument counts the number of times a respondent has used a given hospital and then classifies respondents as frequent, moderate or non-users.

The second element is the traditional cognitive approach to attitude development and change. Smith (1982) described this theoretical position as consisting of two major factors. The first is a belief/schemata/perceptions dimension in which the individual develops his/her concept of the characteristics of the target object. The second is the evaluative factor that creates an affective reaction to the object. These two factors then produce a predisposition to behave positively or negatively toward the object.

The third element in the model combines Fishbein's notion of intentions and Bandura's social learning theory. Ajzen and Fishbein (1980) maintained that "intentions" predict future behavior—the assumption being that there is a high degree of consistency between stated intentions to act and future behavior. At the same time, Bandura (1977) claimed that humans act in accordance with the perceived likelihood and quality of outcomes resulting from a given behavior.

The final element in the model is an involvement dimension. Grunig and Hunt (1984) described the differences between high and low involved publics. One significant difference is the degree to which these two publics seek and process information about the target object.

In summary, the model used in this study assumes that past experience influences future behavior. Second, behavior is influenced by levels of knowledge, or beliefs, about the target object and by the positive or negative evaluations associated with those beliefs. Third, stated intent to behave and perceived outcomes are predictors of behavior. And fourth, different levels of involvement with a target object will influence future communication behavior.

The following section describes the questionnaire developed from the model and how the questionnaire measures each of the elements.

HOSPITAL PUBLIC RELATIONS/MARKETING QUESTIONNAIRE: DESCRIPTION

The questionnaire developed for this study was produced for five public relations/marketing projects contracted through The Blakey Group, Inc. of Tulsa, Oklahoma. Each of these projects was designed to measure public attitudes and perceptions toward a mid-sized community hospital and to develop a public relations/marketing plan based on the results.

The questionnaire was organized in five sections: (a) hospital and physician use; (b) awareness and evaluation of hospital services; (c) evaluation of hospital staff, facilities and overall image; (d) future hospital preference for specific treatments; and (e) a series of demographic questions.

Section I: Past Hospital/Physician Use. This section determines respondent past behavior regarding the hospital and, when requested by the client, physicians. The data produced from this section allows the researcher to describe the current market share of hospitals in the service region for various health care service. The results also provide a basis for determining patterns of hospital use. Past patients can be classified as exclusive users of one hospital or multiple users. Service-use patterns are determined by past patient preference for a given hospital for specific services.

Section II: Awareness and Evaluation of Hospital Services.   In this section the respondent is asked to indicate if he or she is aware that a given service is provided by the hospital. If the respondent indicates that she/he knows that the hospital does provide that service, then he/she is asked to evaluate the service.

The data produced in this section provide an analysis of level of awareness of services in the community. Respondents are asked to indicate if they feel that the service is provided, is not provided or that they are not sure. The evaluation item asks respondents to indicate if they feel that the service is of a "high quality" to "low quality" on a one to five Likert type scale.

Section III: Evaluation of Staff, Facilities, and Overall Image.   The first part of this section deals with respondent perceptions of the staff. Prior research indicated that past patients were most concerned with staff expertise and level of personal concern. This section of the survey assesses respondent's perceptions of the staff's qualifications and the staff's personal concern for patients. Each client is allowed to determine which categories of staff will be included in the questionnaire. Typically the survey asks about nurses, physicians and office personnel.

Hospital facilities are analyzed regarding level of quality, the adequacy for treatments and if the equipment is up-to-date. The overall image of the hospital is assessed by asking respondents if they feel that the hospital provides good overall medical service to the community.

Section IV: Future Hospital Use for Specific Services.   The fourth section of the questionnaire asks respondents to indicate which hospital they would want to use for specific treatments should they or any member of their family need to use such service. The specific services included in the survey are determined by the client. A common set of services included in all five of the projects completed thus far were: major surgery, minor surgery, emergency room, OB/GYN and out-patient services.

Section V: Demographics.   In addition to the past behavior data that is used as a demographic, respondents are asked to provide the following information: (a) if they know an employee of the hospital, (b) how long they have lived in the community, (c) age, (d) major sources of information about the hospital, and (e) location. If the hospital is located in a minor media market, a series of media use questions are included.

HOSPITAL PR/MARKETING QUESTIONNAIRE: RELATION TO PERSUASION MODEL

Element I: Behavior Reinforcement.   The first element in the model assumes that people will be more likely to use a hospital for a second admission if their initial experience was positive. The questionnaire used in this project measures degree of satisfaction with past experiences by combining the data from section I (past hospital/physician experience) with the evaluative data from sections II and III plus the propensity to select results from section IV.

Results are organized according to past hospital experience in three categories: (a) past patients of the client's hospital, (b) past patients of other hospitals and, (c) respondents who have not used a hospital in the past five years. Within these categories it is possible to determine trends in satisfaction by number of experiences (i.e., single admissions vs. multiple admissions, or by type of treatment received).

The data produced in sections II, III and IV also allow the researcher to isolate specific experiences that past patients found to be positive or negative. For example, the five studies completed found different responses to the emergency rooms of each hospital. In three of the cases the "E" rooms produced positive experiences for past patients, and in the other two the "E" room was a negative experience for past patients who had used this service.

As was stated earlier in the chapter, according to Kiesler, Collins and Miller (1969) Hull has demonstrated that positive early experiences have a greater impact on developing use habits than do later experiences. Because a significant number of individuals use the "E" room as their initial encounter, this service has been a factor in overall hospital evaluations. At the same time, most patients go through the "admissions" procedures prior to receiving any treatment. The work done in the studies reported in this chapter have consistently found low evaluations of most hospital admissions procedures.

Element II: Cognitive Beliefs and Evaluations.   The major concern for most hospital clients is the degree to which people in their community are aware of the services they provide. Section II, (awareness and evaluation of hospital services) directly measures this variable. In addition section III (evaluation of staff, facilities and overall image) also measures the degree to which respondents are aware of the hospital's facilities and medical equipment.

Both sections II and III provide evaluative data as well as belief data. The questionnaire uses a 5-point Likert type scale on all evaluative items. Results are analyzed by mean comparisons and distribution comparisons. Analysis by distribution is critical for services that are not highly visible in the community. Often the means for many items tend to cluster around the 3.0 to 3.25 range. In most cases this is caused by a large portion of "neutral" responses rather than a bi-modal clustering of highly favorable and unfavorable responses.

The data from this section are found to be the most useful in developing specific communication goals for future campaigns. In a recent study it was found that public awareness of hospital services had increased up to 30% over a two year period. Although it is not possible to ascribe the gain solely to the public relations campaign, the changes were important to the client organization.

Element III: Intention of Future Behavior. Section IV of the survey questionnaire directly measures intent to behave. The data produced by this section allows the researcher to analyze the propensity of various subgroups to use specific services. Future use patterns have been found in each of the five studies completed using this questionnaire. Clients were provided with results that indicated the services most likely to be in demand at their hospital. The same data were provided for services most likely to be sought from competitors.

The data from section IV are also helpful to clients who are developing long-range marketing plans. Identification of needed new services and potential market strength of these services is critical in deciding to expand certain services, to discontinue services or to add new services. The data also provide an identification of major competing hospitals for specific services. Further subgroup analysis is often requested by clients in order to target specific publics for proposed new services.

Grunig and Hunt (1984) has consistently proposed that the goal of two-way symmetrical public relations is to find a common ground that both the organization and its publics can find acceptable. The data from this section can be used to find those services the community public desires and the services the hospital client can develop.

Element IV: Involvement. Grunig and Hunt (1984) has demonstrated the importance of involvement levels of various publics with the organization in the creation of public relations strategies. The questionnaire used in this project measures involvement in two ways. First, the demographic section identifies respondents who "know" an employee of the hospital. Hamilton (1985) reported that knowing an employee of an organization increases involvement level with the organization. Second, respondent past experience with the hospital is considered to be an indicator of involvement. These two indicators are then combined to produce high or low involved subgroups. Results of this analysis are then used to identify differences, if any, in awareness and evaluation levels, and propensity to use the hospital for specific services. Based on Grunig and Hunt's (1984) description of how high- and low-involved publics respond to various types of communications, a public relations/advertising strategy is suggested for each subgroup.

In summary, this research measures community attitude toward hospitals and is designed to reflect a generalized model of persuasion. The model assumed that future hospital use behavior could be predicted on the basis of past experience; levels of awareness and evaluation of services; evaluations of staff, facilities and overall image; propensity to use the hospital; and degree of involvement with the hospital.

A five section questionnaire was created to measure each of the elements in the persuasion model. The survey instrument asked respondents to report their previous hospital admissions; their degree of awareness of specific hospital services and their opinions about these services; their evaluative perceptions of the hospital staff, facilities and overall image; and finally to indicate their propensity to use specific hospitals for selected services.

The following section of this chapter reports some of the results found in the five research projects completed using this survey.

RESULTS AND TRENDS

The results reported in this section are based on an analysis of the data collected in the five studies that have been completed using this questionnaire. The total N for the five studies is over 2,000. The conclusions below are descriptive and are not based on statistical tests, although the data suggest some obvious trends that could be subjected to further analysis if the situation warranted.

One limitation is the subtle differences in the questionnaire used in each study. In order to adapt the instrument to the specific needs of each client, the questionnaire allowed for differences in the services listed, the types of staff groups and in some cases in the demographic section. However, the basic structure of the questionnaire did remain consistent in all five projects.

Keeping these limitations in mind, the following general conclusions have been found.

1. There is little variation in hospital use. Over 70% of the respondents in these five studies used the same hospital for all of their treatments. A number of factors may explain this result. First, physicians tend to recommend the same facility to their patients. Second, location is a powerful factor in hospital selection. Third, all of the hospitals used in these studies received positive evaluations from their past patients. It appears that once a patient has a good experience with a hospital, he or she continues to use that facility.

2. Most attitudes toward hospitals are formed within the first year of residence in a community. The "years lived in this community" demographic produced consistent findings that people who have been in a community less than one year had very low awareness levels of services offered by the hospitals and their evaluations were moderate to neutral on all evaluative items. However, after one year there was little difference in opinions. The 1–3 year groups did not differ to any greater extent than the other residence groups.

Based on these first two conclusions it would appear that hospitals need to concentrate on new residents in order to expand their census counts. Changing hospital use behavior would be a much more difficult task than influencing initial behavior.

3. There is a very great difference in levels of awareness between traditional hospital services (i.e., surgery, emergency rooms, etc.) and the newer more specialized services such as day-surgery, home health services, swing bed programs, etc. The traditional services typically had awareness ratings of 85% or higher. On the other hand, some of the specialized services had awareness levels as low as 5%.

Involvement is a powerful predictor of awareness. The high involved groups in each of the five studies had significantly higher awareness levels for all services. These same high involved groups reported that they used the media mostly to gain information about the hospital. It would seem that these data support the Grunig–Hunt (1984) model, which predicts that high involved publics are more active seekers of information and tend to expend greater effort in consuming communication about the organization than do low involved groups.

If the low-involved public is the most likely source of new clients for a hospital, it would seem that PR awareness campaigns would be best advised to use short, easy to comprehend messages. Designing messages based on involvement levels is an interesting area for further research.

4. Consistent with most cognitive theories of attitudes, the more information respondents had about the hospitals the more extreme were their evaluations. The mean differences between high and low informed Ss ranged from 0.2 to 2.5 on a 5-point scale.

The direction of the evaluations was not related to information level to the same extent as the affective response. Although there was some support for a conclusion that increased levels of information lead to a positive evaluation, it was not strong. These data indicate that hospitals cannot merely inform the public about their services, they must add some sort of persuasive dimension to their public relations efforts.

5. The least informed subgroups in all five studies were new community residents. However, a somewhat surprising finding was the lack of information about hospital services that older respondents and people who had lived in their communities for over 10 years have.

One hospital CEO suggested that these data indicate that older residents established their perceptions and attitudes before new services had been introduced. Once these attitudes were formed they are resistant to change. All of the hospitals involved in this project were subjected to "institutional stereotyping" by elderly respondents.

6. Respondents who attribute high expertise to a staff subgroup also attribute high levels of personal concern to the same group. This finding was strongest for nurses and weakest for physicians.

This preliminary finding offers interesting avenues for further research. It may suggest that there is some attribution process that links both dimensions, or it may be that health care professionals who have high levels of expertise may also be personally concerned for patients.

7. In four of the five studies used in this project, respondents rated people higher on the evaluate items than they rated facilities or equipment. This result is probably a function of the hospitals used in these projects. All five health care facilities were moderate-sized community hospitals. A comparison with larger urban hospitals would be interesting.

In summary, the data generated from these projects has provided insight into hospital selection behavior. The final section of this chapter describes some of the public relations/marketing plans that were developed based on the results of these research surveys, although it should be noted that a more statistically based analysis would be needed if the conclusion described above were to be used as a basis for more formal research, instead.

USE OF SURVEY RESULTS IN DEVELOPMENT OF PUBLIC RELATIONS MARKETING PLANS

The data produced by the questionnaire used in these studies provides a basis for developing health care services and communication plans.

Health Care Service Planning

As competition for patients increases, hospitals are offering more diverse services in an attempt to increase their census counts. The research produced in these studies identifies the services most needed in the client's community, services patients use at competing hospitals, and the propensity to use a new service if it were offered.

The hospital administration staffs should conduct a cost/benefit analysis of any proposal based on the data produced by the survey.

Communication Planning

Obviously the major concern of this paper is the use of the research in producing effective public relations programs. The plans presented to the client follow a traditional communication format of determining what to say, to whom, and through which channel.

The content of the proposed PR campaigns are determined by the perceptions held by the target public toward the client's hospital and the communication goals. The communication plan must determine if the primary need is information of change in evaluative. Typically, new services need to start with an information campaign whereas negative perceptions of traditional services need an evaluation change project.

Target public analysis is critical to using any theory-based public relations campaign. Both demographic and psychographic data are used to determine specific content strategy. Involvement with the hospital, extremity of attitudes and past experiences with the hospital and its competitors are some of the variables used in strategy development. These variables are used to establish types of appeals to make, length of messages, and channels of communication.

Selecting specific publics as targets of the public relations campaign is the second part of the communication plan. Publics are analyzed on the basis of the probability of success compared to degree of effort needed to achieve the communication goals of the project.

In one study, for example, the data indicated that the client would be best served by concentrating the public relations campaign in a limited geographic area. This area had a high number of people who traveled some distance to seek a new treatment the hospital was developing. At the same time they had neutral to positive opinions of the hospital. Finally, the target public had no strong pattern of using a specific competing health care facility.

The channels of communication used are influenced by content of the message, the communication habits of the target public and the level of involvement of the target public. Research on the efficacy of different media to carry various types of messages has been used to help develop a media buy strategy. Too often clients want to select media on the basis of cost versus reach. This can result in inefficient use of media and money.

Involvement levels of the target groups are used to determine the complexity of the message. As Grunig and Hunt (1984) point out, low-involved publics are not likely to spend much effort in attending to lengthy messages presented in a channel that requires high levels of energy.

Nonmedia communication strategies are also proposed based on the assumption that face/face communication is a more powerful form of persuasion than a media campaign. The development of health fairs, speakers programs, and free physicals for high school athletes are some of the nonmedia plans that have been used.

A major finding from the research was that an initial positive experience with a hospital significantly increases the likelihood of the patient using that hospital in the future. At the same time the data also indicate that emergency room service is often the first service used by new community residents. These findings produced suggestions to have pre-admission data forms mailed to new residents. The hospital then would enter this information into their computer system and send the potential client an identification card to be used during the admission procedures.

Hospitals have also been encouraged to have a patient advocate in the emergency room and admission area. These would be nonmedical personnel who would attempt to ease the stress generated by health emergencies. Another personal communication program that was suggested was a CEO/patient visitation project. The only topic that was off limits during these conversations was the patient's bill.

In summary all of the communication programs outlined for the client were developed in order to achieve a more positive direct experience for patients or future patients (behavior element); increase awareness of services (belief element); create positive evaluations of services, staff and/or facilities (affective element); or to increase the likelihood of selecting the client's hospital (intention element).

The use of this generalized communication/persuasion model has provided direction and structure for the development of a survey questionnaire designed to collect information to be used in creating an effective public relations program.

It would seem that hospital selection is not an additive process in which each of the elements described in this chapter are equally combined into a decision-making process. What is unknown is the weight given to each of the elements by hospital users. Future research will address this while at the same time individual differences need to be considered because no single pattern of hospital selection has been observed.

As the field of public relations develops more sophisticated theories, the need for research based on these models increases. Basic to any public relations campaign is a well constructed pre-campaign research program. Theory-based public relations campaigns need to use research that reflects the campaign's theoretical orientation.

REFERENCES

Ajzen, I., & Fishbein, M. (1980). *Understanding attitudes and predicting social behavior*. Englewood Cliffs, NJ: Prentice-Hall.
Bandura, A. (1977). Self-efficacy: Toward a unifying theory of behavioral change. *Psychological Review, 84*(2), 191–215.
Grunig, J. E., & Hunt, T. (1984). *Managing public relations*. New York: Holt, Rinehart & Winston.
Hamilton, P. K. (1985). *A quantitative analysis of the effects of perceived employee attitudes on public opinion*. Paper presented to the International Communication Association convention, Honolulu, HI.
Hull, C. L. (1952). *A behavior system*. New Haven, CT: Yale University Press.
Kiesler, C. A., Collins, B. E., & Miller, N. (1969). *Attitude change: A critical analysis of theoretical approaches*. New York: Wiley.
Smith, M. J. (1982). *Persuasion and human action: A review and critique of social influence theories*. Belmont, CA: Wadsworth.

Author Index

Subject Index